AF580459

"THE TALENTED INTRUDER"
Wyndham Lewis in Canada, 1939-1945

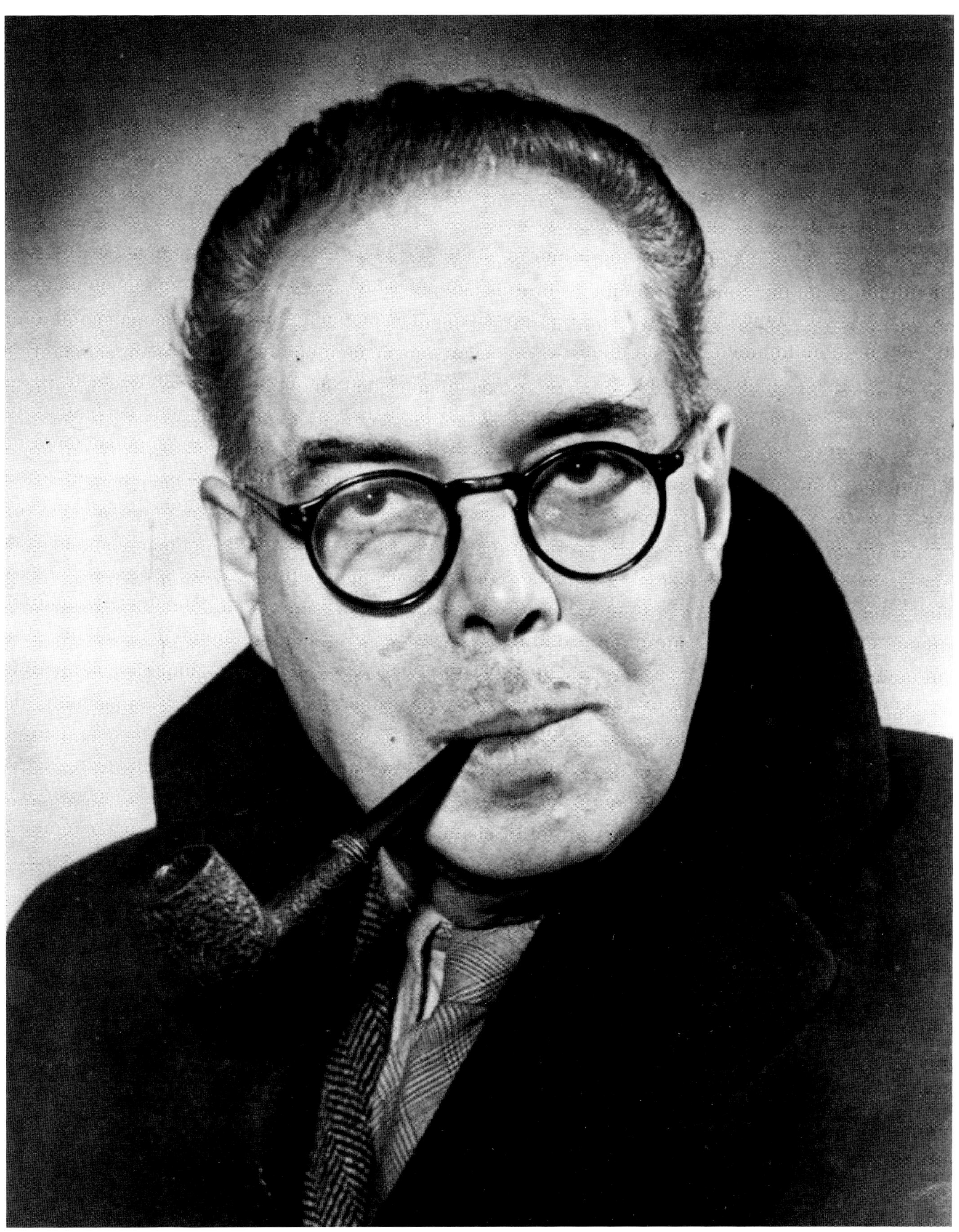

"THE TALENTED INTRUDER"
Wyndham Lewis in Canada, 1939-1945

CATHARINE M. MASTIN
ROBERT STACEY
THOMAS DILWORTH

ART GALLERY OF WINDSOR
Windsor, Ontario
21 November 1992 to 24 January 1993

GLENBOW MUSEUM
Calgary, Alberta
3 July to 15 August 1993

ART GALLERY OF ONTARIO
Toronto, Ontario
23 September to 28 November 1993

Mastin, Catharine M., 1963-
"The Talented Intruder"

Catalogue of an exhibition at the Art Gallery of Windsor, Nov. 21, 1992 to Jan. 24, 1993, the Glenbow Museum, July 3 to Aug. 15, 1993, and the Art Gallery of Ontario, Sept. 23 to Nov. 28, 1993. Includes bibliographic references.

ISBN 0-919837-37-9

1. Lewis, Wyndham, 1882-1957 - Exhibitions.
2. Lewis, Wyndham, 1882-1957 - Criticism and interpretation. I. Stacey, Robert, 1949 - .
II. Dilworth, Thomas. III. Lewis, Wyndham, 1882—1957. VI. Art Gallery of Ontario. VII. Title.
N6549.I49A4 1992 759.11 C92-095213-5

The Art Gallery of Windsor,
445 Riverside Dr. West,
Windsor, Ontario, Canada
N9A 6T8

Editor: Robert Stacey
Design: Scott McKowen, Stratford, Ontario
Translation: Nésida Loyer, Intertext Language Services, Calgary, Alberta
Photography: Barrie Jones, Robert Stacey, Catharine Mastin, Eileen Tweedy
Typesetting and Printing: Beacon Herald Fine Printing Division, Stratford, Ontario
Insurance for this exhibition has been provided by the Department of Communications through the Insurance Program for Travelling Exhibitions.

Front cover: No. 43 (Detail), Wyndham Lewis, *The Mind of the Artist, About to Make a Picture,* 1942, pen-and-ink and watercolour on paper (39.5 x 30.5 cm), M 997. Lent anonymously.

Frontispiece: Wyndham Lewis, in the early 1940s. Wyndham Lewis Collection, Department of Rare Books, Olin Library, Cornell University, Ithaca, New York (hereinafter referred to as " Cornell").

Back Cover: No. 49, Wyndham Lewis, *The Island,* 1942, oil on canvas (56.0 x 78.5 cm), Santa Barbara Museum of Art, Santa Barbara, California, gift of the Women's Board, 1986

ABBREVIATIONS

A.G.O.	Art Gallery of Ontario, Toronto
A.G.T.	Art Gallery of Toronto
A.G.W.	Art Gallery of Windsor
CBC	Canadian Broadcasting Commission (later, Corporation)
C.G.P.	Canadian Group of Painters
C.N.E.	Canadian National Exhibition, Toronto
C.S.G.A.	Canadian Society of Graphic Art
C.S.P.W.C.	Canadian Society of Painters in Water Colour
C.P.E.	Canadian Society of Painter-Etchers and Engravers
N.G.C.	National Gallery of Canada, Ottawa
O.S.A.	Ontario Society of Artists
P.L.S.	Picture Loan Society
R.C.A.	Royal Canadian Academy
S.S.C	Sculptors' Society of Canada
U.C.C.	Upper Canada College, Toronto

Contents

Director's Foreword

WINDSOR, ONTARIO exists as a kind of geographic anomaly: Canada's southernmost city, from which one looks northward, not southward, to the U.S.A. Given the charming peculiarities of this location, which include an intimate conjunction with the metropolis of Detroit across the river, our city has developed a complete personality, at once international and small-town in its makeup. Windsor provides a wide range of amenities, including access to a stimulating range of major centres within and without Canada.

Our community, then, is very much a crossroads, and it is natural that a wide variety of people pass through here, each contributing to the flavour of the place. Thanks to the dynamics of Windsor and its interesting history as a border or frontier town, a surprising number of colourful and influential characters have resided here at least since the awarding of the first land grants, in 1749, and the adoption of the present name, after the royal city of Windsor, England, in 1836. The Canadian-born Wyndham Lewis was definitely one of the more interesting persons to have taken up residence here. With our discovery of the facts of his Windsor sojourn, from 1943 to 1945, the Art Gallery of Windsor was presented with a great opportunity to mount a timely exhibition of the works of this important figure.

To many, Lewis is best-known as a still-controversial writer, but his painting and drawing were of a quality that equalled—some would say surpassed—that of his vast literary production. In both spheres he was a man of insight and discernment, whose attitudes and convictions were often at odds with those of his peers and his time. He seemed to draw strength from this sense of opposition and assumed a kind of "cultural outlaw" persona, even referring to himself as the "Enemy"—an image he promoted in his habits and dress. There is something appropriate about this iconoclastic outsider's having chosen to settle, however briefly, in this border/frontier city.

Catharine M. Mastin, the A.G.W.'s Curator of Canadian Historical Art, has developed a significant thesis with this exhibition and its accompanying publication, which together constitute the first major investigation of Lewis's Canadian years. In both her choice of works and her catalogue essay, she has succeeded in aligning the parallels of his literary and visual arts careers. She has been assisted in this task by the critical insights of Professor Thomas Dilworth, who has contributed a valuable perspective on Lewis's Canadian writings. Similarly, Robert Stacey has provided a counterpoint in his catalogue essay on Lewis's "imaginative" works of the early 1940s. He has also assisted us through the application of his considerable editorial skills. The catalogue was ably designed by Scott McKowen, and the French translation carried out by Nésida Loyer.

This exhibition is one of the more major research projects to have been undertaken by this gallery, and it is with a great deal of pride that we are able to share it with two other institutions and their publics through its national tour. We are grateful to the Museums Assistance Program of the Department of Communications and to the Ontario Arts Council for funding assistance. As well, we wish to acknowledge the efforts of everyone who contributed to the success of this endeavour through their cooperation, technical services, or the lending of artworks. A complete list of acknowledgements follows.

I would like to add one special and very appropriate thank-you to the late the Hon. Paul Martin Sr. and Mrs. Eleanor Martin. It was our discovery of their wonderful Lewis portrait of Mrs. Martin that was the inception of this project. Their enthusiasm and support have been most welcome, and were instrumental in making the exhibition a success. From these almost chance beginnings has evolved a greater awareness and appreciation of our region's history and cultural background.

ALF BOGUSKY, DIRECTOR

Acknowledgements

In the realization of so large an exhibition as this, there are always many people to whom gratitude must be extended, for, without their support and assistance, such endeavours could not be accomplished.

The curator of this exhibition, Catharine M. Mastin, and the catalogue contributors would like to thank, first, the lenders (listed opposite), and the staff at the Art Gallery of Windsor who were involved in this project, including Alf Bogusky, Director; Vincent Varga, Senior Curator; Betty Wilkinson, Registrar; Adele Beitler, Development Officer; Marty Hunt, Senior Preparator; Tony Mosna, Preparator; Dee Douglas, Information Coordinator; and Marie Lopes, Education Curator.

Others who generously provided information and encouragement were: Hugh Anson-Cartwright, Harry Buxton, Oakville Historical Society, Mark Dimunation and Lynne Farrington, of the Department of Rare Books, Cornell University Library, Cy Fox, Robert Fulford, the late the Hon. Paul Martin Sr. and Mrs. Eleanor Martin, Mr. and Mrs. Walter Michel, Michael Power, Victor Russell, City of Toronto Archives, Lois Smedick, Catherine Wallace, and Sheila Watson.

Robert Stacey wishes to acknowledge, in addition to those mentioned above, Dagmar Apel, Peter Caracciolo, Mimi Cazort, Paul Edwards, George Falconer, Robert Fulford, Charles C. Hill, Catherine Johnson, Margaret Keith, Michael Large, John Martin, John O'Brian, Paul O'Keeffe, Michael Pantazzi, Omar S. Pound, Dennis Reid, Douglas Schoenherr, Robert Shamus, and Fred Turner, for information, counsel, criticism, and logistical support. His contributions to this catalogue were completed during the term of his research fellowship at the Canadian Centre for the Visual Arts, National Gallery of Canada, in 1991-92. Thanks for their cooperation to Gyde Shepherd, Assistant Director, Murray Waddington, Librarian, Peter Trepanier, Head of Special Collections; and their staffs.

Permission to quote from Lewis's writings and to reproduce his paintings and drawings, was graciously extended by the Wyndham Lewis Memorial Trust, London.

EXHIBITION, CATALOGUE AND CONSERVATION FUNDING

Funding for this exhibition and its catalogue was provided by the following institutions and individuals: the Museums Assistance Program of the Department of Communications; the Ontario Arts Council; The McLean Foundation; The British Council; Mr. and Mrs. Fred Schaeffer; Christopher Varley; Assumption College, Windsor; and the Travelling Exhibition Insurance Program, Department of Communications, Ottawa.

Many works were conserved for inclusion in this exhibition. Thanks to Assumption College; Keith Bantock, Art Conservation Services, Thamesford, Ontario; Pauline Bondy, Toronto; the Canadian Conservation Institute, Ottawa; Therèse Charbonneau; Mr. and Mrs. Clair Stewart, Caledon East, Ontario; and to Collection Maintenance Fund of the Art Gallery of Windsor.

ACQUISITION ASSISTANCE

We are grateful to the Bobs and Peter Haworth Memorial Bequest, Art Gallery of Windsor and Kenneth Saltmarche, and to the Cultural Property Repatriation Program, Ottawa, for assistance in purchasing two works for the permanent collection of the Art Gallery of Windsor in 1991: *Portrait of the Artist's Wife* (1944; no. 73) and *Landscape* (also known as *Creation Myth*) (1944; no. 74).

Lenders to the Exhibition

CANADA

Shirley Allen, Ottawa, Ontario
Art Gallery of Ontario, Toronto, Ontario
Art Gallery of Windsor, Windsor, Ontario
Assumption College, University of Windsor, Windsor, Ontario
Pauline Bondy, Toronto, Ontario
James Taylor
Dr. Douglas LePan, Toronto, Ontario
The late the Hon. Mr. Paul Martin Sr. and Mrs. Eleanor Martin, Windsor, Ontario
Mark McLean, Toronto, Ontario
Mr. and Mrs. Eric McLuhan, Toronto, Ontario
Corinne McLuhan, Toronto, Ontario
National Gallery of Canada, Ottawa, Ontario
John and Helen O'Brian, Vancouver, British Columbia
Beth Pierce Robinson, Kingston, Ontario
Clair and Amy Stewart, Caledon East, Ontario
Patrick Stewart, Victoria, British Columbia
Thomas Fisher Rare Book Library, University of Toronto, Toronto, Ontario
Vancouver Art Gallery, Vancouver, British Columbia

UNITED KINGDOM

Austin/Desmond and Phipps, London
Bryan Ferry, West Sussex
C.J. Fox, London
Junior Common Room, New College, Oxford
Mercury Gallery, London
Rodney Milne-Day, London
National Portrait Gallery, London
Tate Gallery, London
James H. Winterkorn, Cambridge

UNITED STATES OF AMERICA

Department of Rare Books, Olin Library, Cornell University, Ithaca, New York
The Detroit Institute of Arts, Detroit, Michigan
Herbert F. Johnson Museum of Art, Cornell University, Ithaca, New York
Mary Catherine Lyter, Canoga Park, California
Walter and Harriet Michel
The Museum of Modern Art, New York, New York
Santa Barbara Museum of Art, Santa Barbara, California
Washington University in St. Louis, Gallery of Art, St. Louis, Missouri

We would also like to thank several lenders who wish to remain anonymous.

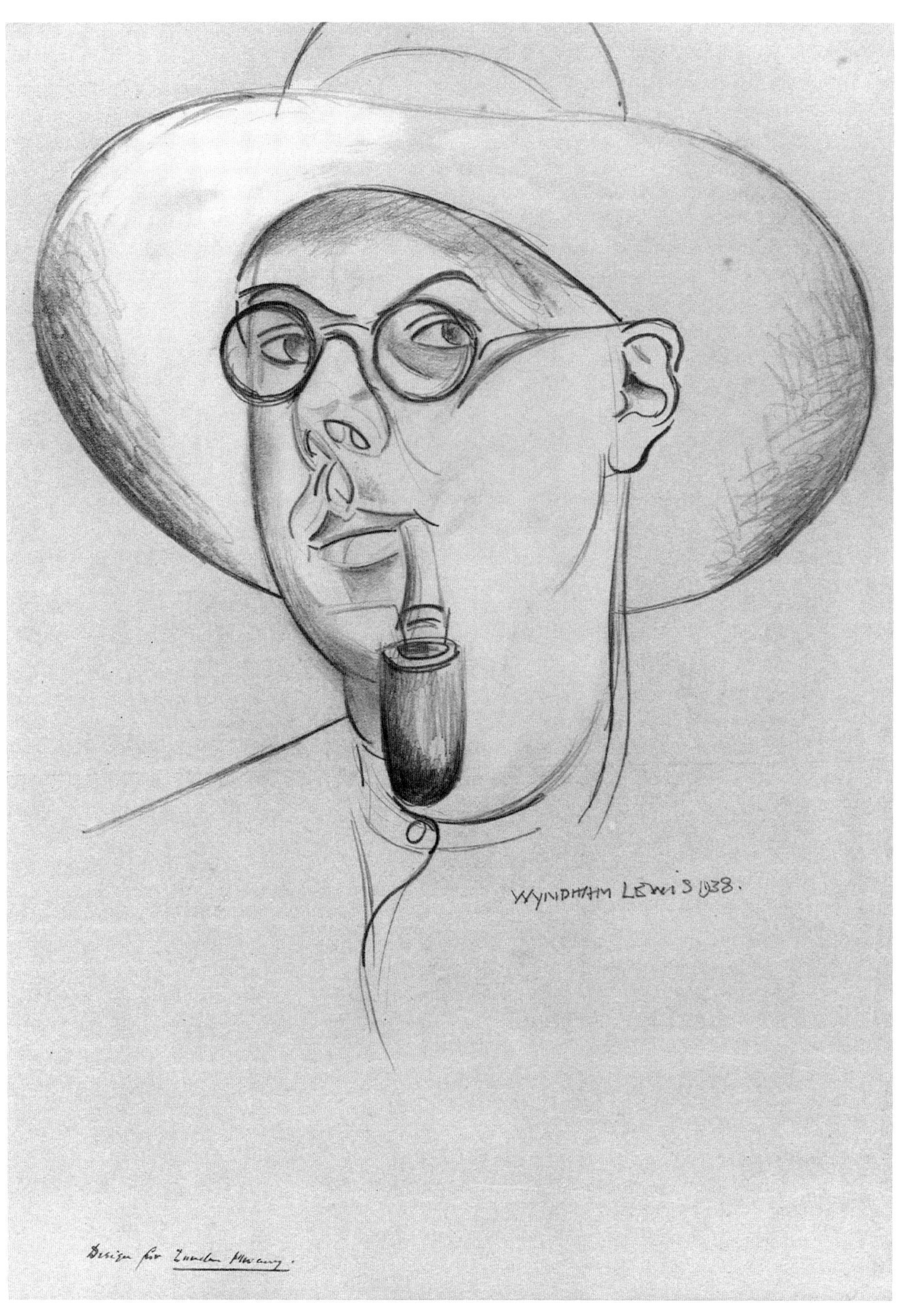
WYNDHAM LEWIS 1938.
Design for London Mercury.

Introduction

CATHARINE M. MASTIN
and ROBERT STACEY

Opposite page:
Fig. 70 *Self-Portrait With Pipe*, 1938, graphite on paper (49.5 x 38.5 cm), M 922. Poetry Collection, State University of New York at Buffalo.

EARLY IN DECEMBER 1930 H.O. McCurry, the director of the National Gallery of Canada in Ottawa, received a letter from Wyndham Lewis accompanying the "first half of a talk or lecture" and a typewritten, hand-corrected sheet of "Representative Opinions", which was obviously intended to impress the recipient. The first of these was by no less a personage than T.S. Eliot, a sometime friend, adversary and sitter of the artist, who is quoted as stating:

> 'Mr. Lewis is a magician who compels our interest in himself: he is the most fascinating personality of our time ... In the work of Mr. Lewis we recognize the thought of the modern and the energy of the cave-man.' *T.S. Eliot.*[1]

The other comments are primarily by writers such as Osbert Sitwell, Herbert Read, Francis Birrell and David Garnett, all of whom concentrate on Lewis's literary accomplishments, the sole judgement by an artist being that of the veteran painter Walter Sickert, who is quoted as declaring that "Wyndham Lewis [is] the best portraitist of this time or any." Almost as unusual as the fact that the Canadian-born British painter, novelist, critic, philosopher and pamphleteer Percy Wyndham Lewis (1882-1957) should have chosen, in a letter to the influential director of a public gallery, to dwell less on his artistic career than on his authorial one, is his selection of commenders, several of whom he had attacked, at one time or other, mercilessly in print. That he felt the need to accompany his covering letter to McCurry with this mini-anthology of accolades from sources he himself considered, for the most part, to be dubious, followed by a list of "prominent sitters" of whom he had made portraits, suggests that he had little confidence that his reputation as a painter and commentator, then in eclipse in Britain, had preceded him to Canada's capital.

Nevertheless Lewis was pleased, at least initially, with his reception in Toronto and Ottawa, as an optimistic letter to the American critic Geoffrey Stone, written shortly after his return to Toronto, indicates:

> For the first time since our arrival [in Canada] I now have a chance of establishing myself: Next Thursday [i.e. 11 December 1940] I give the first of three talks on the radio. Up at Ottawa again I arrived at a moment when 'war-records' were uppermost in the mind of the director of the museum. He has asked me to give a lecture there...and he proposed that I do five portrait-drawings of prominent army and navy personalities... . Also he is confident he can obtain portrait-commissions for me in Ottawa. Further, I met many personages in Ottawa who showed benevolence....[2]

However, no such commissions seem to have materialized—not the first time Lewis was to be disappointed in such hopes—and the fact that only the opening section of the proposed lecture was sent to McCurry suggests that it was not completed and perhaps not delivered.

This fragment was, Lewis explained, "the first half of a talk or lecture. It is really an answer to 'Why Art?' — the recurrent question. The full answer is to come in the half that is yet to be written." This "preamble" bears the title "The Importance of the Visual Arts", and is a defence of the truth that, despite being regarded by many as "a frivolous and remote activity" (especially in wartime), "the visual arts are, indirectly, of enormous moment to everybody." He goes on to inquire, in words that indicate a familiarity with the National Gallery's permanent collection, "The El Grecos, Memlings, Veroneses and so on that are to be found in the galleries upstairs — what have they got to do with this little apocalyptic vision of a world gone Doukhobor?"—a rhetorical question to which he offers a decisive answer: "But El Greco, Memling, and Veronese are, upon the *visual* plane, what Shakespeare and Burke are upon the plane of *language*. They are a visual eloquence (that is for Veronese): a visual integrity, order, and beauty (that is for Memling): a visual dream of tragic detachment (that is for El Greco)."[3] As so often is the case with Lewis's descriptions of other art and artists, he could be writing about his own work, for all these adjectives are applicable to the painting for which he had been justly renowned in the 1910s, '20s and '30s, but which the controversies surrounding his satirical and polemical writings had cast under shadow. As this exhibition hopes to demonstrate, the best of the largely underrated and little-known work he produced in the five years of his on-and-off presence in his native Canada would deserve these same modifiers.

As for the superlatives that Lewis quoted in his addendum to his letter to McCurry, they have been confirmed and amplified in the years since his death with the growth of a veritable Wyndham Lewis "industry" not only in Britain and the United States but, significantly, in his native

Canada. The 1992 Imperial War Museum exhibition, *Wyndham Lewis: Art and War*, occasioned a mixed critical reception, for opinion about this endlessly controversial and contradictory figure has been widely and wildly divided ever since his emergence on the British art scene in 1904, when he was included in the *Thirty-second Exhibition of Modern Pictures held by the New English Art Club* at the Dudley Galleries, London. Some random quotations from the (more positive) reviews of *Art and War*:

> Lewis, Canadian-born, was a cerebral and analytical artist. Unlike the leading English modernists of the 1920s and 1930s—Henry Moore, Barbara Hepworth and Ben Nicholson—who drew their subjects from nature, he has seldom been loved by his adopted countrymen.... Lewis, one of the most revolutionary British artists of this century, still faces difficulties.
> — Laurence Marks, "Disquiet on the Western Front", *Observer Magazine* (21 June 1992).

> He's not by any means unheard of, but Wyndham Lewis continues to fail to arrive, and almost everything that's written about him as a painter or a writer begins by lamenting this fact. And it's getting rather boring for everyone, whether partisan or opponent. On one side, he has an eager fan club, who are always in danger of turning into scolds, pushing the same old hard-luck story of neglect because it seems clear to them, as it does to me, that Lewis's story should be central—that he is clearly the most interesting and intelligent British painter of the first half of this century, the most inventive and, come to that, the most beautiful.
> — Tom Lubbock, "Oh, what a lovely war artist!", *The Independent* (London), 28 June 1992.

> ...Lewis was one of the three or four major British artists of this century. British only by the accident of nationality and upbringing, for in other respects the early Lewis was a European artist, turning the technical innovations of Cubism to his individual purposes, rejecting the romantic Futurist preoccupations with movement symbolized for them in trains and aeroplanes, and replacing it with an awareness that the future belonged not to fast-moving machines but to clumsy dredgers and cranes, phallic guns and shells and the men working them. He saw men as both masters and servants of the machines they used.
> — Julian Symons, "Friends of the Enemy", *Times Literary Supplement* (10 July 1992).

"THE TALENTED INTRUDER": *Wyndham Lewis in Canada*—the title is derived from an ironic description of himself Lewis made to a correspondent in early 1940[4]—examines the five years that Wyndham Lewis spent, on and off, in Toronto and Windsor, Ontario, between the fall of 1939 and the summer of 1945. This half-decade is probably the least-studied period of Lewis's life, yet the only two cities in which he had longer residencies were London and Paris.

It was in his adoptive London that he passed his most productive years, achieving there an international status first for the semi-abstract canvases and drawings he produced from around 1912 through 1915. In these years he was the leader of a group of young and radical artists and writers who called themselves Vorticists, prominent among whose adherents were, besides Lewis, Lawrence Atkinson, David Bomberg, Henri Gaudier-Brzeska, Jessica Dismorr, Frank Dobson, Frederick Etchells, E. McKnight Kauffer, C.W.R. Nevinson, William Roberts, and Edward Wadsworth. All of these artists and several others were included in the landmark exhibition held at the Tate Gallery, London, in 1956, *Wyndham Lewis and Vorticism*, in the introduction to which Lewis proclaimed that "Vorticism, in fact, was what I, personally, did, and said, at a certain period." This boast, predictably, drew vehement protests from other ex-members of the movement, most notably from William Roberts.

Although they had certain stylistic and philosophical affinities with the Cubists and the Futurists, the London-based Vorticists had been anxious to dissociate themselves from these European contemporaries. Lewis offered this definition in 1915, just as World War I was bringing the short-lived phenomenon to a close:

> By Vorticism we mean (a) ACTIVITY as opposed to the tasteful PASSIVITY of Picasso; (b) SIGNIFICANCE as opposed to the dull or anecdotal character to which the Naturalist is condemned; (c) ESSENTIAL MOVEMENT and ACTIVITY (such as the energy of the mind) as opposed to the imitative cinematography, the fuss and hysterics of the Futurists.[5]

In the 1956 introduction that got him in so much trouble with his disgruntled ex-cohorts, he explained,

> As regards Visual Vorticism, it was dogmatically anti-real. It was my ultimate aim to exclude from painting the everyday visual real altogether. The idea was to build up a visual language as abstract as music. The colour green would not be confined, or related, to what was green in nature....; in the matter of form, a shape represented by fish remained a form independent of the animal, and could be made use of in a universe in which there were no fish.[6]

The pioneering experiments of the Vorticists are an important contribution to the art history of the early twentieth century, and constitute the first true break with the British academic and naturalistic traditions. Lewis, thanks in part to his skills as a propagandist, self-populist and publicist, was undoubtedly the movement's most visible and effective exemplar and spokesman. He provided both theoretical and pictorial defences of Vorticism by designing, editing and writing for the two issues (1914 and 1915) of the revolutionary art and literary periodical *Blast,* described by Bradford Morrow as the "blueprint to the Vortex."[7]

Lewis's close identification with the Vorticist campaign in part accounted for the fact that the latter phases of his artistic career, especially during and after the Second World War, have been comparatively overlooked. In comparison with the numerous exhibitions and critical studies of his British period, there have been extremely few treatments of his Canadian years, and these have tended to concentrate on his literary rather than his artistic output. Three modest shows were mounted in this country, previous to the present exhibition, one at Victoria College, University of Toronto, in 1950, five years after Lewis had left Canada; another at the York University Art Gallery, Glendon Campus, in 1964, seven years after his death; and a third at the Art Gallery of Nova Scotia, Halifax, in 1982, to mark the hundredth anniversary of the artist's birth in Nova Scotian waters.[8]

For decades, the consensus of opinion has been that Lewis's wartime "exile," as he bitterly termed it, was one of the most desperate and unfruitful experiences of his life; and that these years saw not only a continuation but an acceleration of the decline that had supposedly set in the decade before. Richard Cork, reviewing *Wyndham Lewis: Paintings and Drawings* in 1970, stated flatly,

> Nothing that Walter Michel has uncovered in his exhaustively illustrated new survey of Lewis's complete *oeuvre* can hide the sad deterioration evident in his later work.... Vorticism remains his finest achievement, and the subsequent slow decline amounts to a paradigm of England's refusal to sustain a vital dialogue with the pioneering forms of modern art.[9]

A reviewer of this reviewer belatedly responded to these comments as follows:

> In my view, Cork makes two fundamental, albeit mistaken assumptions. One is to assume that Lewis's post-war art represents a decline from the 'achievement' of Vorticism so ensuring the continuation of that old chestnut about Lewis's being a fragmented artist who, after a progressive start, took fright and rejected abstraction in favour of a tame form of figure painting. It is surely about time that Lewis's *oeuvre* was viewed as a whole rather than as two faces in a Janus-headed conflict.... The quality of the later work can be allowed to speak for itself.[10]

That is the intention of this exhibition, which also hopes to lay to rest the canard that the Canadian hiatus caused an interruption in Lewis's creativity both as a writer and as an artist, a widely held perception that was perhaps best summarized by the editor of his selected letters, W.K. Rose:

> In view of his productivity both before and after, Lewis's American period was indeed barren. He drew a good deal and he painted a few fine portraits, but he did not advance in artistry or in reputation. As a writer he was practically fallow, completing only two

books and one pamphlet, none of them particularly outstanding. Nor was the social side of the venture rewarding. Kind and interesting friends cropped up in several cities. But being uprooted, Lewis never during this time experienced the stimulus of belonging to a community, a stimulus which had been the daily bread of his London life.[11]

Most of the artworks in *"The Talented Intruder"* have never before been shown publicly, and a substantial portion of Lewis's Canadian writings have never been published, much less studied in depth. Jane Farrington's Lewis retrospective at the City of Manchester Art Galleries of 1980 included only three Canadian-period works, out of a total of 159 items. Up to now, no one has examined in detail the role that Lewis's North American years played in the shaping of the last two decades of his life, and where the collective results of that supposedly arid epoch fit within his overall *oeuvre*.

The decision to come to the New World, it is often forgotten, was Lewis's own, as is clear from the title of his semi-autobiographical novel, published in 1954 but begun while he was in Toronto, the city that is so savagely portrayed in the book *Self Condemned*.[12] He came to escape the war, to pursue portrait and exhibition possibilities, and because he believed that he had played out his string in England, as a result of his unfortunate flirtation, in the early 1930s, with Hitlerism, since retracted but too late to reverse the damage.

Lewis helped to perpetuate the misconception of his Canadian sojourn as a creatively desolate one by referring to the native land in which he considered himself to be homeless as "a very small and backward country," and to Toronto as, among other things, "the bowels of the earth."[13] It is evident, however, from both his artwork and his writing that this period was a time of self-assessment and reflection on the future as well as on the past, and that the sojourn definitely and positively influenced the years of work that remained to him. There is even, in the fact that he renewed his Canadian passport in 1950, a possibility that he intended to return.

It would be naive to leave Lewis with the last word on the matter of interpreting his later career and the motivations behind his actions and his stories. His occasional (some would say habitual) distortions and manipulations of the facts to suit his moods and to muster sympathy serve as a warning not to take everything he said about himself and his acquaintances literally. It is more useful to balance between his published and unpublished statements and the comments and recollections of others.

Lewis, a prolific writer and critic of fiction, possessed great skill in arranging the truth according to his circumstances, one of the clearest examples of this tendency being his accounts of his Canadian origins. Although he was born and baptized in Canada, he only began to see the benefit of promoting the fact that he retained Canadian citizenship when he found that he could not obtain landed immigrant status in the United States, the destination of his preference in 1939. A character such as this has to be approached extremely carefully, and any interpretation of his art and writings is, in consequence, both provisional and subject to revision. The contents of this catalogue acknowledge this reality and present a variety of views and viewpoints of, by, and about this prickly, complex and often contradictory personality. *"The Talented Intruder"* endeavours to present for the first time the material that Lewis produced during, and to identify the significance of, his Canadian years. An appreciation of the degree to which his "exile" was a return, if not a homecoming, can only be arrived at by a digging up and scrutinizing of Lewis's well-buried Canadian roots.

WYNDHAM LEWIS was reminded of his Canadian heritage at various times throughout his life. Although he considered himself English, carried a British passport, and spent most of his adult years in London, his birth in Canada, his service with the Canadian War Memorials during World War I, and the extended periods that he spent in Toronto and Windsor during World War II, strongly associate him with his temporarily re-adopted country.

According to his own account, possibly enhanced in the telling, Lewis was born on board his father's yacht, the *Wanda*, when it was docked at Amherst, Nova Scotia (fig. 1), on 18 November 1882, the year the boat was purchased. The date of Lewis's birth is affirmed not only by the record of it in the Canadian War Memorials papers, now in the National Archives of Canada, and in the "Vita" Lewis prepared some time in the early 1940s for Doubleday and Co., New York, but by the existence, also among his own papers now at Cornell University, of an

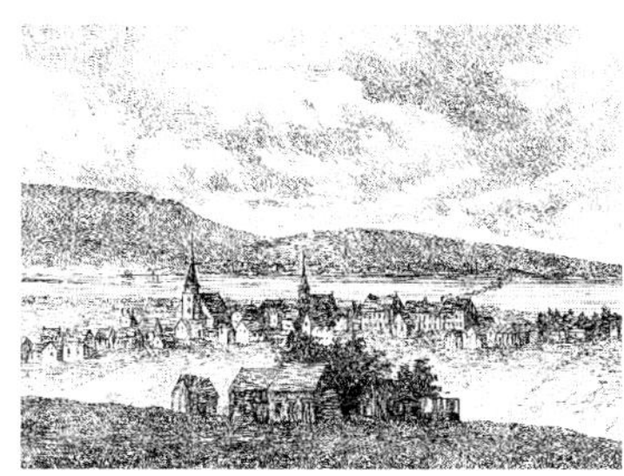

Fig. 1 Albert J. Hill, *Amherst, Nova Scotia*, wood-engraving published in *Canadian Illustrated News* (9 December 1876). National Archives of Canada, Ottawa (C-64729).

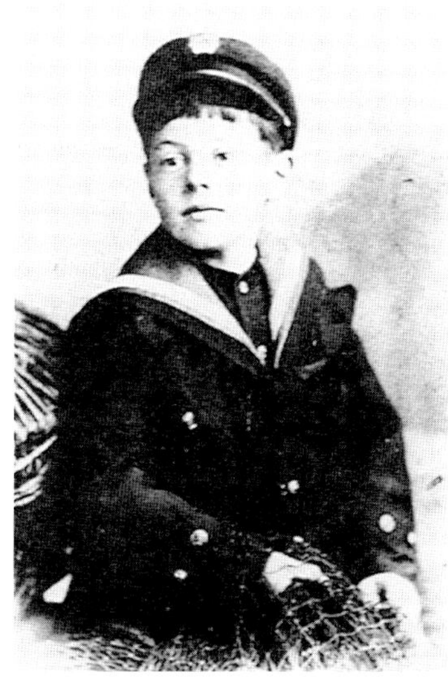

Fig. 2 Wyndham Lewis, c. 1888. Present whereabouts of photograph unknown (reproduced from *The Letters of Wyndham Lewis*, ed. W.K. Rose [Norfolk, Conn.: New Directions, 1963]).

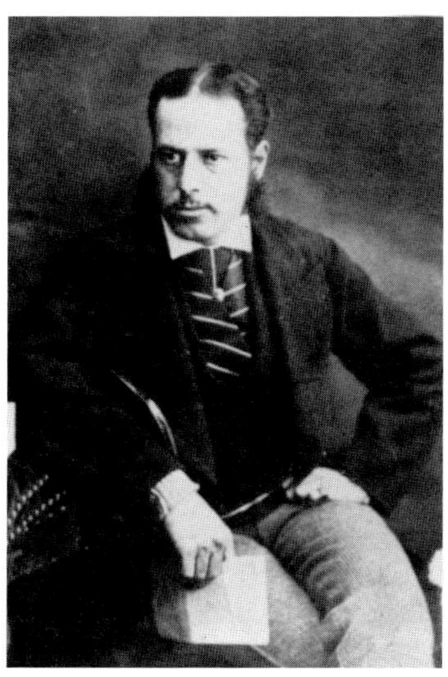

Fig. 3 Charles E. Lewis. Photograph by William Notman and Sons, Montreal, 1870. Notman Photographic Archives, McCord Museum, Montreal.

affidavit signed by his mother, Anne Stuart Lewis, on 16 February 1900.[14] However, his birth was not registered at the time and there is no certificate of it as a consequence. He was, however, christened in Montreal.

Lewis's father, Charles Edward Lewis (fig. 3), a lawyer, wine merchant, sometime writer and full-time practitioner of the "do-nothing mode", was also fond of sailing for both pleasure and business, and regularly visited the Maritime provinces of Canada and the coastal states of the U.S.A. Or as his son put it, "My father travelled to the ends of the earth in search of something in which America is supposed, rightly or wrongly, to be wanting—something that is less like a bivouac and more like a hearth." Despite their differences, there were affinities between the aspirations, if not careers, of the senior and junior Lewises, as the latter recognized. Charles E. was described by relatives as "a dreamer", and, less charitably, by Wyndham as "this fox-hunting, brigantine-owning, essay-writing *bum*", a man "eccentric to the point of madness". His "lack of application" was explained, so the son thought, by the fact that, "Apart from the possession of certain means, which enabled him to do nothing, literary ambition played a great part. He published at his own expense a number of books and papers. He really thought, in spite of all evidences to the contrary, that writing was a worthy occupation."[15] The skewed parallel continues in the strange coincidence that Charles E. Lewis, born probably in New York in 1843, died upon a yacht, near Philadelphia.

Although Wyndham Lewis describes his father as having "ended as he began[,] an American, even a typical American: extremely proud of the gun-metal Grand Army button on his label; very critical of British stick-in-the-mudness",[16] he narrowly escaped being born, like some of his six siblings, in Canada. "My father's family came from Pennsylvania", the memoirist continues; his great-grandfather, Ansel Lewis, was born and married in Boston, and his grandfather, Shebuel [or Shubuel] B. Lewis (1803/4-1890), a Quaker, born in Portland, Maine, was in the lumber business in Philadelphia. "The latter", wrote his grandson, "was a typical patriarch of the old Puritan America."[17] For some reason, Lewis did not see fit to remark that his father's family *also* came from Ontario—and before that, from Quebec.

For not only did Lewis's mother, Anne Stuart Prickett, who married C.E. Lewis in London in 1876, have family in Oakville, Ontario: Shebuel Lewis had moved across Lake Ontario to take up residence in this prosperous harbour town and there married Caroline Romain (1812/13-1884), the sister of a prominent local merchant and developer, William Francis Romain (1818-1911), and Charles Edward Romain, his business partner in Toronto. Their family background was sketched in print in 1885:

> William Romain was born in Quebec, July 15, 1818, and is one of a family of eight children born of Pére and Elizabeth (McDonald) Romain. His father was born in Quebec in 1777 [*sic*; i.e. 1779], and his mother was the eldest daughter of Major McDonald, who was on active service in 1812. Pére [i.e. Pierre] Romain also served in that war as lieutenant.

An interjection is called for here: Pierre Romain (who died in 1858 and is buried in Oakville cemetery, the birthdate on his tombstone being the second earliest in the graveyard), had drawn up terms of apprenticeship with William Ayres, painter and glazer of Montreal, for his son William Frances in 1829, at the age of eleven. However, "Frank" Romain does not seem to have followed "the trade and business of Painter and Glazier with all things thereto belonging" after the age of twenty-one, as the agreement stipulated. Instead, as the 1885 profile continues,

> William Frances Romain came to Little York [Toronto] in May, 1830, and entered the service of Sir W.P. Howland & Brother, of Toronto Township, as clerk. Two years later he became manager for the pioneer store and grain dealer in the present town of Brampton, and was the first post-master of that place. He married Ann, eldest daughter of the late Colonel Wm. Chisholm, and settled in Oakville, Halton County.... Mr. Romain was Reeve of the Township of Trafalgar for two years; and when Oakville was incorporated as a town he served for many years as Councillor, and was twice elected unanimously as Mayor. The Romain Buildings on Kings Street West were built by himself and his brother.[18]

Wyndham Lewis obliquely acknowledged the existence of his Romain relatives in a letter of December 1940:

> The Romain Building is a blackened pile, plastered with statues, dated 1852—erected by my grt-uncle Charles Romain, which gives me a certain sentimental footing. Surely he must have been one of the earliest Torontonians, before the Scotch swamped the original French and English and with their asphyxiating godliness set up a reign of terror for the toper and the whoremaster, which makes life curiously difficult for the person who likes a couple of mild cocktails a day.[19]

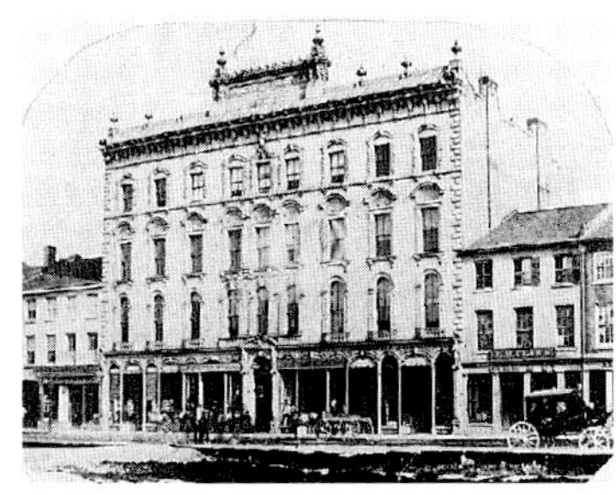
Fig. 4 The Romain Building, King Street West, Toronto, c. 1860s. Metropolitan Toronto Reference Library.

The Romain Buildings (fig. 4), designed by William Kauffmann, the architect of Toronto's Rossin House hotel (1855), the Masonic Hall (1857-58), the Bank of Toronto (1863), and the *Globe* building, were a joint project of W.F. and C.E. Romain. Erected in 1852, these premises, considered "the best piece of architecture of their day", entered the Canadian art-historical record in 1858, when they hosted the exhibition of *Oil Paintings, Water Colours, Engravings and Photographs, from the Private Collections of Gentlemen of Toronto*, mounted in aid of the building fund for St. Paul's Church, Yorkville. This was one of the first public art exhibitions to be held in the city.

Charles Edward Romain, after whom Wyndham Lewis's father was named, was born in Point Lévis, Quebec, in 1820. According to the historian and collector John Ross Robertson, he was "Of Italian descent"—a possibility, but just as likely a way of explaining the possession of a swarthy complexion at a time when having Indian blood was considered shameful.[20] He moved with his family to Toronto, where he received his education at Upper Canada College. "For some time he conducted business in Cooksville, Ont., as general merchant and grain dealer, later returning to Toronto. He took an active interest in civic affairs, sitting in the Council as councillor [for St. James Ward, in 1852-53], and from 1854-5 as alderman [of the same ward].... Later, on his removal to Guelph, he was appointed collector of inland revenue, and afterwards inspector. His death occurred in Guelph, Ont., in 1902."[21] But not before he had tried his hand at politics one more time, running as a reformer for a seat in the Legislative Council in the famous "rowdy election" of 1858—a contest he lost to the Conservative candidate, George William Allan, a former Toronto mayor who went on to become, among other things, the president of the Ontario Society of Artists and the purchaser of the collection of paintings of North American Indian life by Paul Kane that is now in the Royal Ontario Museum.

Lewis alluded to one of the Romain brothers in another letter to the same correspondent: "A little French Canadian cousin of mine (Pierette [Romain])...relates how her grandfather at Christmas would stand in the doorway of the farm to welcome his thirty or forty children and grandchildren, who would kneel and receive his blessing."[22] But if the Romains had kicked off the rural sod in the interim, they had also vaulted into the upper echelons of Oakville and Toronto society. For them to have done so in a single generation is all the more romantic, considering the fact that they may have had Huron Indian blood.

To backtrack: Lewis possibly drew from stories about these exotic ancestors as told to him by the Romain and Lewis relatives he contacted on his arrival in Toronto. He was not long in recasting them in the form of a projected but never-written novel, the title of which was to be *Hill 100*. The outline of this historical fiction begins:

> Story would open in early days of French colonization of Canada. *Hill 100* would be situated in goldmining area of Northern Ontario (border of Quebec, or inside latter province). Story would end upon same hill several centuries hence. Hill would then be marked Hill 100 upon Ordnance maps of the U.S. Army....
>
> Chapter I would reveal Fr.-Canadian, Castou, sitting with Indian at base of hill, covered with bush, gazing into stream.... He dislikes Canada—abominates its wilderness—loathes its Indians. However, he has made his bed, he must lie in it. He is a trapper. He is very far from the hamlet in Calvados from which he came some years before. There is no turning back—....

The Indian is described, somewhat incongruously, as a Dogrib (in actuality a Dene tribe of the Northwest Territories) with "a streak of Iroquois blood", and is named Mitouti, meaning "Wolf's Ear." Despite his antipathy to the race, Castou (whose patronymic is Gaston Laverrière) marries Mitouti's daughter, Kakapo, and they have four children, one of whom, named Antoinette, begins the line of the present-day French-Canadian family of Castou. Lewis continues:

> The next scene (chapter 4?) would show a 'Tory' family, horrified by the cold of the Maritimes, and especially of the unbelievable inclemency of.....in Nova Scotia, to which they have indignantly retired, after their fellow citizens in Philadelphia had parted company with the British Crown and declared themselves "independent"—it would show this greatly-tried and shivering family out to find a warmer place, further inland.
>
> They press on, by road and river...until they reach what then was called Upper Canada. That would be circa 1815, and the region would be that lying west of Kingston, Ontario, Port Grace, they would call it; because being on the St. Lawrence, at the mouth of a muddy little river, it could be called a port....

Chapter five introduces

> a certain Joseph Biggs, operating a rather prosperous store in Port Grace—reputed to be about the richest man in town, and [a] keen politician. This is about 1870. Joseph Biggs looks across the St. Lawrence at the Yankees, and is pretty glad to be a Canadian... [and] a pillar of the Methodist Church, and the Church is a pillar of his business. He had a son, Joseph Jnr., who is ten years old. Next we should move to the heart of the Gay Nineties: Joseph Biggs Jnr. has married a charming girl of "French extraction"—Huguenot, of course —named Antoinette Castou. The Castous turned up in Port Grace way back in the Eighteen Twenties, moving in from Montreal, I guess. (Lots of Huguenots in Ontario, with rather French names, came originally from Montreal.) These Castous had a corn-chandler's and [were] pretty smart people.
>
> The father of Antoinette was a lawyer, doing a big business in Kingston and Toronto. He was a pretty smart man. This was 1895, and Joseph Biggs Jnr. and Antoinette had a boy of ten, who was called Richard Russlyn Biggs. And Dick Biggs became a very smart man indeed.... Dick Biggs was in Toronto.... He was ostensibly interested in agricultural machinery....
>
> But Dick Biggs was not going to spend all his life as a salesman and agent for farm-implements.... No, one day Dick Biggs began prospecting—not himself of course, he was too smart for that, but paying other people to, buying up claims, financing and organizing small companies. By 1940 Dick Biggs was one of the hundred mining millionaires of the great gold and nickel city of Toronto....
>
> Now Mr. and Mrs. Biggs had a solitary child, a son,...named Alistair. Alistair...had met an American girl,...whom he is about to marry. She has come to the Biggs home at Mimico to meet her future father and mother-in-law....

Having thus blocked in the background, Lewis proposed to devote 100 pages to "the miner's life at Timmins", and a similar number to "the social structure of the city of Toronto, which is in fact a vast mining camp." However,

> ...the grand plan of the book is to show first the two European races, the French and the Anglosaxon, in their early colonizing stage. We start with the French trapper, who, like the majority of the early French settlers, married an Indian woman. There are not many French-Canadian families engaged in agriculture along the St. Lawrence who are not partly Indian. Quite half the French Canadians in such a city as Montreal—and *all* the French Canadians in Quebec—are perfectly visibly possessed of Indian blood. Well, it will be our purpose to show this conditioning of the French-Canadian stock in operation. There will be patriarchal scenes (perhaps the one described by Pierette of the arresting of the grandchildren, to the number of 100 at Easter, kneeling outside the front door, being blessed by the *grandpère* before they enter.)[23]

"Like most serious novelists", the editor of his letters insists, "Lewis was essentially an autobiographical writer".[24] There is certainly more than one kernel of the family-historical in this fragmentary outline. Working backwards, we can see that the French Canadian aspect is a reflection of his grandmother's heritage, which was also reputedly part-Indian, a fact of which Lewis was reportedly proud. Northrop Frye, who had criticized Lewis's anti-Spenglerianism in the pages of *Canadian Forum* in 1936, recalled hearing Lewis tell a Canadian audience about his alleged aboriginal origins:

> The only thing I remember discussing with him was his telling me that he was of partly Indian ancestry. I remarked that this threw a different light on *Paleface* [Lewis's 1929 attack on the "philosophy of the melting-pot"—a stance he was later to reverse], and he said that he didn't know himself about his Indian ancestry when he wrote his book.[25]

But Lewis may not have been pulling his listeners' legs about his "savage" heritage. Romain (French for "Roman") also happens to be well-known adoptive surname among the Huron-Wyandot of Quebec, being the patronymic of several generations of hereditary chiefs of the band at Village-Huron outside of Quebec City: André Tsouhahissen Romain, second chief of the Council, was a member of a four-man delegation that went to England in 1824-25 to petition King George for the Seigneury of Sillery, which had been appropriated by the Jesuits; Simon Tegaruilin Romain was grand chief of the Hurons at Lorette from 1845 to 1870, and Aimé Tehariolin Romain held the same post from 1944 to 1947. Wyndham Lewis's fascination with the mixing of the races extended to his description of his Toronto painter-friend A.Y. Jackson as having "the legendary dignity of the Indian, whom he resembles—so much so that, who knows, a Huron or something may lurk in his family-tree."[26] C.J. Fox finds the possibility that something Native might also "lurk" in Lewis's family tree "very interesting":

> And if there *is* an Indian connection, perhaps it would help to explain L's pictorial interest in totems as well as L.'s interest in the French Canadian-Indian kinship and the whole ethos of "Hill 100" and the concept of Paleface, etc. Certainly L's strange physiognomy (like [Pierre] Trudeau's) bears a trace of Can[adian] Indian admixture (via The Fr[ench]-Can[adian]). And note how L (cf. *Rude Assignment)* once compared highbrows (or was it painters?) to a strange tribe stuck on a reservation and visited there by tourist-like pseudo-highbrows. And note L.'s...fascination with the Indian-like Berbers of Morocco and the connection via Atlantis between Europe/Africa and the Mexico of the pre-Hispanic era, and his depiction of the Incas in "Inca and Birds" [i.e. *Inca with Birds* (1933; M P49)], etc., etc. All circumstantial evidence of course, butworth speculation about. Mrs. L. used to say that, at the time of writing "Do-Nothing Mode", L. was going to do something on his N. American family connections.... I think the story of L. delighting in portraying himself as part-Indian is probably apocryphal and his frightening the hell out of the shrinking-violet Bloomsburies in doing so). I seem to remember Mrs. L. laughing at the idea delightedly.... But certainly L.'s warpath orientation fitted this ethnic possibility![27]

There are other morsels of the Lewis/Romain family romance in the outline of "Hill 100." Mention of the town of Mimico, later to be distorted into Momaco in *Self Condemned*, suggests a knowledge of this community on the shore of Lake Ontario between Toronto and Oakville which he may have gleaned from a train trip, Mimico being a station on the line (the name, incidentally, being Mississauga Indian for Place of the Wild Pigeons). The name Biggs was stolen from that of the business partner of Lewis's Buffalo cousin George Chisholm. His shaky Canadian geography places Port Grace (suggested, perhaps, by the real Lake Ontario town of Port Hope, a station on the line between Toronto and Montreal?) on the St. Lawrence but *west* of Kingston, which is some distance from the mouth of that river to the east; perhaps its actual inspiration was Oakville, a small lakeport town, and the adoptive home of his American-born grandfather and French-Canadian grandmother.

As for that fictional family of Tory Loyalists who flee from the Maritimes to Upper Canada: here, surely, is a reference to a Lewis relation by marriage, William Chisholm (1788-1842), a militia officer, farmer, politician, office-holder and businessman whose father, George Chisholm, of Inverness, Scotland, had emigrated to Tryon County, New York and settled briefly in Nova Scotia after the outbreak of the American revolution before moving, by 1793, to what is now Ontario. William Chisholm, who grew up in the area of Burlington Bay, fought with distinction in the War of 1812, later became involved in reformist politics, then joined the Family Compact side against the rebel William Lyon Mackenzie. Not content with farming, he opened a general store, followed by an inn and a still, and by 1822 he was engaged in the burgeoning lumber trade. These interests led him to purchase the Crown land reserved for the Mississauga Ojibwa at the mouth of muddy Sixteen Mile (Oakville) Creek in 1827, his proposal being to develop the site as a shipyard and harbour. Having laid out the town and built a warehouse, he succeeded in 1828 in having an act passed vesting in him the rights for use of the harbour for fifty years. There followed the construction of a series of schooners and steamers (bearing such

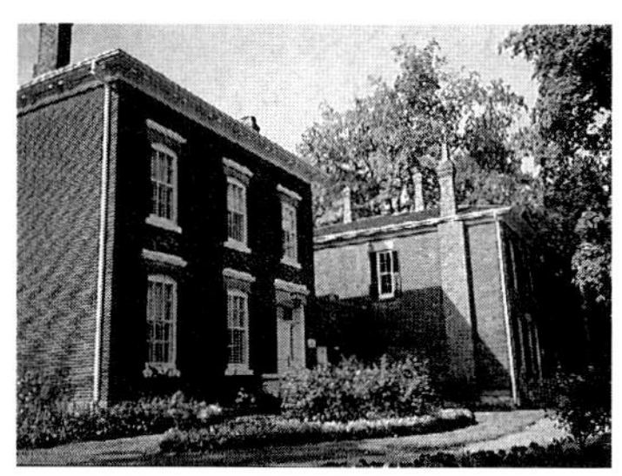

Fig. 5 "Erchless" Estate, Oakville, Ontario, erected 1858, with Custom House to the right, erected 1856; now the Oakville Museum, 8 Navy St. Photograph by Robert Stacey, 1992.

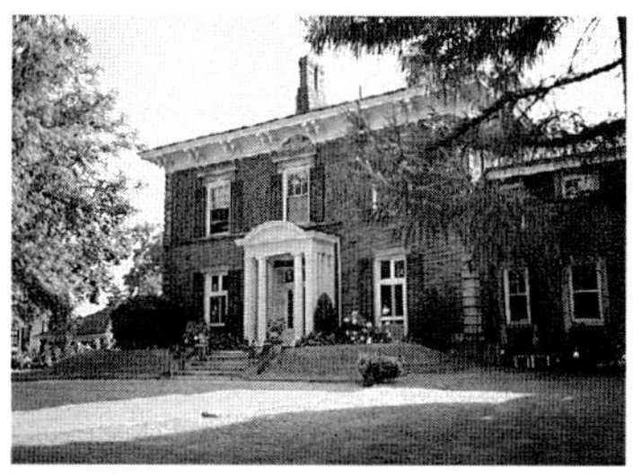

Fig. 6 The Romain House, 40 First Street, Oakville, erected 1855. Photograph by Robert Stacey, 1992.

names as *Mohawk Chief, Mississauga Chief and White Oak*) to transport the squared-timber pine and oak masts and staves that were the mainstay of the British navy.[28] Stories of this enterprise must have influenced Wyndham Lewis's lifelong fixation with ships and the sea, as much as the unusual circumstances of his own maritime birth.

It was William Chisholm's identification with Oakville's white-oak stave trade that earned him from the local Indians the epithet "White Oak"—one of the inspirations, incidentally, for the surname of the dynasty chronicled in Mazo de la Roche's hugely popular saga, *Jalna* (1927) and its sequels, which were written at nearby Clarkson. William Chisholm's third surviving son, Robert K. Chisholm (1819-1899), however, more likely provided the main source for the series' chief character, Rennie Whiteoak. After taking over from his deceased father as Oakville's Customs Officer and owner of Oakville Harbour in 1842, "R.K." became effectual head of the clan, and stood *in loco parentis* for his frequently embarrassed brothers, sisters and cousins. In 1856 R.K. Chisholm became engaged to, and in 1858 married Flora Matilda Lewis (1835-1918), daughter of Shebuel Lewis and Caroline Romain, and built for her a large brick Georgian-style mansion at the foot of Navy Street overlooking the harbour, which was named "Erchless" after the seat of the Chisholm clan in Inverness, Scotland; this imposing structure, with the former Custom House immediately to the southeast, today houses the Oakville Museum (fig. 5). One of four children, Wyndham Lewis's beloved Aunt "Tilly" (after whom the family firm had named a fifty-ton schooner) was to extend to his mother much-needed moral and financial support after her wayward husband, Charles E. Lewis, ran off with the maid in 1893.

Meanwhile, William F. Romain, described in the 1851 Census as a "general merchant, forwarder & agent for life, marine & fire insurance", and later as a "dealer in dry goods, groceries, provisions, hardware, etc.", had consolidated his position in Oakville by marrying Esther Ann Chisholm, oldest daughter of William Chisholm and his wife Rebecca *(née)* Silverthorn, of a locally powerful family whose nearby house, Cherry Hill, had come into the hands of their nephew, William Stanislaus Romain, by profession an actor. (Another Romain, Zamer, a merchant at Port Credit, had married William Chisholm's niece Elizabeth Rebecca Silverthorn.)

William and Esther had six children, who with their cousins were educated by tutor in the family's large, elegant brick house, built at 40 First Street in 1855 (fig. 6). The central window of the façade of the Romain House (as it is still called) was embellished by a crest depicting a fleur-de-lis, representing Romain's French-Canadian background, and the Cross of St. Andrew, representing his wife's Scottish Chisholm ancestry.[29] In 1854 he formed a grain-shipping partnership with Peter McDougall, who had married another of Chisholm's daughters, and two years later built a stone granary (still standing). Also in 1854, Romain financed the construction of the three-storey limestone Navy Block (also still standing), on the second floor of which Lewis Hall, "the only public hall in the village" was opened, and here auctions were conducted. However, like his father-in-law, Romain overextended himself and, with the collapse of the grain-shipping industry in 1869, was forced to declare bankruptcy, losing his house and its furnishings to his creditors. Although he was able to re-establish himself on a lesser scale as a general merchant, he never regained the splendid property he had been forced to forfeit.

Economic and other disasters seem to run through Chisholm, Romain and Lewis history—no demise being so novelistic, perhaps, as that of the bankrupted William Chisholm's profligate grandson Thomas Charles Chisholm, who disappeared in 1873 on a trip to New York, his body finally being found floating in the river in which it had been dumped by his probable assassin. (Lewis may have had this lurid incident in mind when devising the fate of Dougal Tandish, the rich playboy who is shot and thrown into the Thames by the counterfeiter Halvorson and his accomplice, Vincent Penhale, in *The Vulgar Streak*, written in 1940 and published in 1941.) Fire as well as financial problems seems to be a common denominator in these catastrophes, a phenomenon that may have added a certain *déja-vu* quality to Wyndham Lewis's own experience of the spectacular Tudor Hotel blaze of February 1943. During a dry spell in October 1871 Chisholm's Bush caught fire, the town itself being saved only by a shift in the wind. Then, in 1883, Oakville's worst conflagration nearly wiped out the entire business section, taking with it the handsome Romain Block and the adjoining stores. Nor was Lewis's grandfather spared this bane. As the great-granddaughter of Col. William Chisholm relates,

> The fire brigade was quite powerless to act when the brick house of Shubel [sic] Lewis, built in 1874, caught fire on a February day in 1888. The house, turreted like a castle and impressive if ugly, stood in a thick grove of trees high on the bank overlooking the lake on the west side of the harbour. On the day of the fire the temperature was ten

degrees below zero, and icebergs extended so far out into the lake that the fire hose could not reach the open water. The firemen were obliged to stand by while the house burned to the ground.[30]

Some thirty years earlier, on his retirement in 1859, Shebuel Lewis had moved his family to the idyllic western New York village of Nundā (pronounced Nunday), where he "indulged his inordinate weakness for horseflesh", but by 1873 the Lewises returned to Canada. Both of Wyndham Lewis's grandparents are buried in the iron-fenced Chisholm plot in Oakville St. Mary's Cemetery (fig. 7). It is not known whether, in the 1940s, Wyndham Lewis was able to pay a visit to Oakville, where Chisholms were still in residence, however precariously, at Erchless, but the reduced fortunes of his once-prosperous Canadian relatives must have proved a major disappointment to someone as habitually insolvent and in search of financial relief as himself. He was aware that some members of the extended family had done well for themselves in the United States: for instance, Charles E. Lewis's elder brother was the director of several banks and utility companies and president of the Bell, Lewis and Yates Coal Company of Buffalo, which at one point was producing a million tons a year. But when, in Buffalo in the fall of 1939, Lewis had looked up his cousins Alfred George Lewis Jr. and George and Harry Lewis, the sons of his aunt Matilda, he found that "The family had lost their considerable wealth and social status, but not their snobbish pretentions; Lewis thought they were 'shits' and satirized them as the Grahames"[31] in *America I Presume* (1940). His Toronto uncle, Albert Lewis, a lawyer and "the *Gelehrter* [scholar] of the family," had run through "three fortunes."[32] On the other hand, Lewis found his cousin Pierrette Romain "good value"—probably because she was able to supply him with colourful anecdotes of Romain family history and legend.[33] Perhaps it was his belated reclamation of his own French-Canadian ancestry that induced him to make an "Address to French-Canada" over the C.B.C. in which he explained that his license to speak in French (however fractured) derived not only from his having spent "la moitié de sa jeunesse en France", but because "Ma grand mère était Canadienne. Sa langue à elle était française. Il se peut bien qu'il y aient parmi vous qui à cette heure m'écoutent des cousins—aussi loin que ce soit. (Sa famille s'appelait *Romain*. It peut bien se trouver des *Romains* dans cette auditoire aerienne.)"[34]

Unfortunately, Lewis's removal from the New World to the Old in 1888, when he was six, happened too early in his life for him to have formed an identity as a North American. The occasional word from across the Atlantic came through the correspondence Anne Stuart Lewis maintained with such Oakville and Toronto relatives as Matilda Chisholm and Albert Lewis, who in 1899, when his nephew was attending the Slade School of Art in London, received from his brother "Char" a sketchbook of young Wyndham's which prompted this approving reply:

> I am not artist but shd. think Percy had a decided inclination for Art—and should give it full encouragement.
>
> It's a good thing for one's boys to be included to some good and use[ful] calling—you are to be congratulated in Percy's bent for something providing he has some purpose, economy, and the power of sticking at what he undertakes, and will make the most of it.[35]

However, the tie with any sense of Canada as "home" had effectively been snapped when Charles Lewis abandoned his wife and son, who in consequence became extremely close. Wyndham Lewis's at best ambivalent and at worst openly hostile feelings toward his birthplace may have had something to do with the fact that his father returned to North America and was an unreliable source of support of his deserted family until his death.

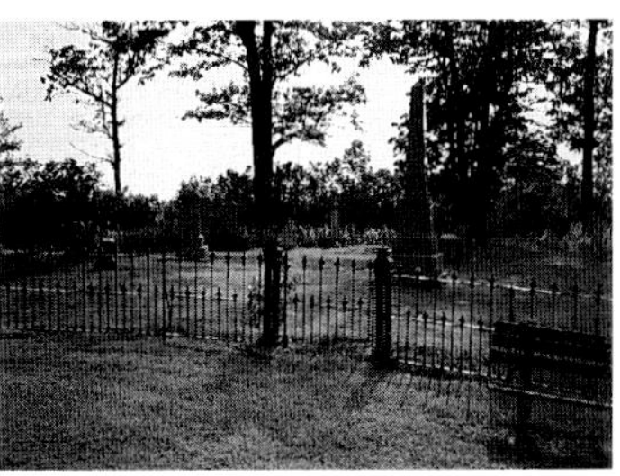

Fig. 7 The Chisholm/Lewis family plot, Oakville St. Mary's Cemetery, Oakville, Ontario, showing (l. to r.) gravestones of Shubuel (*sic*)and Caroline (*née* Romain) Lewis, William and Rebecca (*née* Silverthorn) Chisholm, and Robert K. and Matilda (*née* Lewis) Chisholm

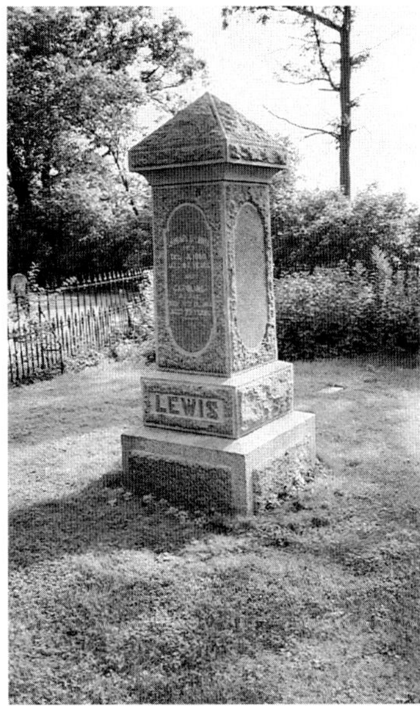

Fig. 8 Tombstone of Shubuel (*sic*) and Caroline Lewis. Both photos by Robert Stacey, 1992.

LEWIS'S CASTIGATIONS of Toronto in particular, and of Canada in general (as exemplified by his description of the latter as "the most parochial nationette on earth"), have not deterred Canadians from playing leading roles in the revival of his reputation and the editing, publishing and critical study of his visual and literary production. In fact, the negativity of the Enemy's pronouncements about his native land, while generating mixed feelings of guilt and resentment, has indirectly led to a concerted campaign to right wrongs, defend against unjust slurs, correct misconceptions, set the record straight, and above all make amends for the slights and neglect that, real or imagined, Lewis suffered while "trapped" in Toronto and Windsor. The disproportionate number of writers, academics, art historians, curators, critics, bibliographers and publishers quoted in these pages and listed in the selected bibliography who have been instrumental in doing Lewis at least posthumous justice and who also happen to be Canadian natives, or at least are Canadian-based, is neither accidental nor evidence of citational chauvinism.

Perhaps the first Canadian to have a direct effect on Lewis's career was the Toronto-born friend and executor of Oscar Wilde, Robert Ross, who had called Lewis "a buffalo in wolf's clothing". Ross was the founding director of London's Carfax Gallery, where Lewis participated in three group shows in 1911 and 1912; in his capacity as advisor to the British War Memorials Committee, he had influenced the format of Lewis's *Canadian Gun-pit*, painted for the Canadian War Memorials in 1918, by recommending Paulo Uccello's *The Battle of San Romano* in the National Gallery, London, as being "a very charming size" for such an undertaking. The New Brunswick-born Lord Beaverbrook it was, of course, who established the Canadian War Records Office, which got Lewis out of the trenches and back to the easel. The other Canadian art dealer to take up Lewis was Douglas Duncan, proprietor of the Picture Loan Gallery in Toronto. Douglas, though unthanked for his efforts, represented, collected and supported Lewis in the darkest days of the 1940s, and subsequently lent works to exhibitions which planted the seeds of interest in Lewis in a variety of inquiring minds. Two of Lewis's publishers have been Canadian: Lovat Dickson (the "discoverer" of Grey Owl), who brought out his anti-war pamphlet *Count Your Dead, They Are Alive!* in 1927; and Lorne Pierce, for whom he wrote *Anglosaxony: A League that Works* in 1941. The torch of Lewis championship was passed from the Alberta-born, University of Toronto-educated Marshall McLuhan, who befriended and promoted his prickly mentor in Windsor and St. Louis, Hugh Kenner, another U. of T. graduate, who met McLuhan in 1946 at St. Michael's College and at his suggestion applied for and obtained a teaching position at Assumption College, going on to publish the first comprehensive survey of Lewis and his work in 1954 (a study McLuhan himself had contemplated writing); to Vernon Van Sickle,[36] an Ottawa admirer of Lewis from the mid-1930s following his reading of *Men Without Art*, and a founder of the Ottawa Film Society, who awakened the interest of a young scientifically minded protégé, Walter Michel, who, after getting his masters degree in fine art at New York University, published his Wyndham Lewis *catalogue raisonnée* published in 1971, with an essay by Hugh Kenner; to the Newfoundland-born, London-based journalist C.J. Fox, who befriended the blind Lewis and his wife in London, compiled with Michel the anthology *Wyndham Lewis on Art,* founded and edited *Lewisletter* (later renamed *Enemy News*), and has long served as a member of the Wyndham Lewis Memorial Trust; and to the Toronto antiquarian bookdealer Hugh Anson-Cartwright, who was put onto Lewis by Mrs. Shirley Van Sickle and went on to form one of the best collections of his books and drawings in private hands. This legacy of service to the sometimes seemingly lost cause of Wyndham Lewis has been furthered by the work of such Canadian writers, critics and editors as Sheila Watson, George Woodcock, Rowland Smith, Toby Foshay, Bryant Knox, Linda Sandler, Robert Fulford and B.W. Powe.

"The Talented Intruder" is offered as a continuation of the past work of these distinguished precursors and as an invitation to scholars and artlovers of the future to carry forward from here the collective project of recovery and rediscovery, for, to paraphrase Lewis, "The present cannot become yesterday until it has been revealed to us."

The Talented Intruder

CATHARINE M. MASTIN

"A Question of Force Majeure"

IT WAS DURING WORLD WAR I that Wyndham Lewis received his first opportunity to put his Canadian citizenship to use by signing on as a war artist with the Canadian War Memorials in 1917. Earlier that same year, he had joined the British Royal Garrison Artillery as a gunnery officer. A bout of trench fever, and first-hand experience of the horrors of the front, had made Lewis less than enthusiastic about remaining in a combat role. Even before enlisting in 1916, he had written to a hoped-for patroness (and lover) of his fear that he "must join the Army" and that he had "as little reason to be shot at once and *without a hearsay* as any artist in Europe, but have certain accomplishments...that might be more of use to pen-polyglot alliés than my trusty right arm, which, I flatter myself, is rather a creative than a destructive limb."[1]

On compassionate leave in London in November 1917 to visit his mother, who had taken seriously ill with pneumonia, he was advised by his flat-mate and patron, Captain Guy Baker, to apply for a war-artist position. The Canadian War Memorials scheme was set up a year before by Sir Max Aitken (Lord Beaverbrook), the New Brunswick-born press magnate and wartime minister of information in the British government, to provide a visual record of Canada's involvement in the conflict, and to commission mural-scale paintings to decorate the Parliament Buildings in Ottawa. Beaverbrook was serving as historian and archivist for the recently established Canadian War Records Office in London; assisting him in choosing participating artists, British as well as Canadian, was P.G. Konody, the art critic for the *Observer* and a cautious friend of the English modernist movement, whose leadership Lewis had lately assumed. It was thanks not only to his Canadian birth but to his direct experience as a gunner that Lewis won his commission; further, his Vorticist style, a response to the Machine Age, was considered to give him an advantage in the depiction of heavy artillery and violent action.

Lewis and a fellow graduate of the Slade School, Augustus John, returned to France toward the end of 1917, with directions to report to Canadian Army Headquarters at Vimy Ridge. Lewis sketched, in ink, graphite and watercolour, such subjects as shell-firing, digging pits for guns, and the frequent intervals of inactivity between bombardments during which the officers lounged about, smoked, and drank rum. His thorough understanding of the mechanical forms and technical functions of the guns and other weapons also provided him with abundant material for pictures.

The most significant work resulting from Lewis's involvement with the War Memorials was the monumental, *A Canadian Gun-Pit* (1918) (fig. 9)—the largest canvas he ever completed. In preparation for it, Lewis had studied the mural-scale paintings of three great war artists, Paulo Uccello (1397-1475), Francisco Goya (1746-1828) and Diego Velasquez (1599-1660), which he had seen on display in the National Gallery, London, and at other galleries and museums in Europe.

In addition to gaining experience in the construction of large pictures for the historical record, Lewis also further developed some of the stylistic elements of his earlier, Vorticist mode. The forms of his war works are simplified, angular, and painted with bold colours, such as yellow-ochre and cobalt and navy blues. As Lewis retrospectively observed, "War, and especially those miles of hideous desert known as 'the Line' in Flanders and France, presented me with a subject-matter so consonant with the austerity of the 'abstract' vision I have developed, that it was an easy transition."[2] A more-or-less naturalistic painting, *A Canadian Gun-pit* differs significantly in style from the flattened space and geometricized abstraction of his Vorticist-period works; the figures are recognizably human, despite their mechanical postures, and the space, though compacted, recedes logically from foreground to middle-ground and background. The expressionless faces and rigid poses of the officers, who stand idly in the foreground, contrasted with the insect-like bustle of the soldiers in the background and middle-ground, make a strong statement about the monotonous yet constantly threatened daily life of the battery. The blasted, lifeless trees, stripped of all foliage, the gloomy sky, and the dark, cold colour-scheme reinforce the mood of desolation and danger. Lewis remarked in the foreword to the catalogue of his important exhibition, *Guns,* held at the Goupil Gallery in January 1919: "I have attempted here only one thing: that is in a direct, ready formula to give an interpretation of what I took part in in France. I set out to do a series dealing with the Gunner's life from his arrival in the Depôt to his life in the Line."[3] *A Canadian Gun-pit,* and such preparatory works-on-paper as the sketch bearing the same title (c. 1917-18; fig. 10), can be considered the first examples of Lewis's art that are directly associated with his native land.[4] One of the first Canadian critics to respond to the work was a recent arrival from Yorkshire, Barker Fairley, who in 1919 astutely observed that

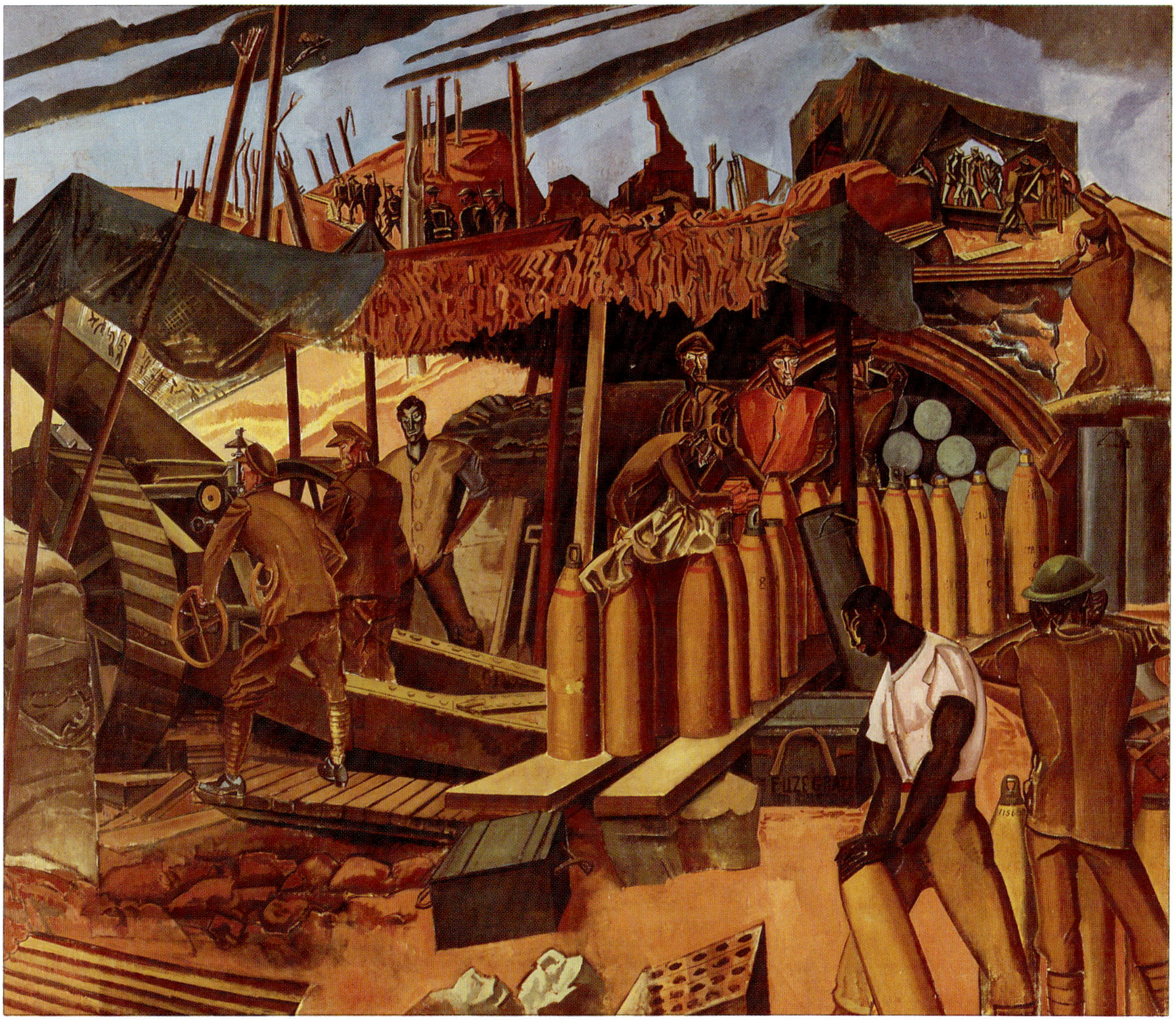

Fig. 9 Wyndham Lewis: *A Canadian Gun-pit*, 1918, oil on canvas (305.0 x 335.0 cm). National Gallery of Canada, Ottawa, transfer from the Canadian War Memorials, 1921.

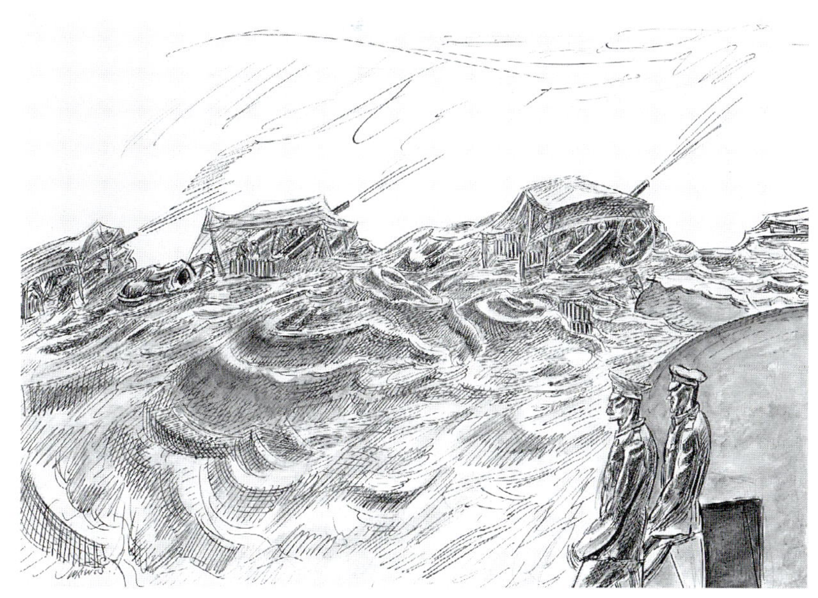

Fig. 10 Wyndham Lewis: *A Canadian Gun-pit*, c. 1917-18, pen and dark brown ink over graphite with watercolour wash on wove paper (35.4 x 50.9 cm). National Gallery of Canada, Ottawa, transfer from the Canadian War Memorials, 1921.

> If the War had come ten years earlier it is unlikely that Paul Nash's "Void", Wyndham Lewis's "Canadian Gunpit" or [C.R.W.] Nevinson's "Roads to France" would have been executed in anything like their present form.... Quite early in the war it was noticed that the breath-taking experiments of the years immediately preceding, the cubism and the vorticism and what not that had seemed so outrageous and even inexplicable to an overwhelming majority of normal human beings, had received at least a partial justification in the actual experience of men, both in what they had before their eyes and in what they felt within themselves. This is but another instance of the connection, causal or otherwise, that is so frequently found to exist between what is apparently unrelated in a given period of civilization. It is disturbing to healthy pluralistic minds but is has to be faced, and, if possible, explained.[5]

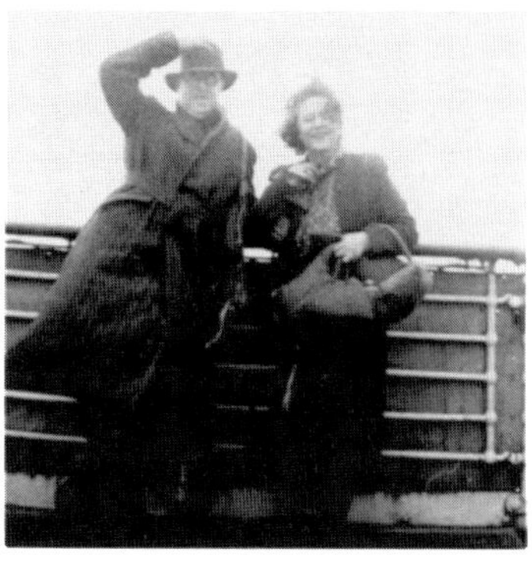

Fig. 11 Wyndham and Anne Lewis on board *The Empress of Britain* en route to Canada, September 1939; or on board the *Strathden* en route to England, August 1945. Photograph: Cornell.

WYNDHAM LEWIS'S BOND WITH CANADA was unintentionally though signficantly strengthened during the Second World War. He and his wife, Gladys Anne Lewis (nicknamed "Froanna"), had planned to sail to New York City in the early summer of 1939. However, because Anne Lewis was superstitious about sailing on a Friday, they rebooked their tickets, embarking instead on board *The Empress of Britain* (whose cargo, incidentally, included oil paintings from British public collections which were bound for safe-keeping in the National Gallery of Canada in Ottawa). The switch to another vessel was indeed fortunate, as the one that sailed on that fatal Friday ended up being torpedoed by a German submarine. The trans-Atlantic voyage was extended by a detour into Arctic waters to avoid attack by submarines, as described by Lewis:

> The sea got rougher and rougher, the temperature colder and colder. We were going north. We were on our way to Greenland. We had cut off our radio and were holding no communication with the outside world. We were just seeking safety among the ice-floes; and now, all our portholes and saloon windows blacked out, and our decks hemmed in with canvas, to make us invisible to an external enemy, we were all by ourselves, in an icy sea, plunging along at top speed in the general direction of the Northwest Passage.[6]

The Lewises probably disembarked at Quebec City and took the train to Toronto, staying there for no more than a fortnight before to moving on to Buffalo and New York City, where they ended up spending the better part of a year.

The reasons for the move to North America are complex, but one fact that can hardly be disputed is that Lewis wished to avoid the devastation that the war would bring to England, and especially to London. Even without the threat of invasion and bombardment, a pessimistic outsider like Lewis could hardly have been sanguine about an improvement of the hostile political and economic climate of the late 1930s. Although he had publicly rejected his previous stance in favour of Hitler, written early in the 1930s before news of Nazi brutality had leaked to the West, he was reluctant to be conscripted by the government propaganda machine, as was expected of members of the intelligentsia who were too old to fight, nor was the old combatant likely to have joined the ranks of the conscientious objectors whose passivity, if not pacifism, he despised. Rightly or wrongly, he believed there was no alternative to the course he took. Lewis may well have been encouraged to make the move by his first editor and publisher, the novelist Ford Madox Ford, who had been teaching at Olivet College in Michigan, an institution at which Lewis himself later unsuccessfully sought employment. Ford and Lewis were part of a veritable exodus of writers, musicians and artists who quit Europe on the eve of war, significant among whose numbers were W.H. Auden, Christopher Isherwood, Thomas Mann, Berthold Brecht, Vladimir Nabokov, Arnold Schoenberg, Igor Stravinsky, Benjamin Britten, Salvador Dalí, André Masson, Amédée Ozenfant and Yves Tanguy.

Lewis had made two previous trips to New York, the first in 1927 and the second in 1931. His decision to return in 1939 must have been based on the supposition that he could support himself and his wife in the New World by writing and painting portraits. "My presence on the North American continent", he optimistically wrote to the publisher of his novel *The Vulgar Streak* in the spring of 1939, "is a question of force majeure. I can earn a living here whereas I doubt if I could in England. When the war started I wanted to go back, but at the time was going through a major economic Blitz of my own, and had not the necessary jack."[7] Certain of his success in America, Lewis in 1940 confidently and accurately described himself, for self-promotion purposes, as "the famous novelist, essayist, pamphleteer, editor, poet, painter and draughtsman."[8] He claimed that he wanted to make quick money so as to enable him to erase a series of debts that he had left behind in England, and to provide himself with a financial cushion for the future. To his dismay, however, Lewis soon discovered that New York was "crowded with people on the same errand as myself."[9] His finances had been crippled by a number of serious illnesses that he had suffered during the 1930s, and by the eclipse of his critical reputation, which he blamed on the machinations of his arch-enemies, the Bloomsbury Group and the Sitwells. So devastating was Lewis's predicament that he had to turn to his few remaining friends for payment of his medical expenses over the better part of the decade. Beleaguered as he was by "Doctors and dentists bills, butcher bills, rent," he lamented, "War itself, when it came, would, I knew, complete my economic frustration."[10]

Despite his often justified complaints about being an unknown or forgotten figure in the United States and Canada, Lewis was also faced with hostility on the part of those who did know of him, through his reputation if not through his actual writing and artwork. Nowhere in Lewis's explanations for his North American sojourn, however, does he mention the real cause of his notoriety, which erupted in 1931 after the publication of his controversial book *Hitler,* in which he approvingly observed the rise of the Fascist régime in Germany. Although he does not seem to have considered himself a political exile in Canada, but rather, as he termed it in the novel he based on his Canadian experience, a "self condemned" one, the views expressed in *Hitler* did him permanent damage. So sensitive was he to the harm done to his credibility by the earlier publication that, when his young disciple Hebert Marshall McLuhan (1911-1980) asked him to sign his copy, Lewis tore it up and threw it into a nearby incinerator.[11]

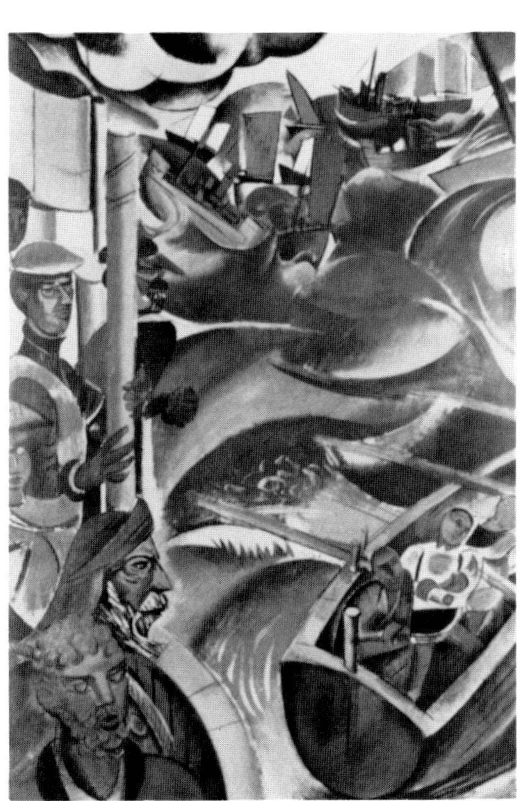
No. 1 *Newfoundland,* 1937, oil on canvas (70.5 x 49.5 cm), M P67. Junior Common Room, New College, Oxford.

Lewis had been seduced by the concept of the German "New Democracy," and naively believed Adolf Hitler to be a man of peace. At the time Lewis wrote *Hitler,* after a visit to Berlin in 1930, the Nazi leader had promised that destructive weapons would not be used against his political opponents. He believed that the National Socialist system proposed by Hitler would provide artists and writers with leading roles in the creation of the "new society." By the mid-1930s, circumstances were changing rapidly in the politically volatile Germany, and Lewis attempted to retract his original support for Hitler with the publication of *Left Wings Over Europe* (1936), *The Jews, Are They Human?* (1939), and *The Hitler Cult and How it will End* (1939). However, it was his previous polemic that was remembered and his later, more liberal publications, which continued to warn against the coming global conflict, were ignored by his North American critics.

Lewis had also wanted to research his North American family background, and soon located relatives in Toronto, New York and Buffalo.[12] He had demonstrated his interested in his Atlantic coast origins in the preceding decade when he included the painting *Newfoundland* (1937; no. 1) in a series of pictures depicting Nordic nautical and military exploits, a subject that had stimulated his imagination since his Vorticist years.[13] *Newfoundland* pays homage to the Norse explorers and fishermen who discovered and settled this island long before it became a British crown colony; it may also be a commentary on colonization and the depredations of the as-yet unspoiled New World by the marauding Europeans. Judging from his writings, Lewis was not much interested in later developments in Canadian history, and in his rare comments about his hosts he clearly favoured the culture and society of Quebec, with its mixed Norman and Indian roots, than that of English-speaking Canada.

Once in New York, the Lewises were prevented by several complications from being able to return as soon as they had hoped to London, the continuation of the war over nearly six years rather than the anticipated six months being the main cause of delay. As the conflict progressed, strict regulations were imposed upon currency transferral and Atlantic travel; Lewis spent all the money he had brought with him within a few months, and for the next six years he was unable to afford passage back to England.

AFTER A YEAR, which Lewis spent painting portraits and writing books and articles in the cities of Buffalo and New York, the couple's U.S. visitors' visas expired and they turned to Toronto as their next place of residence. The decision to move to this city, usually referred to an unfortunate occurence in Lewis's life, was, however, far more calculated on his part than has previously been understood. The Lewises' brief visit in mid-September 1939 stemmed from his friendship with John Reid, a young Toronto writer then working for the National Film Board, whom Lewis had met in England in the summer of 1939, and who also returned to Canada on board the *Empress of Britain*. An ardent admirer of Lewis's work, Reid had sought out the author's advice on a novel he was then writing, entitled *Puppet's Dream*.[14]

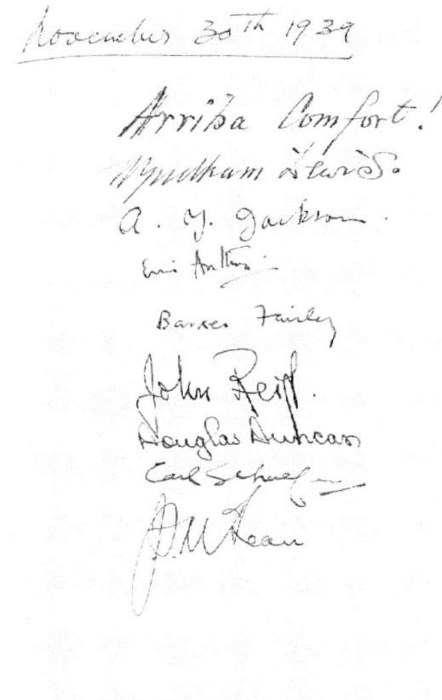

Fig. 12 Entry in Charles and Louise Comfort's guest-book, 30 November 1939, with signatures of Wyndham Lewis, A.Y. Jackson, Eric Arthur, Barker Fairley, John Reid, Douglas Duncan, Carl Schaefer and J.W. Mclean. National Archives of Canada, Ottawa, gift of Charles and Louise Comfort, 1992. Photograph by George Falconer.

Throughout 1939 and 1940, the Lewises maintained communications with Reid and other acquaintances whom they had met through him. Reid and his friend Terence W.L. MacDermot, the principal of Upper Canada College, a private boys' school in Toronto, were convinced that Canada needed Lewis's talents and tried to come up with employment opportunites for him.[15] MacDermot's position at U.C.C. gave him access to the city's wealthier set, who, he hoped, would provide Lewis with portrait commissions. In addition, MacDermot, like Reid, was highly impressed with Lewis's reputation as an internationally respected writer, and sought ways of getting him involved in the founding of an independent Canadian literary periodical.[16] "We need pens in this country—badly, as any perusal of any 'Canadian Litterchoor' will show", he wrote to Lewis in June 1940.[17]

Lewis made a second trip to Toronto in mid-November 1939, staying this time for about two weeks. According to John Reid's recollections, on 30 November a dinner was held in Lewis's honour at Toronto's York Club, hosted by the president of Canada Packers Inc., J.S. McLean, the city's most prominent collector of contemporary Canadian art. Also present on this occasion were three of the most prominent Canadian artists of the day: Charles F. Comfort (b. 1900), A.Y. Jackson (1882-1974), and Carl Schaefer (b. 1903); as well as John Reid, the art dealer and connoisseur Douglas M. Duncan (1902-1968), the architect and architectural historian Eric Arthur (1898-1982), and the aforementioned Barker Fairley (1887-1986), the founding editor of *Canadian Forum*, a teacher of German literature at the University of Toronto, an internationally recognized Goethe scholar, and one of the first and most vocal champions of the Group of Seven (fig. 12). Lewis had met Jackson during World War I at the London offices of the Canadian War Records, where he may also have encountered such fellow war artists as J.W. Beatty (1869-1941), David B. Milne (1882-1953) and Frederick H. Varley (1881-1969). The son of the president of Provincial Paper Limited, Duncan was an independently wealthy bibliophile and bookbinder who in 1936 co-founded the Picture Loan Society, an alternative gallery and art-rental service on Toronto's Charles Street, at which Lewis's "imaginative" watercolours were to be on display on several occasions between 1941 and 1943. Over several years Lewis maintained an acquaintance and correspondence with McLean, who in January 1940 wrote to him regarding a possible meeting in New York to view the Picasso exhibition at the Museum of Modern Art. Schaefer, a painter of rural Ontario landscapes and later a war artist, also kept in touch with Lewis after this meeting.[18]

At first hopeful that this clique of admirers would be able to supply him with lucrative contacts and employment, Lewis soon began to find fault with Toronto generally and in particular with certain aspects of its art scene and arts community, which, he felt, was not doing enough on his behalf. Besides, compared to what he was familiar with in England, the city struck him as being small-minded and parochial, and he could not resist poking fun at its apparent lack of history and culture. The events of a visit to the University of Toronto's Hart House (on the afternoon of the York Club dinner), during which he was given a guided tour of this men's facility by its warden, Burgon Bickersteth, were semi-fictionalized in Lewis's *America, I Presume*, published in April 1940, while the author was living in New York. Lewis's contempt for the place was clearly expressed in his description of the recently completed Hart House chapel murals by the Canadian painter, Will Ogilvie (fig. 13). Ogilvie had intended the scheme, dating from 1936, to mimic Italian altarpieces while also reflecting aspects of the Canadian landscape. Lewis did not see the murals that way, however, and it is on account of such derogatory remarks as those expressed in the following passage that he met with a certain degree of hostility when seeking to make his *entrée* in the small and self-protective Toronto art scene, for both Hart House and its patrons, the wealthy and powerful Massey family, were sacrosanct in Toronto:

Fig. 13 William A. Ogilvie (1901-1989), *Study for Hart House Chapel Mural: Adam*, c. 1936, oil on canvas (45.7 x 121.8 cm). National Gallery of Canada, Ottawa.

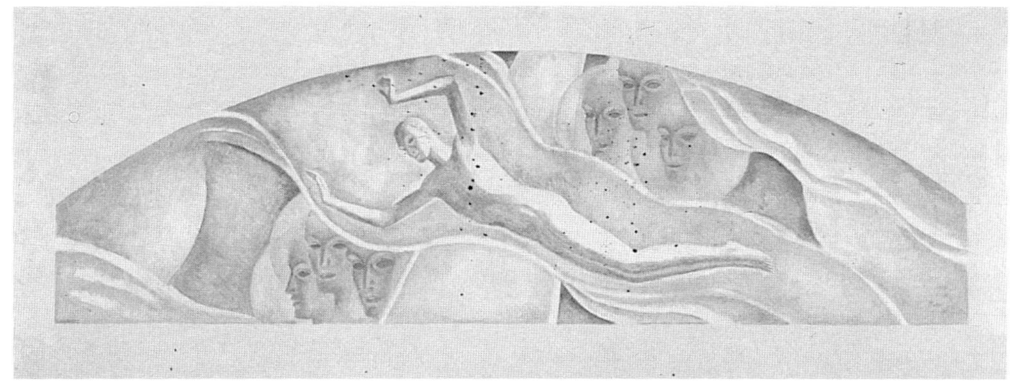

> More pictures! Murals of hundreds of horrid little angels, all with the same face, like strings of quintuplets. Like that Johnny Blake, that kind of thing. Spooky and ugly. Hope I don't go to heaven if it looks like that.
>
> The place was too small to be of any use. Only intended for prayer he said, but who prays, except at church? Apart from Catholics. The whole set-up had a rather popish look to me. Again a chapel, like a lavatory, oughtn't to be kept locked. What would you do if you wanted to pray? Go to the Warden and say: "Please, sir, may I have the key of the chapel? I should like to pray."
>
> I sat down—didn't know what was expected of me. Really felt quite like prayer—The Good Lord deliver us part of the Litany—when Brandelboyes [i.e. his guide, the Hart House Warden, Burgon Bickersteth] hissed in my ear, for we whispered to each other while we were in there— "Jolly little place, rather? No? We're rather proud of it. Took a lot of trouble trying to get it right."

Lying, Lewis replied to Bickersteth:

> "I think it's quite beautiful," I said. It's so peaceful."
> "Isn't it? But I can't get the lighting right."
> "No? It seems to me... Well it's jolly nice. Topping little retreat for the footsore and weary."[19]

Realizing how offensive he had been in his description of this occasion, Lewis later attempted to explain away his satirical comments of the building and its ambience, but even his rationalizations had a sarcastic edge. He wrote to MacDermot:

> The more I think of that Hart House burlesque, the more I feel that if the master (whom I rather highhandedly borrowed to have a little fun with) realized how impressed I was for I can say with my hand on my heart that I do not believe another such educational, or recreative, wonder is to be found anywhere on this earth, and that it is a tremendous feat to have built up that hive of collegiate activity — he would not mind the burlesque form my admiration took.... It is what is so wonderful in America and could be found in no other country.[20]

WHEN THE LEWISES ARRIVED IN TORONTO on 18 November 1940,[1] they took up residence in the Tudor Hotel (fig. 14) at 559 Sherbourne, just south of Bloor Street. Douglas Duncan previously had recommended the Tudor to the painter and printmaker David Milne, whose agent he had become in 1938, as a reasonably priced and conveniently located place to stay after his departure from Six Mile Lake in 1939, and it is likely that he also steered Lewis there as well. Milne had relocated to Uxbridge, north of Toronto, before Lewis's return to Toronto, but both artists undoubtedly met once Lewis began showing at Duncan's Picture Loan Gallery in 1941. Although the Tudor was intended as an interim address, the Lewises were to spend almost all of their stay in Toronto at this somewhat seedy hotel, remaining there until June 1943 when they moved to Windsor. Lewis frequently referred to these years as his "Tudor period"[2]—an ironic reference to his incarceration in the half-timbered fake-Tudor encasement where he rented an apartment consisting of "one big room, kitchen and bathroom" for fourteen dollars per week.[3]

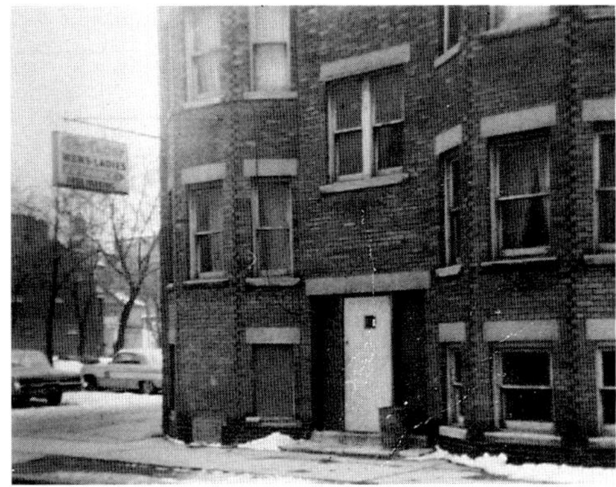

Fig. 14 The Tudor Hotel, Sherbourne St., Toronto, c. 1960 (remaining original section after fire of 1943). Photograph: Cornell.

The Lewises were not being excessively critical when they described the shortcomings of their cramped and overheated apartment. The Tudor was situated on what was then considered the "wrong" (i.e. working-class) side of Toronto's main north-south thoroughfare, Yonge Street, and attracted (thanks to the rowdy bar on the premises) a somewhat undesirable clientèle, who, however, Lewis found more interesting or at least more amusing than most of the academics, culturati and businessmen who crossed his path. After a year and a half of living there, Lewis wrote to an American friend, "the present phase of my existence is amazingly un-pleasant. I am an involuntary squatter in this drab wilderness".[4] To an American correspondent he vowed, "If I ever get out of this hotel room alive... I shall look back on it as on a black pit."[5] Anne Lewis responded with less hostility to the hotel and to Toronto in general than did her husband, and she found that, because of the wartime atmosphere, "a kind of community spirit emerged" at the Tudor.[6]

Despite the noisiness, overcrowding and general squalor of the hotel, Lewis for the first month after his arrival was reasonably confident that he would be able to work and make a living in Toronto, and that his circumstances were preferable to those of the previous year. "After the winter of my discontent in the long and chilly shadow of that Statue of Liberty", he wrote to the American critic Geoffrey Stone in December 1940, "I feel as if I had come up out of a coalmine or a dungeon into the fresh air again."[7] Canada, he informed this same correspondent, "seems a 'land of opportunity' though of course one's problem is to keep calm while this or that opportunity is pruned down and secured to one."[8] And Toronto, he confidently told Stone, "is turning out more promising than anticipated".[9] Lewis explained that he expected to obtain several portrait commissions within the few weeks following his arrival.[10] After a brief trip to Ottawa and Montreal, he had secured promises of public lectures, portrait commissions and opportunities to write short articles for the Toronto press.

Lewis's derogatory comments about Hart House and its well-respected warden, as recently published in *America I Presume,* and his freely expressed criticisms about the city of his reluctant adoption, ensured that his reception into the close-knit and in some respects exclusive Toronto art community would not be as rapid or as unequivocal as he had anticipated. Nor was he prepared for the fact that, while slanted reports of his somewhat intemperate political stances had preceded him, other less pejorative reports of his reputation had failed to make their way across the Atlantic. Then in his late fifties, Lewis seems to have felt that he should have been able to rest on his laurels as a great modern artist and writer. Although his fame carried him some distance towards his goal of finding remunerative work and generous patrons in Canada, he badly misjudged the economic and cultural climate of a country that had just barely emerged from the throes of the Depression and whose energies and attention were now almost entirely concentrated on helping to win the war overseas. His bitterness about his failure to make a deeper and more positive impression was noticed by Lorne Pierce, the director of Ryerson Press, which published the only book Lewis completed in Toronto, his polemical pamphlet *Anglosaxony: A League that Works* (1941). Pierce remarked that "Lewis was very restless, critical of Toronto, and, I seem to recall, the world, if not indeed the cosmos."[11]

Many people in Toronto were more familiar with Lewis's pro-Hitler book than with his three subsequent retractions and counter-attacks. Word spread quickly about his controversial views, and in one instance *The Hitler Cult,* not published until after Lewis's arrival in New York, was even confused with *Hitler*. A.Y. Jackson recalled, "Lewis left England after he had written an article [*sic*] in which he said that some of the Nazi ideas weren' t at all bad. It was very bad form of course, when England was at war with the Germans, and feeling ran pretty high."[12]

Aware that his readers were probably not familiar with his new book, Lewis quickly addressed the problem through the local press. The *Toronto Daily Star* headlined an article announcing his presence in the city by driving home his revised assessment of the Nazi leader: "Snow 'His Passion' Famed Artist Here: Wyndham Lewis, Toronto Resident, Now Calls Hitler Bluffer."[13] The first part of the title is ironic, considering the fact that Lewis, who suffered from numerous bouts of influenza during his Canadian residence, hated the extremes of the climate, especially the cold of the (to him) interminable winter months. On the other hand, he lauded A.Y. Jackson's treatment of snow in his paintings, and recommended the winter landscape to Canadian artists as a distinctive and characteristic theme for their brushes.

Lewis was commissioned to deliver three radio addresses for the Canadian Broadcasting Corporation in December 1940. In the first talk, he promoted the strengths of liberal democracy and laid out the British position on the subject to a Canadian audience. To gain his listeners' sympathy, he stressed his Canadian background and explained his current views on freedom and democracy, unfavourably comparing Germany to Britain by pointing out differences in manners and the absence of the freedom of speech and the right to vote under Hitler's dictatorship.[14]

In another of his radio broadcasts, Lewis again drew attention to his Canadian ancestry, this time appropriately emphasising his French-Canadian roots.[15] The text of his "Address to French-Canada", delivered in Lewis's idiomatic Parisian French, concentrates, however, on the need for the country's francophone and anglophone communities to put aside their traditional differences and recognize their shared cultural heritage and values, and prophetically speaks of the need for national reconciliation at a time when ancient territorial rivalries in Europe were threatening to destroy civilization and replace democracy with a global reign of terror:

> Ma foi, ça serait bien malheureux si nous autres, pour de bagatelles—pour ainsi dire pour des caprices de vanité sécondaires—perdraient de vu nos intêrets primordiaux, et si notre *effort commun* languissait à cause de cela.
>
> Voilà pourquoi *Canadians* autant que *Canadiens* devient fair bien attention, dans *les petites choses* de la vie; prendre garde qu'il soient pas coupable de vanités *nationalistes*: qu'ils ne cherchent pas à tirer profit de l'accident de la naissance, ou de traiter *race* comme si elle était *classe*. - C'est nationalisme, n'est pas? c'est *racisme*, que nous voudrions bannir du monde. Soyons logiques! Supprimons cette chose malpropre et stupide--chassons-le de chez nous.
>
> De l'imagination de l'habitant—de l'imagination du pionier écossais—jaillissent images contradictoires du même objet. - C'est affaire de *gout*. Mais il y a rien là de fondamentale....
>
> Quant au Canada, c'est une collaboration émouvante, que cell-ci: entre les fils de deux grands peuples—aventuriers dans un nouveau monde, fraternisant de cet façon dramatique--si loin de leur terres d' origine—et unissant leurs destinés.[16]

Behind Lewis's call for a united Canada was a concern for the threatened British and European society and culture with which he more closely identified with than with his tenuous North American connection. In this respect his defence of "Anglosaxony" as a commonwealth of shared traditions, language and interests can be seen as a mid-century throwback to the Greater Britain imperialism of the Victorian era, for Lewis strongly believed that it was the duty of the former colonies and dominions to come to the aid of the Mother Country—just as it was French-Canada's obligation to fight for the deliverance of France. Lewis's public appeals to Canadians to put their patriotism in action for the salvation of the Old World contrast starkly with his private disparagements of the country about which he spoke so glowingly over the national airwaves.

QUITE ASIDE from Lewis's contentious political opinions and brusque manner, he had his own ways of thwarting his admission into Toronto' s art, intellectual and social circles. Such portrait commissions as he was able to obtain, for example, were not always well-received on completion. Lewis's first such effort, begun soon after his arrival in Toronto, was a wedding portrait of J.S. McLean's daughter. According to the sitter, *Portrait of Mary McLean* (1940-41; no. 3) was undertaken at her father's request as a gesture of support for the debt-ridden Lewis. Unfortunately,

Miss McLean was preoccupied with plans for the wedding ceremony, and the timing of the commission was not appropriate. Her tight schedule and Lewis's time-consuming working method led to considerable conflict between herself and the painter, which is graphically reflected in the portrait. That the almost daily three-hour sittings did not help the matter is suggested by the sitter's awkward pose and tense facial expression. Her bent left leg, pulled up onto the chair, stretches her dress tightly across her right thigh, resulting in a posture that conveys a sense of impatience and unease. The subject stares directly out at the viewer, her features overly pronounced and her expression grim and self-conscious: her nose is flattened unnaturally into a cartoon-like profile, her lips are painted brightly, and her eyelashes are unnaturally lengthened. The two stiff, tunnel-like curls in her hair seem exaggerated, even beyond what may have been the style of the day. The colour-scheme is quite daring: the sitter's mauve dress contrasts with the red-and-green chintz fabric of the chair, against a green background.

As with so many of Lewis's portraits, completion of the picture was fraught with complications and difficulties. When Mary McLean and her new husband, Douglas Stewart, moved to Vancouver in the New Year, her portrait was still not finished and Lewis was left with a photograph to work from. Some months later, after the family had repeatedly asked Lewis about it, he eventually brought the painting to J.S. McLean. Mary Stewart recalls that her father "had no idea what he was getting into at the outset of the commission."[17] The response Lewis received when he finally delivered was less than enthusiastic. J.S. McLean' s wife remarked that it made her daughter "look like a horse", and Lewis was consequently ordered to take it away from the McLean residence.[18]

Mary Stewart finally saw her portrait in the late 1950s, after Lewis's death in 1957. Today, she regards it as a handsome work of art, despite her feeling (shared by many Lewis sitters) that it failed to do her justice or indeed even to closely resemble her.[19] The sitter recalls that she and Lewis "really disliked each other", and considers in retrospect that he "wasn't a very nice man and was bitter about the Toronto establishment".[20] A.Y. Jackson, a friend of J.S. McLean's as well as of Lewis's, remarked, "he dwelt on her bad points and the portrait was quite cruel. Mary didn't like Wyndham Lewis and he didn' t like her. All his dislike showed in that portrait."[21]

Considering the reception of this uncomplimentary wedding present, it is surprising that Lewis received any further portrait commissions in Toronto. Even more surprising is the fact that the next commission was a portrait of Lewis's first Canadian patron—J.S. McLean himself. Although the work was officially commissioned by McLean's employees at Canada Packers, as a commemoration of his forty years of service there, McLean must have influenced the choice of the artist hired to portray him.[22]

Despite the fact that Lewis spent considerable time working on *Portrait of J.S. McLean* (1941; no. 4), the McLeans did not find his second attempt at depicting a member of the family any more successful than the first. Both Mary and her sister Amy felt that the work was not a good likeness (their standard of comparison being a portrait photograph of McLean taken by Yousuf Karsh).[23] A.Y. Jackson agreed, adding that "the staff were very disappointed."[24] The painting was so disliked that it was removed from its stretcher, rolled and stored, and was not restretched and framed until it was conserved for inclusion in the present exhibition.

Because of McLean's prominence both as a businessman and as a patron of the arts, Canada Packers hosted a public event to celebrate the unveiling of the portrait. The *Toronto Daily Star*, in reporting on the presentation of the picture at the head offices of Canada Packers on 18 April 1941, described it as follows:

> The portrait is a harmony in blue, green and brown, and is a subtle study in strong shades cleverly balanced. Dressed in a blue business suit, the industrialist sits is front of a pale-bluish-green background. A section of a Canadian painting in the upper left [right] symbolizes Mr. McLean's interest in art, and the books on the table at the lower right stand for the sitter's wide reading.[25]

Lewis is quoted in this account as follows: "I was thinking of Mr. McLean more in his private than his business life. His two greatest interests are art and literature"[26] As an homage to Jackson and as a reflection of McLean's collecting interests, Lewis included, in the upper-right comer of the portrait, a section of *Mining Town*, a painting Jackson did of Cobalt, Ontario around 1935.[27]

Lewis made a somewhat patronising statement about his subject at the unveiling of the J.S. McLean portrait, perhaps as a means of deflecting anticipated criticism and appeasing his patron:

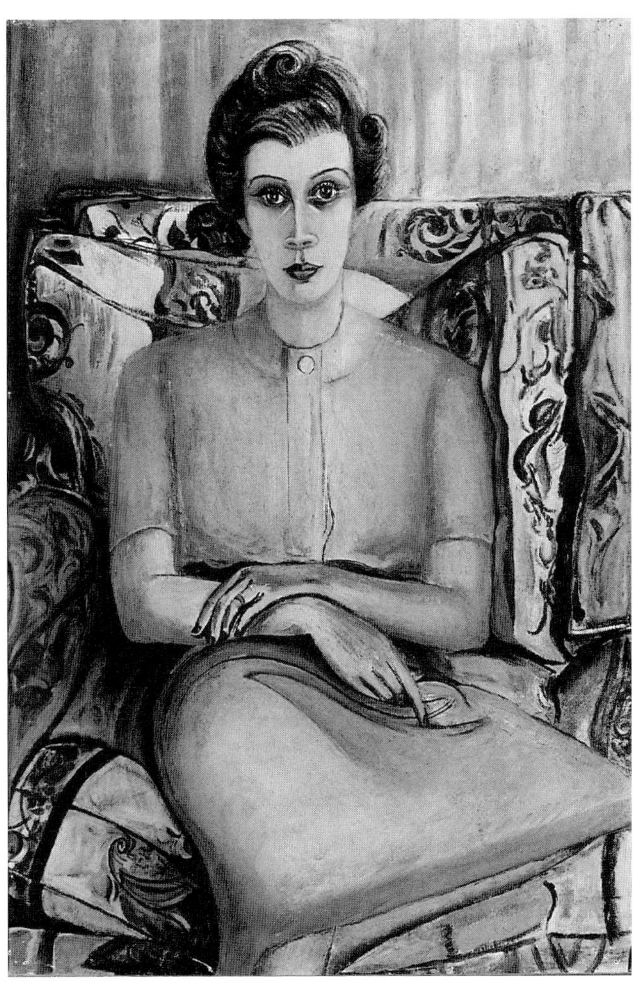

No. 3 *Portrait of Mary McLean*, 1940-41, oil on canvas (73.5 x 51.0 cm), M P100. Patrick Stewart, Victoria, B.C.

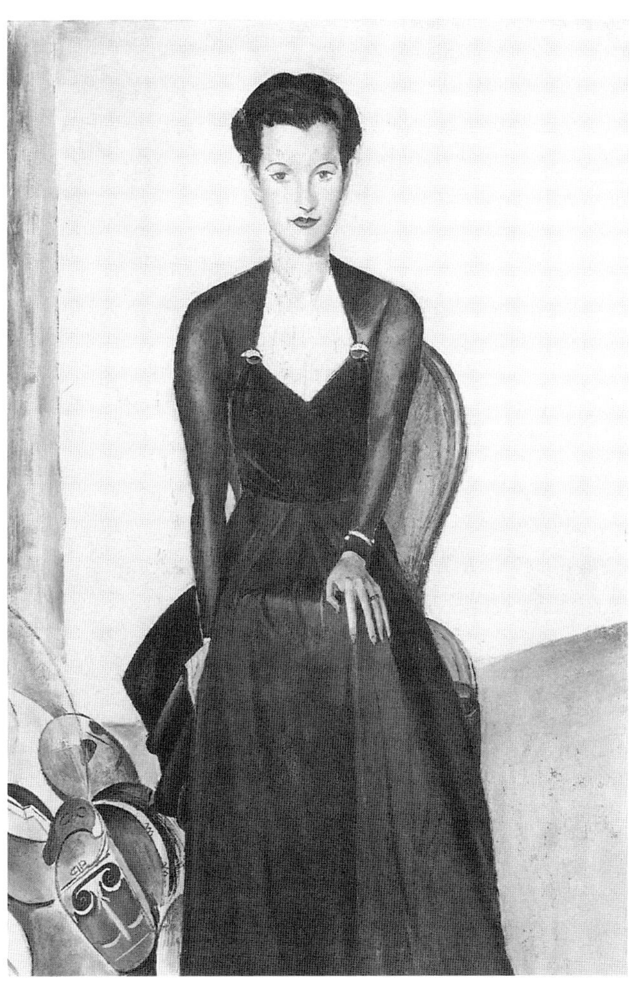

No. 5 *Portrait of Mrs. R.J. (Lisa) Sainsbury*, 1941, oil on canvas (89.0 x 58.5 cm), M P103. National Gallery of Canada, Ottawa, gift of R. J. Sainsbury, London, 1964.

> In my portrait I have said--more concisely and precisely--than it is possible to do in words—what I think of the very distinguished man who is President of this company. It has been a great privilege to have been selected to record, in this way, the personality of a great business leader, who appears destined to play an increasingly important part in the life of this young and vigorous nation. As an artist, I can say that I regard myself as extremely fortunate to have had so interesting a subject to paint, and also a man like Mr. McLean, has found time, in the midst of a strenuous business career, to give his attention to cultural matters and especially to the particular arts that I practice.—All in all, the painting of this portrait has been for me a great and pleasurable experience.[28]

Opposite page: No. 4 *Portrait of J.S. McLean*, 1941, oil on canvas (106.0 x 77.0 cm), M P101. Mr. and Mrs. Clair Stewart, Caledon East.

The sincerity of the concluding remark we must judge for ourselves.

Whether or not he was disappointed with Lewis's depiction of himself and his daughter, McLean was responsible for two more commissions coming to Lewis: *Portrait of Mrs. R.J. (Lisa) Sainsbury* (1941; no. 5), and another portrait of the same sitter, the now-unlocated *The Red Hat*. These were intended as gifts for his friend Robert James Sainsbury, head of the London-based Sainsbury food-store chain.[29] Mrs. Sainsbury was then living in Toronto to avoid the war in Britain, having been advised to move to the city by J.S. McLean. *Portrait of Mrs. R.J. (Lisa) Sainsbury*, although less cruel than *Portrait of Mary McLean*, is nonetheless stiff and formal in comparison with Lewis's best portraits of the 1920s and '30s. It portrays the sitter in a severely frontal aspect, revealing little depth of space or character. It may be that Lewis was more sympathetic to the interests of Sainsbury than to those of his wife, for the African masks in the lower-left corner of the canvas refer to the former's well-known collection of primitive art.[30] The grid-structure, evident beneath a thin layer of paint in the subject's throat and facial area, suggests that Lewis again worked, as was increasingly his custom, from a photograph, scaling up the easel portrait from the smaller reference image. Such a technique would in part explain the formality and flatness of this portrait. Lisa Sainsbury, who is so placed in the chair as to appear to defy gravity, seems to be suspended in the air, especially when one studies the curious location of her knees in relationship to the height of the chair. The work is roughly painted and perhaps even unfinished in places, such as the sitter's neck and the background area. Even as a gift from a friend, the painting was not gratefully received; its recipient, Lord Sainsbury, lamented on donating it to the National Gallery of Canada in 1964, "I must confess that I do not think that the result is either a very good picture or very worthy of Wyndham Lewis."[31]

What McLean thought of his own, his daughter's and the two Sainsbury portraits remains a mystery. Either he felt that they were not as harsh as his family and friends believed, or he had other reasons for encouraging and assisting Lewis. Until he sat for Lewis in 1941, McLean did not have a painted likeness of himself, and he may have been convinced that the painter's considerable reputation as a portraitist would have guaranteed that the job would be done well. Like Douglas Duncan, McLean was also extremely supportive of Lewis, offering and lending him money, buying his art, and providing him with introductions that might lead to future commissions and purchases.[32] These gestures may have stemmed from McLean's respect for Lewis's renown as a member of the British cultural élite, and as a highly esteemed portrayer of fellow artists and writers and other notables, as typified by such works as *Edith Sitwell* (1923; Tate Gallery, London), *T.S. Eliot* (1938; Durban Municipal Art Gallery, Durban, South Africa), and *Ezra Pound* (1939; Tate Gallery).

Of the four portraits that McLean commissioned from Lewis, that of himself is arguably the most successful both as a likeness and as a work of art. It would seem from these canvases that Lewis was more comfortable when portraying dynamic and powerful men than when he had to depict women whose social station relegated them to comparative idleness and ineffectuality. By contrast with the Mary McLean and Lisa Sainsbury portraits, that of J.S. McLean reveals how well Lewis could penetrate the character and temperament of a male sitter, especially when set in the context of a career or avocation—as indicated, in McLean's case, by the allusions of his literary and artistic interests. When portraying women with whom he was not amorously involved, Lewis seems to have been unable to put aside his personal prejudices, which over time took on an emphatically misogynistic tone. Although he appears to have softened some of his more immoderate views during his Canadian sojourn, if only to gain the confidence and sympathy of an audience he deemed (with some reason) to be hostile, Lewis's behaviour toward the opposite sex was fundamentally that of an anti-feminist, if not a misogynist. In Canada, he continued to repress his wife's untapped natural talent in art, and generally led a very dominant role in their relationship.[33] Although, before his marriage, Lewis had attracted an array of hand-

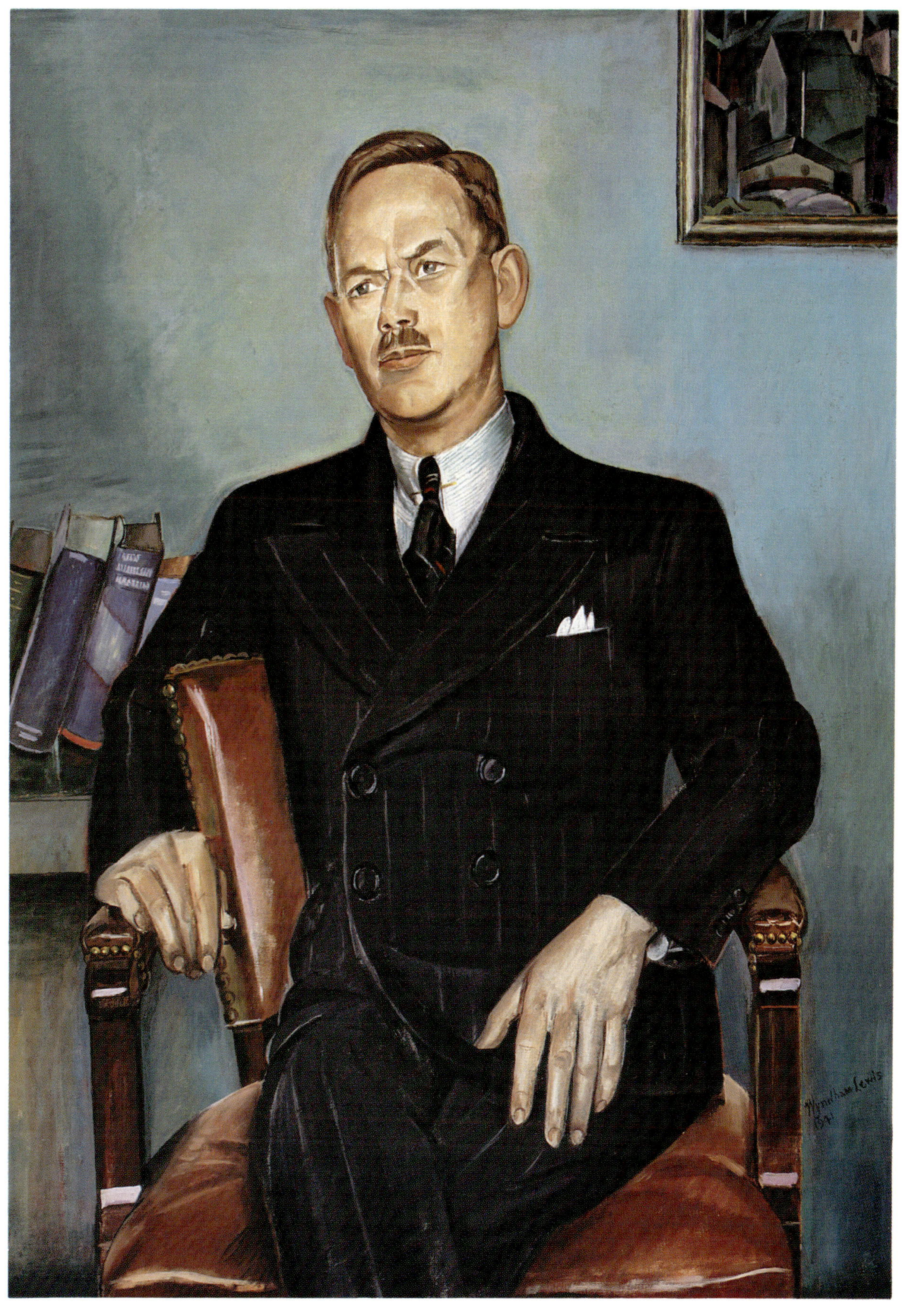
Wyndham Lewis

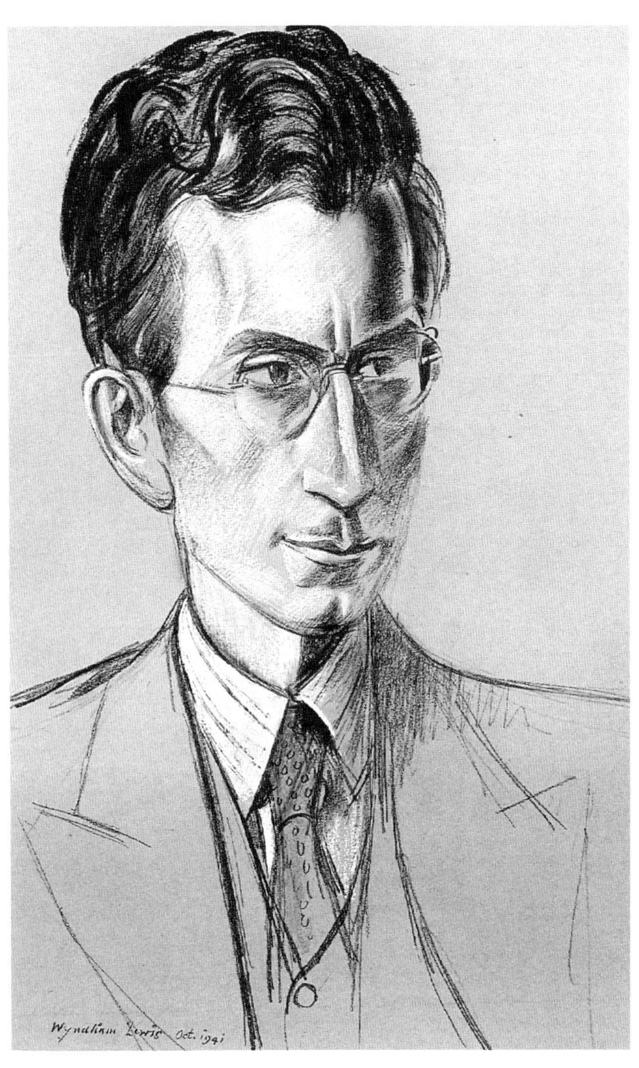

No. 6 *Portrait of Dr. Lorne Pierce*, 1941, black and coloured chalks on blue paper (48.5 x 31.0 cm), M 978. Beth Pierce Robinson, Kingston, Ontario.

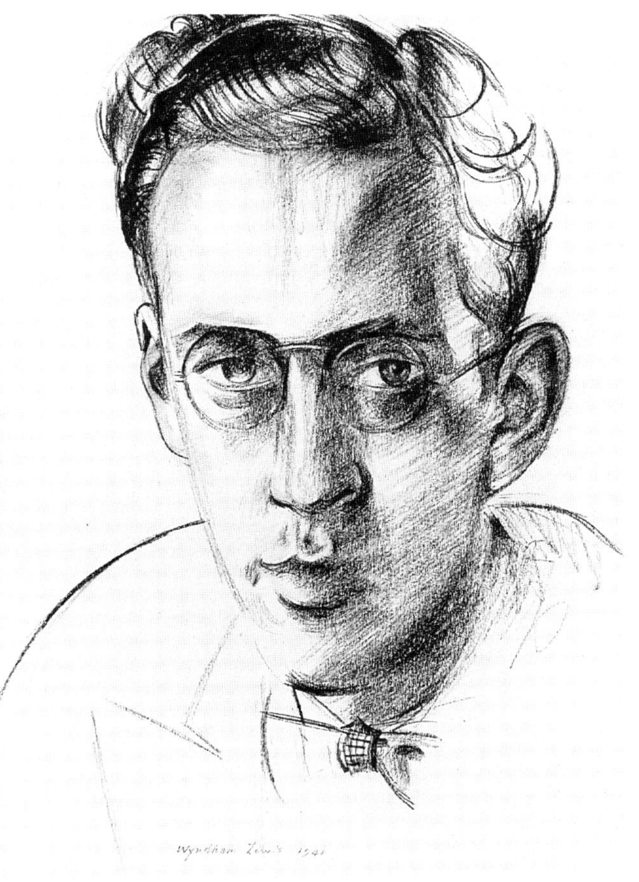

No. 7 *Portrait of Douglas LePan*, 1941, black chalk on paper (38.0 x 28.0 cm), M 1071. Dr. Douglas LePan, Toronto.

some and intelligent women, such as Nancy Cunard and Iris Barry (who later became the curator of film for the Museum of Modern Art in New York), he did not believe that women shared intellectual equality with men, and considered their efforts to create genuine works of art to be largely wasted. For Lewis, women were most useful as sexual objects and domestic helpmeets. These outdated opinions had not grown any more liberal in the 1940s, as is revealed by his remark in a lecture that "a woman, her face, her figure, are ultimately utilitarian".[34]

Two of Lewis's most effective Toronto-period portraits are those of the publisher Lorne Pierce (1890-1961) and the poet Douglas LePan (b. 1914). Lewis got to know Pierce because of his contractual relationship with Ryerson Press, the publisher of *Anglosaxony: A League That Works*, which Lewis had begun early in 1941. His acquaintance with him developed at a remove, through correspondence and the correcting of proofs; in May 1941 Lewis had taken up a studio in Montreal, at 430 Prince Arthur Street, remaining there until mid-July, the purpose of the move being the pursuit of new portrait commissions. As on other occasions, this mission proved futile, although Lewis had relatives in the city where he had been baptized, as well as the support of the influential John Lyman.

Although *Portrait of Lorne Pierce* (no. 6) is dated October 1941, the idea of drawing his publisher was possibly conceived while Lewis was writing *Anglosaxony* earlier in the year, as part of a projected series of portraits of North American personages that would complement his *Thirty Personalities and a Self-Portrait*, published as a portfolio in 1932. Lewis and Pierce got along quite well and this cordiality clearly affected the portrait. Pierce described Lewis as "a veritable volcano of energy, for ever sending up showers of ideas, hunches, imprecations, and the odd benevolent blessing."[35] In this complimentary likeness, Lewis depicts Pierce in a pensive mood, the impression of quiet, reserved intelligence being emphasized (as in his strikingly similar portrait of Julian Symons, begun in 1939 but not completed until 1949) by the concentration on the sitter's high and massive brow. Both Lewis and Pierce considered the drawing a success, the former describing to the latter his objectives in these terms:

> In doing you I wanted to arrive at something very serious, even severe, as becomes your record in the intellectual life of Canada: in a word, to show the intellectual man, rather than the social man. (If it were my task to portray a prosperous man, of more pedestrian destiny, then I should concentrate upon the animal spirits—the [J.B.] Priestleyesque and "bonne enfant" side of my sitter. This is, as a matter of fact, the side that the majority of sitters deserve to see brought out: and where there is nothing else to bring out, one is very content to do so).[36]

The portrait was not completed without conflict, however. As Pierce recalled, Lewis arrived at his office unannounced, proclaiming his desire to draw him in chalk. Although Pierce was busy, Lewis pressed the matter, explaining that he had no work and that Pierce's consenting to sit for him might assist with the search for further (paid) portrait commissions. Pierce did not agree to pose formally, but allowed Lewis to sketch him while he worked in his office. This setting, and the fact that the work was not commissioned, gave Lewis considerable freedom of creative expression, and the drawing is one of the finest portraits he did in Canada.[37] Pierce describes the sitting as follows:

> He worked away on a large sheet of paper, thumb-tacked to a board, but suddenly rose, and in disgust rolled the sheet into a ball, strode to the wpb (waste paper basket), and threw it in. He tore out of my office without a word, banged the door and was gone. Some days later, he returned, and without knocking entered, sat in an arm chair near me, and began working again. He repeated this a day or so later, and then showed me the result, a striking study, vigorous, probing, his commentary on the sitter and not a flattering "likeness". I liked it, of course, and asked him why he went to so much trouble over an unknown. He replied that he was interested in my face and head, that it represented a challenge to him, and that it reminded him of [the Irish prime minister Eamon] De Valera and Mephistopheles! He said this laughing, and I was bound to laugh with him.[38]

Besides the four portrait contracts he obtained from J.S. McLean, Lewis only received one other commission during his residence in Toronto, and that was not from a socialite but from a young writer, Douglas LePan, whose poetry Lewis admired.[39] At that time, Lewis's much reduced fee for a chalk-on-paper portrait was approximately fifty dollars.

LePan, who served as an artillery officer in the Italian campaign during World War II and then joined the department of External Affairs, met Lewis at a dinner party held at Lisa Sainsbury's Forest Hill residence, in the summer of 1941, and offered him the commission on the spot.[40] Not one but two portraits resulted, these being completed over four afternoon sittings in September.[41] Only one of the two chalk drawings of LePan is included in this exhibition, the whereabouts of the second being unknown. LePan described the process of posing for Lewis in his autobiography:

> As I found out when I presented myself for the first sitting, it was a bed-sitting room that he had rented in a boarding house; and it was suitably, and oh! so tastefully fitted out with crocheted doilies on the tables, and potted plants by the windows overlooking the street. The contrast between the surroundings and the impression I had formed of the buccaneer—or perhaps I should say, "blaster" or "bombardier"—who was to do my likeness was almost too much, and was increased, if that were possible, by the fact that he greeted me wearing a flat-crowned, flat-brimmed black felt hat and never took it off while he was with me either that afternoon or during afternoons that were to follow. The effect was to make him seem even more piratical than ever and even more out of place among the doilies and the anti-macassars. But he was either oblivious to the surroundings or undaunted by them. We had tea and then he set to work.
>
> Occasionally we would fall silent for five minutes or so when he was particularly intent on what he was doing.[42]

The subject describes *Portrait of Douglas LePan* (1941; no. 7) as showing him "as a young, tolerably handsome intellectual, with wavy hair, thin ascetic cheeks and deep-set eyes. That was the one I liked."[43] On the second, now-unlocated portrait LePan remarked:

> The other was more like a mask, a death-mask, with my head cut off at the top of my forehead. That was the one Wyndham Lewis liked.... Ten years later the drawing I preferred was almost a mockery of me, I had changed so much. The drawing he preferred, on the other hand, had become me to the life.[44]

Economic necessity dictated that Lewis spend a significant amount of his time in Canada painting or seeking portrait commissions. Grateful though he was for such jobs, they consumed a considerable amount of what he considered to be his creative time, a fact that Lewis understandably resented. As he lamented in a letter, "we all waste our lives. I reckon I waste 99 per-cent of mine, without ever getting reconciled to it."[45] Perhaps his anger at having to support himself and his wife with what he considered to be hackwork and potboiling partly accounts for the complaints of several of his sitters that he executed cunning, unflattering, often caricaturesque likenesses which tell us more about the artist's state of mind than about the subjects'. In very few instances did Lewis attempt to present his sitters to positive advantage, at least according to their own lights. More frequently, he concentrated on their less-attractive aspects; hands, body-positions and facial features and expressions were all studied with acute calculation as a way of telegraphing character. This tactic is demonstrated to advantage in the exquisite drawing of his wife's clasped hands, simply titled *Hands* (1940-45; no. 97). Moods specific to the moment during which Lewis was actually painting or drawing his sitter are often conveyed, as in *Portrait of Mary McLean*, in which the artist emphasized rather than attempted to disguise (as an ordinary society portraitist would have done) the tension he had deliberately or indeliberately created. In this respect, Lewis's admiration for the introspective and analytical portraits of Velasquez, Rembrandt, Goya and Van Gogh is evident;[46] lacking in most of his "public" portraits, however, is the element of sympathy or empathy with the subject that all—even the often merciless Goya —were capable of imparting in paint.

One of the dilemmas of portrait painting, for Lewis, was his feeling that the subject, more often than not, was uninteresting, and the rendering process correspondingly monotonous. He complained that he did not find the human species "physically impressive" and "that the human face as a rule was not particularly expressive", concluding that "the grossest flattery is demanded of the artist."[47] The artist, Lewis explained, was under a heavy obligation not only to the subject but to posterity: "every portrait painter should feel in a peculiar relation to a sitter. For he is probably prolonging her or his life in an uncanny manner. There his sitter will be sitting and looking at the world long after they are both dead."[48] Too often, however, he either did not take this counsel to heart when depicting his own sitters for cash or future considerations. He laid the blame for his failures squarely at the feet of those who sought out his services, complaining to a correspondent that

> portrait-painting...is very gruesome work struggling with people about the shapes of their noses and the size of their feet: and being so small and backward a country does not make it any easier. The "Royal Academy" seems to them a quasi-divine institution: and although I give them something worthy of the Uffizi or Prado the fact is that if Bellini or Goya came to Toronto they would probably be regarded as "reds" or "bums". I feel that until the war' s end something taking with it a regular salary however small, and some time on the side to do my work as is what I should try and get....
>
> ...I know more about painting than most people—I mean modern painting—and removed from the necessity of painting portraits I should be able to do non-pot-boiling work....[49]

The exceptions to the generally uninspired quality of the portraits Lewis made for hire remain those that he painted or drew on his own terms, where he could exercise his remark able facility in draughtsmanship, and could experiment more freely with colour, composition and setting. The numerous portraits of his wife Anne (discussed below), and of other sitters who were probably residents of or casual visitors to the Tudor Hotel, including such works as *Sybil (sic;* i.e. *Sibyl?), Estelle with Kerchiefed Head , New Orleans in Toronto, Turbaned Student*, and *Pensive Girl*, all from 1942 (nos. 34-39), and possibly also *Matilda* (1940; no. 2), which is believed to have been done in Toronto, fall within this category of "private" pictures.

Probably the most impressive feature of Lewis's portrait drawings is the technique employed. Sometimes, in a single, continuous line extending the length of a torso or limb, without break or hesitation, varying in thickness according to the amount of pressure brought to bear on the graphite, he was able to suggest subtleties of depth, shape, atmosphere and form. That these qualities could be rendered without supplementary modelling through shading demonstrates Lewis's dextral skill and command of his medium. Not needing to please his sitter proved a considerable advantage, in consequence of which his analysis of character is both probing and sensitive. The drawing seems almost to have been intended as a means of communication between artist and sitter, rather than a sarcastic comment or covert attack.

Nowhere else does Lewis better exhibit his extraordinary draughtsmanship than in his many portraits of his most constant sitter—his wife Anne. He had depicted Anne on various occasions during the earlier years of his career, one of the best, and best-known, likenesses being *Froanna--Portrait of the Artist's Wife* (1937; Glasgow Art Gallery and Museum). In Canada, Lewis continued to sketch "Froanna," perhaps as a way of passing the time during his enforced periods of idleness and ill-health, perhaps as a meditation on the domestic life the couple led together in the claustrophobic confines of their bunker-like apartment in the Tudor Hotel. *Head of a Woman* (1941; no. 8), one of the earliest-dated Toronto-period portraits of Anne Lewis, shows the greatest intensity of expression of all the likenesses of his wife that Lewis did in Canada. She is depicted deep in thought, her prominent eyes gazing away from the viewer. By contrast, in *Head of Anne* (c. 1940-45; no. 96) a softer expression is rendered by means of a much lighter pressure of the medium on the paper, and by the use of coloured chalks, which makes for more graduated contrasts than those achieved with black chalk or charcoal. The subtlety of toning gives this work a more tender mood than is usual in Lewis's portraits, even those of lovers and close friends. The delicately rendered graphite drawing entitled *Pensive Girl* (1942; no. 39), a portrait of Anne dozing over her book, is a loving response to the vulnerability and secret inner life of the sleeper. Lewis also completed several drawings of Anne knitting, such as *Figure Knitting* (1942; no. 54) and *The Ball of Wool* (1942; no. 55).[50]

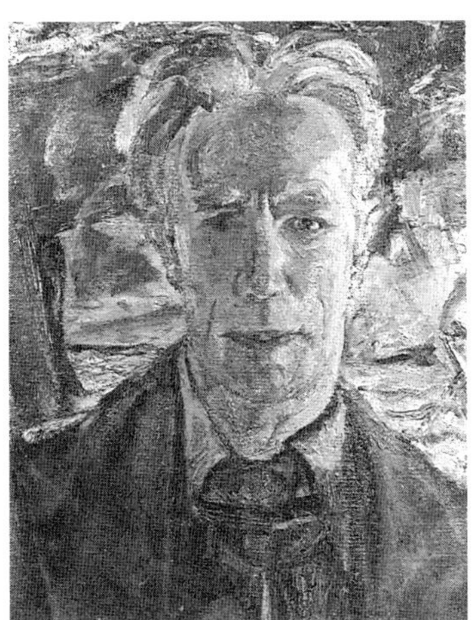

Fig. 15 Frederick H. Varley (1881-1969): *Self-Portrait, Days of 1943*, 1945, oil on canvas on masonite (49.5 x 40.7 cm). Hart House, University of Toronto.

His negative feelings about portraiture notwithstanding, Lewis was forced to continue his search for employment in this genre in order, as he remarked, "to keep the wolf from the door."[51] The summer of 1941 proved to be disappointing for Lewis, and he soon came to realize that the prospects of obtaining publishing contracts and portrait commissions were not improving, nor were they likely to do so in the near future. Lewis felt so unlucky in his search for regular remuneration that he attempted, unsuccessfully, to return to England, despite the continuation of the war and the poor economic climate.[52] Ironically, at least in comparison to other Canadian portrait painters with national reputations, he did relatively well by his portraiture, especially given the times and the circumstances in which he worked. Frederick H. Varley

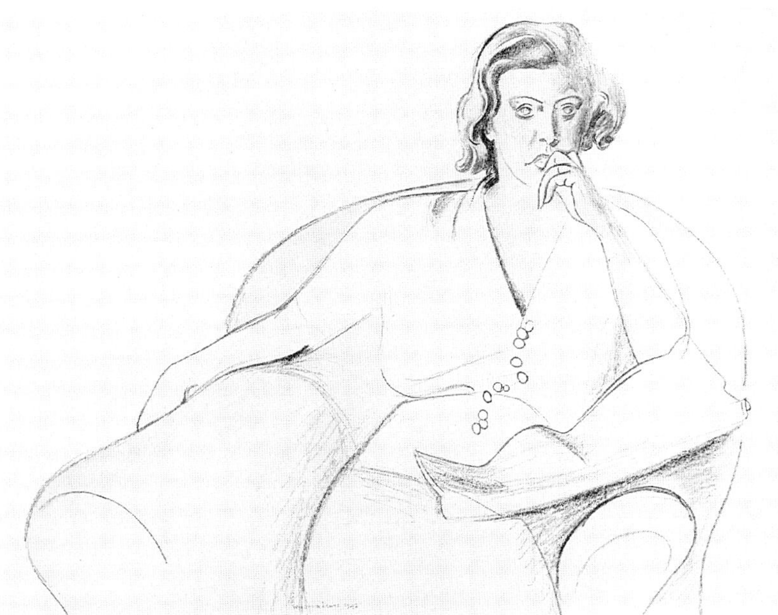

No. 34 *Sybil*, 1942, black chalk and watercolour wash on paper (35.0 x 50.0 cm), M 1019. Lent anonymously.

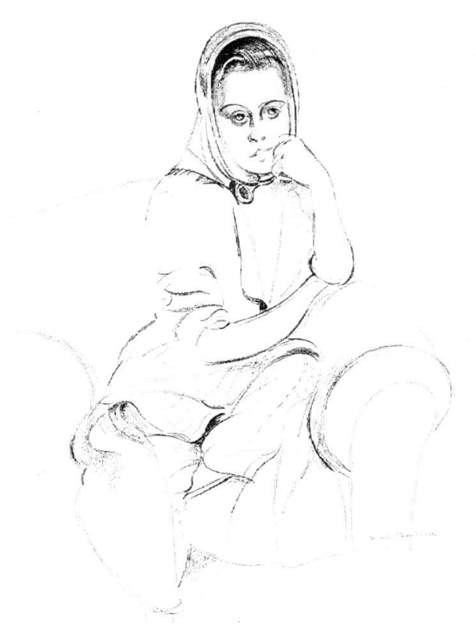

No. 35 *Estelle with Kerchiefed Head*, 1942, graphite, chalk and wash on paper (35.0 x 44.5 cm), M 1013. Private Collection.

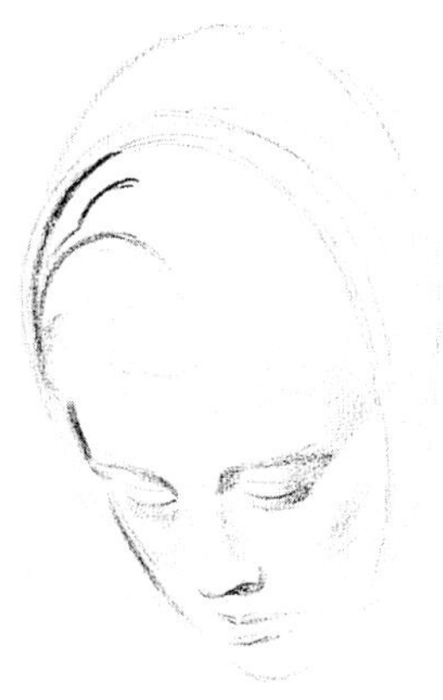

No. 36 *Kerchiefed Head, Looking Down*, 1942, black chalk on paper (25.5 x 25.5 cm), M 1025. Lent anonymously.

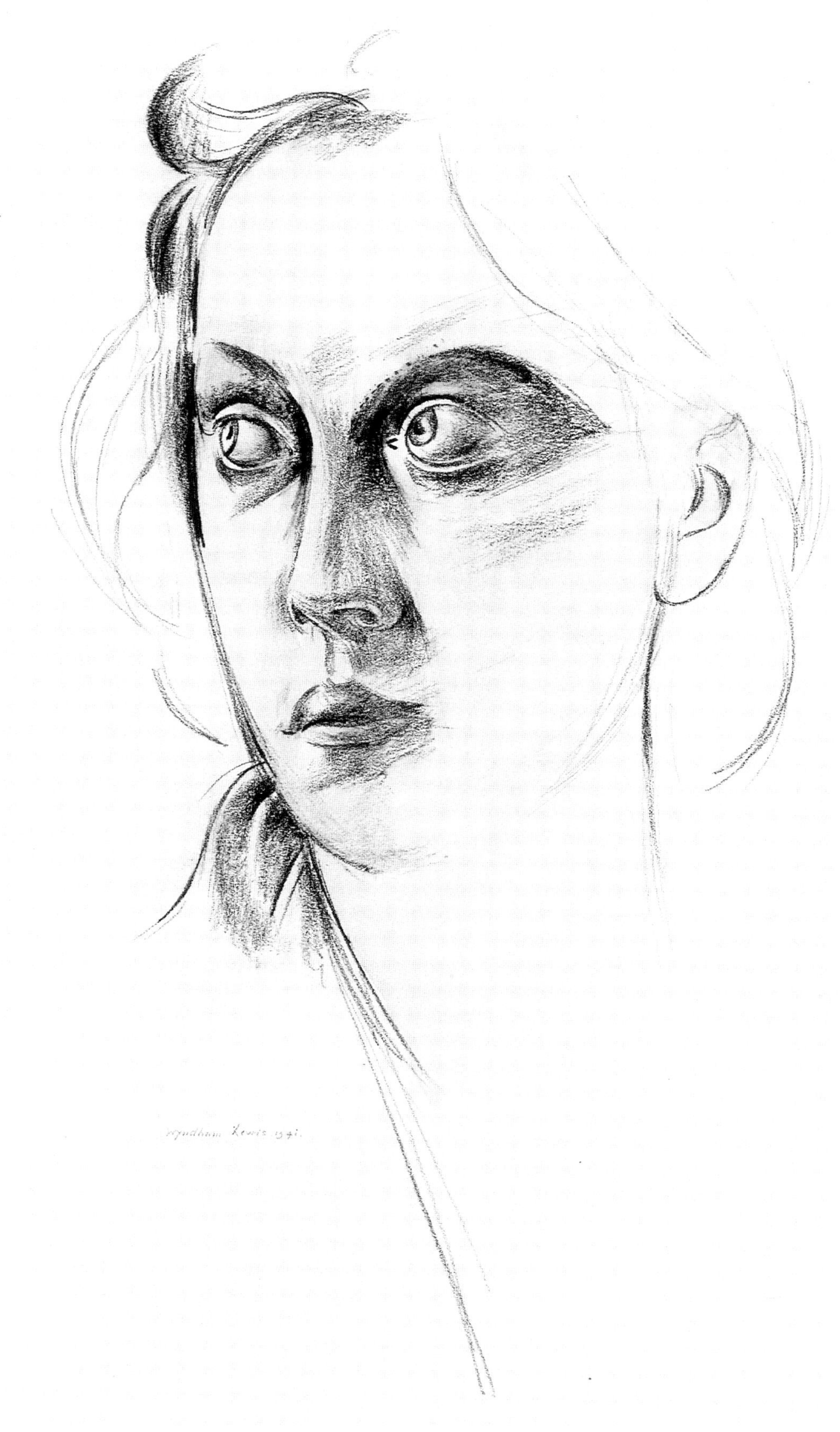

No. 8 *Head of a Woman*, 1941, black chalk and watercolour wash on paper (48.5 x 32.0 cm), M 973. Lent anonymously.

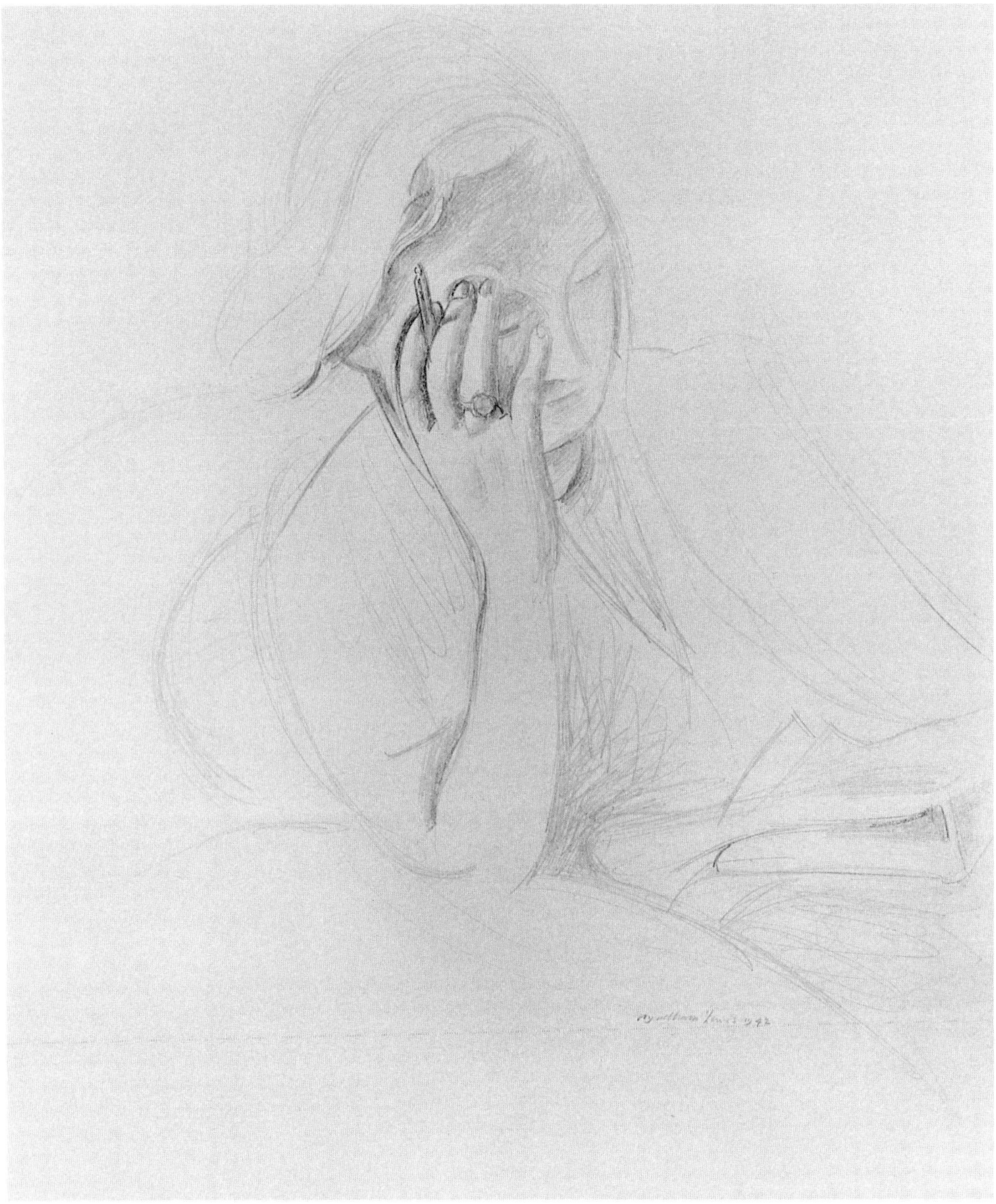

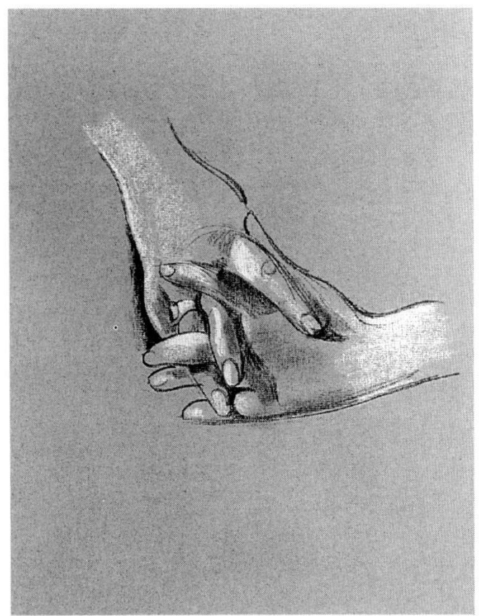

No. 39 *Pensive Girl*, 1942, graphite on paper (47.5 x 37.5 cm), M 1017. Lent anonymously.

No. 97 *Hands*, n.d. (c. 1940-45), black and coloured chalks on green paper (48.5 x 32.0 cm), M 1067. Lent anonymously.

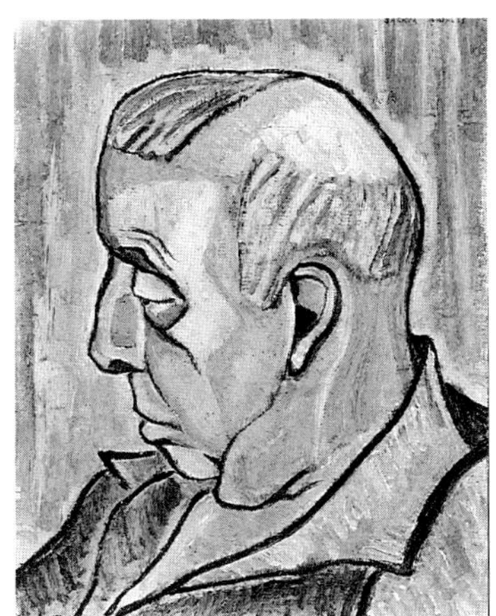

Fig. 16 Barker Fairley (1887-1986): *Portrait of A. Y. Jackson*, 1939, oil on canvas (36.2 x 28.6 cm). Art Gallery of Ontario, Toronto, purchase, 1962.

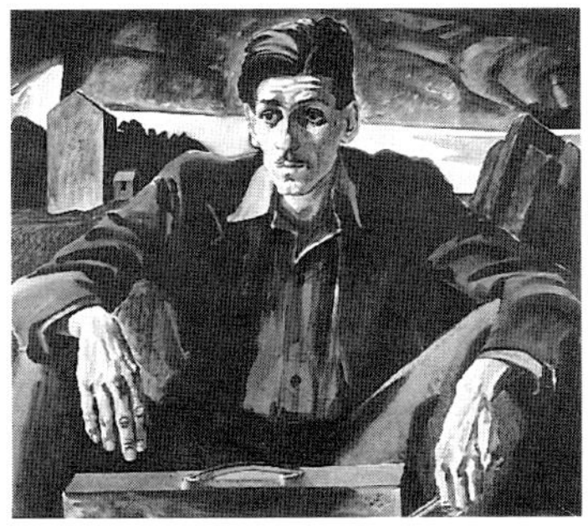

Fig. 17 Charles F. Comfort (b. 1900): *Young Canadian* (portrait of Carl Schaeffer), 1932, oil on canvas (91.4 x 106.7 cm). Hart House Art Gallery, University of Toronto. Photograph by TDF Artists Ltd., Toronto.

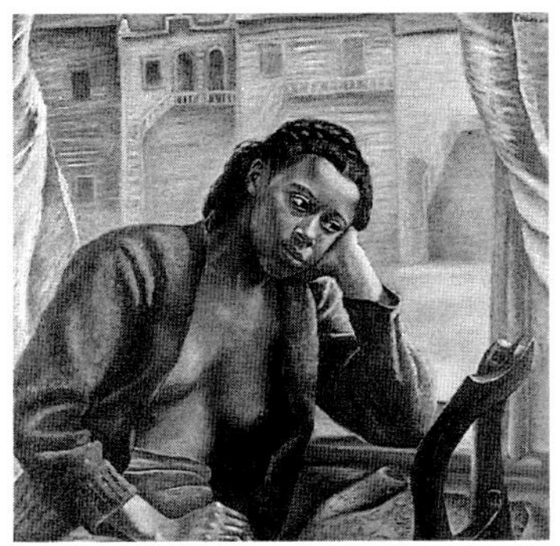

Fig. 18 Prudence Heward (1896-1947): *Girl in the Window*, 1941, oil on canvas (86.4 x 91.5 cm). Art Gallery of Windsor. Photograph by Gary Drouin.

(1881-1969), by far the best Canadian portrait painter of the day, received only one official commission throughout the entire war, in receipt of which he may have been in direct or indirect competition with Lewis.[53] His soul-searching *Self-Portrait, Days of 1943* (1945; fig. 15) insightfully conveys the emotional (and financial) desolation that artists faced during the war years.

Like most other Canadian artists, Varley was unable to live by means of his art alone. Those who did not enter the services or were appointed as war artists had to resort to teaching or to working as commercial artists to support their painting. Before Lewis's arrival in Canada, most of the available portrait commissions went to Varley and a few more conservative contemporaries, such as Sir E. Wyly Grier (1862-1957), John Russell (1879-1959), Archibald Barnes (1887-1972), Allan Barr (1890-1959), and Lilias Torrance Newton (1896-1980), and their French-Canadian counterparts.[54] Barker Fairley, who was one of Canada' s most interesting experimental portraitists, fared as poorly as Varley during the war, receiving not a single commission. Essentially a talented amateur, Fairley was known for his angular style, pronounced use of outline, expressive, non-naturalistic approach of colour, and blocky handling of forms, as can be seen in his *Portrait of A.Y. Jackson* (1939; fig. 16). Nor did Charles Comfort receive any portrait commissions during the war, despite the remarkable aptitude for characterization that he displayed during the 1930s, as exemplified by his *Young Canadian* (1932; fig. 18), a haunting depiction of Carl Schaefer as a rural victim of the Depression.

The austerities and redirected priorities of wartime alone do not account for the paucity of portrait commissions during the Forties, but these factors certainly added to the difficulties experienced by artists, many of whom had been existing at a subsistence level since the Crash of 1929. This decade-long drought forced figurative painters to turn their attention to larger social and political issues. One of the most outstanding painters of this period was the Montreal-based Prudence Heward (1896-1947), whose *Girl in the Window* (1941; fig. 18) would appear to address the changing role of women (black women specifically) in modern society, the pensive figure retreating into her own thoughts while simultaneously gazing out onto the world through the windowpane.[55] Another popular theme was the figure in the landscape, a motif explored by such painters as Heward, Edwin Holgate, Charles Comfort, Randolph Hewton, Will Ogilvie and Dorothy Stevens. As Robert Stacey' s contribution to this catalogue reveals, Lewis followed their lead in resorting to similar subject matter in the absence of gainful employment as a portraitist, at least until he landed a teaching position toward the middle of his third year in Canada.

WHILE PORTRAIT COMMISSIONS or the pursuit thereof constituted about half of Lewis's easel-time during the Canadian years, he also executed a surprising number of modestly scaled but powerfully drawn and composed drawings and watercolours on paper which he described as "works of the imagination",[56] and which Walter Michel has designated "the Toronto drawings." Mostly dating from 1941 and 1942, the series is unquestionably the most interesting and inventive product of Lewis's Canadian exile, and arguably of the last twenty years of his life. Although few were exhibited or sold before his return to England (or indeed before his death), Lewis considered them especially significant, as is revealed in a letter he wrote to Alfred Barr, director of the Museum of Modern Art, in November 1941: "I have an important group of drawings which I have done in Canada during the last twelve months and which I feel sure you would like."[57] Unfortunately, Barr did not rise to the bait.

These "works of the imagination" were made entirely on Lewis's own terms, and because of this he was free to address the philosophical, aesthetic and sexual issues that most deeply concerned him. Coherent (if inherently mysterious) as a series, they fall into a number of sub-sections: the Creation Myths, the Crucifixions, the Bathers, and the loosely related fantastic works depicting human suffering in wartime, the conflict of good and evil, and various mythological and religious themes.

These mixed-media pictures frequently combine graphite, conté crayon, gouache, watercolour and ink, occasionally all in the same work. The time required to make most of them was probably limited to a few hours; however, despite their spontaneous, unpremeditated appearance, they indicate considerable concentration on subject matter and formal concerns, such as composition, colour, and the balance of graphic and painterly elements. As a result, the group falls into a hybrid category existing between drawing and painting;

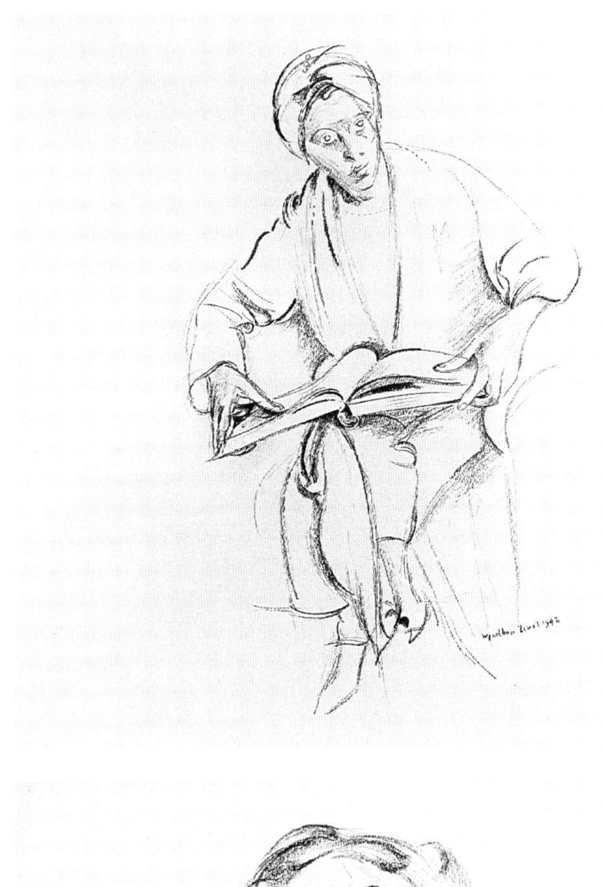

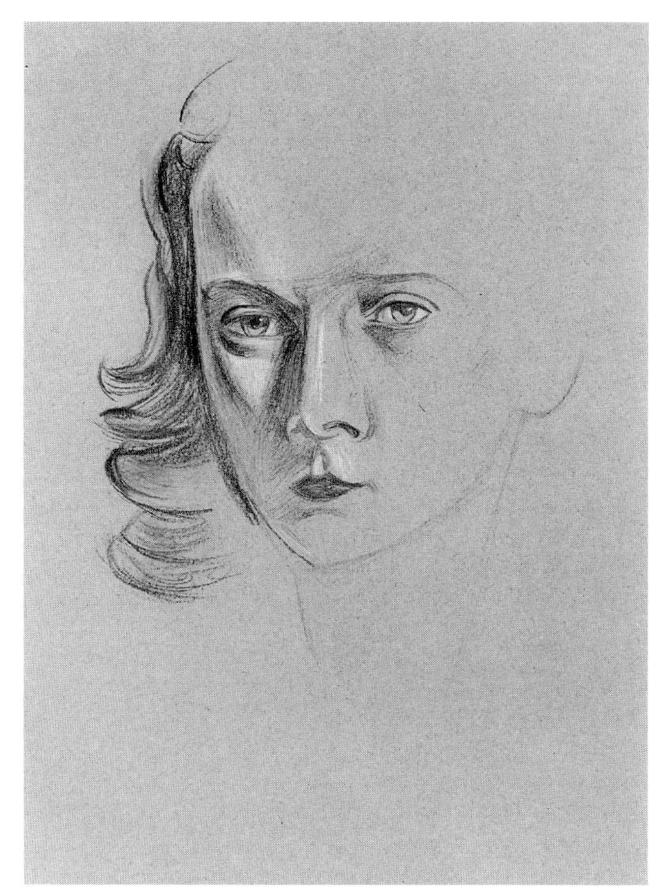

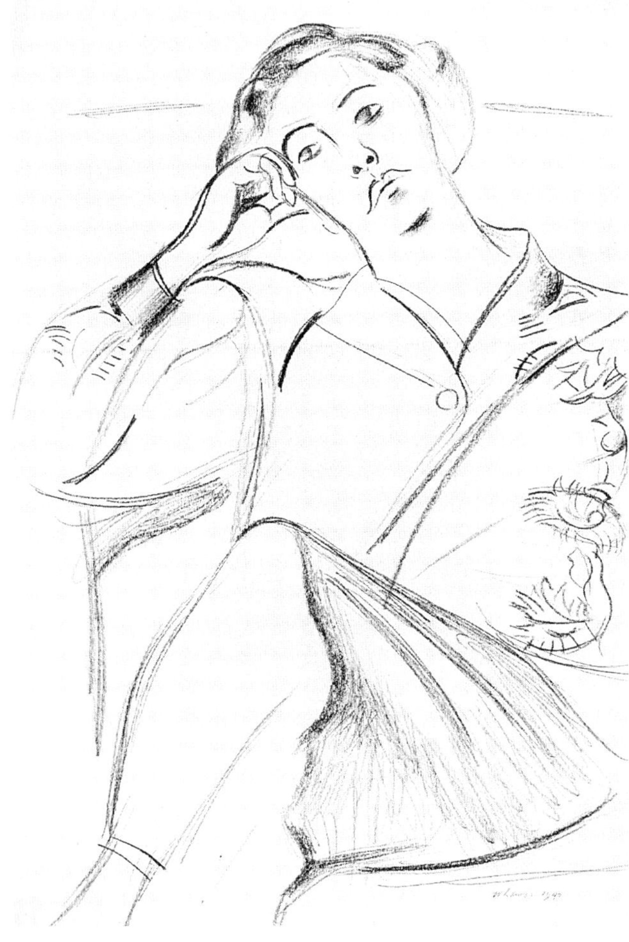

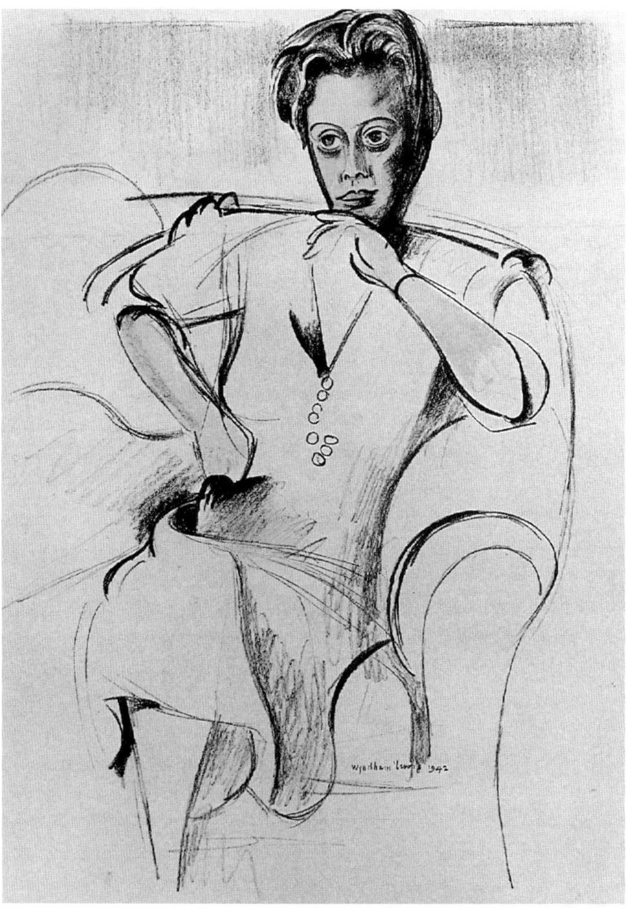

No. 55 *The Ball of Wool*, 1942, graphite and wash on paper (34.5 x 25 cm) M 1009. Shirley Allen, Ottawa.

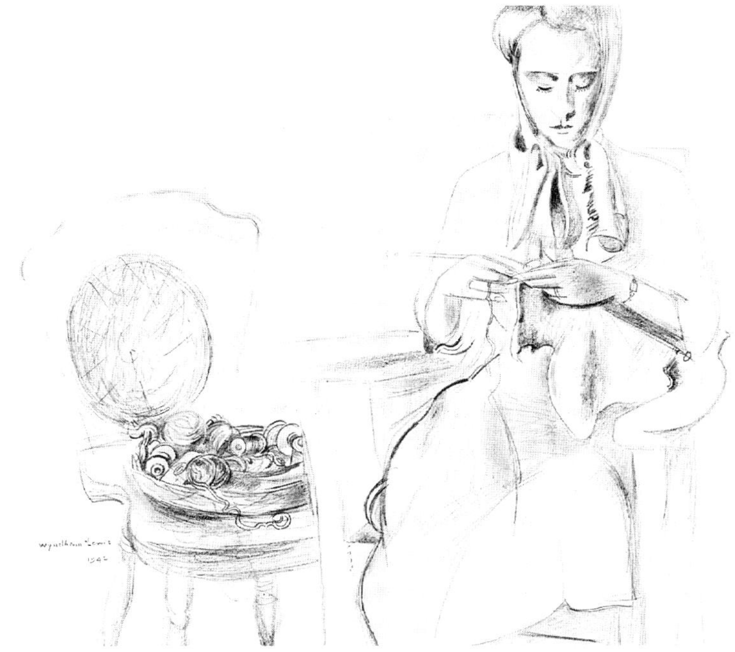

No. 54 *Figure Knitting*, 1942, graphite, coloured chalks and watercolour wash on paper (35.0 x 50.0 cm), M 1014. Mercury Gallery, London, England.

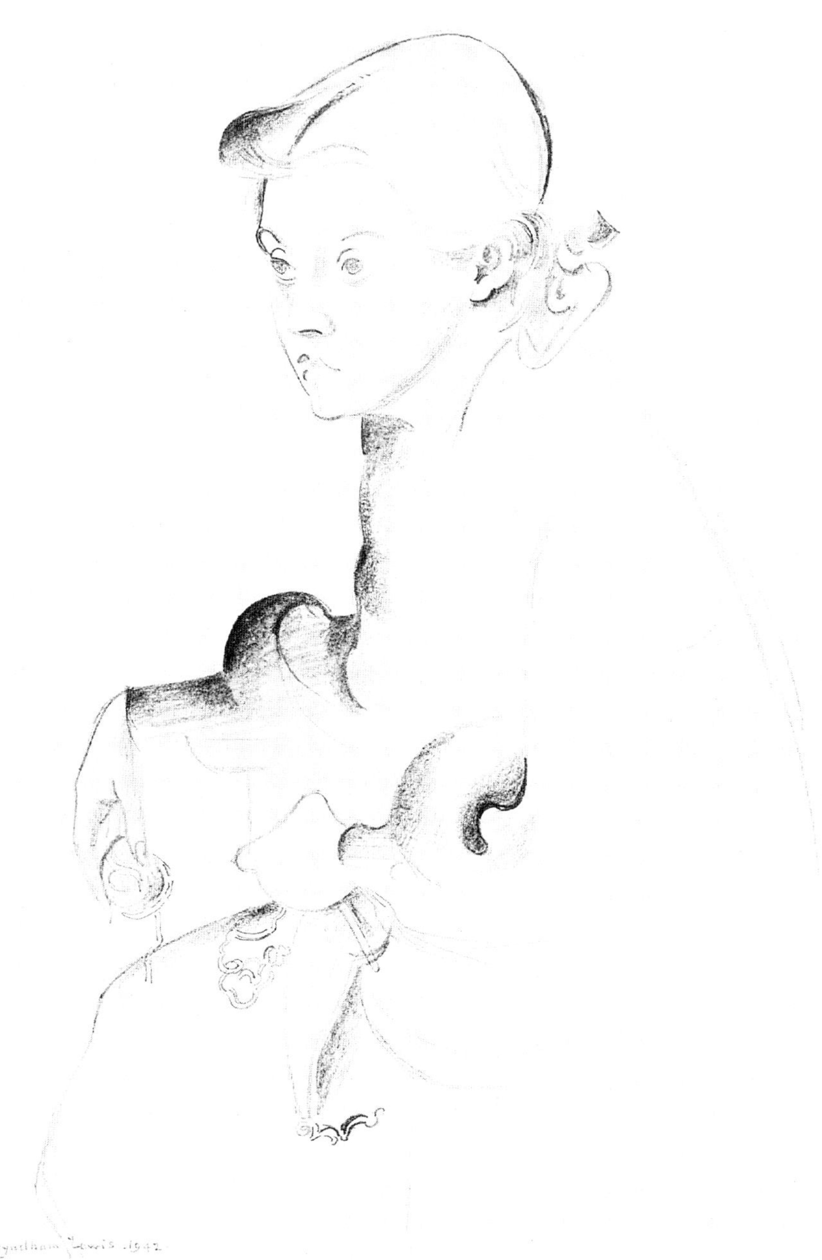

Opposite page (clockwise from top left): No. 38 *Turbaned Student*, 1942, black chalk on paper (45.5 x 37.5 cm), M 1020, Lent anonymously; No. 96 *Head of Anne*, c. 1940-45, black and coloured chalks on brown paper (24.5 x 18.5 cm), M 1065, Walter and Harriet Michel; No. 37 *New Orleans in Toronto*, 1942, black chalk, graphite and watercolour on paper (35.0 x 25.0 cm), M 1016, Lent anonymously; No. 2 *Matilda*, 1940, black chalk on paper (45.5 x 30.5 cm), M 959, Lent anonymously.

each is a unique and complete work of art, yet so connected thematically and stylistically to the other parts of the series as to take on a larger entity as a succession of images that circles back on itself.

No. 43 *The Mind of the Artist, About to Make a Picture*, 1942, pen-and-ink and watercolour on paper (39.5 x 30.5 cm), M 997. Lent anonymously.

The contrast with Lewis's commissioned portraits is perhaps best demonstrated by *The Mind of the Artist About to Make a Picture* (1942; no. 43), an enigmatic and beguiling work reflective of Lewis's reliance on the powers of the imagination to guide his hand in the creative act. The title, inscribed on the *verso* in Lewis's hand, suggests that the image is as much about the *process* of conceiving a work of art as about the physical making of it. Although the drawing could represent any and all artists, it is highly likely this is a symbolic self-portrait. If such is the case, it is the only such work that Lewis produced in Canada. It functions both horizontally and vertically, although Lewis's signature on the lower right suggests that the latter is the proper orientation. A forward-leaning figure is shown in profile, in the act of painting (or reading?), perhaps in his studio. His eyes are closed and he appears to be dreaming, in a trance, or at least in deep meditation. The book beneath the figure may be a reference to Lewis's dual calling of writer and painter. There is also an implication that the creative artist is in some way a stand-in for the universal Creator, whose world-begetting Word is rendered into Law in the form of The Book.

In the Creation Myth series--a revival of a sequence begun as early as 1912—Lewis attempted to visualize the creation of the world and of life from the void of space. The group dating from 1941-42 includes *Creation Myth No. 17, Creation Myth: Maternal Figure, Creation Myth* (nos. 26-28), and probably several other works of the same period possessing similar visual qualities, such as *Dragon's Teeth, The Sage Meditating Upon the Life of Flesh and Blood, Jehovah the Thunderer*, all dating from 1941 (nos. 9, 17-18), and possibly *Still Life: Figures in the Belly of a Duck* (1942; no. 52).[58]

Creation Myth depicts a cosmic landscape in which floating, planet-like forms soar through a space defiant of gravity. The picture may represent the creation of Adam, who is supposed to have been moulded by God's hand from red clay ("Adam" being derived from the Hebrew word *adamah*, meaning "earth"; cf. *Genesis 2*, 7, "And the LORD God formed man *of* the dust of the ground..."; inside the larger black circle is a figure in red and green. The compositional similarity and use of floating forms suggest that *Dragon's Teeth* may be a companion-piece to *Creation Myth*. Here, the main circle in the foreground contains two figures, one of which is distinctly male, the other probably female. If, as in the first instance, the male figure represents Adam, then, in *Dragon's Teeth*, he is probably accompanied by his counterpart, Eve. However, the title of this work reminds us of the Greek myth in which the dragon's teeth sown by Cadmus spring up as fully armed soldiers—another of Lewis's frequent allegorical allusions to war in general and World War II in particular.

Reproduction and regeneration would seem to be the subject of *Creation Myth: Maternal Figure*, also known as *Gestation*, and *Creation Myth No. 17*. In the former work, an ever-changing, amoebic, womb-like form can scarcely hold the bustling brood of shifting leaf-like shapes within. *Creation Myth No. 17* is the most explicit image of the group, depicting a form resembling a phallus emerging from a large circular base, surrounded by smaller, semi-circular, spliced forms, resembling a piece of fruit cut open to reveal the seeds of life. The phallus-form sprouts folial extensions suggestive of rejuvenation and new growth. In *Still Life: Figures in the Belly of a Duck*, Lewis seems to be examining the moment of creation as told in *Genesis*, specifically that section of the story in which God is described as having created the birds of the air and the creatures that inhabit the waters. Two egg-shaped forms are placed within a nest below (rather, as the title indicates, within) the belly of a large duck, in which two miniature human beings or homunculi are seen huddled together. (One cannot help but wonder whether Lewis might be pulling our collective leg with this mystifying image.)

Despite the implied emphasis on death and suffering, the four works in the 1941 crucifixion series, *Small Crucifixion Series, I, Small Crucifixion Series, II: Pietà, Crucifixion Series, III* (nos. 23-25), and *Crucifixion Series, IV*,[59] also suggest the possibility of resurrection and rebirth. The torso and upper limbs of Christ are adorned with burgeoning plant-sprouts and other leaf-like forms, indicative, perhaps, of a conflation of druidic Green Men and their Christian replacement. The lower figure, perhaps representing the Virgin Mary or Mary Magdalene, also has vegetal appendages bursting from her right side. Lewis may have been alluding here to pre-Christian mythology, specifically to the gods of vegetation and fertility who die in the fall, only to be reborn in the spring, as exhaustively chronicled by J.G. Frazer in *The Golden Bough*. This was a key book for Lewis, who, despite his professed distaste for the "primitive" and the savage state, was obsessed with the ancient tribal customs and sacrificial rites which he saw being re-enacted on a

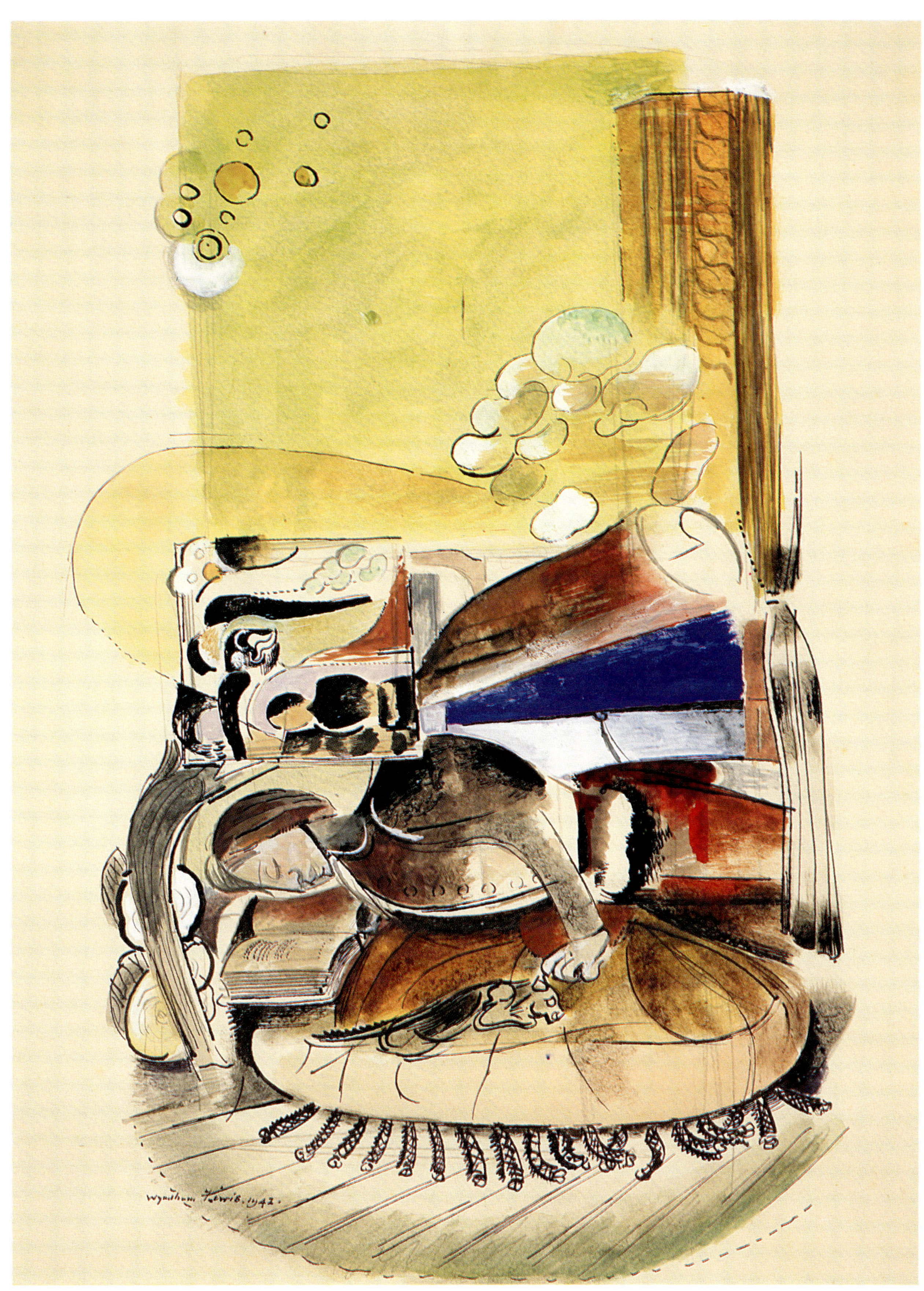
Wyndham Lewis. 1942.

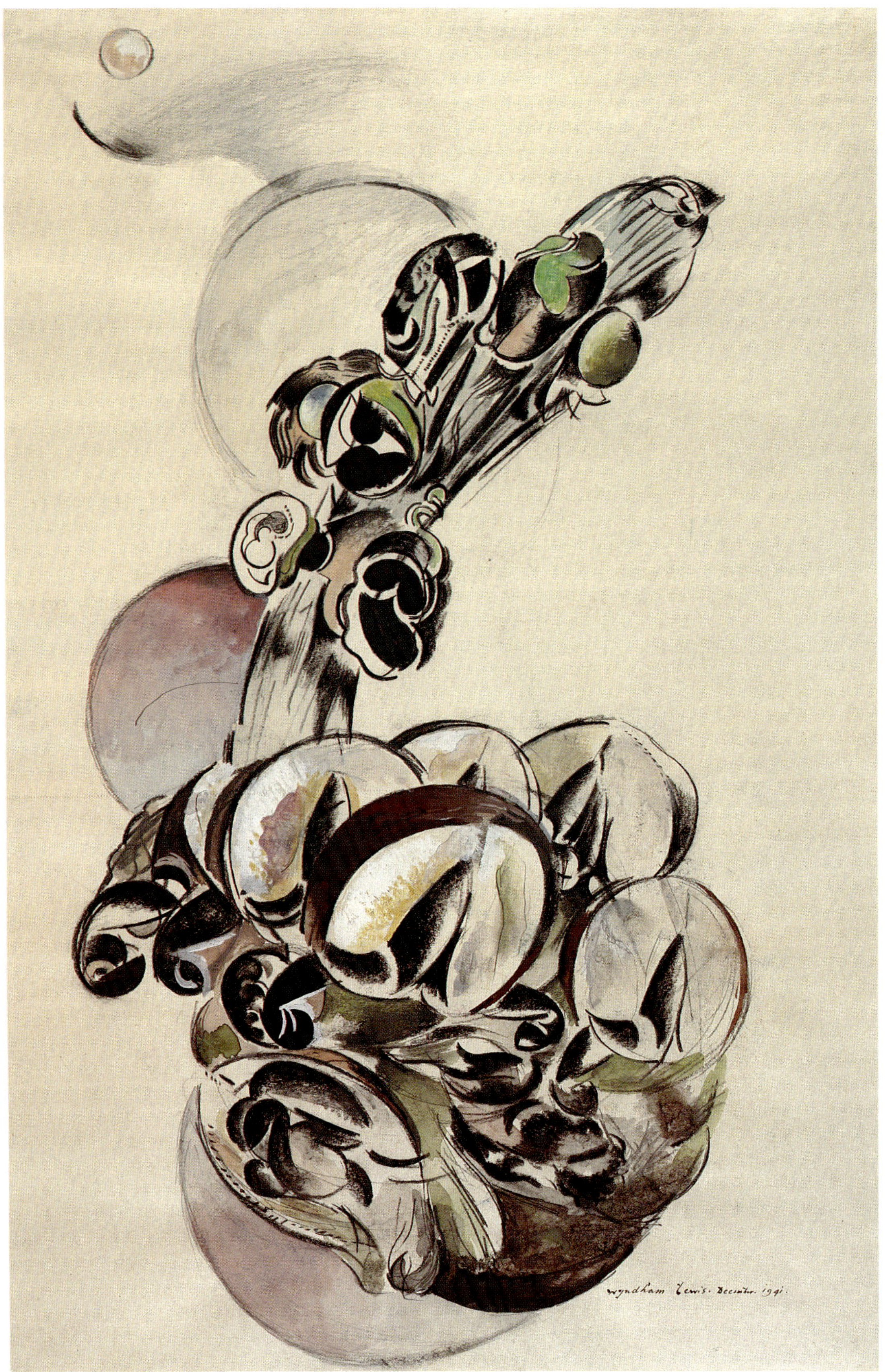

This page:
No. 26 *Creation Myth, No. 17*, 1941, charcoal, gouache and graphite on paper (50.2 x 34.9 cm), M 968. National Gallery of Canada, Ottawa, gift of the Douglas M. Duncan Collection, 1970.

Opposite page:
No. 19 *Jehovah the Thunderer*, 1941, graphite, ink and water-colour on paper (37.0 x 25.5 cm), M 975. Lent anonymously.

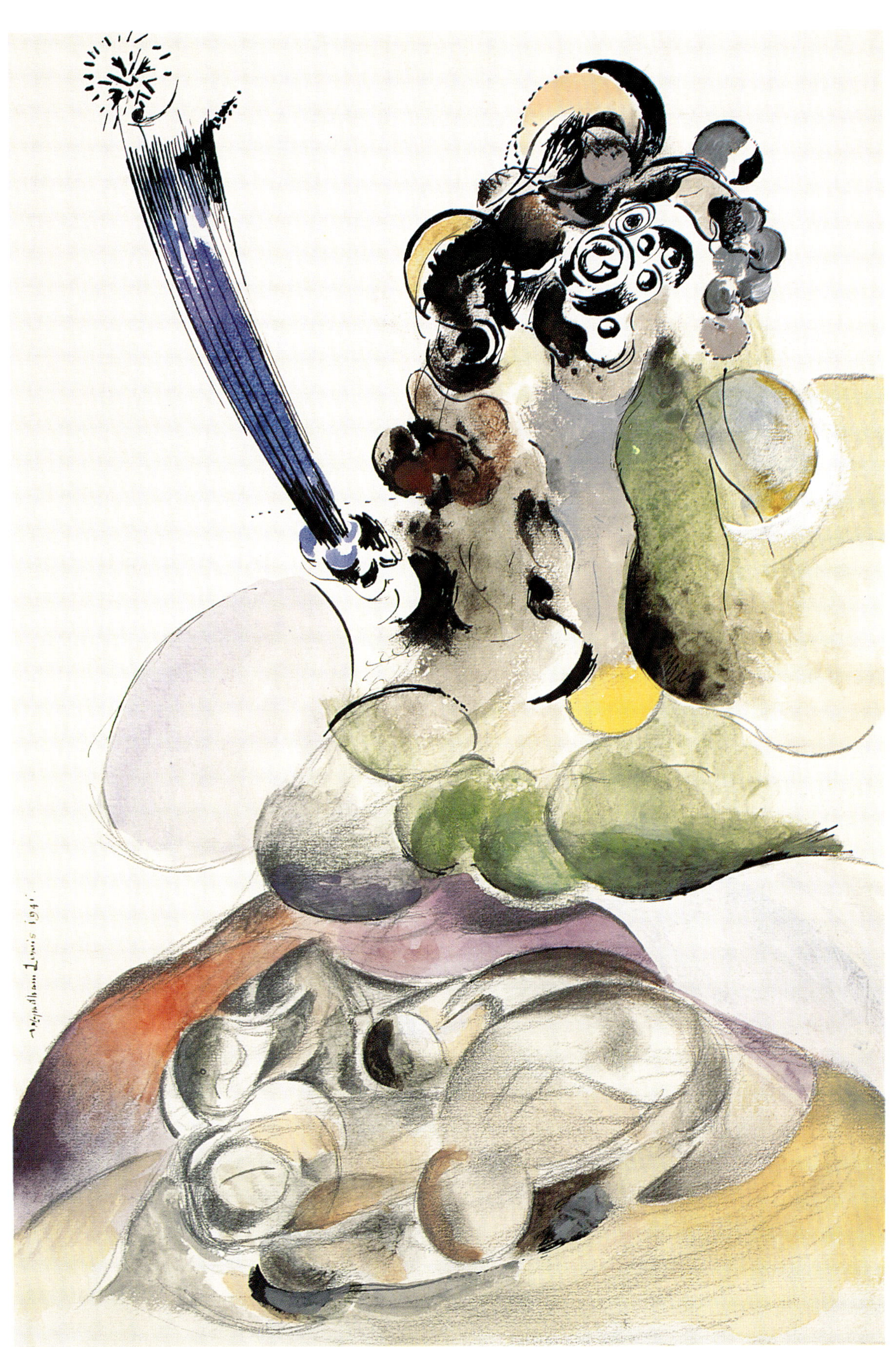

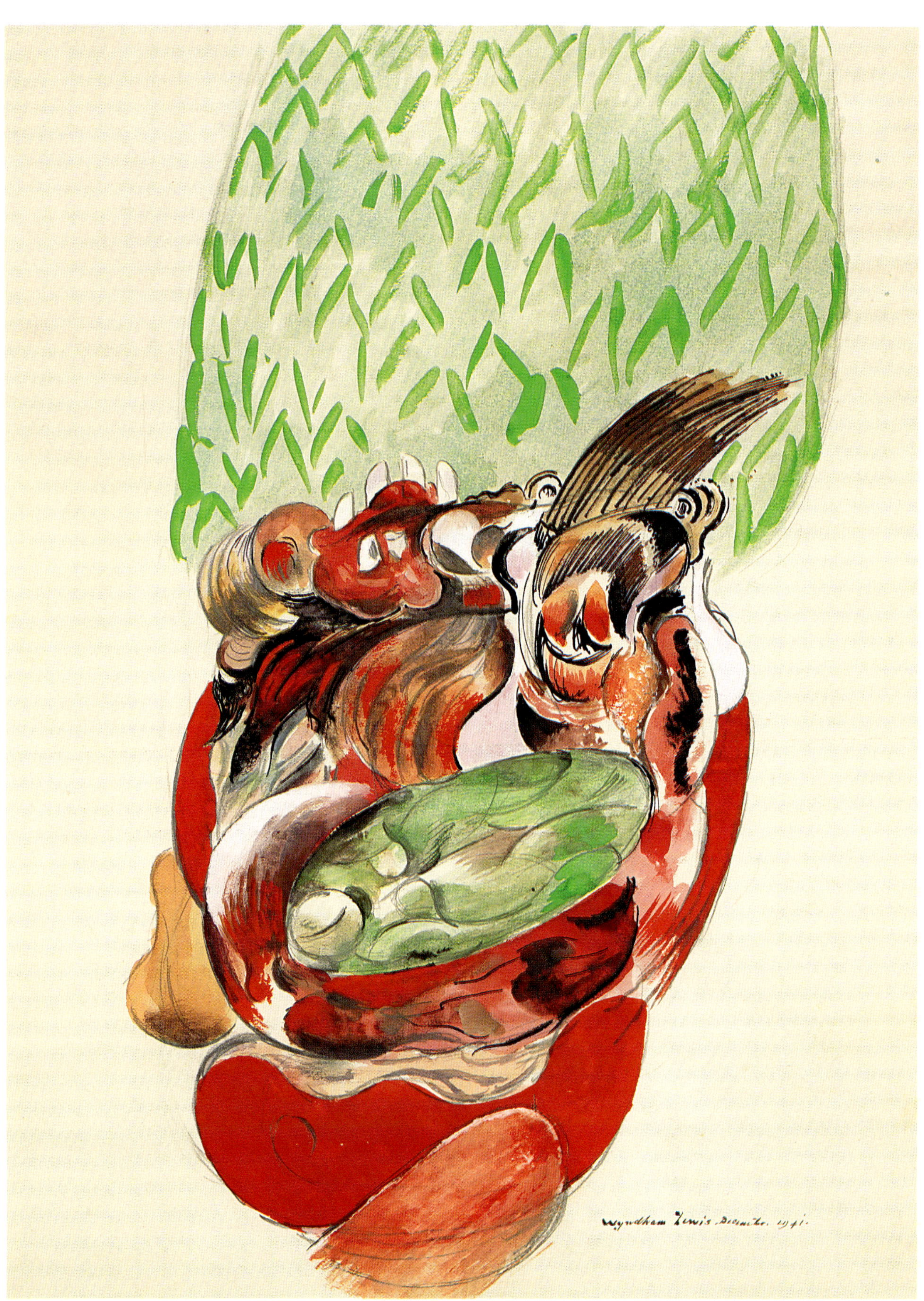
Wyndham Lewis. December. 1941.

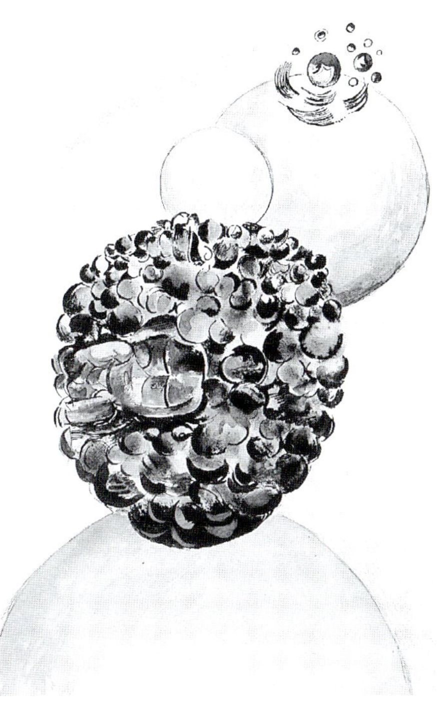

No. 28 *Creation Myth*, 1941-42, pen and ink, pencil and watercolour on paper (37.0 x 25.5 cm), M 987. Walter and Harriet Michel.

Opposite page:
No. 17 *The Sage Meditating Upon the Life of Flesh and Blood*, 1941, graphite, ink and gouache on paper (40.0 x 33.5 cm), M 979. Lent anonymously.

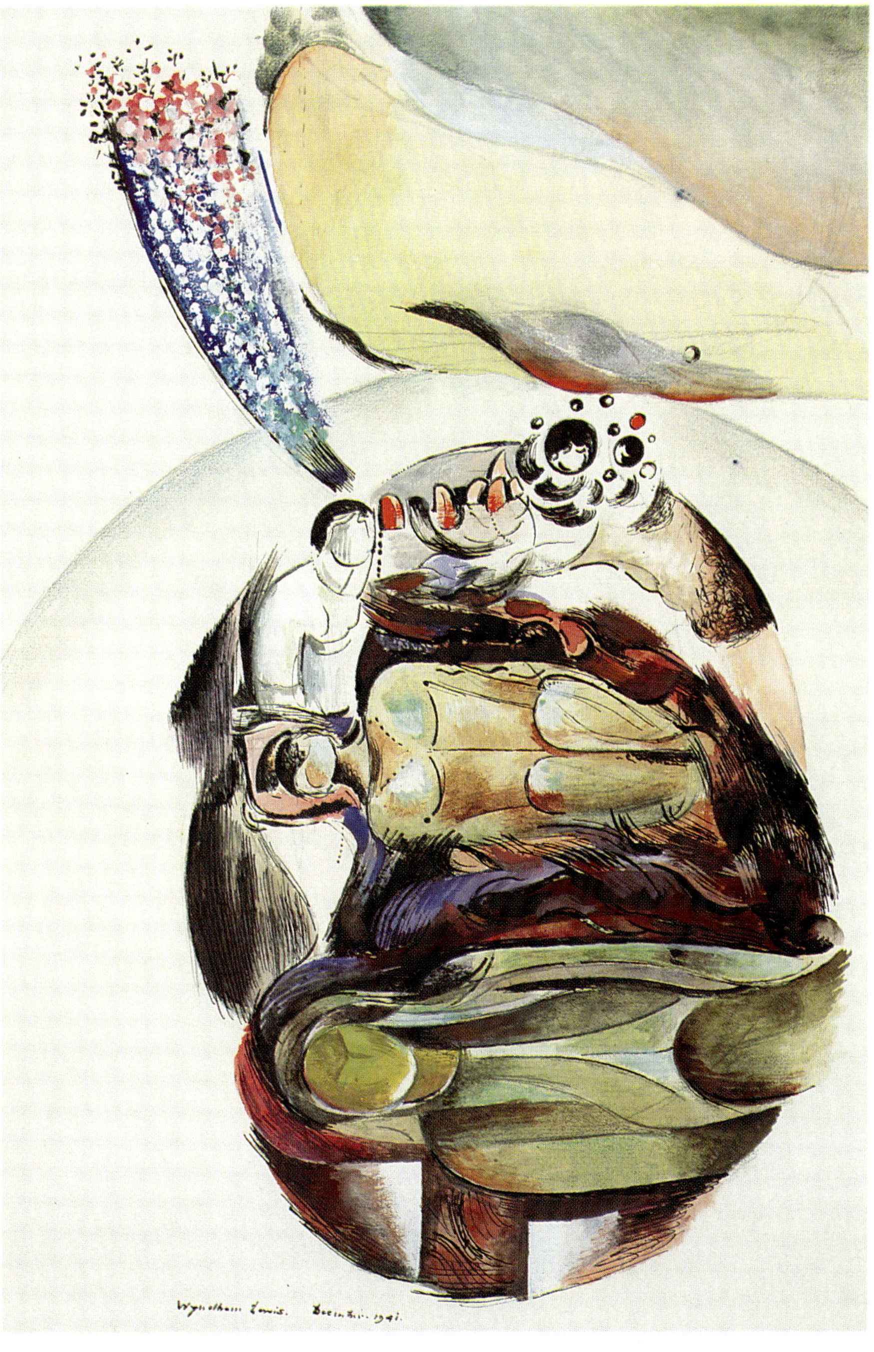

No. 9 *Dragon's Teeth*, 1941, watercolour, ink and graphite on paper (35.5 x 25.0 cm), M 969. Lent anonymously.

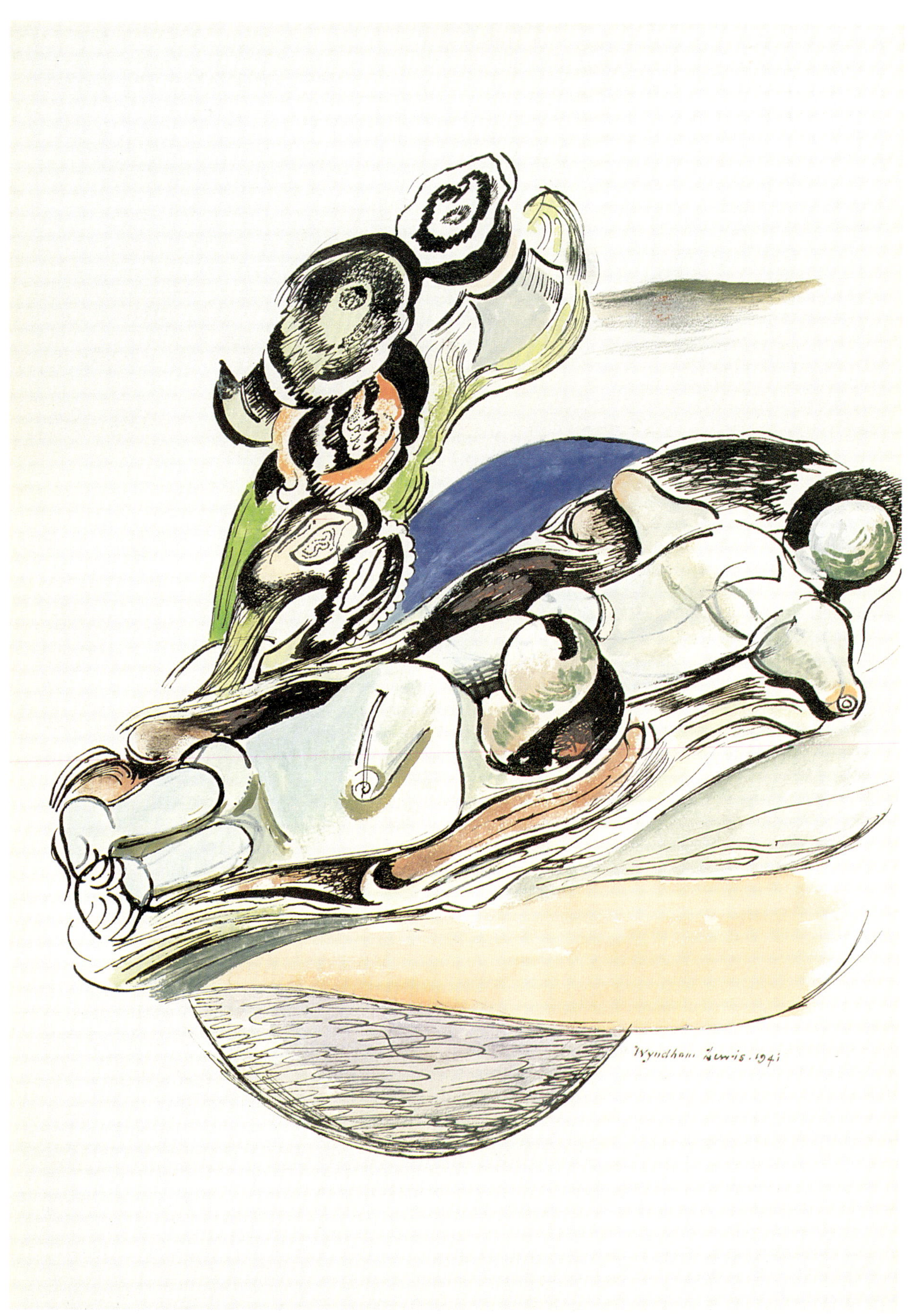
Wyndham Lewis . 1941

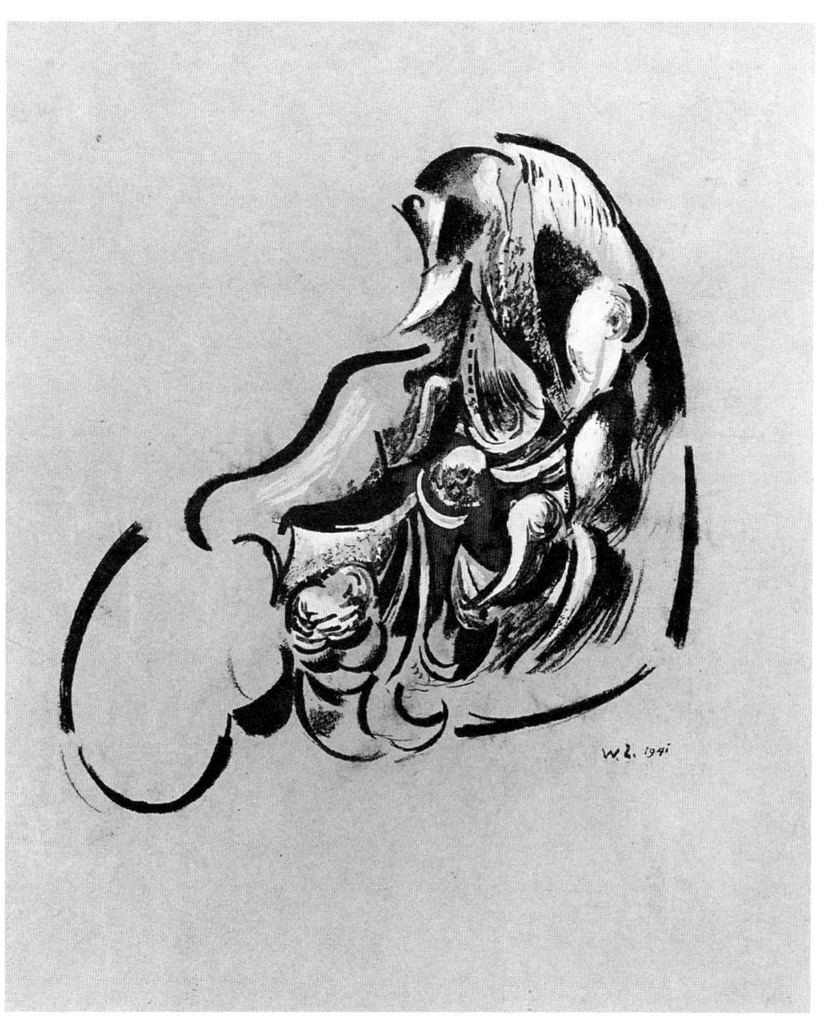

No. 27 *Creation Myth: Maternal Figure* (also known as *Gestation*), 1941, crayon and coloured chalks on blue paper (30.0 x 24.0 cm), M 971. Lent anonymously.

No. 52 *Still-life: Figures In the Belly of a Duck*, 1942, graphite and watercolour on paper (35.0 x 25.7 cm), M 1005. Vancouver Art Gallery, purchase, 1970.

Opposite page:
No. 23 *Small Crucifixion Series, I* (or *III*), 1941, graphite, ink and watercolour on paper (35.5 x 25.0 cm), M 980. Lent anonymously.

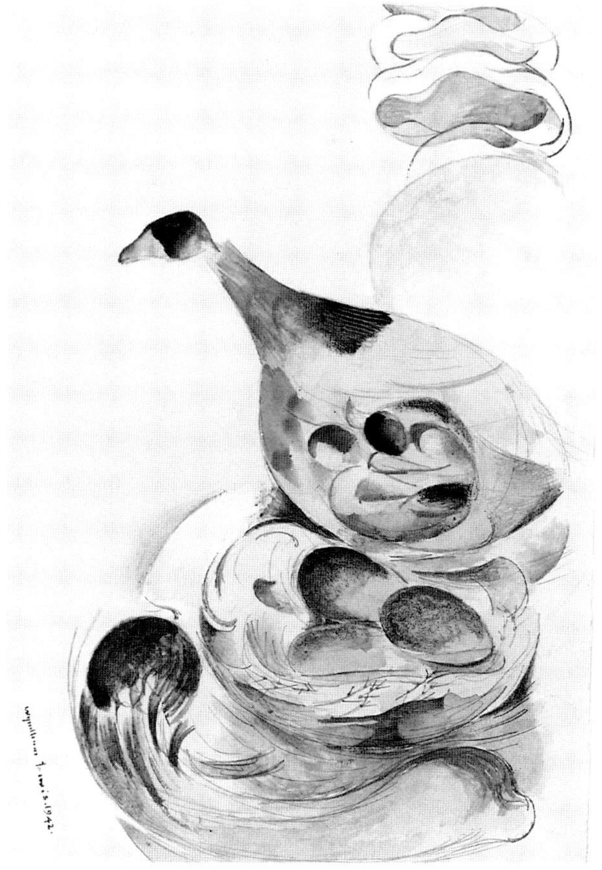

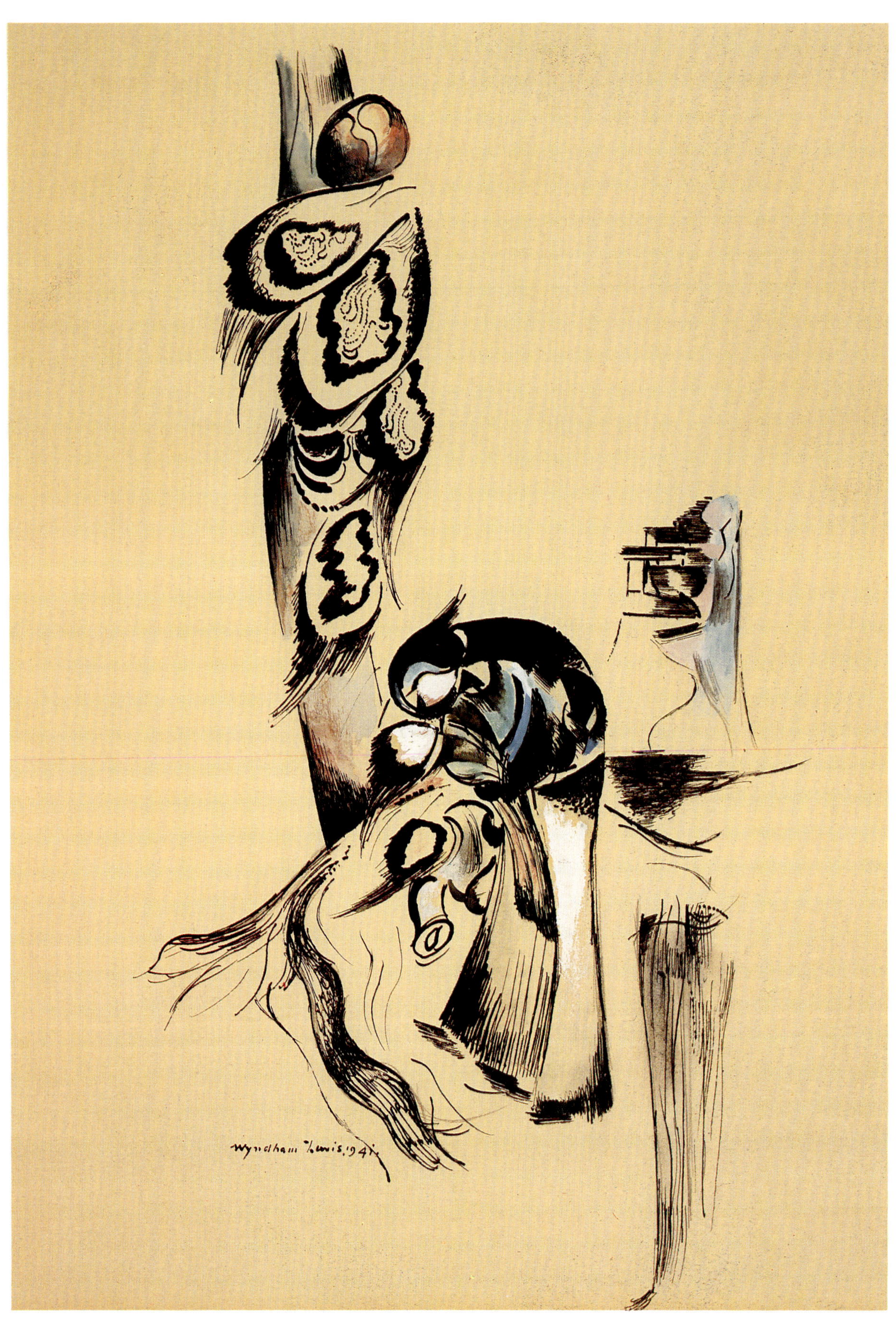
Wyndham Lewis. 1941.

This page:
No. 25 *Crucifixion Series, III*, 1941, graphite, ink and watercolour on paper (35.5 × 25.5 cm) M 982. Lent anonymously.

Opposite page:
No. 24 *Small Crucifixion Series, II: Pietà*, 1941, pen-and-ink and watercolour on paper (33.0 × 25.5 cm), M 981. Rodney Milne-Day, London, England.

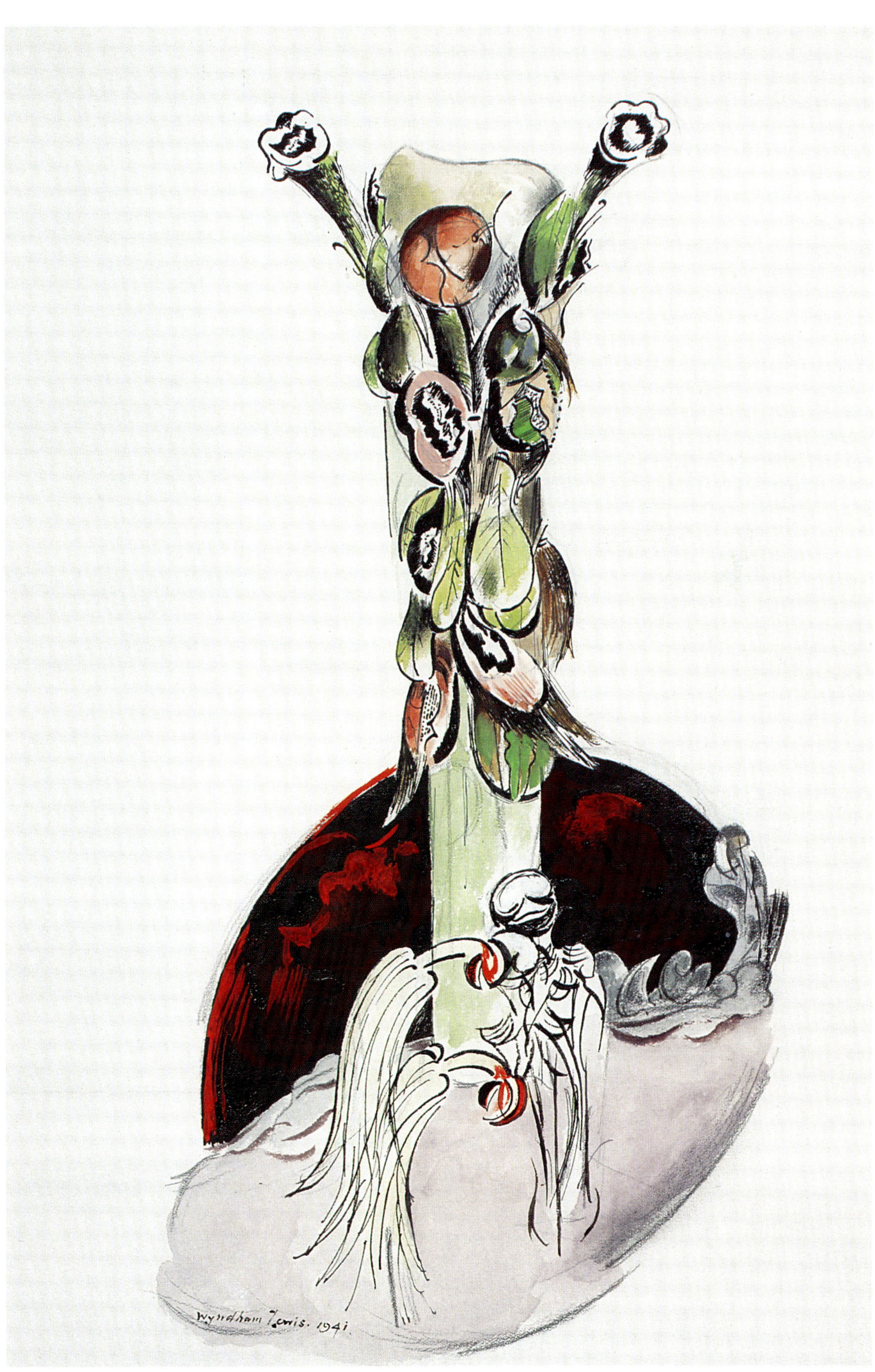

global scale in the person of the nameless, faceless Crowd as it rose to meet its fate on the battlefield of universal war.

In *Crucifixion Series, I,* above the mutilated, partly de-limbed body lying on the ground, is a semi-abstract shape ascending from the corpse, perhaps symbolic of the resurrection or ascension of Christ. Union and bonding of male and female, as well as the more traditional lament for a slain but redemptive god, are alluded to in *Crucifixion Series, II: Pietà.* In traditional Christian iconography, the crucifixion scene frequently includes the Virgin Mary and Mary Magdalene mourning the death of the saviour. Here, however, Lewis has introduced a new figure arrangement suggestive of an entire family, including what appears to be a larger male figure and a small child. *Supplicating Figures*, a pen-and-ink of 1941 (no. 22), appears to represent apostles praying before the body of the slain Christ.

The other imaginative works of this period which do not belong to any specific sequence concentrate on mankind' s confrontation with the darker forces of creation, including the diabolical. In *Figure on Horseback* (1941; no. 11), a man is shown about to stab a serpent (likelyintended here to symbolize Satan). In *Witch on Cowback* (1941; no. 10) and *Witches Surprised by Dawn*, (1942; no. 51), leaping animals charge through undefined, ambiguous space. In the former work, the beast of the title is obviously terrified by something in the distance, as is indicated by its wide-open eyes, flaring nostrils and frightened expression. In the latter, the witches of the title are shown fleeing away at the arrival of daylight. Several different groups of horses and riders, positioned near and far, give an unusual depth to the image. The range and intensity of colour—blues, greys, black, orange, purple and lime-green—also suggest this picture's onieric inspiration.

Human relationships, particularly those of mother and child, are depicted in complex configurations in another body of works dating from 1941-42. *Adoration* (no. 21) is the most specific treatment of this theme; the subject is actually the adoration of the infant Christ by the Magi. Lewis altered the story from the New Testament source, however, by posing the Madonna and Child in an architectural setting, and by depicting the three Wise Men on horseback.

Two further investigations of figural relationships are *Mother and Child*, also known as *Pietà* (1942; no. 40), and *Pietà*, alternately entitled *Madonna and Child* (1942; no. 41), both depicting the Virgin Mary and the Christ Child, as in *Adoration*. These two overtly religious images may also be related thematically to works like *Mother Love* (1942; no. 42) and *Mother and Child, with Male Figure*, also known as *Family Group* (1943; no. 56), in which Lewis continues to explore the maternal/filial bond (or bind). In *Mother Love*, the figures are dressed in military uniform and have a distinctly martial air to them, implying yet again a satirical wartime subtext; the child pushes against its mother, who tries to embrace it. The complexity of human relationships is taken one step farther in *Mother and Child, with Male Figure,* in which a triangular tension is established between the three figures, the union of mother and child contrasting with the isolation of the distant male figure standing in the background, separated by the placement of horizontal bars in the middle ground.

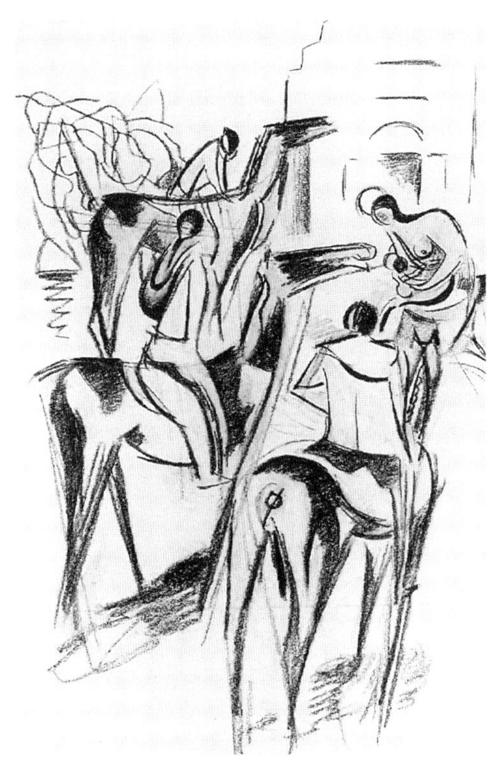

No. 21 *Adoration*, 1941, black and white chalk on paper (38.0 x 25.5 cm), M 963. Walter and Harriet Michel.

If there is a theme common to the imaginative pictures, it is that of mankind's frailty and suffering, and of the ability of the species to survive in the face of the forces of universal destruction. These contrastingly despairing and optimistic views of the human condition do battle with one another in the form of the harsh realities of poverty in *The Three Beggars* (1942; no. 53) and the joyous and brilliantly coloured Creation Myth series. There is, however, no single answer as to what impulse or compulsion prompted Lewis to produce the imaginative works of the early 1940s. Such diverse factors as the state of his exile, his oncoming blindness, his precarious finances, and his doubts about the possibility of peace and justice triumphing over the forces of war and state-sanctioned evil, all no doubt contributed to this extraordinary outpouring. (During his stay in Canada, Lewis had been diagnosed as suffering from glaucoma by a Toronto eye-specialist, although the cause of his eventual blindness in 1949 was a large brain-tumour which was pressing on the optic nerve.)

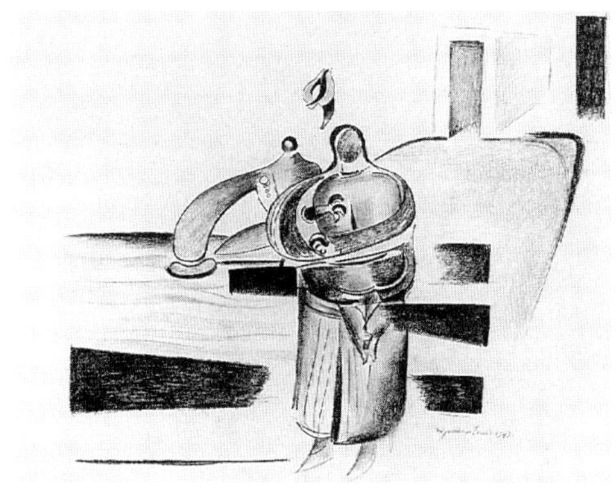

No. 56 *Mother and Child, with Male Figure* (also known as *Family Group*), 1943, graphite and coloured chalks on paper (28.0 x 37.5 cm), M 1023. Mr. and Mrs. Eric McLuhan, Toronto.

In his writings and public lectures of the 1940s, Lewis envisioned the advent of a global harmony, and his interests in Roman Catholicism and Christian themes, as portrayed in his Creation Myth and Crucifixion series pictures, may well have

No. 11 *Figure on Horseback*, 1941, black chalk on paper (26.5 x 35.5 cm), M 970. Austin/Desmond and Phipps, London, England.

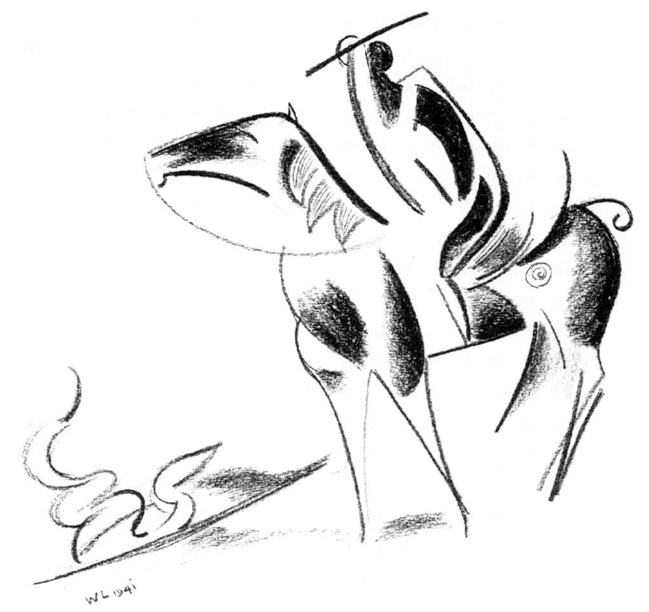

No. 10 *Witch on Cow Back*, 1941, charcoal with watercolour and ochre pastel on wove paper (29.0 x 43.6 cm), M 985. National Gallery of Canada, Ottawa, gift of the Douglas M. Duncan Collection, 1970.

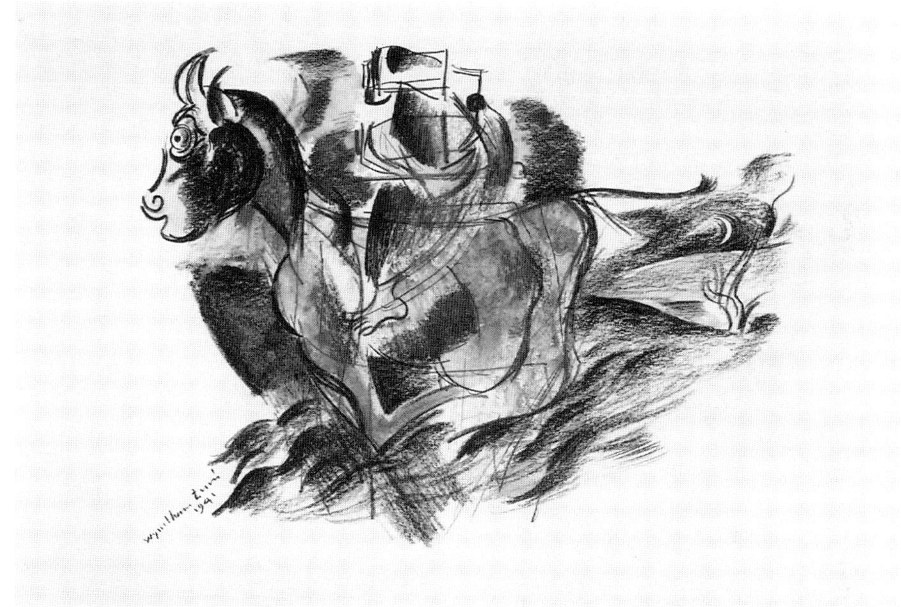

No. 51 *Witches Surprised by Dawn*, 1942, black chalk and watercolour on paper (29.0 x 43.0 cm), M 1008. John and Helen O'Brian, Vancouver.

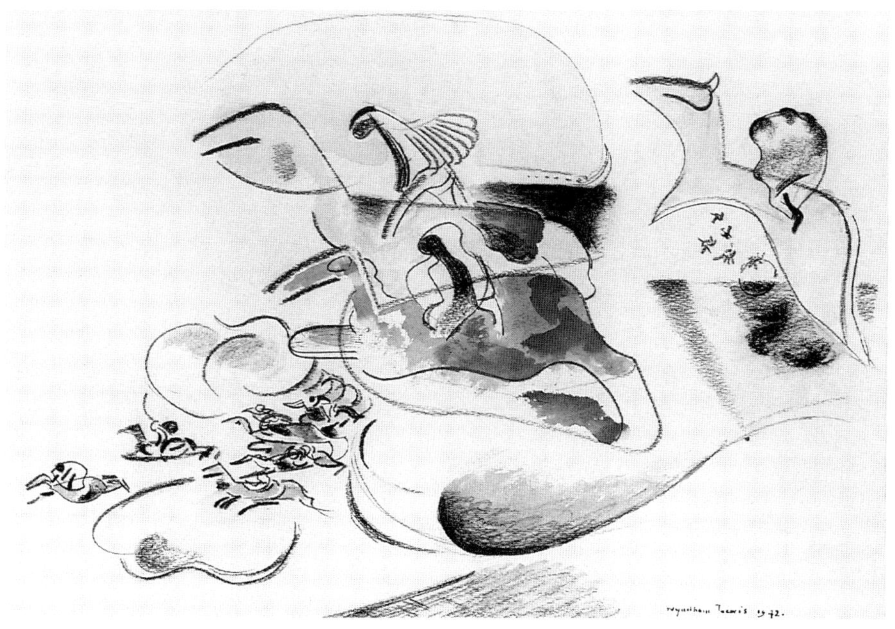

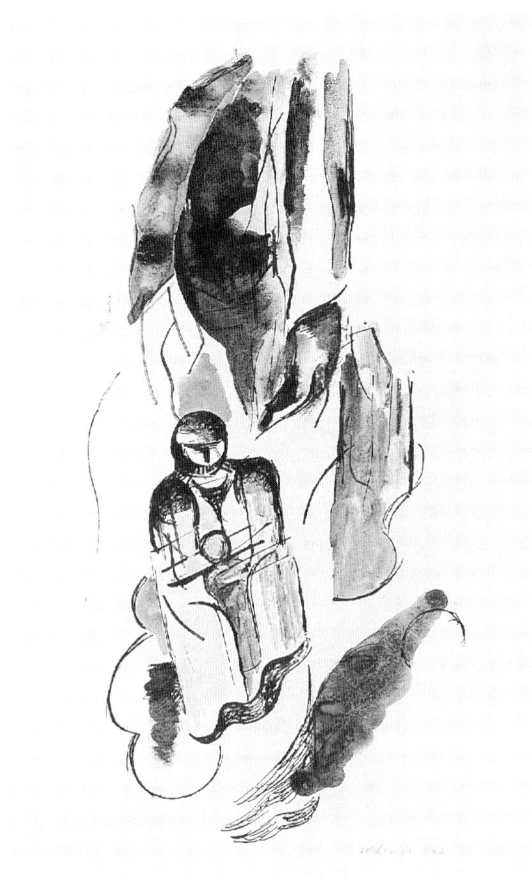

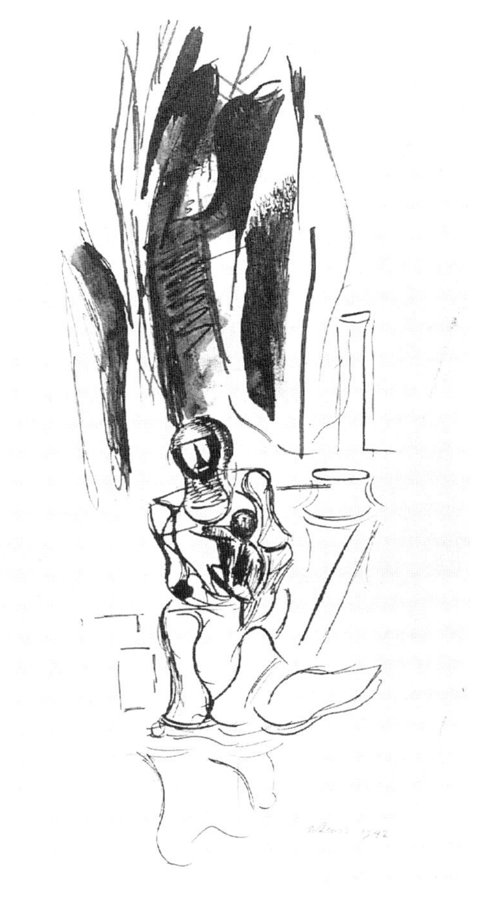

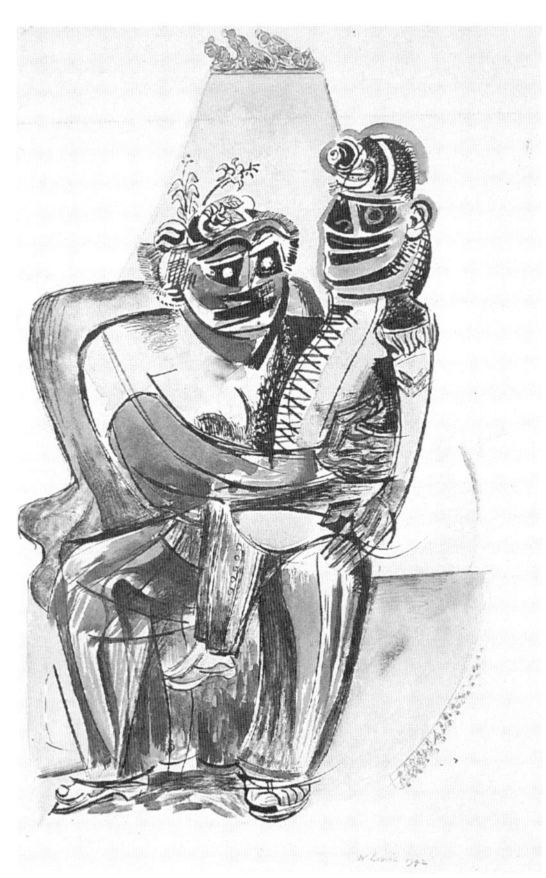

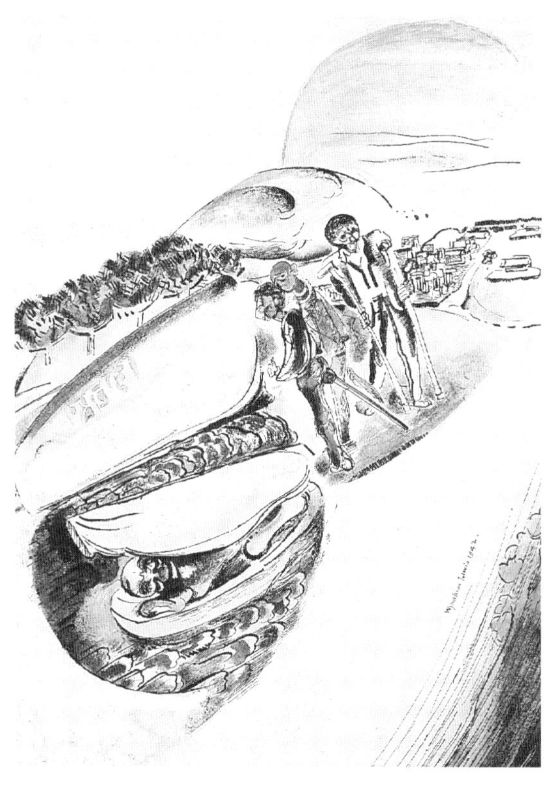

Opposite page (clockwise from top left): No. 40 *Mother and Child* (also known as *Pietà*), 1942, pen-and-ink and watercolour on paper (38.0 x 23.0 cm), M 1001, Lent anonymously; No. 41 *Pietà* (also known as *Madonna and Child*), 1942, pen-and-ink and wash on paper (38.0 x 24.0 cm), M 1002, Herbert F. Johnson Museum of Art, Cornell University, Ithaca, New York, gift of Walter and Harriet Michel; No. 53 *The Three Beggars*, 1942, pen-and-ink and watercolour on paper (37.0 x 27.5 cm), M 1007, Lent anonymously; No. 42 *Mother Love*, 1942, pen-and-ink, graphite, watercolour and wash on paper (45.5 x 28.5 cm), M 998, Lent anonymously.

been an attempt to prophesy a world order of the postwar future. In 1946 he had optimistically predicted,

> Actually we are beginning to have a genuine international, or cosmic culture; even though, alas, no world-state is yet in sight.... We are in transition from being a number of locked-in, parochial, national communities, to a cosmic social unity of some kind.... Manners of expressing ourselves in the past have had the stamp of a locality and race very strong on them, in the arts as in everything else. But a "regionalist", or a nationalist today, anywhere, is the last of his species.[60]

Artists had not lagged behind writers in considering the possibility of non-Biblical origins of the human species in the wake of the publication of Darwin's theory of the evolution of species in 1859. Gradually a consensus emerged that, while Judeo-Christian chronology could not account for the duration of time required for the formation of the universe and the development of life on Earth, science alone could not explain the coming into existence of matter or the beginnings of the cosmos, nor could it define, much less give a rationale for, the life-force of consciousness. Lewis, living in the aftermath of these heated debates, appears to have been fascinated, like so many of his contemporaries, by the subject of creation and its aftermath, and his pictures represent his own resolution of traditional Judeo-Christian themes and their relationship to modern science. Lewis's Creation Myth and Crucifixion series can be interpreted as a visual monologue on a complex subject that became something of an obsession among intellectuals during the 1920s and '30s, as epitomized by Darius Milhaud's jazz-oriented ballet score of 1922-23, *La Création du Monde*. The desire to explore spiritual or metaphysical realms and to penetrate the principle of growth and decay was also a concern of the English-born Canadian artist, designer and writer Bertram Brooker (1888-1955), who had been painting semi-abstract images of the creation of the world as early as 1927 (fig. 19). The Scottish-born painter J.W.G. Macdonald (1897-1960), then based in British Columbia, was painting a series of pictures he termed "modalities." These unique landscapes, such as *Departing Day* (1935) and *Etheric Form* (1935), he said, "lift me out of the earthliness, the material mire, of our civilization."[61] Similar motifs, such as sprouting, regenerative leaf-forms, are found in both Lewis's Crucifixion series and Macdonald's *Winter*(1938; fig. 20). Lewis's crucifixions also coincided with David Milne's religious sequences, typified by the Ascensions, the Resurrections, the Day of Judgement and the Saint pictures of his late maturity, as typified by *Ascension I, Uxbridge* (1943; fig. 21).[62]

The semi-abstract, semi-naturalistic style Lewis was developing during the 1940s may also relate to his views on the future role of the artist in society and his increasing critical response to abstraction. He feared that "the Artist—as painter of easel-pictures, 'oil-paintings'—is in the first stages of dissolution, so within an easily foreseeable future there will be no Artist either.—Unless the state steps in, and becomes society."[63] Lewis predicted widespread visual illiteracy, observing that the problem lay in the perceived relevance of the two-dimensional arts in contemporary western culture. Painting and drawing, he believed, faced challenging competition from radio and telecommunications, a concern later expressed in the influential writings of Marshall McLuhan.[64] Lewis's solution was the reintegration of art into society by returning to the naturalism of the immediate early-modern period of the 1910s, though not to the false, imitative realism associated with the Royal Academy, which had, in 1938, rejected for exhibition his famous *Portrait of T.S. Eliot,* a decision that led to Augustus John's resignation from the Academy.

Lewis felt, rightly or wrongly, that there was only a limited place for non-objective abstract art in contemporary painting. His gradual rejection of abstraction, following the demise of the Vorticist period, and the evidence of the semi-naturalistic pictures of the Toronto years, confirm that he held true to this belief. Predicting that the era of abstractionism had come to its natural end, he insisted, "all along the line nature has won", and that "there was no further excuse for it [abstract art]".[65] According to Lewis, "There is emotional appeal in the visual arts, but it resides altogether in the human reference, not in the nature of form or of colour itself."[66] Like other fads and phases in the history of art, abstraction, Lewis felt, had outlived its usefulness:

> Abstract Art died of acute boredom...boredom on the part of both public and artist.... While the idea of a visual music was still a novelty, everything went swimmingly. But it turned out that the visual world could not be reduced to those terms, and is so much more interesting than "abstract volumes" of our visual-musical world could ever be.... Abstract art had to be attempted but it was a fantastic branch of architecture rather than anything else.[67]

Lewis's concern about current tendencies to non-objectivism in American painting related directly to his vision of the role of the artist in modern society. The general current of art in the U.S., which had been so dynamically energized by European emigrés in the 1930s and '40s, was inexorably towards Abstract Expressionism. During the Depression and the subsequent world war, however, artists had been concerned to make socially committed statements about their roles and functions in a society that had little use for non-commercial culture in an epoch dominated by technology, mass-marketing and global industrialization. It was widely be-lieved, during these years of conflict, that art could not survive if it were to continue unimpeded on its course toward total formalism and self-referentiality. Always *engagé,* however alienated he may have been from the society in which he worked and fought, Lewis strongly supported the view that artists should turn to social and political issues for their *raison d'être,* which perhaps explains why he showed appreciation for the intensively localized Canadian and American Regionalist landscapes of the 1930s and 1940s, while lamenting the relative calm and complacency that prevailed on the North American political scene during these years of international trauma and crisis. This bias also explains why he continued to favour the quasi-realistic landscapes and cityscapes of the Group of Seven and the Canadian Group of Painters over the work of their more abstractionist contemporaries and successors.[68]

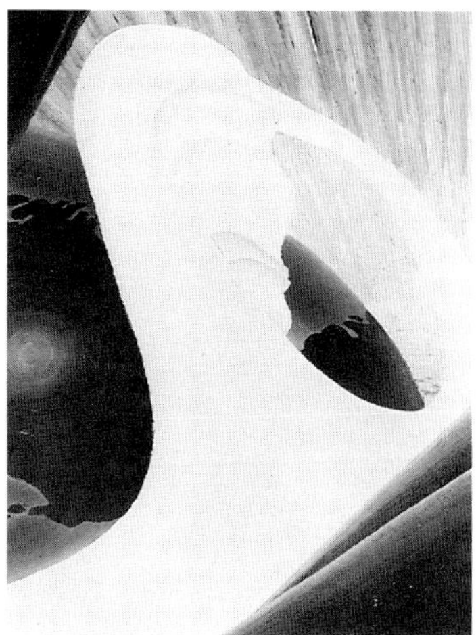

No. 19 Bertram Brooker (1888-1955): *Creation,* (c. 1972, oil on board (60.9 x 43.2 cm), Private collection. Photograph: National Gallery of Canada, Ottawa.

The role of art and the artist in modern society, which had preoccupied Lewis since the outset of his career, was a topical one throughout the 1930s and '40s, as the British art critic Herbert Read's *Art and Society* (1937) indicates. The question was the subject of much discussion in Canada during the early 1940s, coming to a head in June 1941 in the form of the Kingston Conference of Canadian Artists, held at Queen's University in Kingston, Ontario. Although Lewis was then living in Montreal, and his name does not appear in the conference's attendance list, virtually every Canadian artist of any consequence was present at this symposium, led by the Swiss-born artist and teacher André Biéler, who had invited the American Regionalist painter Thomas Hart Benton to be a keynote speaker. Lewis knew of this pivotal event, as he had been invited to attend a party at the Toronto residence of Isabel McLaughlin, held in honour of those West Coast artists who were on their way to Kingston. Among the guests were the painters Jack Shadbolt, Jock Macdonald, Charles Scott, Paraskeva Clark, Peter and Bobs Cogill Haworth, and André Biéler.[69] The conference resulted in the formation of several important organizations, including the Canadian Arts Council (now The Canada Council) and the Federation of Canadian Artists, the founding of which responded to the need for the kind of support structures for artists that would potentially have relieved some of the difficulties experienced by Lewis.[70]

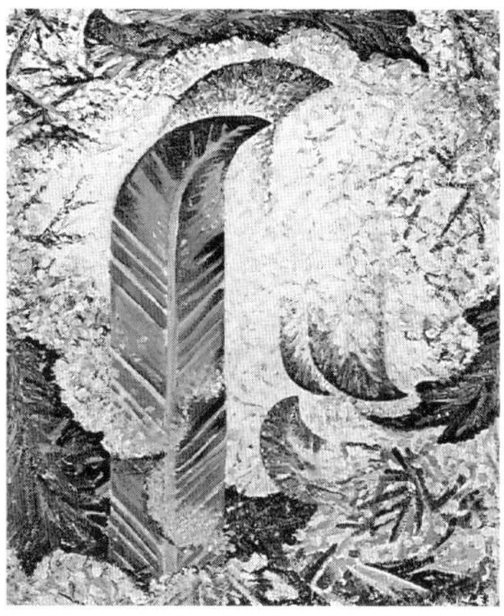

Fig. 20 J.W.G. Macdonald (1897-1960): *Winter,* 1938, oil on canvas (56.0 x 45.8 cm). Art Gallery of Ontario, Toronto, gift of Miss Jessie A.B. Staunton in memory of her parents, Mr. and Mrs. V.C. Staunton, 1961.

The Kingston Conference occurred at a time when Lewis was voicing increasingly vociferous complaints about the weakness of the Canadian art community and the lack of opportunities for advanced painters such as himself to make a living from their work. It reflected, in a single gathering, the amount of cultural activity that really was taking place in Canada, despite the formidable odds against its flourishing. A substantial number of the artists in attendance were based in Toronto, and Lewis would certainly have known of most of them, even if he had not made their acquaintance. By November 1941 he could comment, "I have painted all the more or less intelligent people here (a handful)",[71] and by May 1943 was writing, "nothing pleasant has happened to me here. But I don't think that anybody coming in from the outside —from Europe—would have a very nice time in this place. This is a province; but with a provincialism that has no equal for exclusiveness and jealousy."[72] Had he attended the Kingston Conference, he would have encountered a spirit of openness, cooperation and camaraderie that contradicted these perceptions, but then Lewis was so confirmed a non-joiner, and so fundamentally opposed to the idea of artists taking political action, that the notion of his mingling with his numerous colleagues at Kingston becomes too fanciful to contemplate. Instead, he went on insisting that "Real whole-time artists do not abound in Canada,"[73] and—with considerably more accuracy—that "Canada possesses no writers so far of the imaginative range of Hemingway or Faulkner."[74]

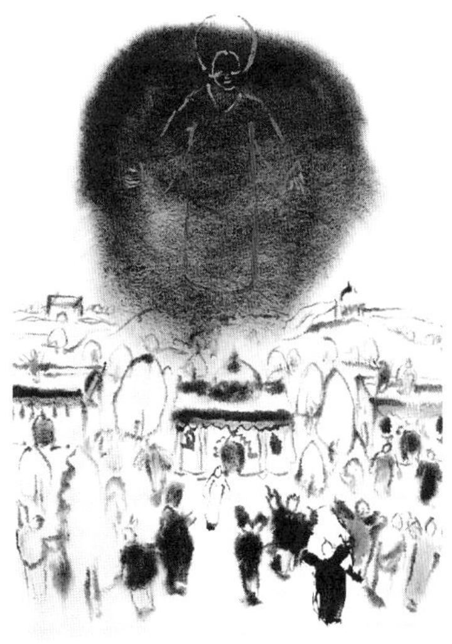

Fig. 21 David B. Milne (1882-1953): *Ascension I. Uxbridge,* 1943, watercolour over pencil on paper (55.6 x 38.8 cm). National Gallery of Canada, Ottawa (acc. no. 16515).

Virtually the only positive remarks Lewis made about the Canadian art scene were on the subject of the Group of Seven, a nationalist landscape-painting movement that had been launched in 1920 and was considered to be somewhat *passé* by the younger, more socially committed regionalists and modernists of the 1930 and '40s. The Group had been dissolved as an exhibiting unit in 1932, then succeeded by the larger and more progressive Canadian Group of Painters, founded in 1933 and active until 1954. The depiction of wilderness landscapes gave way to the painting of current events and such crucial issues as the Great Depression, the war, aspects of industrialization, the dereliction of the countryside, and social conditions in the inner city. Lewis expressed cautious support of a few of the younger artists who then were coming into the fore in Toronto, but his allegiance remained with the older school:

> in the art of painting something has really happened, in spite of a cramped social system. Canada has what is, in my view, the most important school of painting upon the North American continent. To be specific: I would as soon possess a watercolour picture by Carl Schaefer as I would a good early Birchfield [*sic;* i.e. Charles Burchfield] with whom Schaefer has obvious analogies, and the latter is regarded as one of the most distinguished artists in the States. A fine Jackson, or one of the best Tom Thompsons [*sic*]...is a match, in my humble opinion, for any canvas in the Whitney Museum of American Art in New York.[75]

In a private letter written shortly after Lewis expressed these affirmative opinions, however, he openly admitted that he had exaggerated the strengths of the arts in Canada for public consumption:

> I am reduced to writing articles to fill in time—and my pocket—on "Will there be a Canadian Renaissance?" The bigger I picture the "renaissance" (whatever they mean by that) the more money I get. So I make it quite a spectacular explosion of intellectual energy. The only intelligent people here—like the painter, Jackson,—regard a marriage with the States as their best bet, and I think the same. Meanwhile I cudgel my brains to imagine Toronto as a sort of Florence or Padua in a great cultural birthroe [i.e. birth-throe]. By the time I cross that frontier of yours again I shall be a semi-idiot.[76]

The friend at whose suggestion Lewis had originally come to Canada bore the brunt of his dissatisfaction with Toronto. According to John Reid, "Lewis suddenly turned on me: I was to blame for all his troubles; behind his back I had spread stories about his life in England."[77] Reid was so offended by Lewis's accusations, which were exacerbated by Lewis' s failure to pay him for some books, that he threatened to commence legal action. He felt badly about the turn in their formerly amicable relationship, especially as "more than anyone else except Lewis I was to blame for him coming to Toronto."[78]

Lewis's largely negative generalizations about Canadian culture and society suggest that he knew little in advance about what he was going to encounter when he arrived on these shores. Shortly before and after his departure from England he could have availed himself, in preparation for his stay, of two important international exhibitions organized by the National Gallery of Canada. These were *A Century of Canadian Art,* a large historical survey of painting, sculpture and indigenous art, was shown at Tate Gallery, London in 1938; and the survey of contemporary Canadian art selected by five leading Canadian art societies—the Royal Canadian Academy, the Canadian Society of Painters in Watercolour, the Canadian Society of Graphic Art, the Canadian Group of Painters, and the Sculptors' Society of Canada—for the New York World's Fair in 1939, at which Lewis's painting *The Siege of Barcelona* was included in the *Exhibition of Contemporary British Art.*

Despite the bleak picture Lewis drew of cultural conditions in Toronto, he was actually positioned at the centre of a fairly vibrant and progressive community of artists and writers, at least until early 1943, when many of their number joined the armed services and went overseas.[79] If Lewis felt that little was being done in Toronto to nurture the arts, his perspective was a reflection of, and reaction to, his own isolated and economically uncertain situation. That Lewis found Toronto as unpalatable as he did had as much to do with his personality as it did with the city itself and the transitional period in which he lived in it. The extent of his alienation —or indifference—is demonstrated by his apparent absence from the Toronto opening of the *Britain At War* exhibition in November 1941, which included his *A Canadian Gun-pit.*[80]

Despite his complaints about being ostracized and ignored, Lewis was as closely connected to the Toronto art scene as any non-Canadian artist could have expected, being supported (for a time, at least) by its two most important patrons, by the contacts he established through his painting activities, journalism, and rare appearances in society, and by other means. His first studio, rented between November 1940 and March 1941, was at 22 Grenville Street, at the heart of Toronto's miniature version of Greenwich Village, the main thoroughfare of which was nearby Gerrard Street West. Grenville Street boasted an arts supply store, two commercial galleries, and many artists' and craftsmens' studios. Number 18-22 Grenville was the site of the Jenkins' Studio Building, opened across the street from the former Jenkins Art Gallery, which was housed in an Art Nouveau addition on the back of the Queen Anne-style College St. house built for the nineteenth-century landscape painter Lucius O'Brien (1832-1899), where the Ontario Society of Artists (O.S.A.) had been founded in 1870.[81]

By March 1941 Lewis had moved into the Studio Building on Severn Street(fig. 22), a fair distance to the north, on the fringes of the upper-class enclave of Rosedale, where he probably worked until the end of May. This building, erected in 1913 by Lawren Harris and Dr. James MacCallum, served as the main studio space for the painters who formed the Group of Seven in 1920, and continued to be a wellspring of artistic activity until a new owner evicted most of the tenants in the 1950s. Although, by the 1940s, only A.Y. Jackson of the original Group was still renting quarters there, its other tenants, representing a younger generation of painters and designers—Charles Comfort, Kathleen Daly (b. 1898), Thoreau MacDonald (1901-1989), George Pepper (1903-1962), and Lowrie Warrener (1900-1983)—were beginning to make their mark. Lewis moved into the studio vacated by Lawren P. Harris (b. 1910), the son of Lawren S. Harris, who had been conscripted as a war artist in early 1941.[82] Comfort, who had first met Lewis at the dinner hosted by J.S. McLean at the York Club in November 1939, recorded an uncomfortable *rencontre* with his co-tenant in 1943, which graphically illustrates the temperamental volatility induced by Lewis's difficulties and frustrations at the time of the *Canadian War Factory* commission. "The feature" of a train journey between Ottawa and Toronto in December 1942, Comfort wrote in his unpublished autobiography,

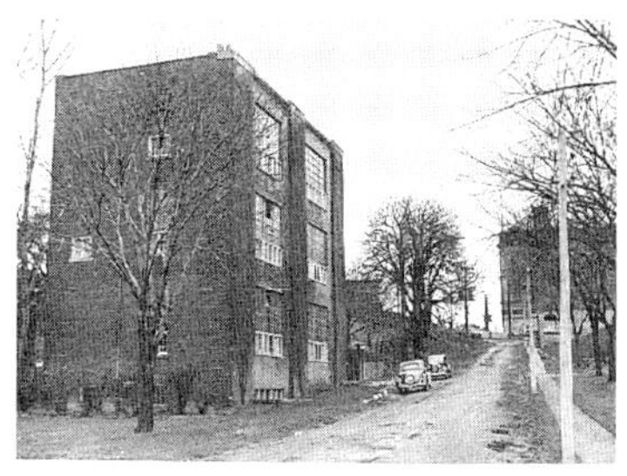

Fig. 22 The Studio Building, Toronto, erected in 1913 by Lawren Harris and Dr. James MacCallum. Photograph by Charles F. Comfort, 1938. Charles Comfort Papers, Documentary Art and Photography Division, National Archives of Canada, Ottawa (acc. no. 1991-306).

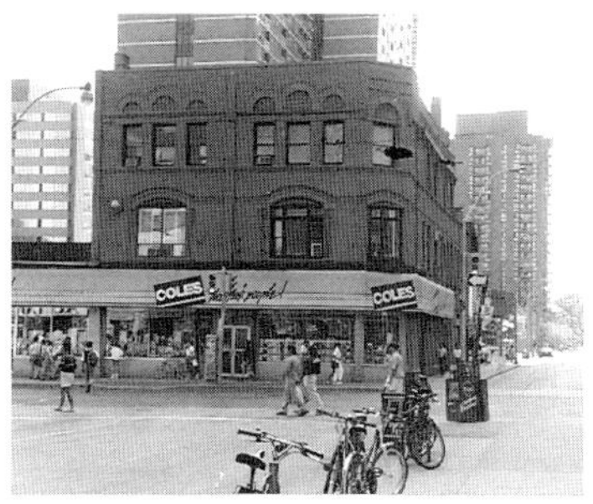

Fig. 23 Former location of the Picture Loan Gallery, 3 Charles St. (at Yonge), Toronto. Photograph by Robert Stacey, 1991.

> was my brush with the sardonic Wyndham Lewis. Shortly after leaving Brockville I was moving down the swaying coach when I suddenly saw him sprawling in the last seat, where one expects to find one of the trainmen. Readers will recall the unmistakable fact that he was a neighbour of mine in the Studio Building at 25 Severn Street. I addressed him civilly. He lifted his head, turned a daemonic eye on me and said, "What do you want? Bugger-off and leave me alone!" Knowing Lewis, I was not shocked, but I was surprised. He appeared to be in a particularly evil mood. I answered, "Just a minute. I would not dream of interrupting your ugly reveries. I am leaving for England in a few days and I shall report your characteristic behaviour to Mr. [Vincent] Massey [Canada's high commissioner in London] and Sir Kenneth [Clark]." I wandered back to my seat, wondering if I had done the right thing. Evidently I did, because while the engine was coaling up at Belleville, he approached with a smile, said he regretted his rudeness, that I had caught him in a mood of resentment following the failure of an interview in Ottawa. He said he hoped I would overlook the incident and inquired in what capacity I was going overseas. I was in battle-dress with captain's rank on my shoulders. I told him I was attached to the Historical Section and would function as a war artist. His bitterness turned to friendliness and he confessed that he envied me. I never did discover the purpose of his visit to Ottawa, but Malcolm MacDonald was alluded to.[83]

It was with A.Y. Jackson, of all the artists in the Studio Building and indeed in Toronto, that Lewis was most closely associated (fig. 23).[84] Lewis appreciated his outgoing personality and generosity, affectionately writing of this colleague and benefactor, "He received me, coming from a foreign milieu, like a brother."[85] The two artists spent a considerable amount of time discussing Canadian geography and topography as a subject for painters, particularly that of the North, and these discussions subsequently found their way into Lewis' s review article, "Nature's Place in Canadian Culture." He used the occasion to pay tribute to Jackson and his work:

> There is gaiety sometimes in Jackson, but it is rationed. His vision is as austere as his subject-matter, which is precisely the hard puritanic land in which he always had lived: with no frills, with all its dismal solitary grandeur and bleak beauty, its bad side deliberately selected rather than its chilly relentings. This is a matter of temperament: Jackson is not a man to go gathering nuts in May. He has no wish to be seduced every Spring when the sap rises—neither he nor nature are often shown in these compromising moods. There is something of Ahab in him; the long white contours of the Laurentian Mountains in mid-winter are his elusive leviathan.[86]

In 1943 Lewis wrote to Malcolm MacDonald, "As you no doubt realised, the main object of my article [i.e. "Nature's Place in Canadian Culture"] was to do personal service to Jackson. I made myself his advocate, and was glad to stress the publicity value to Canadians of their zero-land. (Why mind being treated as snowbound 'hicks'?)"[87]

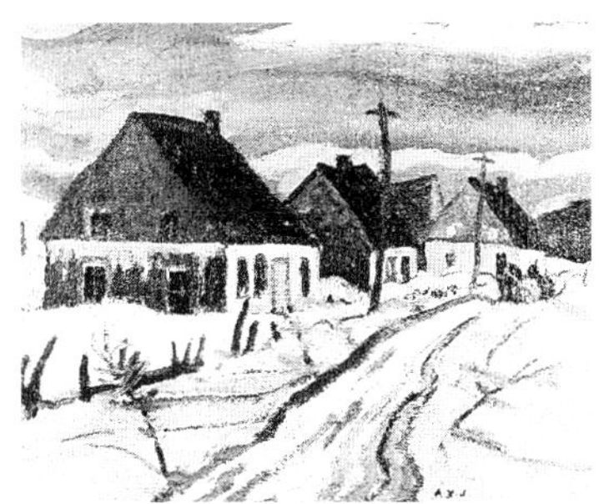

Fig. 24 A.Y. Jackson (1882-1974): *Les Eboulements, Winter*, n.d., oil on canvas (35.6 x 43.7 cm). Art Gallery of Windsor, gift from the Douglas M. Duncan Collection, 1970.

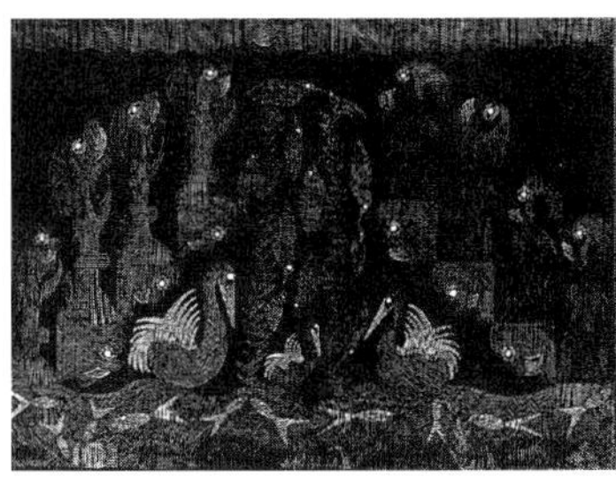

Fig. 25 Scottie Wilson (1888-1972): *The Stream of Life*, n.d. (c. 1940s), crayon and ink on paper (38.7 x 53.3 cm). Art Gallery of Windsor, gift from the Douglas M. Duncan Collection, 1970.

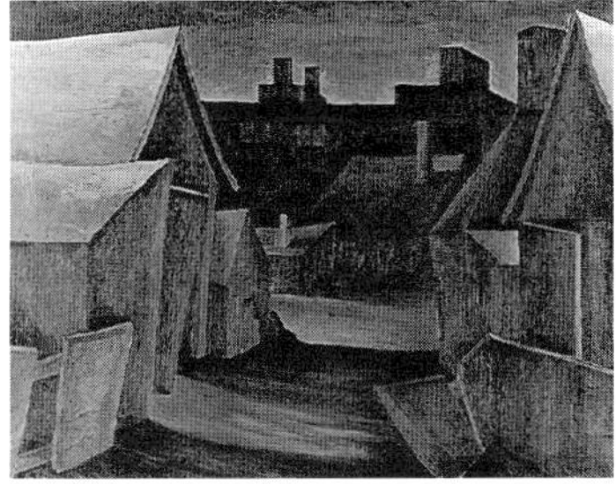

Fig. 26 Caven Atkins (b. 1908): *Night*, 1932, oil on canvas (53.3 x 71.1 cm). Art Gallery of Windsor, gift of the artist, 1990.

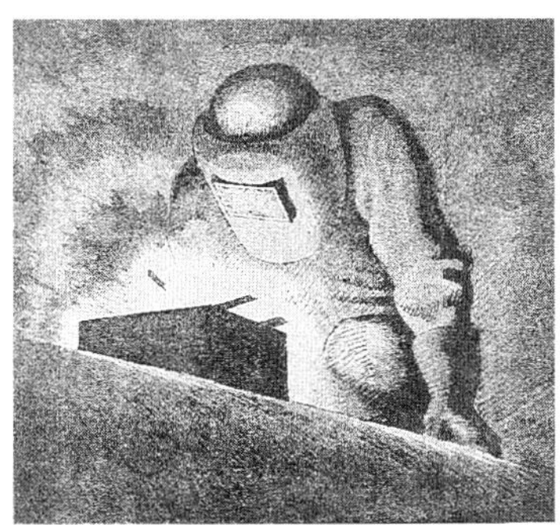

Fig. 27 Frederick B. Taylor (1906-1987), *Welder*, 1944, soft-ground etching and aquatint, state II, 2/2 (28.1 x 33.4 cm). Art Gallery of Windsor, purchase, 1989.

Jackson in his turn admired Lewis and valued his strengths over his weaknesses. "In Toronto", he remarked, "only a few people realized what an important figure he was in both art and literary circles."[88] Elsewhere, he recalled:

> I liked Lewis. He dropped into my studio quite frequently while he lived in Toronto and would exchange views. I let him do most of the talking. I felt it was a priviledge [*sic*] to listen to him. I was not always in accord with him. He had strong dislikes. But I admired many of the people who were his good friends and his views on art and artists were quite above the level of most of our art critics.[89]

Lewis also had a high regard for Carl Schaefer, who was especially fond of Lewis's imaginative pictures, which he considered to be "very fine works of art, although Lewis rarely discussed them."[90]

Douglas Duncan also kept Lewis informed of doings of the various artists then active in Toronto, most of whom were associated with his Picture Loan Society(fig. 23), where Lewis could have made the acquaintance of such co-founders of this cooperative gallery as H. Garnard (Rik) Kettle (b. 1906), Erma Lennox, Norah McCullough, Gordon McNamara (b. 1910), Pegi Nicol (1904-1949), and Gordon Webber (1909-1965). There could have seen the work of the numerous artists for whom Duncan organized solo and group shows in the early Forties, such as Will Ogilvie, Carl Schaefer and David Milne, and the British primitive Surrealist, Scottie Wilson (1888-1972), who lived in Toronto from the early 1930s to 1945.[91] Among the Wilson works shown by Duncan were several that dealt with the idea of creation, such as *The Stream of Life* (fig. 25). These artists, other artists who periodically exhibited at the P.L.S., including André Biéler, Jack Bush (1909-1977), Caven Atkins (b. 1907)(fig. 26), Isabel McLaughlin, Paraskeva Clark (1898-1986) and L.A.C. Panton (1894-1954), were to have a lasting impact on the development of modernist Canadian painting throughout the 1940s and thereafter.

Besides the Picture Loan Gallery, there were only a limited number of spaces available for artists to exhibit in Toronto, chief among them being the Art Gallery of Toronto, in addition to which there were at least three commercial galleries: Mellors-Laing, on Yonge Street at Bloor, and the Malloney and Roberts galleries, then on Grenville, as well as the art galleries housed in the Eaton's and Simpson's department stores.[92] Lewis was lucky to have the opportunity to exhibit and sell his pictures, as he had brought very few with him from England and it took him the better part of two years to create a new body of work for exhibition and sale. He was grateful to Duncan for his support, once revealing to J.S. McLean, "Douglas Duncan has helped as much as is humanly possible and far more than I could expect."[93] (This indebtedness—which was financial as well as moral—did not prevent Lewis, however, from cruelly caricaturing Duncan as the effeminate, unreliable and snobbish Cedric Furbish in *Self Condemned*.) Two of Lewis's new works from this period, *Allégresse Aquatique* (1941; no. 32) and *Lebensraum I: The Battlefield* (no. 14), were purchased by the Art Gallery of Toronto, indicating that for a time, at least, the social élite that controlled this institution looked favourably upon the painter.[94]

Considering the austerities of wartime and the depletion of the artistic community, the Toronto art scene was surprisingly robust during this period. There were regular exhibitions at the A.G.T. of works by members of the Canadian Group of Painters, the Ontario Society of Artists, the Royal Canadian Academy (founded in 1880), the Canadian Society of Graphic Art (founded in 1904 and reorganized in 1925), the Canadian Society of Painters in Water-Colours (founded in 1925), and the Canadian Society of Painter-Etchers and Engravers (founded in 1919), among other national and local groups and organizations. Given that Lewis's work was included in the 1942 C.S.P.W.C. and C.S.G.A. exhibitions[95] (for details, see the appendix in this catalogue entitled "Wyndham Lewis: Exhibition History in Canada"), one would have hoped that he would have taken the initiative to view his own works and those of his Canadian contemporaries at these venues, but there is no evidence that he did.

The A.G.T., the main public gallery in Toronto at the time and Canada's second largest art museum, also held solo exhibitions and dedicated space to exhibitions featuring the war effort, such as the annual war poster competitions of 1940, 1941 and 1942. In 1943 the O.S.A. and C.S.P.W.C. mounted a special show at the gallery marking Canada' s production of raw materials and munitions supplies.[96]

Another body committed to the advancement of art in Toronto was the Arts and Letters Club, founded in 1908 to provide a meeting-place for artists, writers, architects, musicians and other members of the cultural community. Lewis's name does not appear in the scrapbooks or other records of this private men's club, where lunchtime speakers were much in demand, but

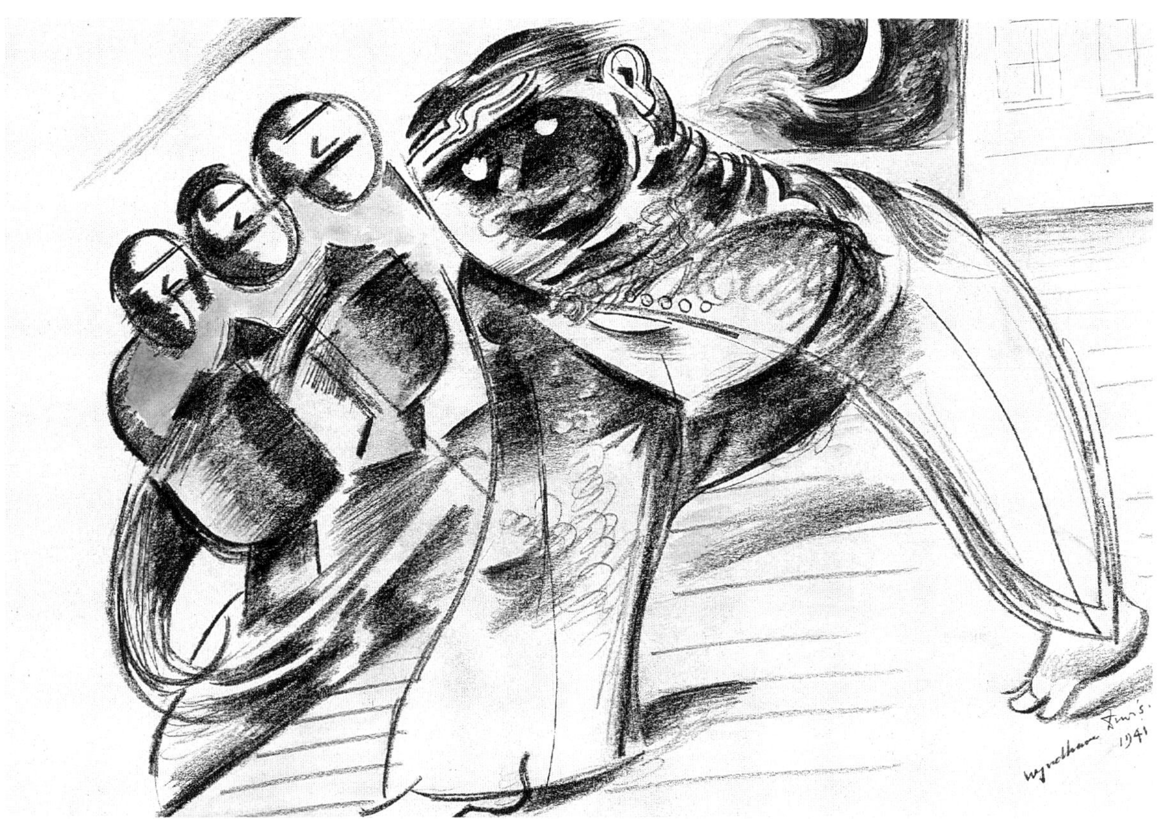

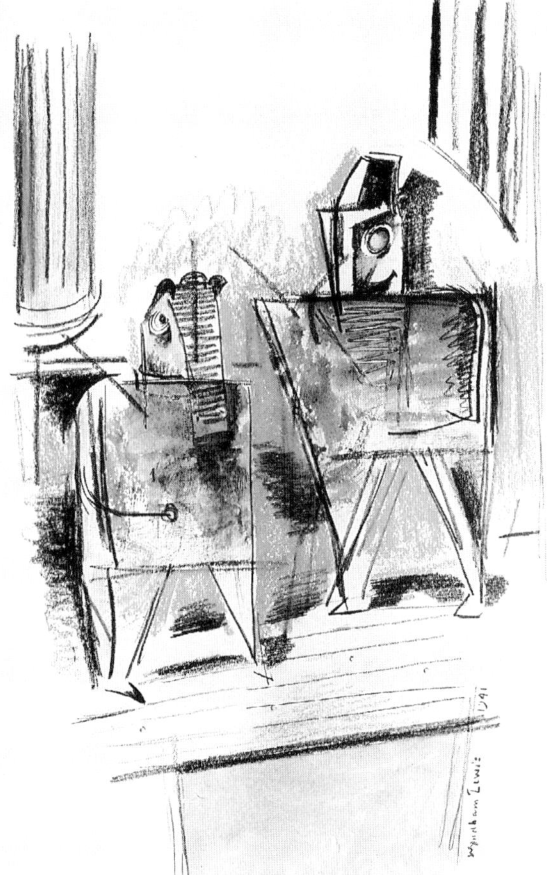

No. 15 *Armless Man on Stage*, 1941, black chalk and wash on paper (28.5 x 44.0 cm), M 966. Lent anonymously.

No. 20 *Untitled*, 1941, crayon, coloured chalks and watercolour on paper (48.0 x 28.0 cm). Mr. and Mrs. Clair Stewart, Caledon East, Ontario.

with long stretches of uncertainty and insolvency. Nonetheless, he once admitted his preference for being poor in Canada to being poor in England, explaining to John Rothenstein, "I don't want a fare back without some guarantee that at the other end I shall not be plunged into economic miseries worse even than before.... I will not ever return to my hand to mouth existence in London. I have a great horror of it."[105]

Throughout 1942 Lewis was constantly in search of teaching jobs and commissions. Such was his desperation that for a while he even contemplated following Malcolm Lowry's footsteps and decamping to Vancouver, British Columbia. This he hoped to do with the promised assistance of an eccentric correspondent by the name of David Kahma (b. 1919), a young, ambitious, wealthy, but hopelessly untalented writer who tried to interest Lewis in the intellectual centre he proposed setting up in Vancouver. A long and detailed correspondence ensued between Kahma and Lewis throughout 1942, but nothing resulted from this scheme. As the editor of Lewis's letters relates,

> Funds were lacking, but they would be supplied in plenty by an inheritance the young enthusiast was about to receive. Sceptical but fascinated, Lewis found himself drawn into a prolonged, sometimes hectic correspondence which continued till the end of the year, when it became apparent that Kahma's dream was not to be realised. In the course of this, Kahma revealed his own ideas about writing, and Lewis offered advice and encouragement. Then after a lapse of more than four years, Kahma revived the association. He had vast manuscripts to show—projects in drama, fiction, poetry, criticism. He wanted to send food parcels. Lewis, still interested in his unseen disciple, accepted the gambit, and the two corresponded from 1947 to 1955.... Though Kahma's volubility was unbeatable, Lewis more than held up his side. Out of a possible escape in the dark days of Toronto had emerged one of the most curious and touching relationships in Lewis's later life.[106]

IN THE MEANTIME, Lewis had turned his attention to completing an important commission for the British Ministry of Information's War Artists' Advisory Committee, and to writing articles and public lecturing (see Thomas Dilworth's essay "Out of Canada" for a discussion of his articles for *Saturday Night*).

Ever since his arrival in Toronto in December 1940, Lewis had hoped to become involved in the War Artists' Advisory Committee programme.[107] His participation was confirmed by early 1943, when he was assigned to record Canada's war effort on the home front. However, because of the currency-exchange freeze then in effect, the transaction was extremely complicated. Involved in the commissioning process were H.O. McCurry of the National Gallery of Canada and the British high commissioner, Malcolm MacDonald. MacDonald's Ottawa office then liaised with its equivalent in London, England, the Canadian High Commission, headed by Vincent Massey. Kenneth Clark, then director of the National Gallery in London, wrote to Massey in July of 1942 that "we are anxious to employ him [Lewis] as a war artist, and there are plenty of fine subjects in the Canadian war effort which he could do for us."[108]

Lewis had already completed several works during 1941 and 1942 based on various responses to the war and its disasters, including *Lebensraum I: The Battlefield* and *Lebensraum: The Empty Tunic* (1941; fig. 28). Several other works of this period are concerned with the horrors of human conflict, a deeply troubling group that includes *A Man's Form Taking a Fall From a Small Horse* (1941; no. 13), *Three Gladiators, Armless Man on Stage* (1941; no. 15), and possibly *Untitled* (1941; no. 20).

Among the subjects that Lewis suggested for his proposed War Artists' Advisory Committee painting were depictions of silver and nickel mines and smelters in Cobalt and Sudbury, steel plants in Sault Ste. Marie, Northern Ontario logging camps, and "the nitration of wood pulp into gun cotton at Nobel, Ontario."[109] He also wanted to paint shipping activities along the St. Lawrence River and at Halifax. Because of restricted finances, however, by late March Lewis had settled on depicting the Anaconda American Brass Foundry, in New Toronto, to the west of the city. This scheme reduced his travel expenses but still provided him with access to the manufacturing aspect of Canada's war effort. Lewis found the mechanical side of the brass works "wildly interesting". He described the scene in a letter to Malcolm MacDonald:

> At the glass factory there is a great tank-like monster they have christened "Winnie" which bears down upon the furnace, puts a great claw inside, and

draws out in its clutch the white-hot jar full of molten glass. My assignment, being "Canada's War Effort", and Canada being mainly an agricultural and raw-material country, I am logically attracted to the raw-material end of the industrial process.[110]

For several weeks Lewis made preparatory sketches of workers and machinery at the foundry, later incorporating these observations into his easel painting, *A Canadian War Factory* (1943; no. 58). However, his initial plans for the picture remain unknown, because, of the many such on-site drawings Lewis claimed to have made, only one directly related sketch, *Workman* (1943; no. 59), has been located. *Head from a Casting Shop* (1943; fig. 29) was also done in preparation for this painting, but could not be located for inclusion in this exhibition. Both works, which are portraits of figures who do not appear in the final oil-on-canvas, are of interest because, part-way through the completion of the painting, and after having been paid in full for it, Lewis decided that the result was not satisfactory and began anew.[111] Trying to put off demands for delivery of the picture, Lewis in 1944 explained to Malcolm MacDonald why it remained unfinished:

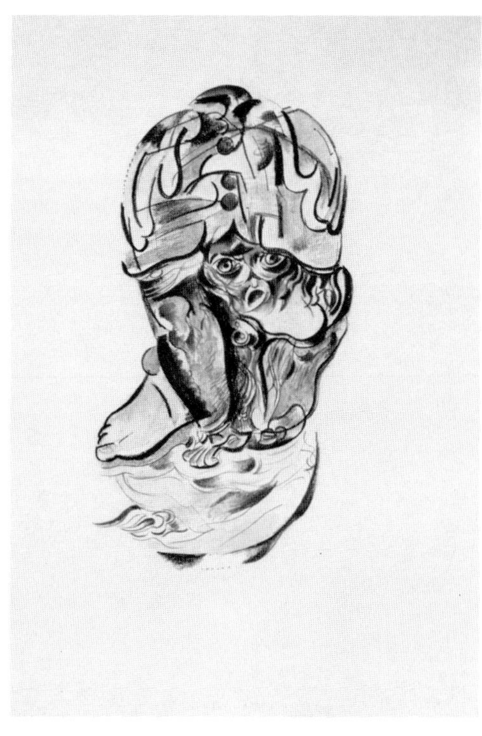

Fig. 28 *Lebensraum II: The Empty Tunic*, 1941-42 watercolour, chalks and Indian ink on paper (38.0 x 24.0 cm). Private collection, London, England.

> It is a busy scene in a factory, with all the contraptions that pertain to such a scene, and there are two ways of approaching it. One could be described as the "impressionistic" approach. That would entail no great accuracy of detail. Even the purpose of the various objects need not be studied—such as the casts into which the molten metal is run, for instance, or the hoods which are swung over the furnaces to catch as much of the smoke and fumes as possible and pass them along into the shoots. What I was looking at was most of the time indistinct, as there was a great deal of smoke and steam, and not a great deal of light. I had been working there (drawing—sketching—that is) for a couple of weeks before I discovered (from the superintendent) the meaning of a certain cleft shape in the hoods. It turned out to be an extra bit they had added on, because the original hood was not large enough. Thereupon, in between the shifts, I made a close-up drawing of a hood just in case I should need to use this particular shape.
>
> I started with the "impressionistic" approach in my mind, especially as I came to realize, the more I studied my subject, how long it would take to build up this scene into a solid documented work of art. For six weeks of the allotted three months I worked in the casting-shop doing preparatory drawings and I have I should think a hundred of these factual notes; quite unsaleable, since they are in the first place very dirty and they are in the main nothing but notes of how all these things function, their relative propositions and positions....
>
> At last I started in on my canvas and perforce my aim was to paint an impression rather than what Cézanne called "quelque chose de solide et durable comme l'art des musées." That I completed at the time I told you...at the end of 3 months...I revised my approach. I switched from the "impressionistic" to a more solid and detailed one—and one, I may add, more in harmony with my own tastes and manner of work....
>
> Meanwhile one part after another took body and bristled with factual stuff. So that at last it all has to be brought in to far more solid pattern. And for that task I shall require yet more time.... I compute that another six months will be necessary—I mean to do all I should wish to do with this picture. And I am asking the War Artists Committee to leave [it] with me for that period at least.[112]

Opposite page:
No. 58 *A Canadian War Factory*, 1943, oil on canvas (114.3 x 85.7 cm), M P105. The Tate Gallery, London, England (T00135).

A Canadian War Factory was eventually finished, but it was not delivered to its permanent home, the Tate Gallery, until after Lewis's death in 1957, several unsuccessful attempts to claim it having been rebuffed by the artist in the meantime.[113]

THE MOST IMPORTANT lecturing opportunity that came Lewis's way while he was living in Toronto was provided by Father J. Stanley Murphy, then residing at the University of Toronto's St. Michael's College. Father Murphy had launched the Christian Culture Series at Assumption College, Windsor, Ontario (since 1962 a part of the University of Windsor, but then associated

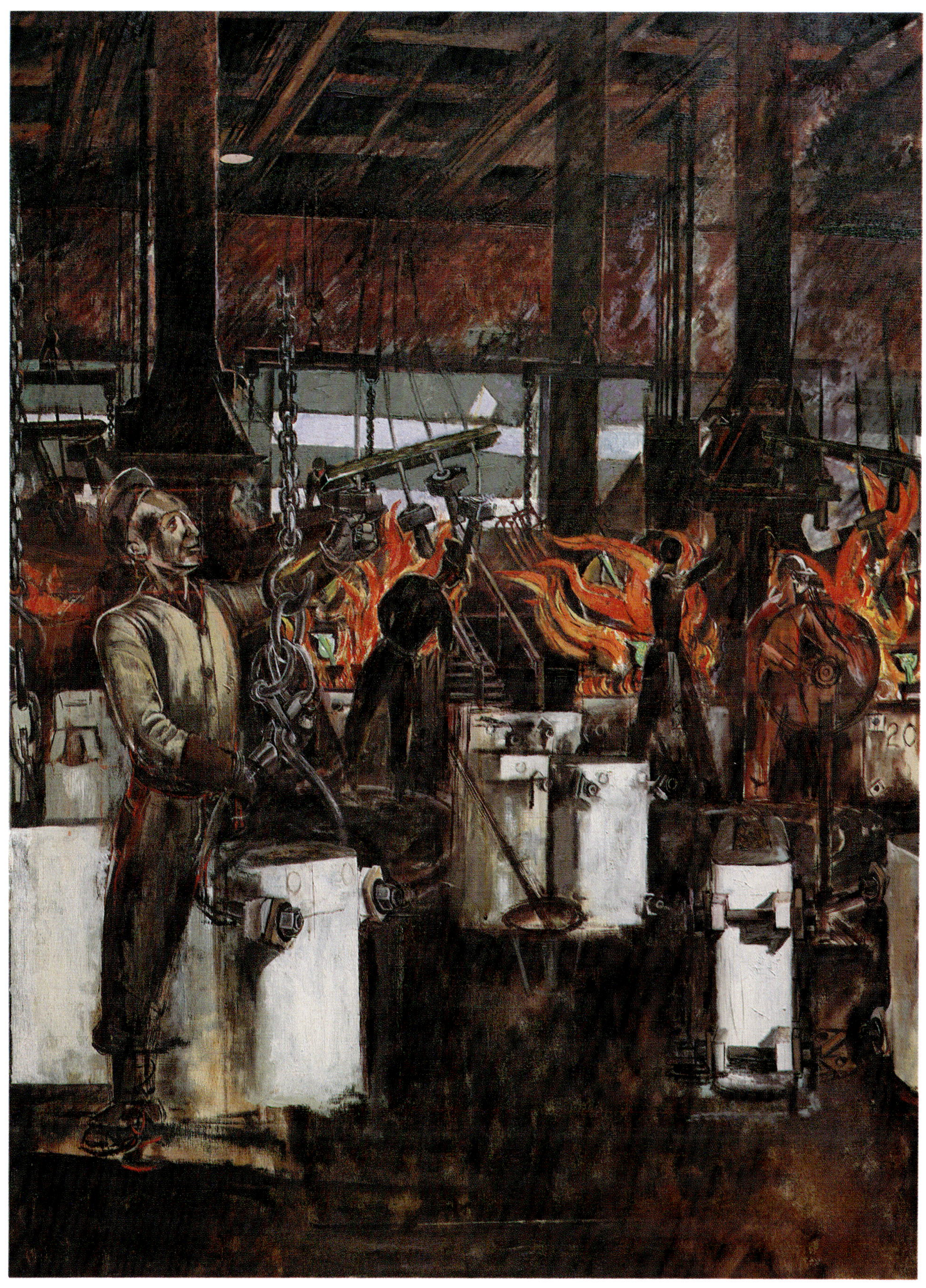

with the University of Western Ontario) in 1934. The Christian Culture Series was a lecture program that elicited contributions from leading intellectuals in the United States, Europe and Canada. Murphy had taken on the project in addition to his positions as associate professor of English and registrar at Assumption College. This Roman Catholic institution, founded in 1857, was then considered to be the most liberal of the Basilian teaching orders of priests in Canada, and prided itself on its distinguished program.

Father Murphy paid a visit to Lewis in his Tudor Hotel apartment in the summer of 1942, having discovered that his quarry was in Toronto through Cecil J. Eustace, the publisher of *The Vulgar Streak* (1941) and a Christian Culture Series lecturer in 1942. Murphy felt that Lewis's wide knowledge of art and philosophy, and his familiarity with the work and thought of Etienne Gilson (1884-1978), the founder in 1929 of St. Michael's College's Pontifical Institute of Medieval Studies, and Jacques Maritain (1882-1973), who had lectured annually at the Institute from 1932 to 1945, would make an important contribution to the series.[114] Lewis became one of an extraordinary roster of speakers, which also included Maritain, Bishop Fulton J. Sheen, and Marshall McLuhan.

During Lewis's initial meeting with Father Murphy, it was agreed that he would present a lecture combining his knowledge of art, philosophy and religion. His talk, "Religious Expression in Contemporary Art: Rouault and the Painter of Original Sin", was delivered at the Vanity Theatre on Ouellette Avenue on 7 February 1943. The subject of the lecture was the expressionistic religious paintings of the French artist Georges Rouault (1871-1958), which in some respects were closely aligned with the concerns Lewis was exploring in his imaginative works of the early 1940s. On the importance of Rouault's vision of the contemporary world, Lewis wrote:

> There has been nothing since monastic times quite so uncompromising, so opaquely dark. And perhaps why so many people today have turned to such images of life as these, rather than to the more delectable ones, is because our present world had gradually become so unbelievably bleak, charged as it is with a hundred unresolved and brooding storms, crowding behind the particular hurricane of the moment.[115]

In many respects, the Rouault lecture was an assimilation of ideas developed by Lewis in both his art and his writing during his Toronto period. He stated in the talk that humanity was entering a "Dark Age" and that "it is little wonder that we demand something fairly bitter in our imaginative art."[116] Lewis approved of Rouault's work because of its ability to re-interpret traditional religious themes within a modern context, and because it addressed such crucial issues as the future of mankind and the role of art in contemporary society. A century of industrial "progress," Lewis believed with Rouault, had ultimately been detrimental to the advance of humanity and of civilization:

> it is the idea of Progress—and everything that goes with it—that occupies the first and dominant place, both in England and on the North American continent: the belief of the well-fed, and the well-to-do man, that, in the first place, everybody is considerate, and very anxious to please, without an unkind thought in their hearts, bless them, good bodies that they are!—that Nature having been at length tamed and the rougher side of human nature smoothed out to a sleek and comfortable finish, humanitarian principles happily supreme—that now at last we were out of the wood, or rather out of the jungle, and a new and enlightened age had begun. When we reflect what a shock was involved in waking out of a dream of that order and of that intensity—for it had all the convincing authenticity of the external world sense—we see at once that the world is not necessarily quite so dark as it must appear just now by contrast. It is merely dark in comparison with the nineteenth century which was a slightly unreal interlude.... Industrial technique will go on turning out its mechanical marvels every week-end, when "peace" sets in.... Remove, abruptly, the

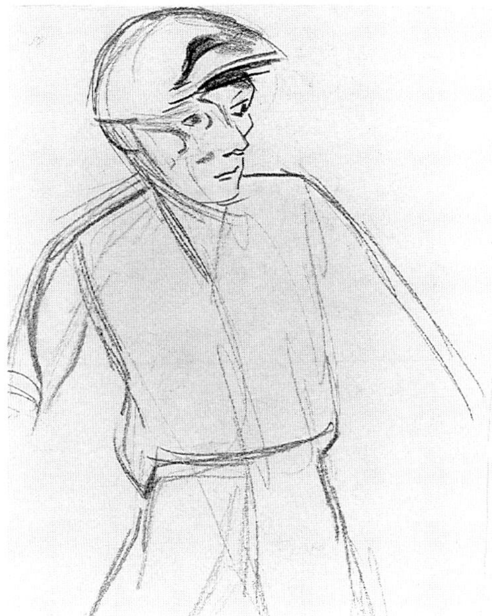

No. 59 *Workman*, 1943, black chalk on paper (35.5 x 28.0 cm), M 1033. Herbert F. Johnson Museum of Art, Cornell University, Ithaca, New York, gift of Walter and Harriet Michel.

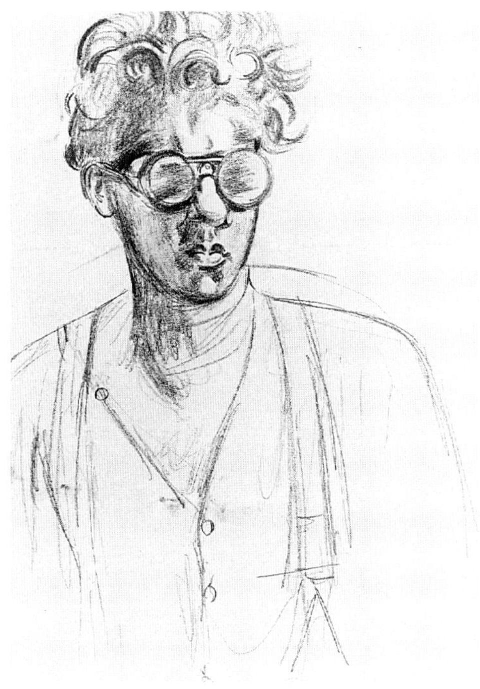

Fig. 29 Wyndham Lewis, *Head from a Casting Shop*, 1943, black chalk on paper (dimensions unknown). Present whereabouts unknown. Photograph: National Gallery of Canada, Ottawa.

> notion of Progress, from beneath the Modern World where it has been for so long solidly based, at the very centre of the popular belief. What will happen then? Something terrific, that is to say when the full effect has registered. It will leave a vacuum so great that it will alter the thinking of everybody: it will be in the class of Darwin or the internal combustion engine.[117]

Lewis claimed Rouault to be the most significant modern artist painting religious subjects, describing him as "one of those who have been called to fill that vacuum: that pit—that bottomless bomb-crater—left by the exorcism of the notion of Progress, among other things, in our society."[118] Toronto, like Buffalo, New York or London, or, for that matter, any other western city in which Lewis might have chosen to live, was engulfed by the same problems of industrial "progress," at the same time being confronted by the spectre of a war that, in 1943, still had no certain outcome and might yet result in the defeat of the Allied cause.

Father Murphy also arranged for Lewis to present a lecture at Marygrove College, Lansing, Michigan, delivered on 8 February 1943. This talk, entitled "Modernism in Art", reiterated many of the issues discussed in the Rouault lecture, addressing as it did the history of society's relation to art and the utility of the arts at different periods in time. Lewis was concerned to expose his audience to the reality of a what society would be like if it were to be deprived of its artists, drawing upon his 1934 polemic, *Men Without Art,* for ammunition. Once again he reverted to his preoccupation with the decreasing value given to culture in western society, stating that "modern art of the highly experimental sort, is at an end.... There has never been such as thing up to now as men without art. It seems to me perfectly feasible, and even likely, that that may happen in the near future."[119]

Father Murphy approved so highly of the content of Lewis's two lectures that he arranged for him to become a resident lecturer at Assumption College for a one-year term, beginning in the summer of 1943. The Lewises would have remained in the Tudor Hotel until the summer term began in Windsor, were it not for the disastrous fire that broke out on the morning of 15 February 1943 (fig. 30). Nearly all of the main building of the hotel was severely damaged. The Lewises' "Tudor period" thus came to an end one week after Wyndham returned from Windsor and Detroit.

The fire took place on one of the coldest nights in the winter; the *Toronto Daily Star* recorded the temperature as being at twenty-one degrees below zero Fahrenheit. Retrospectively, in his novel *Self Condemned,* Lewis described the surreal effects and results of the fire:

> It was a flaming spectre, a fiery iceberg. Its sides, where there were no flames, were now a solid mass of ice. The water of the hoses had turned to ice as it ran down the walls, and had created an icy armour many feet in thickness. This enormous cocoon of ice did not descend vertically, but swept outwards for perhaps fifty yards, stopped by the wall of the Friseur, half-submerging the Beverage Room in its outward progress. The flames rising into the sky seemed somehow cold and conventional as if it had been their duty to go on aspiring, but they were doing it because they must, not because they had any lust for destruction. These were the flames that still reached up above the skyline of the facade. But a new generation of fiery monsters, a half-hour younger, appeared behind them, a darker red and full of muscular leaps, charged with the authentic will to devour and consume. And there were dense volumes of black smoke too, where fresh areas were being brought into the holocaust.[120]

The fire somehow epitomized Lewis's negative feelings about Toronto, and provided further evidence of a rejection that was more imagined or symbolical than actual. He claimed that he had lost "two valuable portraits, two unfinished manuscripts and hundreds of books" in the fire.[121] A much greater loss for the Lewises, however, was that of the one friend they had made at the Tudor, the Scottish manageress immortalized as the eccentric "Affie" in *Self Condemned,* who in the novel is murdered by the arsonist who sets fire to the building (of which he turns out to be the owner) to cover up his deed.

In the interim, the Lewises moved to the nearby Selby Hotel, on the west side of Sherbourne Street, where Ernest Hemingway had rented a room in the 1920s during his stint as a reporter with the *Toronto Star.* By the end of Lewis's residence in Toronto, his views had extended to the larger context of Canada generally:

> A nation, like a woman, has to make itself attractive, if it is going to attract. And it must attract in order to grow and increase. To stop drably and dowdily at home and tell the

rest of the world to go hang is no way to live. If a nation wants to repel rather than attract, it only has to neglect its social equipment and throw away its manners. But no modern nation can afford, any more than a modern woman, to neglect those arts and graces that advertise it, and make people seek its company.

Now, greatly daring—but the very friendliest motives—I am whispering a few things in Canada's pretty ear. For what is written here will not go beyond the frontier of Canada. I am saying that Canada should give more care to making itself agreeable and gracious, in its intercourse with strangers. For this new country needs—paradoxical as that may sound—new blood. All new countries do....

One feels that in Upper Canada—Anglosaxon Canada—there is a sort of pride in being repellent, rather than attractive, to the stranger within-the-gate. What the Canadian of these parts tells you is that the social organism to which he belongs is snooty.[122]

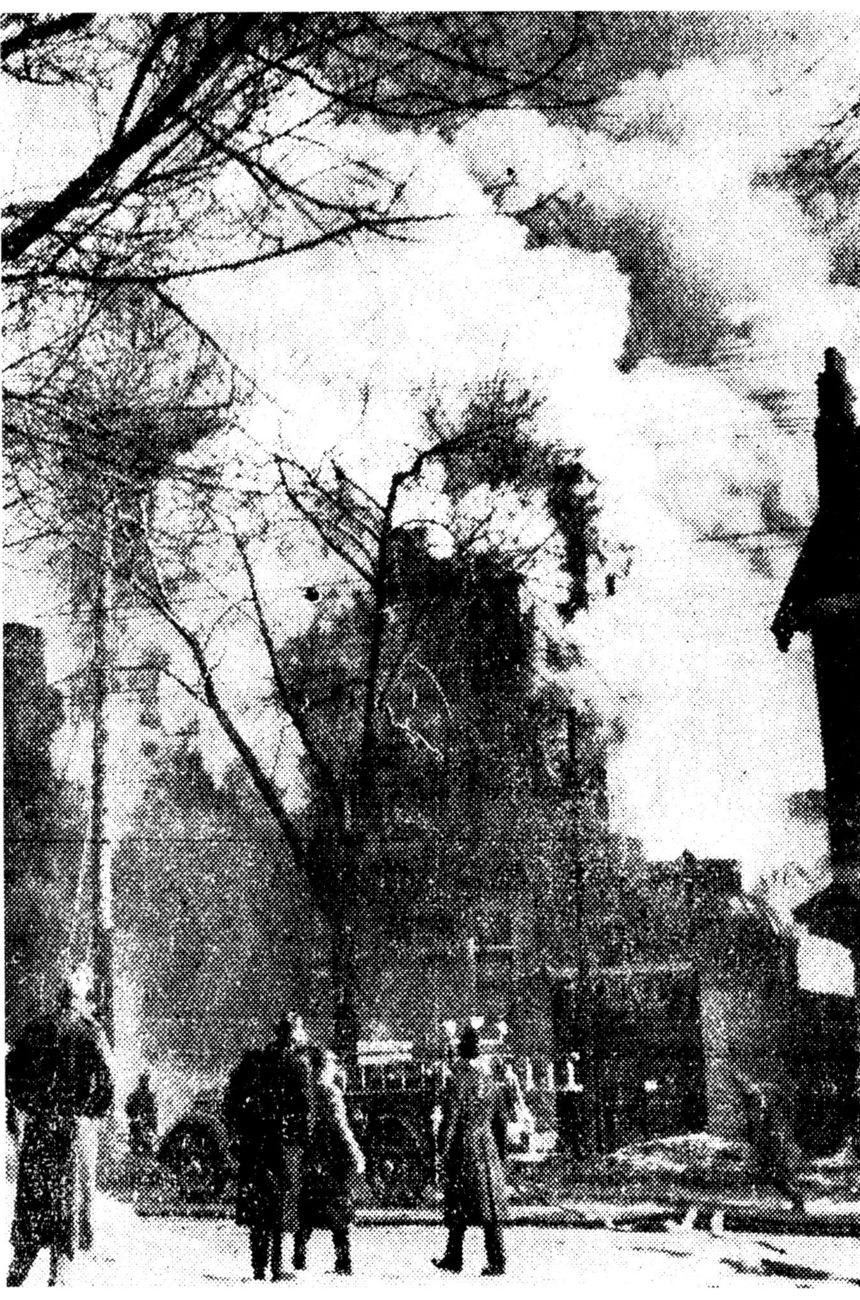

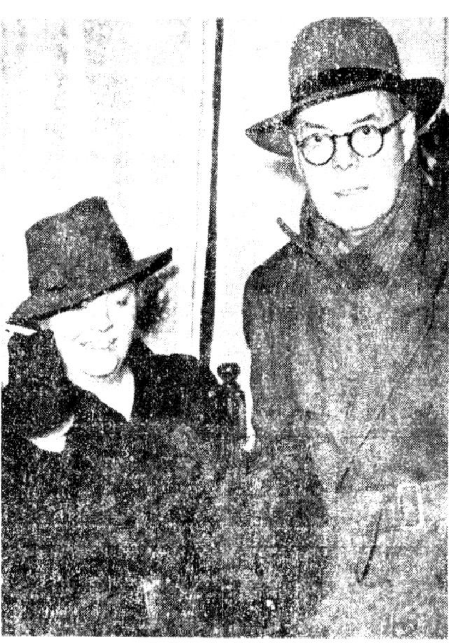

Fig. 30 The Lewises and the Tudor Hotel fire, 1943, from the *Toronto Daily Star*, 15 February 1943. Photograph: Metropolitan Toronto Reference Library.

LEWIS'S APPOINTMENT AS A LECTURER on art and philosophy at Assumption College, in Windsor, Ontario, began in early July 1943 (fig. 31). The Lewises moved from Toronto to Windsor at the end of June and, aside from two stays in St. Louis, Missouri in 1944, they spent the better part of two years in this small, working-class, industrial city, finally departing in April 1945. The Royal Apartments, at 30 Ellis Street East, sarcastically described by Lewis as "a somewhat deceptive address: I have no Clark to 'keep' my Rowlandsons"[1]—the ironic allusion being to Sir Kenneth Clark, Surveyor of the King's Pictures at Windsor Castle from 1934 to 1944. Although the accommodations were not much of an improvement over their room at the Tudor Hotel, Lewis was happy to be regularly employed and gratefully accepted the offer to sublet an apartment from a Windsor family.[2] His eager acceptance of the teaching position was communicated in a letter to Father J. Stanley Murphy:

> I am delighted to learn that I am to come to Assumption College, and I am personally enormously obliged to you, for bringing to so happy and expeditious a conclusion this plan you spoke to me about while I was in Windsor. I cannot imagine for myself more congenial surroundings: and I greatly appreciate the favorable periods of work you outline, though you must not hesitate to ask me to do more, if and when that is desirable.—I hope you will express to Fathers Lee and Garvey, and to Father Young, my thanks for the ready welcome they accorded your proposal. I know I shall work alongside them harmoniously.[3]

In contrast to the bitterness that Lewis felt in Toronto, he found Windsor to be "a very agreeable little city, and quite charmingly arranged."[4] Especially considering his propensity for making enemies and ruffling feathers, Lewis could hardly have hoped for a better end to his two-year search for an artist/writer-in-residency or teaching appointment.[5] That the offer came unsolicited from Father Murphy made Lewis feel even more appreciated. He wrote that "The college priests are very pleasant and do not mind my not being catholic. They accept me as a well-wisher; they respect the principles of others...they have treated me with great kindness, as also the nuns." In the same letter, Lewis observed that "This place is actually *south* of Detroit, and one participates more in the life of the States than in Toronto."[6] To a new acquaintance, Marshall McLuhan, he complained that "A Professor —— of Toronto University...wrote me the other day asking me to speak to his students. Can you beat it? We were nearly 3 years in that disgusting spot. The moment I came down here, they learn that I am in Canada."[7]

Lewis might have liked Windsor not only because it had offered a comparatively warm welcome after what he interpreted as the cold-shoulder treatment meted out to him by Toronto, but because of its mixed British, French and Indian heritage (the city, in a sense, combining his own ethnic makeup), as well as its close proximity to the United States and its position in the "sunbelt" of Ontario. (As Canada's southernmost city, Windsor enjoys a milder climate, longer summers and shorter winters than Toronto.) Another positive factor was that Windsor is older than Toronto, having been visited by French explorers and Jesuit missionaries in the seventeenth century, with permanent settlement following the founding of Detroit by Antoine de la Mothe Cadillac in 1701 and the issuance of the first land grants in 1749.[8] Toronto (originally Fort Rouillé, then York), on the other hand, had remained a minor trading post and garrison until John Graves Simcoe made it the capital of Upper Canada in 1794. Windsor was incorporated as a village in 1854 and as a town in 1858,[9] one year after the founding of Assumption College (incorporated as the University of Windsor in 1962).

Lewis was treated very well at Assumption, in terms both of salary and of the amount of time he was required to devote to his duties; he was paid the then-generous fee of $200 per month for a ten-month period, with three paid months off in between, and he generally had to conduct only one session, of fifty-minute duration, per day. His classes consisted mainly of nuns, student teachers and auditors. Lewis enjoyed teaching and remarked that he "found his pupils very responsive".[10] A colleague at Assumption who sat in on Lewis's class remembers that singing and whistling were part of his teaching method.[11] Marshall McLuhan, who also audited some of his lectures, recalled that Lewis's "classroom manner was greatly appreciated by the students."[12] His appreciative reception did not prevent Lewis, however, from characterizing colleges like Assumption and such neighbours as the University of Michigan and Michigan State University as consisting of "A group of old hacks teaching English, though they have some difficulty in speaking it, supported by a deferential group of young hacks, [who] entertain one to liqourless and beerless six o'clock suppers.... What the devil they or their students think they're doing I don't know."[13]

The interests of the organizers of the Christian Culture Series programme were happily in tune with Lewis's own preoccupations in a variety of disciplines, touching as they did not only on art and literature but on philosophy, history and politics. Several of the series' guests whom Lewis met, such as Bishop Fulton J. Sheen and Jacques Maritain (fig. 32), approached their work from an interdisciplinary perspective that was comparable in certain respects to Lewis's. These thinkers also shared views concerning the need to achieve a permanent global peace through some kind of world confederation and the defeat of atavistic nationalist tendencies, a theme that resurfaced throughout Lewis's Windsor lectures and ultimately formed the gist of his 1948 book, *America and Cosmic Man.*[14]

The courses that Lewis taught demanded extensive reading and laborious preparation. Because of this, the Windsor period differs greatly from his experience in Toronto, being primarily focused on teaching and public lectures rather than on the artmaking or creative writing. As a consequence, his production of "imaginative" pictures significantly decreased; the *Creation Myth* series essentially ceased, there being only one drawing, *Landscape* (also known as *Creation Myth*), dated 1944 (no. 74), that is related, albeit marginally, to the previous group. A reflection of the ongoing presence of the war, it depicts a mythological landscape with a large striding figure (strongly evocative of a Chinese dragon-dance mask) on the left, perhaps in a state of transformation between the vegetal and the animal, or between the animal and the totemic. Barbed wire (or shrubbery?) fills the middle-ground, and in the right foreground a group of ambiguous figures are huddled in an oval formation below an embankment (or is it the hull of a ship or ark?); they may even be sunbathers, shaded by a lop-sided beach-umbrella (which would relate this strange image at least tangentially to the Bathers series discussed by Robert Stacey in his essay in this catalogue).

In his private works of the Windsor period, Lewis continued to explore the themes of the intimate portrait study, the still life and the domestic interior, which he had resumed inToronto as both a graphic exercise and as a way of coming to terms with his uncertain circumstances. Anne Lewis, however, appears in these drawings less frequently as a subject than she did in the late 1930s, being depicted in only three works from the 1943-45 years: *The Sullen Eye* (no. 57), *Reading the Newspaper* (fig. 33), and *Portrait of the Artist's Wife* (no. 73). Like 1942's *War News* (present whereabouts unknown) and perhaps *Sybil (sic;* i.e. *Sibyl?),* the latter two pictures are reflections on the continuing global conflict, the nail-biting subject being shown perusing what we must assume to be disturbing reports from overseas, and then turning away to pondering the implications of what she has read. The grave facial expression of the figure in *The Sullen Eye* suggests that this drawing, too, is a meditation on wartime doubts and fears. The tactic of combining a figure or portrait study with implied references to the larger world beyond the confines of the home and the home front was turned to by other artists during this troublous time: for example, the Polish-born Canadian painter and sculptor Nathan Petroff (b. 1916) played a social-realist variation on it in his *Modern Times* of 1937 (fig. 34).

Also during his Windsor sojourn, Lewis began another variation on the domestic interior images that he had begun in Toronto with a group of chalk drawings depicting the English tea ceremony. Works belonging to this series, all dating from 1943, include *Table with Tray and Arm-chairs, Table with Tray and Cups*, and *Tray with Cups* (nos. 60-62). Each conveys a sense of intimacy by presenting the subject at sharp angles, looking directly down upon the service, as if the viewer had just walked into a private room. The high quality of draughtsmanship and unusual perspective are the most outstanding features of these unusual drawings. Although Anne Lewis is not the centre of attention here, the tea-service drawings are clearly a continuation of the intensely personal and observant domestic portraits of the artist's wife dating from 1941 and 1942. For example, *Table with Tray and Armchairs*, with its discarded newspaper hanging over the couch arm, relates to the Toronto- and Windsor-period portraits of Anne anxiously scanning the headlines, as in *War News, Sybil, Reading the Newspaper*, and *Portrait of the Artist's Wife*.

Like many other ideas and images Lewis explored during his Canadian years, these scenes hark back to earlier series and groupings, being a continuation of still-lifes begun in the 1930s, as represented by *The Room* (1936) and *The Full Table* (1938). Similar subjects served as backgrounds of and complements to his portraits of the same period, including *Froanna—Portrait of the Artist's Wife* (1937), *Girl Reading* (1921), *The Reader* (1936) and *Ezra Pound* (1939).[15]

Opposite page (clockwise from top): Fig. 31 Wyndham Lewis (back row, ninth from left) with colleagues at Assumption College, Windsor, Ontario, 1943, photograph: Cornell; Detail of Fig. 31; Fig. 32 Wyndham Lewis (left) with Jacques Maritain at Assumption College, Windsor, 1943, photograph: Cornell.

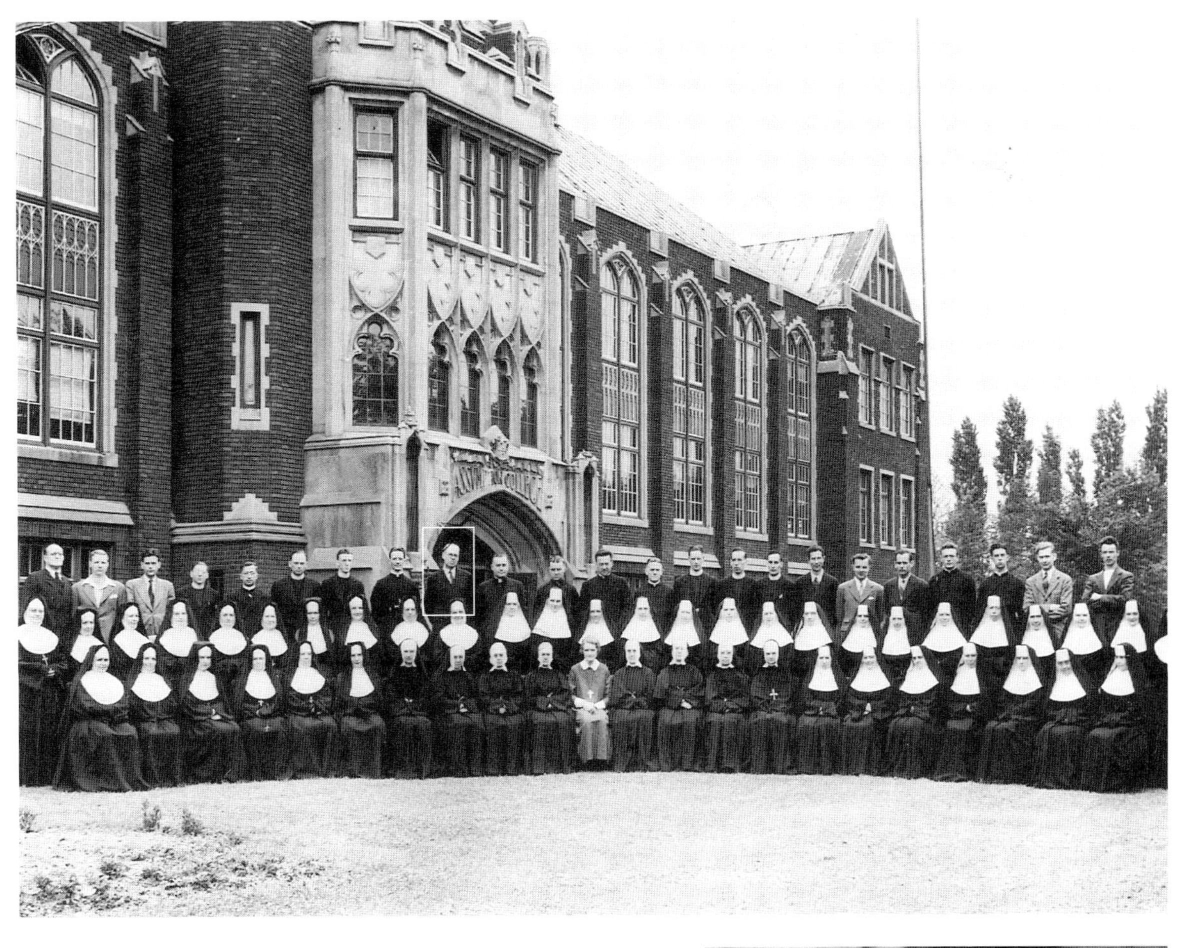

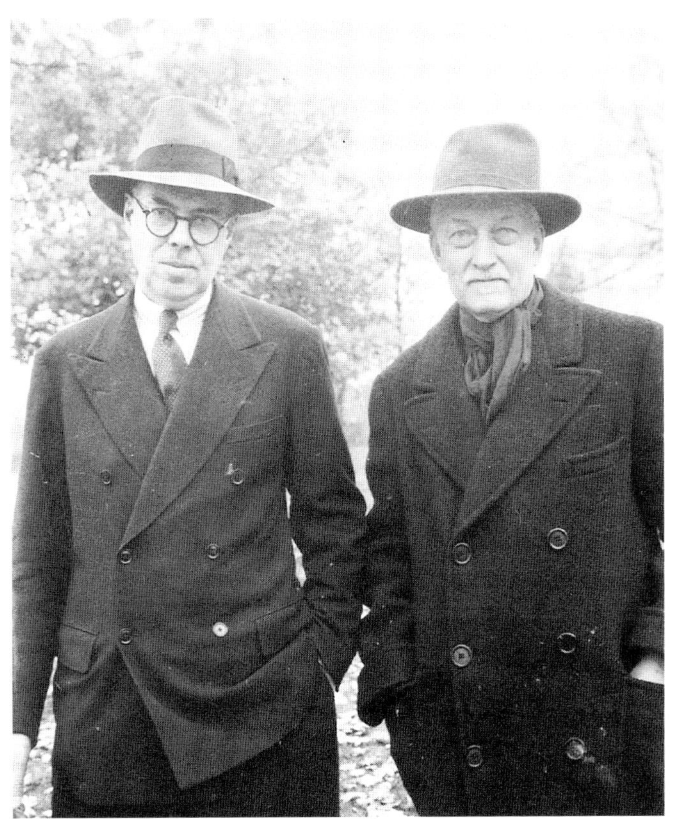

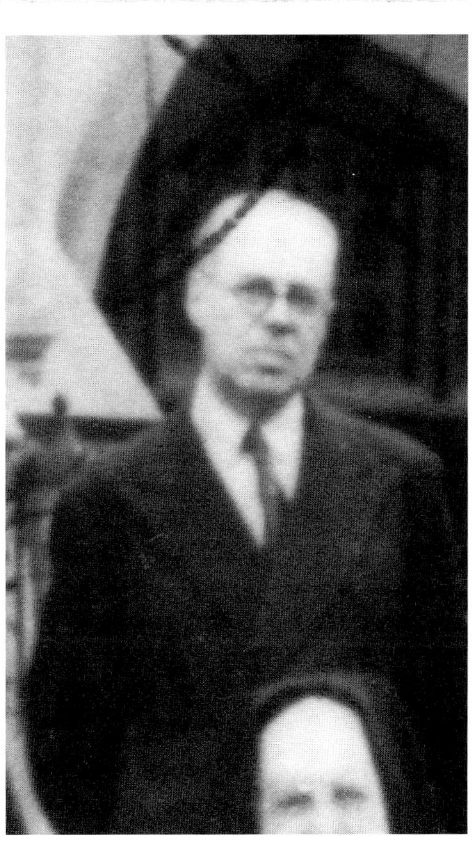

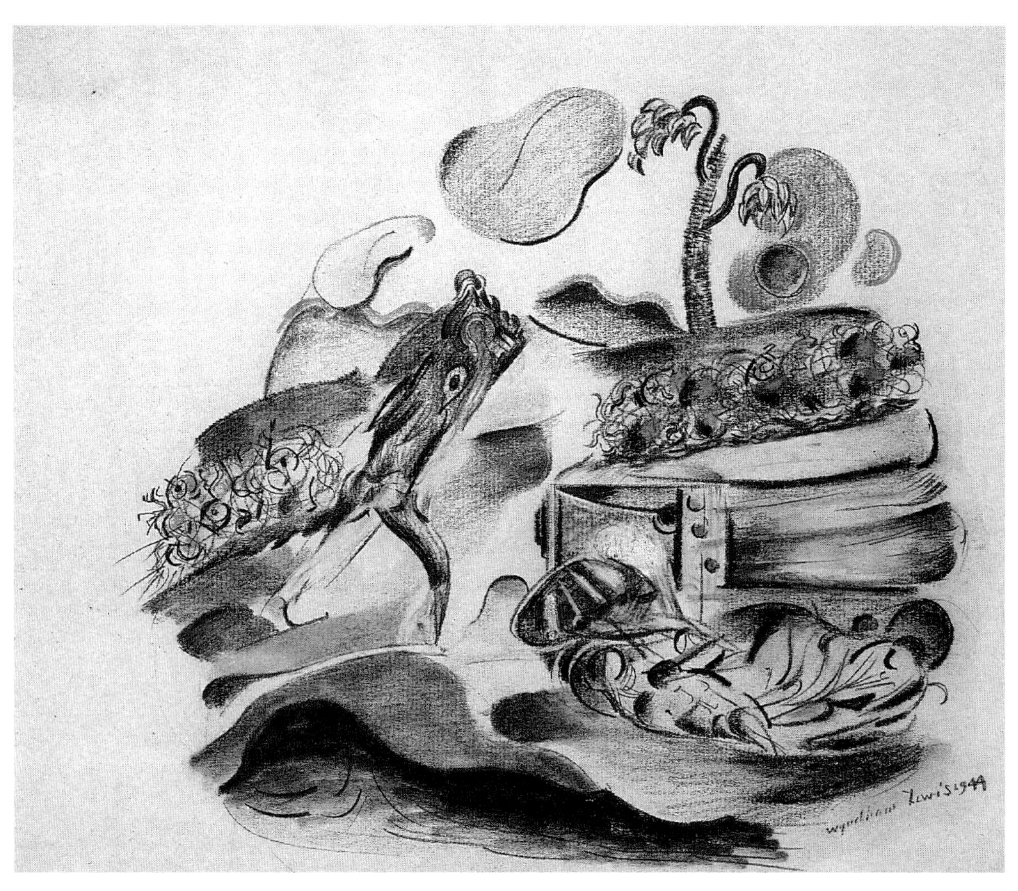

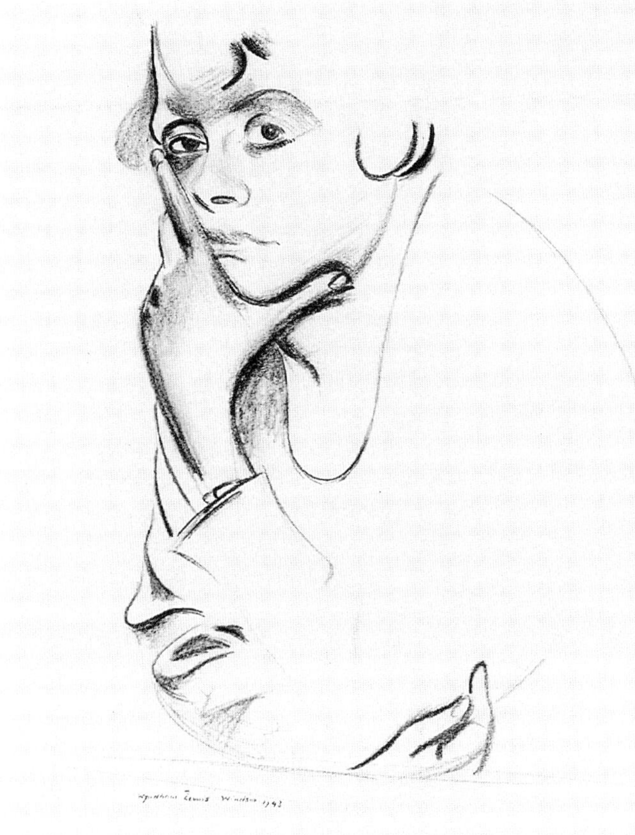

No. 74 *Landscape* (also known as *Creation Myth*), 1944, black and coloured chalks over graphite on paper (28.0 x 37.5 cm), M 1045. Art Gallery of Windsor, Windsor, Ontario, purchased with funds from the Bobs Cogill and Peter Haworth estate and the assistance of the Government of Canada through the Cultural Property Export and Import Act, 1991.

No. 57 *The Sullen Eye*, 1943, charcoal on paper (42.5 x 32.5 cm), M 1029. Mercury Gallery, London, England.

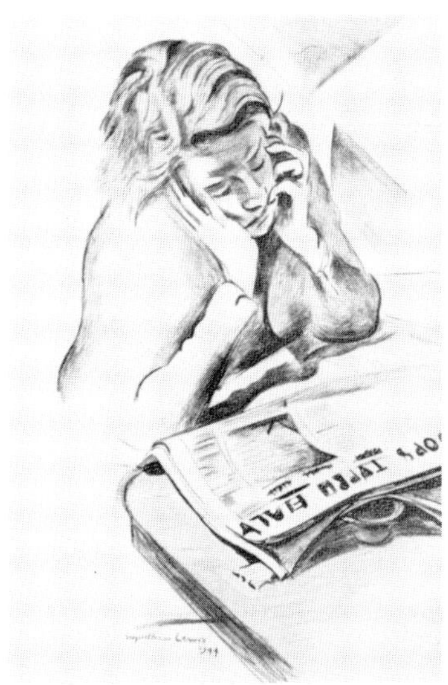

Fig. 33 *Reading the Newspaper*, 1944, black and coloured chalks (37.0 x 26.5 cm), M 1050. Present whereabouts unknown (ownership indicated in Michel, *Wyndham Lewis: Paintings and Drawings*, p. 416, as collection of Mrs. E.W. Stix).

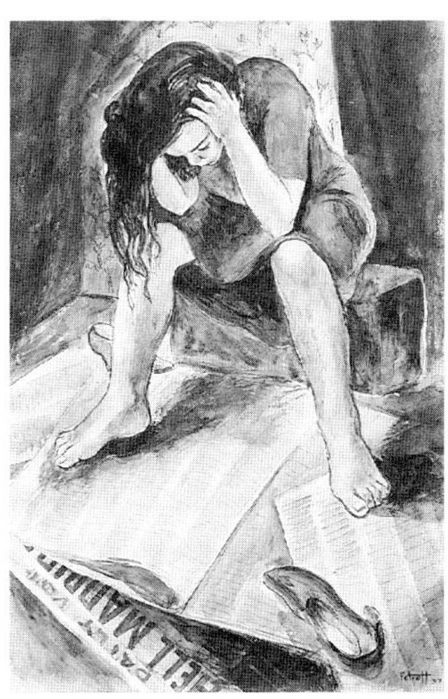

Fig. 34 Nathan Petroff (b. 1916), *Modern Times*, 1937, watercolour over graphite on wove paper (57.5 x 39.2 cm). National Gallery of Canada, Ottawa.

IN THE FIRST COURSE that Lewis taught at Assumption, a six-week summer session that took place during July and August of 1943, he discussed "The Philosophical Roots of Modern Art and Literature." Like most of Lewis's Windsor lectures, this course was concerned with providing a general audience with the criteria for evaluating subjective aspects of art and literature, such as the concept of beauty. The difference between popular art and creative expression, Lewis explained, was to be found in the degree to which the author or artist had observed society. Of the popular side of literary production, he pointed out: "It is a hard, brittle, shallow, materialist society[,] it must be recalled[,] that these books are written to mirror and to amuse. On the lower levels they have[,] in order to succeed, to be slick and streamlined, and to vie with each other in sentimentality or violence."[16] Cautioning his students against measuring success by an economic yardstick, Lewis argued that good art was "not to be the dialect or common speech of man, but a purged and selective human expression.... Literature cannot in the nature of things be edifying" but it must be "elevated" and "rational".[17] Among the examples of such superior writing cited by Lewis were his own *Left Wings Over Europe* (1936) and *Men Without Art* (1934), and the works of Tolstoi, Dostoevsky, Nietzsche, Spengler, Steinbeck, Hegel and Voltaire—writers who, in other contexts, he had occasion to criticize with greater and lesser degrees of severity according to the nature and purpose of his polemic.

In the visual art section of this course, Lewis brought Canada into the discussion by reading an article he had begun in the spring of 1943, the aforementioned "Canadian Nature and its Painters."[18] In this overview, Lewis praised the Group of Seven for the critical position it had taken on the northern landscape and its spiritual associations with the Canadian identity. That Lewis supported the leading representational Canadian school of painting is not surprising, given his increasingly conservative views on contemporary trends in abstractionism.

In two Assumption lectures on "Abstract Art", Lewis maintained the stance he had taken in his 1940 article, "The End of Abstract Art." He outlined the history of abstraction in the modern era, drawing particular attention to the differences between visual art, music and architecture. Although, in music and architecture, such abstract qualities as tone and form alone could provide valid subjects and evoke feeling, this was not possible, Lewis contended, in visual art, where the formal qualities inherent in the medium were not sufficient in themselves to engage the viewer on an emotional level. He phrased the task faced by the modern artist in these words: "What to do next in art, so as to restore painting to its old position of creative mastery: so that it should cease to be a plaything—a joke for the rich."[19]

In the early fall of 1943 Lewis taught a course which he called "The ABC of the Visual Arts", the title of which was perhaps inspired by Ezra Pound's *ABC of Reading*, first published in 1934.[20] His main concern was the future of the arts in society, claiming in the keynote lecture in the series that "The visual arts not only are a derelict craft surviving into the industrial era, but they are perhaps a psychological anachronism."[21] Stressing the importance of art as a language to be learned and appreciated, he proclaimed that "Not imitation of nature but imitation of the world of art is the first thing.... Therefore it is more important[,] to start with[,] to copy a picture of a tree than to copy a tree," the result being "a stylized selection of the chaos of nature". As examples of such selective artists Lewis cited Whistler, Gauguin and Picasso, who respectively derived their inspiration from the Japanese printmakers, from the carvers of the South Pacific, and from African sculpture.[22]

Later in the fall of 1943, Lewis prepared twelve lectures for the Heywood Broun Memorial Series, a program affiliated with the Christian Culture Series, also directed by Father Stan Murphy. In these lectures, delivered in both Windsor and Detroit between 7 November to 19 December 1943, Lewis discussed "The Concept of Liberty from the Founding Fathers of the U.S.A. until Now". Along with a speech presented at the Detroit Institute of Arts, entitled "The Frontiers of Art or The Cultural Melting Pot", these lectures formed the basis for Lewis's *America and Cosmic Man*, which, however, did not appear until after his return to England.[23] Anticipating the prophecies of his disciple Marshall McLuhan, Lewis envisioned a political, cultural, racial and social coalescence through "air transport, ocean liners [and] television."[24] In his Detroit lecture, Lewis announced that "hourly the frontiers of art are melting away. In the cultural field we are in the presence of a cultural melting pot.... Lying half way between Europe and Asia, it is destined by nature to be the meeting-place, a mingling place, of all the nations of the earth."[25]

The two points of convergence that Lewis most strongly emphasized were political and cultural. In his mind, America (specifically, the United States; Canada seems largely to have been left out of the equation) had the benefit of a traditionally capitalist political system, which he

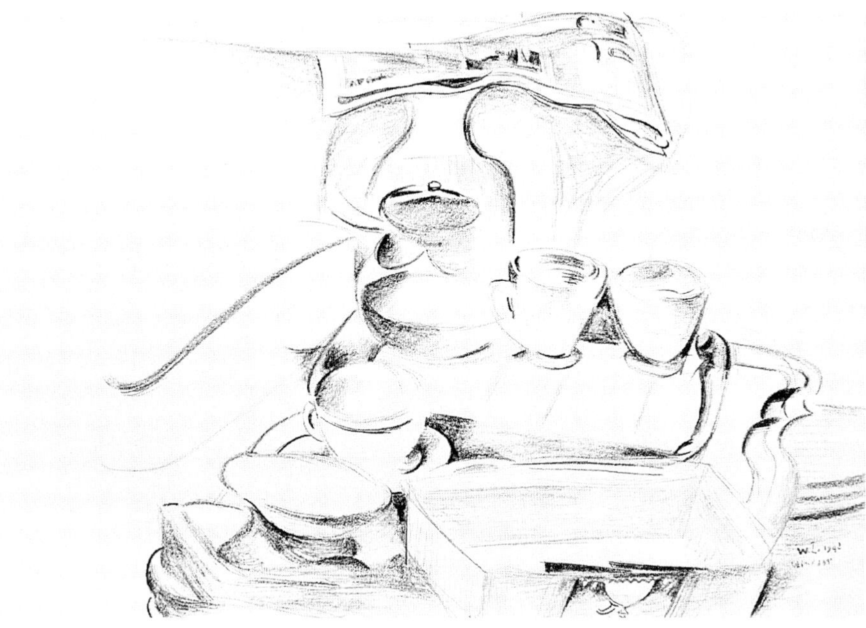

No. 60 *Table with Tray and Armchairs*, 1943, black chalk on paper (13.8 x 19.8 cm), M 1030. Herbert F. Johnson Museum of Art, Cornell University, Ithaca, New York, gift of Walter and Harriet Michel.

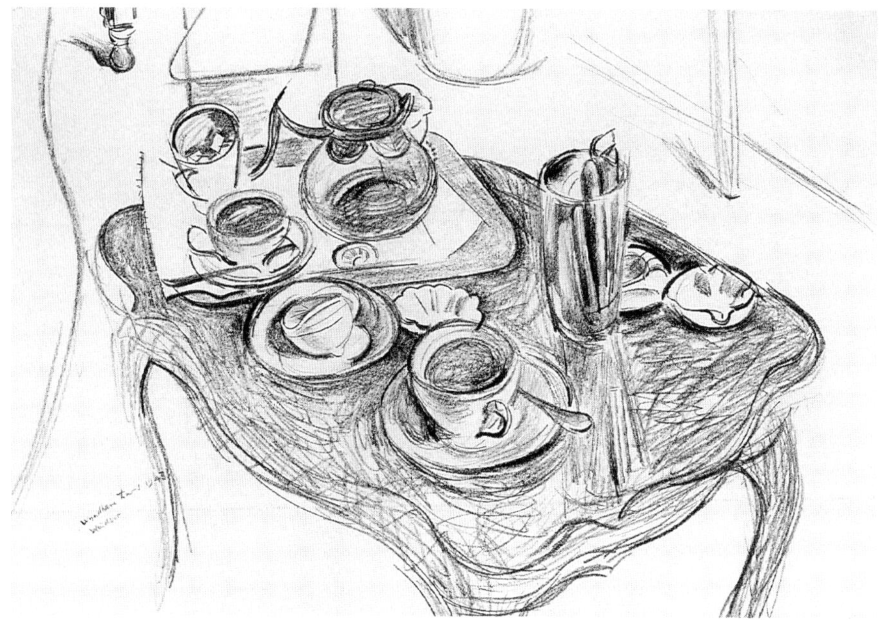

No. 61 *Table with Tray and Cups*, 1943, black chalk on paper (35.5 x 48.5 cm), M 1031. Lent anonymously.

No. 62 *Tray with Cups*, 1943, black chalk on paper (35.5 x 48.5 cm), M 1032. Lent anonymously.

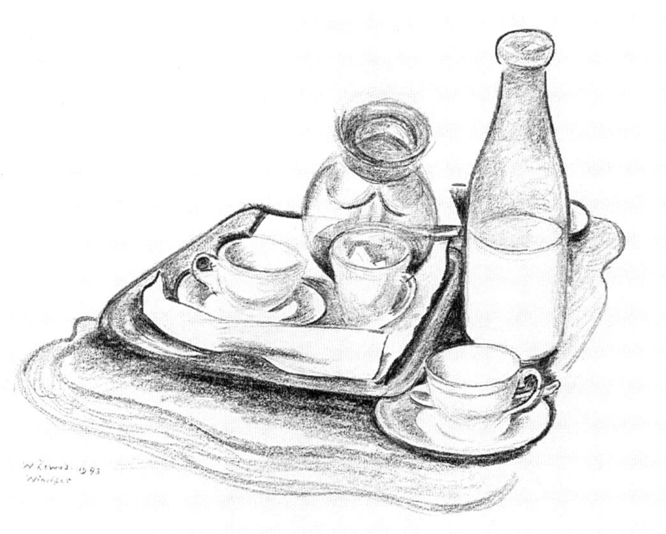

Opposite page:
No. 73 *Portrait of the Artist's Wife*, 1944, black and coloured pencil, black and coloured chalks on paper (37.5 x 28.0 cm), M 1048. Art Gallery of Windsor, purchased with funds from the Bobs Cogill and Peter Haworth estate and the assistance of the Government of Canada through the Cultural Property Export and Import Act, 1991.

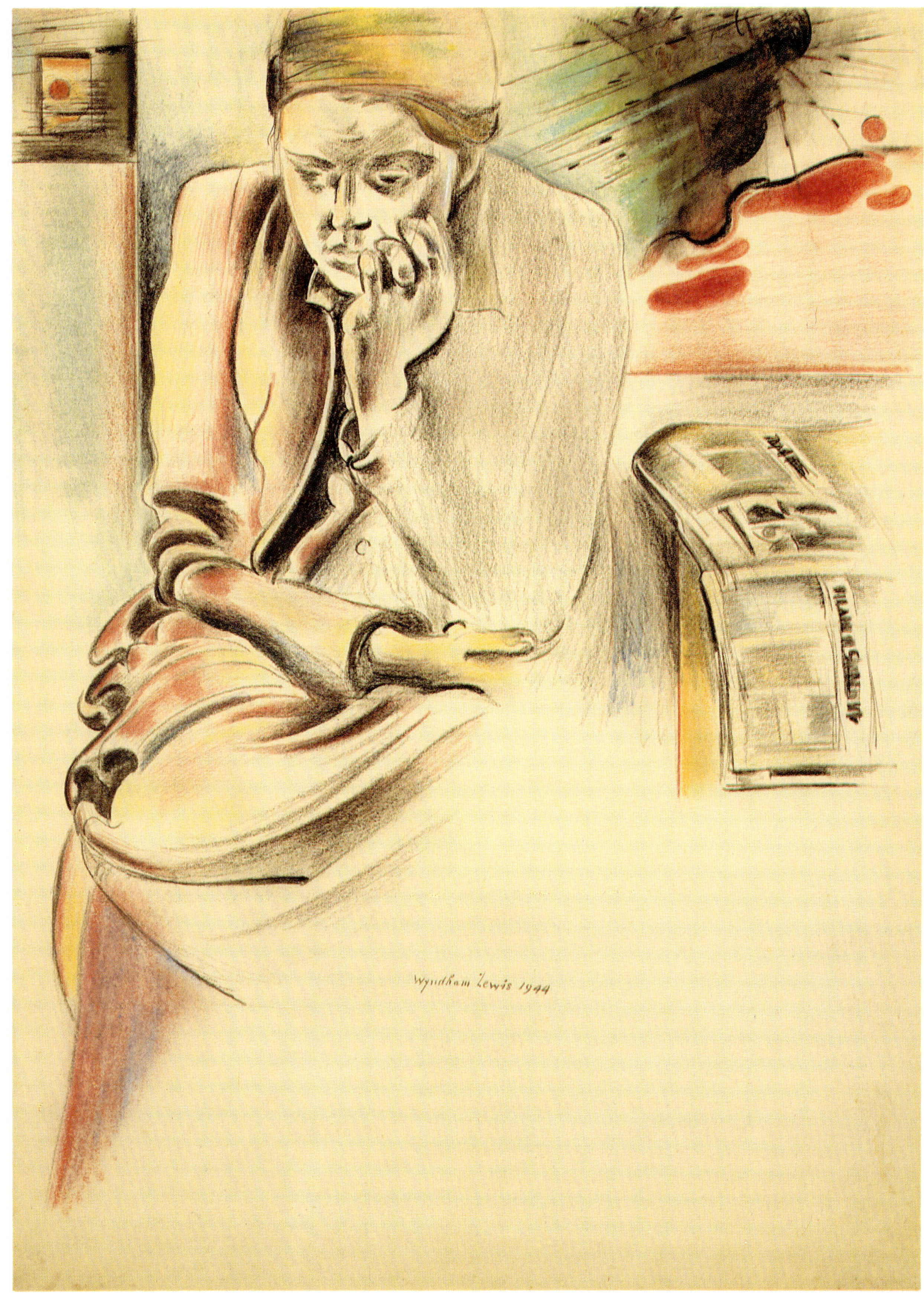
Wyndham Lewis 1944

learned about by studying, on McLuhan's recommendation, Henry Jones Ford's *The Rise and Growth of American Politics* (1898), and, in a more contemporary political context, as exemplified by the doctrines of Wendell L. Wilkie and Henry A. Wallace, both of whom campaigned for world harmony and unification.[26] Although Lewis was concerned with larger global issues, it is interesting that he sought, as he had done in the preceding decade, to find a single nation to uphold his vision of the future. Central to his vision of the United States becoming a leader in the search for world peace and an international culture was his observation that the centre of the western art world was shifting from Europe to North America. He noted the decline of Paris as the world's artistic capital and its relocation to New York City. "Will Paris be the place for cultural centrality?", Lewis asked, answering his own rhetorical question by replying, "After this war France will be propped up by one or the other of the five big power groups to look as like its old self as possible, but it will be a shadow of what it was, with its rapidly dwindling population."[27]

Lewis prophesied that North America would produce the first examples of a new strain of humanity. Such beings, he idealistically declared in *America and Cosmic Man*,

> are, it seems to me, dedicated to the future more than any other people: and it is my argument in this book that we can read our own future by an imaginative scrutiny of what is occurring, and what is so plainly destined to occur there.... The earth has become one big village with telephone and air transport.[28]

Compared to other nations, America was a harmonious racial "melting-pot", or so he over-optimistically conceived on the basis of his somewhat limited experience of the U.S.A.:

> America stands out as the one great community in which race had been thrown out, and the priests of many cults have been brought together, in relative harmony—in a world in which obstinate bottle-necks of racial and religious passion, whether in Europe, Asia, or Africa, are in process of being overcome.[29]

Except for this book, Lewis's forays into the analysis of contemporary politics were confined to the Heywood Broun lectures.[30] In his course on "Creative Literature", taught at Assumption in the winter of 1944, he returned to the topic of criteria used in the evaluation and creation of art. Such concerns are reflective of his own interests, and also provide an insight into his own work of the period. He emphasized the importance of writers searching within themselves for their subject matter, of the need to consider personal feelings as relevant, and of the uselessness of formal teaching in literary technique:

> Education must be got rid of before CREATION can begin.... There is and can be no such thing as AUTHENTIC ART until you have liquidated all the influences you have submitted to—Until you have broken up and thrown away all that cultural equipment which Education gives. Until you have regained for your mind its INNOCENCE. Until you have purged your eye of that complexity of vision which knowledge produces. This is the doctrine of the EYE OF THE CHILD. These are the creative conditions necessary for the vision of Blake's 'Songs of Innocence'.[31]

From this recommendation it would appear that Lewis's theory of the best art coming from other art—from the copying of art rather than of nature—was at variance with his formula for the best writing, but elsewhere he dwelled on the obligation of painters to consult their own imaginations and emotions in the creating of personal universes alternative to the flawed organum of observable reality.

The course included his students' participation in the writing of their "most disagreeable experience up-to-date.... Know thyself, You will learn a great deal about yourself, if you do it properly. And then one of you may begin creating."[32] Lewis felt that this would produce the following results, which were in accordance with T.S. Eliot's call for a dissociation of sensibility:

> What you will find, as you peer back, into this dark tunnel, that you see other people, or certain scenes more clearly than yourself. The memory of other people will go farther back than memories of yourself.... You will remember lots of things vividly, but you yourself will be an as-it-were disembodied spectator.[33]

Lewis enjoyed his classroom encounters and intended to continue teaching until the end of the spring of 1944, when, thanks to the encouragement of two young and eager intellectuals then on the faculty of the Saint Louis University, the Canadian-born Marshall McLuhan and his

American colleague, Felix Giovanelli (1913-1962), Lewis departed in February 1944 for St. Louis, Missouri. Lewis had met these two young supporters, who greatly admired both his writings and his art, in Windsor in the summer of 1943. McLuhan particularly esteemed Lewis's *The Art of Being Ruled* (1926), *Time and Western Man* (1927), *The Lion and the Fox* (1927), *Paleface*, and *The Apes of God* (1930), which he had read as a Cambridge undergraduate in 1936, and was enthusiastic about Lewis's recently published *The Vulgar Streak*, reviewing it for a literary club in St. Louis.

Both McLuhan and Giovanelli were astonished to find so eminent a modern intellectual as Lewis in a southern-Ontario backwater like Windsor. Just shortly after Lewis moved to this border city, McLuhan had been informed of his presence by his mother, Elsie McLuhan, who had attended the Christian Culture Series lecture on "Rouault, Painter of Original Sin." McLuhan wrote to Lewis from St. Louis in July 1943, expressing his hope that they might get together for "a chat" after the end of summer school.[34] The following August, McLuhan and Giovanelli took the train to Windsor to meet Lewis.

The two professors returned to St. Louis with the idea of assisting Lewis by obtaining for him some portrait commissions, public lectures and teaching jobs. In the hopes of mounting an exhibition of his work, they arranged a meeting with Charles Nagel, then director of the St. Louis Museum of Art. By 17 August 1943 McLuhan could write to Lewis that he had arranged a lecture and had lined up "one serious (!) sitter—that is one intelligent person of small means who would pay for a pencil drawing or study"—but that further jobs and commissions would not likely be forthcoming until the fall and winter.[35] In addition, McLuhan had written to several American universities in an attempt to find Lewis a teaching post. As Lewis had no further guarantee of a position at Assumption College after the spring session, the St. Louis venture seemed opportune, if not essential, although in fact he had not completed his term at Windsor. Luckily, the ever-accommodating Father Murphy was able to take over his class until the end of the spring.

By February of 1944 it had been arranged that Lewis would give two talks in St. Louis and execute at least one portrait, that of Ernest Hemingway's mother-in-law, Edna Gellhorn.[36] McLuhan remained sanguine, however, about the potential for further opportunities in the city, claiming that

> We shall probably wangle a really large reception for you on Thursday the 17th which will be attended by all the new wealth of St. Louis plus some of the old.... Everybody wants to see some of your work, so we are combing the libraries of the country for a set of Thirty Personalities [a portfolio of portraits Lewis published in 1932]. They would make a suitable show by themselves.[37]

Lewis's first talk in St. Louis was at the Wednesday Club, a high-society women's organization, in which Lewis nostalgically gossiped about the "Famous People I Have Put on Canvas and in Books", impressing his listeners with anecdotes about such personages as James Joyce, T.S. Eliot, Ernest Hemingway, William Faulkner, Edith Sitwell and Gertrude Stein.[38]

Lewis also delivered, on 21 February 1944, a lecture at the opening of the thirty-seventh annual exhibition of *American Painting of Today*, organized by the City Art Museum of St. Louis. This exhibition was a survey of painting from various states, ranging in style from contemporary experiments in abstraction to regionalist "American Scene" painting. In his address, entitled "The Role of Art in Ordering Nature", Lewis not surprisingly favoured the more naturalistically based exhibits.[39] He explained his views on abstraction in a letter to Charles Nagel:

> I shall prefer probably the non-abstract to the abstract pictures (most of the latter are not very good I'm afraid), there are very few abstract pictures as a matter of fact, that seem to me to have any great interest: most are pretty futile reflections of what occurred in Europe a quarter century ago. But I am quite ready to explain, in the simplest vocabulary[,] the principle of all such attempts at abstraction (which can be[,] however seldom in fact they are that—very serious experiments).[40]

That same February, Lewis presented a third lecture, this time at the Twentieth Century Club in Chicago, in which he discussed concepts of beauty, once again using the work of Georges Rouault as an illustration:

> PURE ACTION and PURE FEELING are very closely allied. It is in the arts of painting, more than any other, that this particular controversy rages.... There is no artist more greatly admired. There is no uglier painter.... Beauty is the last thing that Rouault ever

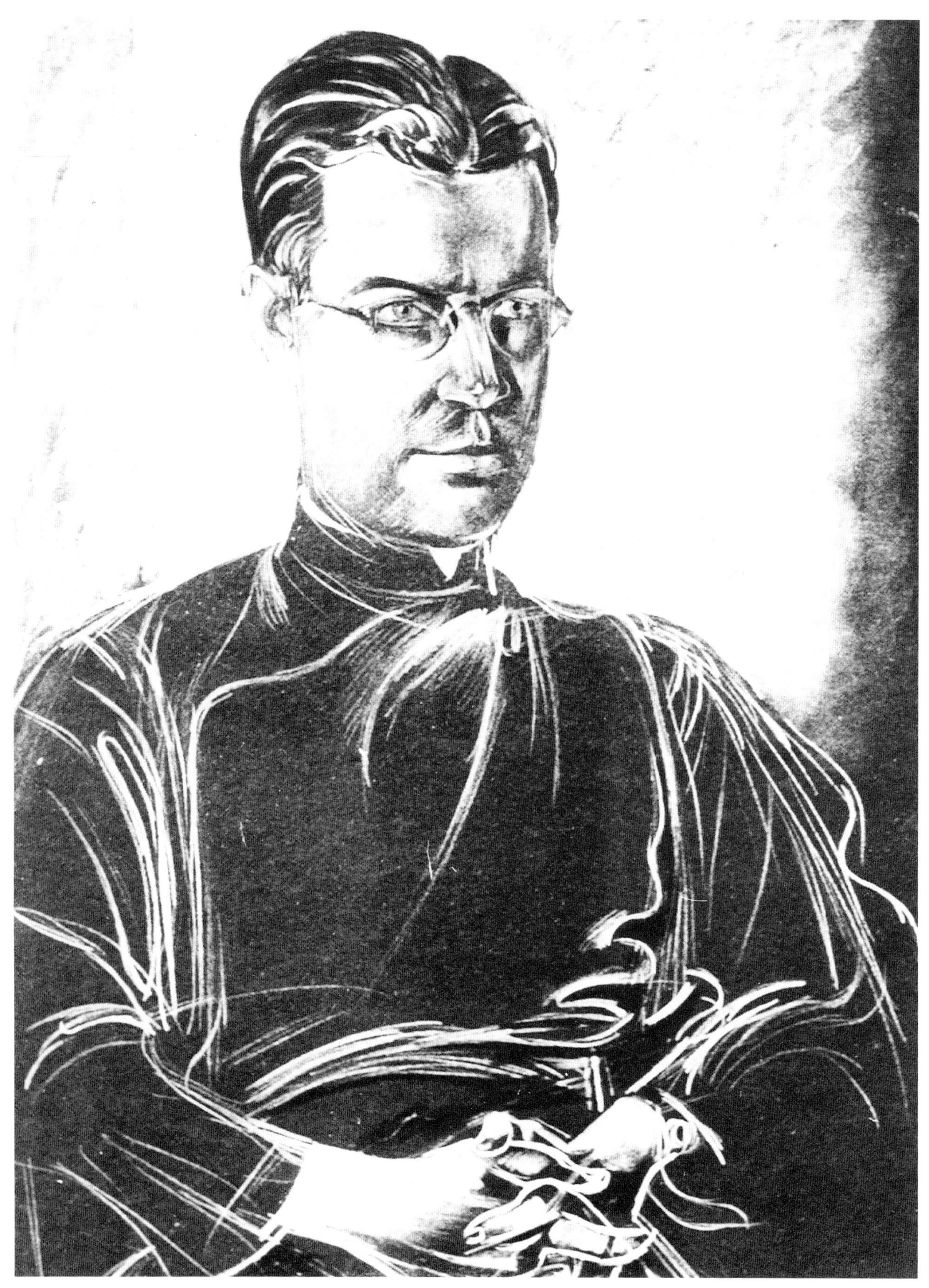

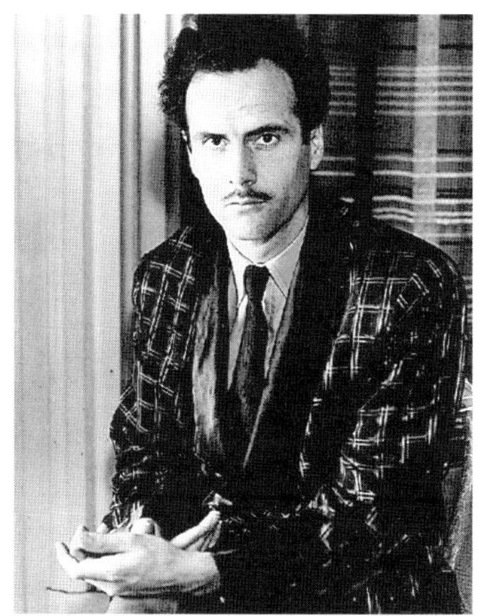

Fig. 36 Herbert Marshall McLuhan, c. 1944. Photograph: Cornell.

Right: No. 67 *Portrait of Marshall McLuhan,* 1944, black chalk on paper (37.5 x 23.5 cm), M 1046. Corinne McLuhan, Toronto.

Opposite page:
Fig. 35 *Portrait of Father J. Stanley Murphy,* 1944, coloured chalks on paper (49.5 x 32.0 cm). Photograph: Sheila Watson, Nanaimo, B.C..

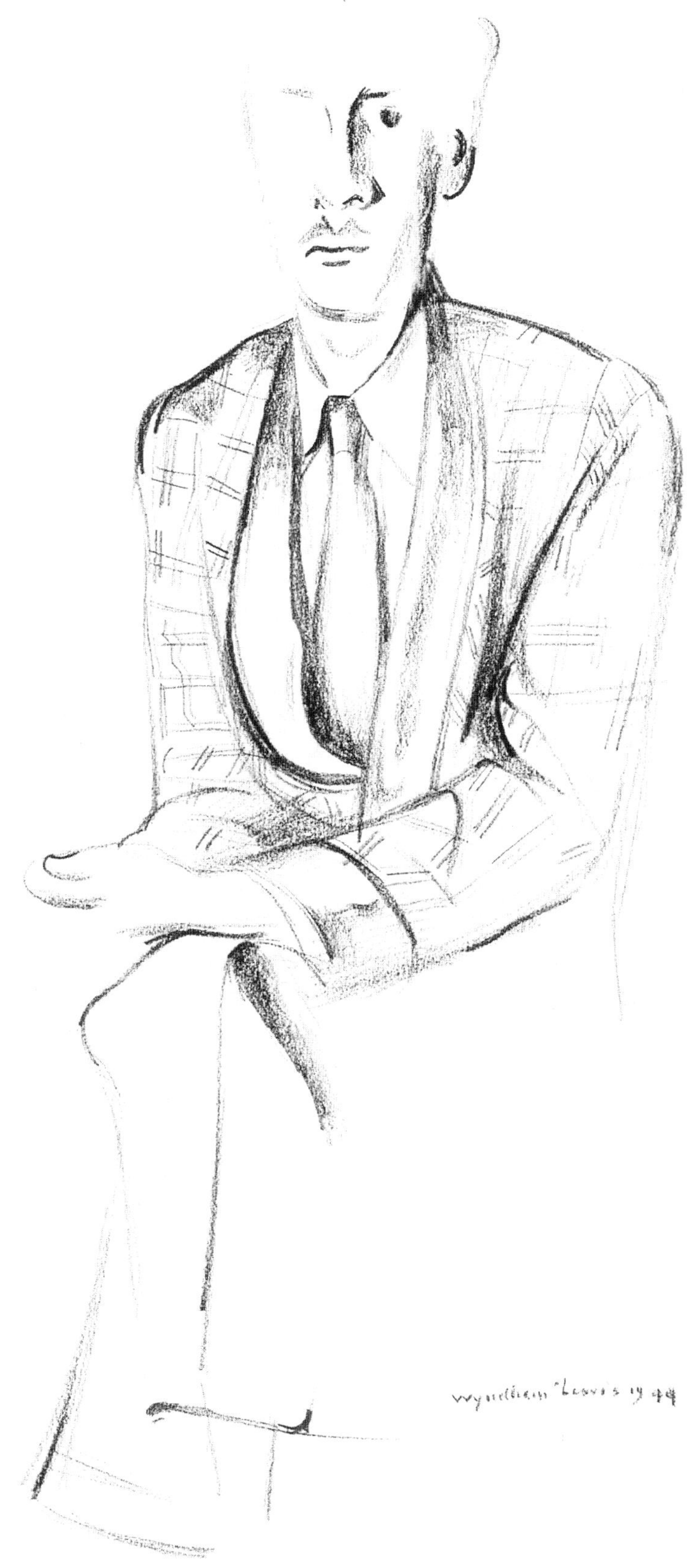

entitled *Portrait of Pauline Bondy* (nos. 69-70), and *Portrait of a Young Lady* (no. 71), as well as an oil, *Portrait of Pauline Bondy* (no. 72), all executed in the summer of 1944. Of all the portraits Lewis did in Canada, this group of works demonstrates most comprehensively the preparations he made for a larger oil-on-canvas easel painting.

Pauline Bondy remembers sitting for her portrait through several hot summer sessions in the Lewises' apartment.[58] The thick wool suit she was wearing was, she thought, painted accurately, but Lewis took a particular fancy to her broad-brimmed black hat and used it as a formal device to create three quite different moods in the oil and in two of the chalks.[59] (Only *Portrait of a Young Lady* lacks the hat.) The three drawings reveal Lewis's consideration of the various poses in which his subject could be portrayed. In making the three chalk drawings, the artist paid close attention to the hands, face and seated attitude of his sitter. These works show an attractive young woman of slender frame, looking directly at the viewer with a self-assured, confident expression, the impression conveyed being one of an open and pleasant disposition.

The oil portrait of Pauline Bondy was not directly based on any of the three drawings, although these works no doubt assisted Lewis in making decisions about the pose, mood and attire of the final painting. Miss Bondy thought the summer background, which does not appear in any of the drawings, had nothing to do with the reality of the setting, although it was almost certainly a view through Lewis's apartment window overlooking the Detroit River. The sitter faces the viewer, leaning further forward than in the chalk drawings, her expression more reserved than confident. Unlike so many other female subjects of Lewis's, Pauline Bondy considers her portrait to be a flattering likeness.[60]

Lewis had hoped to resume teaching at Assumption College but reduced enrolment forced spending cutbacks and his appointment was not renewed. In the meantime, Father Lee, one of the Basilian Fathers at Assumption, had vacated his post as head of the Department of English. Marshall McLuhan, having recently obtained his doctorate, had been brought on as staff for the summer of 1944 to teach English, and when the position officially became vacant in the fall, it was given to McLuhan. As McLuhan's biographer, Philip Marchand, has noted, the "job [was] immediately offered to him when he applied for it at Lewis's suggestion."[61] Despite his having recommended McLuhan, however, considerable bitterness on Lewis's part eventually erupted as an indirect consequence. Father Murphy had anticipated both the decision and the potential conflict, and wrote to Lewis:

> In view of the possible reduction of the number of college students next year...the powers-that-be will be especially cautious (probably too cautious) regarding the expenditure of every hundred dollars. I am morally certain that they will continue McLuhan after Summer School in view of Father Lee's going away.[62]

According to McLuhan, the friction had begun earlier, in St. Louis, where Lewis had initiated or encouraged contention between himself, the McLuhans and the Giovanellis by making unfortunate and critical comments about their efforts to assist him. The numerous letters between Lewis, Giovanelli and McLuhan substantiate the latter's claims about the clash.[63] So embittered by the experience was McLuhan that he wrote to a colleague, the Canadian-born poet and academic A.J.M. Smith, to warn him about Lewis's mercurial and vindictive temper:

> He accused me of vile intrigues against him in Windsor. I had inveigled him down to St. Louis and then shot up here to steal his job—and, of course to avoid the draft, which wasn't ever close to my neck at any time.... I lived daily with Lewis for 6 months and gradually became acquainted with his labyrinthine ways.[64]

Even before the outbreak of hostilities, however, McLuhan had run into difficulties with Lewis over money, as he explained in his letter to Smith:

> Gradually I became aware of Lewis's totally irrational motivations in these matters. Gio[vanelli] understood too. Gio. had lent him 400 bucks which he never asked for again. In fact he wrote Lewis a note cancelling the debt, That didn't allay Lewis's fears a bit. Lewis had me assume the debt, in writing. Meanwhile Lewis had borrowed considerably from me promising to paint a portrait of Corinne [McLuhan's wife]. Well I didn't care about the money or the portrait, but Lewis hates and fears anybody to whom he owes money. So that was finis for us.[65]

Opposite page, clockwise from top left: No. 71 *Portrait of Pauline Bondy,* 1944, black and coloured chalks on green paper (47.0 x 33.0 cm), M 1035. Mary Catherine Lyter, Canoga Park, Calfornia; No. 69 *Portrait of Pauline Bondy,* 1944, oil on canvas (72.5 x 45.5 cm), M P106, Pauline Bondy, Toronto; No. 70 *Portrait of Pauline Bondy,* 1944, black chalk on paper (39.5 x 31.0 cm) M 1036, Lent anonymously. No. 70 *Portrait of Pauline Bondy,* 1944, black chalk on paper (39.5 x 31.0 cm) M 1036, Lent anonymously; No. 72 *Portrait of a Young Lady* (i.e Miss Pauline Bondy), 1944, black and coloured chalks on paper (46.5 x 32.0 cm), M 1049, Bryan Ferry, West Sussex, England.

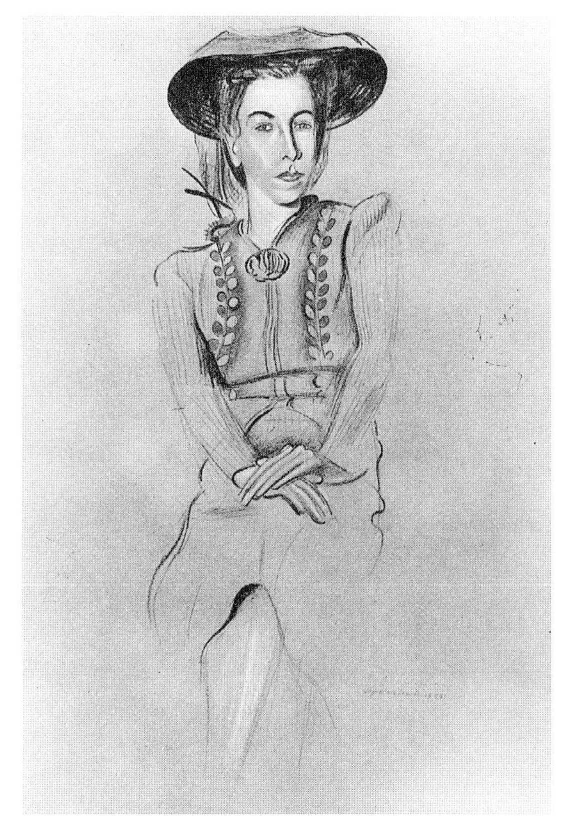

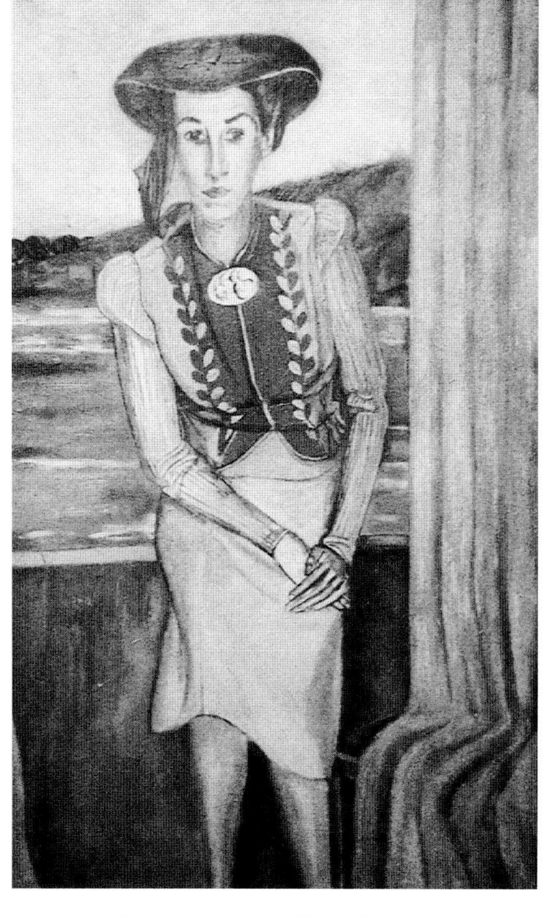

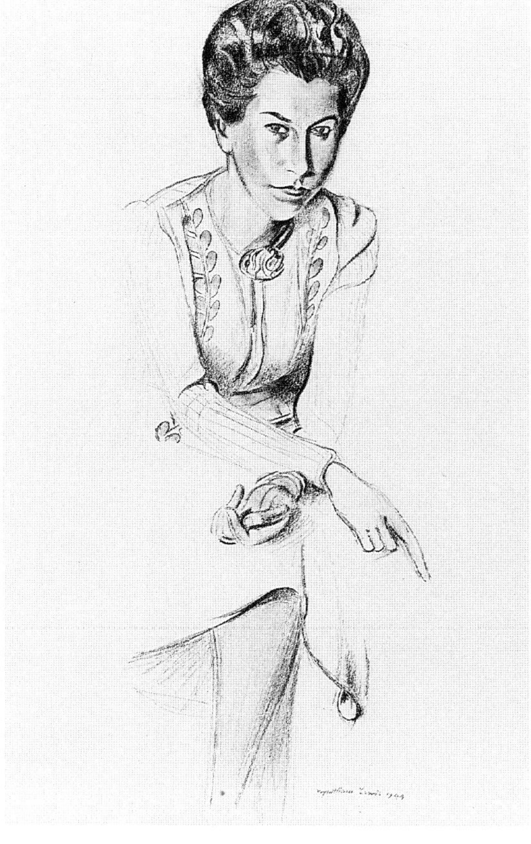

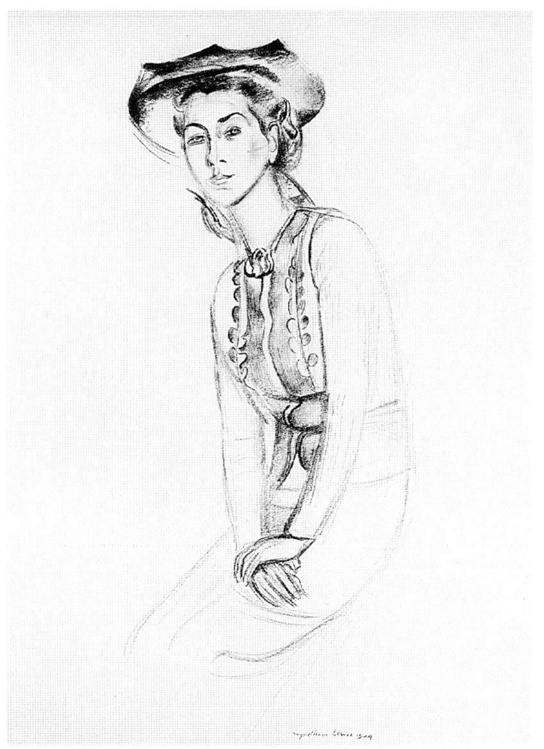

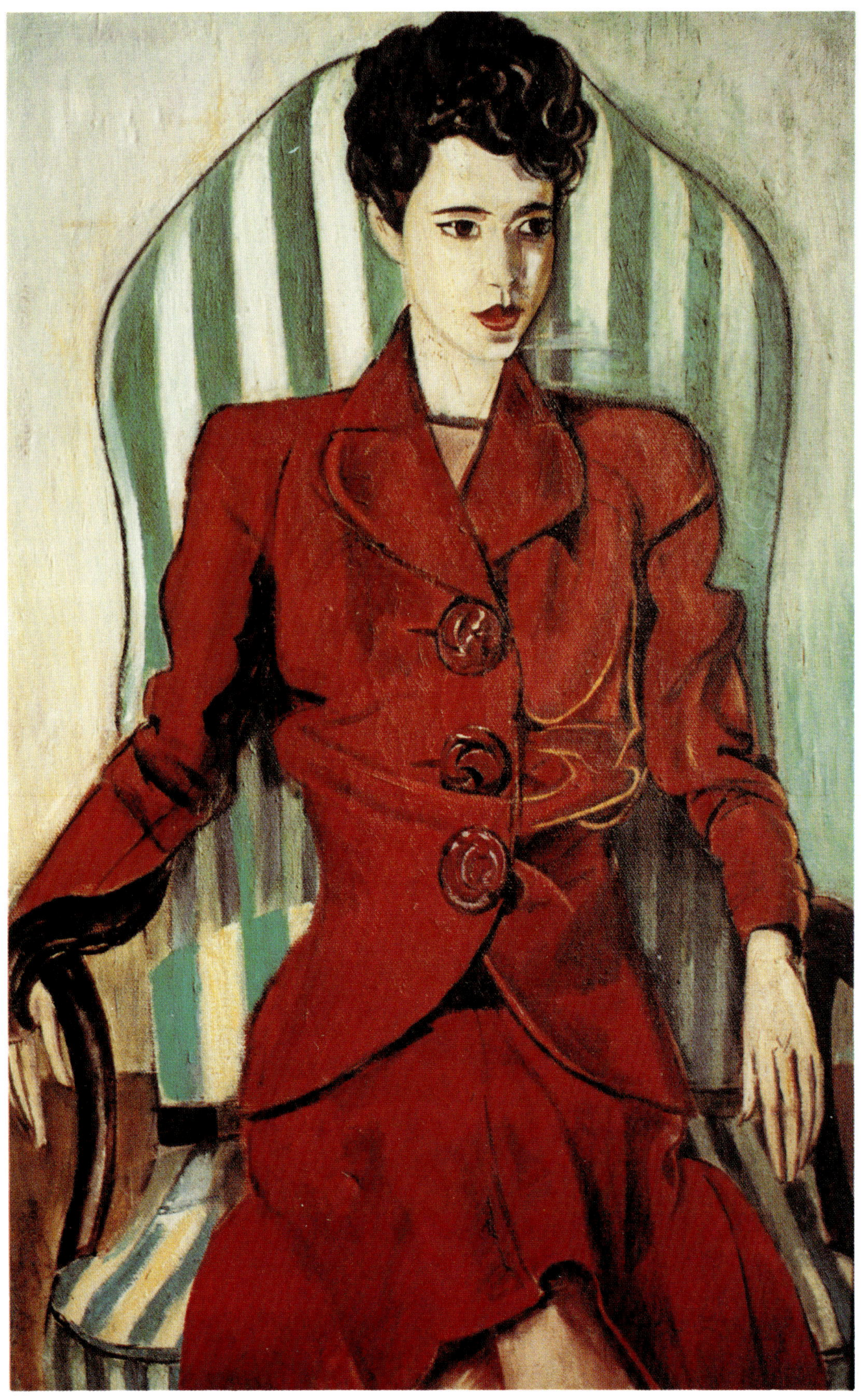

No. 85 *Portrait of Mrs. Margaret Giovanelli*, 1944, oil on canvas (63.5 x 41.0 cm), M P109. Bryan Ferry, West Sussex, England.

No. 89 *Portrait of Mrs. Paul Martin*, 1945, oil on canvas (114.8 x 71.5 cm), M P122. The late the Hon. Paul Martin Sr. and Mrs. Eleanor Martin, Windsor, Ontario.

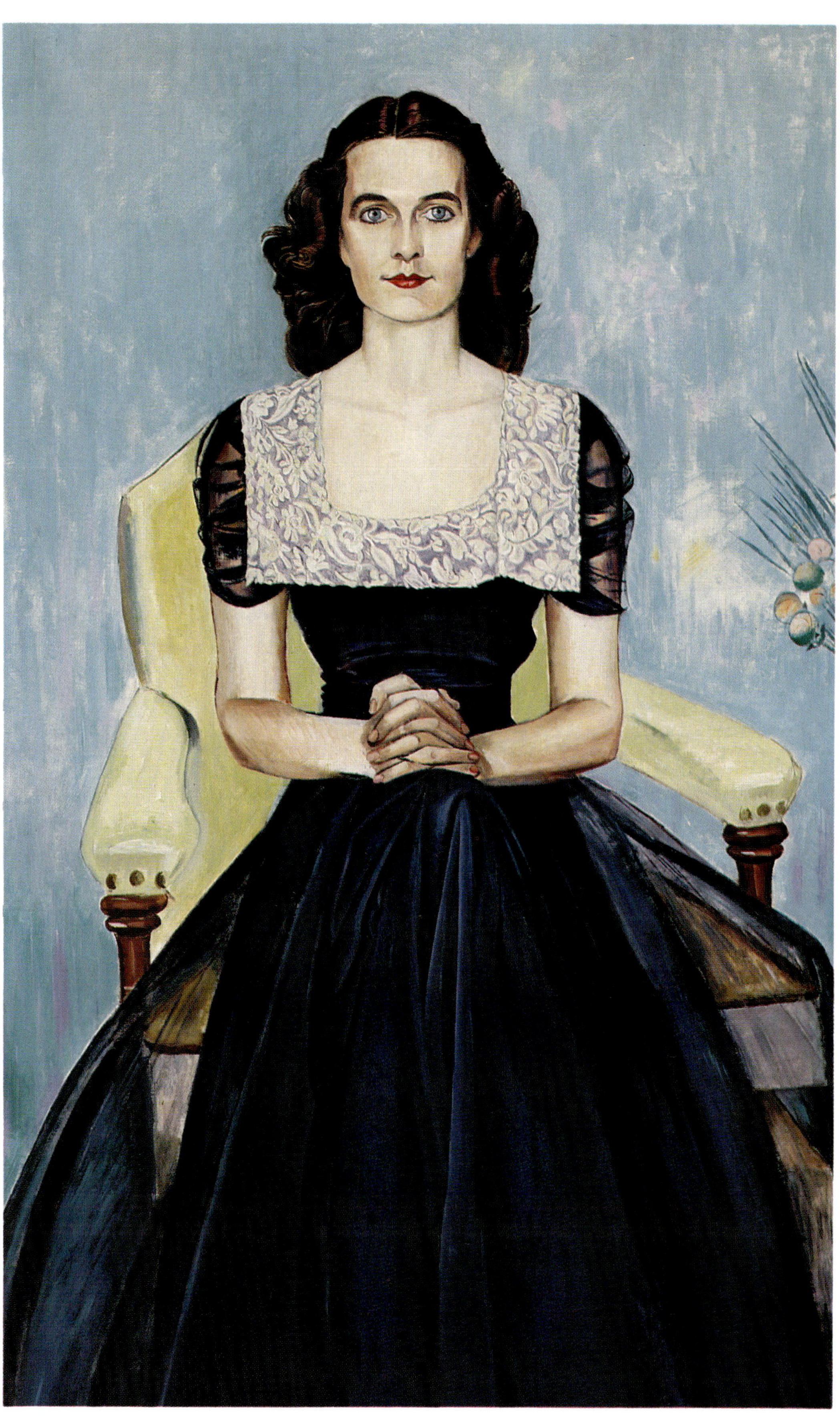

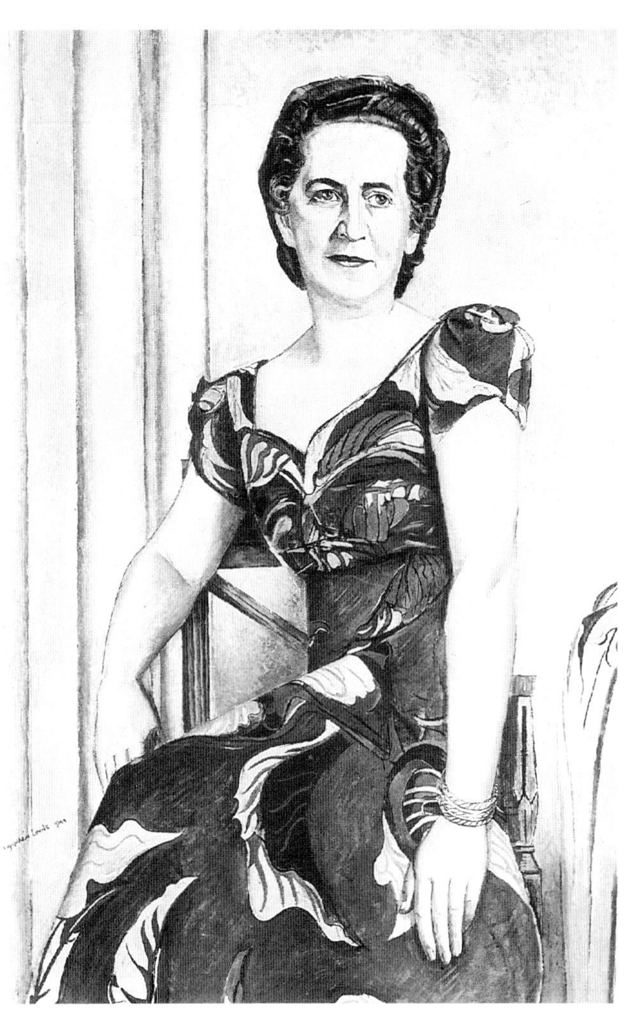

No. 64 *Portrait of Mrs. Ernest W. Stix,* 1944, oil on canvas (117.0 x 81.5 cm), M P110. Washington University in St. Louis, Gallery of Art, St. Louis, Missouri.

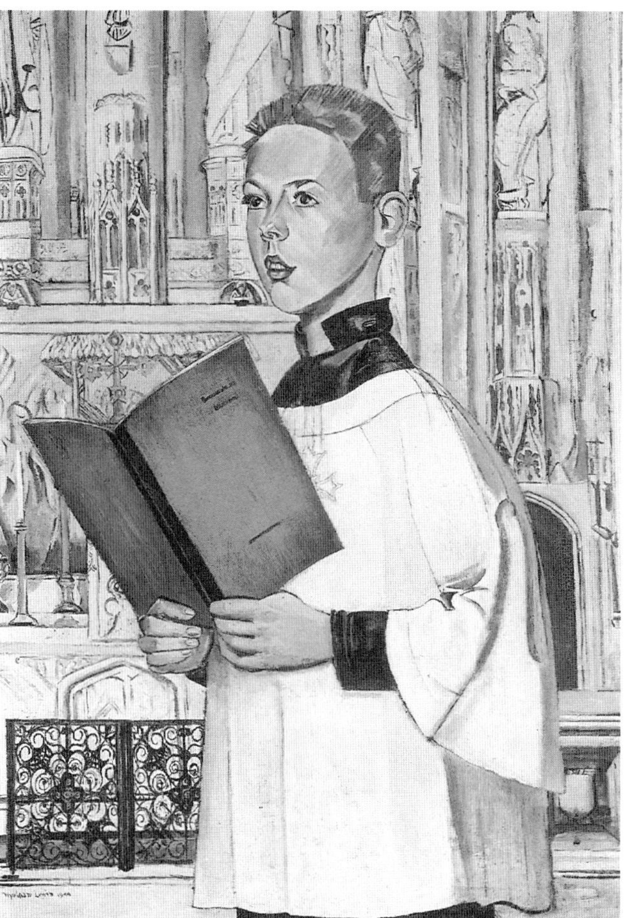

No. 66 *Portrait of James Taylor,* 1944, oil on canvas (76.0 x 52.0 cm), M P111. James Taylor.

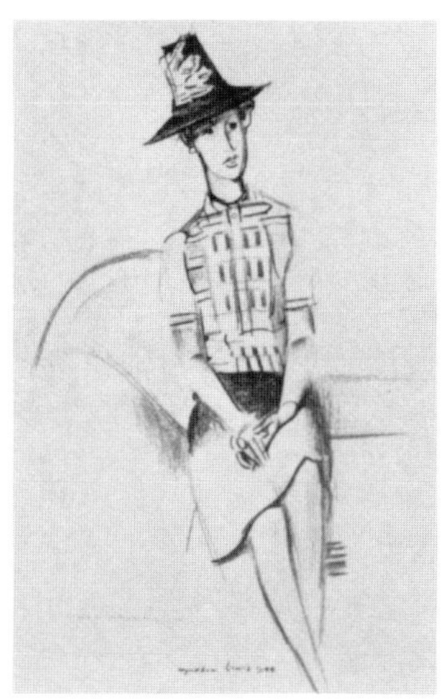

No. 37 *Corinne* (McLuhan), 1944, black chalk on paper (33.0 x 24.0 cm), M 1037. Private collection.

The bad feelings that came to a head in 1944 carried on for some years hence, although Lewis renewed contact with his erstwhile disciple in the spring of 1953 and the correspondence resumed.[66] So antagonistic had their relations become in Windsor, however, that McLuhan believed, with some justice, that Lewis had caricatured him as Prof. Ian Mackenzie in his semi-autobiographical novel of 1954, *Self Condemned*, in which the Scots expatriate (actually quite a sympathetic portrayal, compared to other targets in the book) is described as "a little routine teaching hack," possessed "of a very good mind of a routine kind."[67] McLuhan was by no means being unreasonable in this suspicion, as Lewis had made a regular habit of satirizing his friends, lovers and patrons as well as his innumerable enemies in his novels and stories, perhaps most notoriously in his attack on Bloomsbury, *The Apes of God*. The conflicts of the Windsor and St. Louis years may even have found their way into several of his Windsor-period portraits.

Portrait of Marshall McLuhan (1944; no. 67) is probably the most cutting of all these likenesses. Although it is not known whether or not this work was commissioned, Lewis had borrowed money from McLuhan and the drawing may have been offered in repayment.[68] The fact, however, that Lewis most likely did not work directly from the sitter but rather from a photograph (fig. 36), which he closely followed, suggests that he was not very enthusiastic about the job, which McLuhan may have been pressing him to complete even after they had had their falling out. Lewis strayed from his source image by shifting his subject farther up the picture plane than in the photo, sketchily adding crossed legs and cropping McLuhan's head at the hairline, and leaving out the sitter's right eye and the right side of his face and brow. He retained the tweed sports-jacket of the photograph (toning down somewhat the rather loud check-pattern) and the curious positioning of the hands, which appear to be fiddling with a pipe. Lewis had experienced McLuhan's intelligence first-hand, and the deletion of his cranium leaves little doubt that the artist intended this gesture to be an insult or check to this extremely ambitious and talented young acolyte, who clearly represented a threat to the distrustful old prophet-in-exile.

Lewis also made two portraits of McLuhan's wife, Corinne, one of which remains unlocated and the other of which is now in a private California collection. Both were also based on photographs and cannot be described as flattering portrayals of Mrs. McLuhan's stunning classical features. *Corinne* (1944; fig. 37) is essentially a mirror-image of a photograph now in the Lewis papers at Cornell. However, in the drawing Corinne McLuhan's figure is pared down to a thin, doll-like body, and the face conveys little sense of her pleasant, outgoing personality. As in his portrait of Marshall McLuhan, Lewis concentrated his attention on the subject's fashionable clothing, especially, in this case, her decorative hat. Corinne McLuhan's Catholic godmother, Pauline Bondy, remarked, "Lewis deliberately made her look awful."[69] And yet the portrait does not seem overtly unfriendly.

Despite conflicts with the McLuhans and Felix Giovanelli, Lewis appears not to have held any grudges against the beautiful Margaret Giovanelli, the subject of one of his finest portraits of the Windsor-St. Louis period. This extraordinary likeness was probably begun in 1944,[70] but was not finished until after Lewis's return to England in 1945. The sitter in *Portrait of Mrs. Margaret (Felix) Giovanelli* (no. 85) is shown seated on a green-and white-striped chair wearing a vibrant red suit with yellow-ochre highlights. Her features are handled with subtlety, care and tenderness; her mood seems introspective and the sitter looks relaxed and easy-going. Lewis has captured this sensitive moment by using a three-quarter view of Margaret Giovanelli's face, which softens the effect of the portrait, particularly when compared with those of Mrs. Robert Sainsbury and Mary McLean. In portraits that strike us as confrontational and awkward, Lewis has almost invariably employed a full-frontal perspective; the slightly averted gaze of the sitter invites a regard that is curious and sympathetic rather than hostile or confrontational, the result being, ironically, a greater degree of psychological probity on the artist's part rather than a lesser.

In the early fall of 1944 the Lewises gave up their apartment on Sandwich St. and moved back to St. Louis, where he completed the previously ordered *Portrait of James Taylor* (no. 66)[70] and carried out an important commission, *Portrait of Mrs. Ernest W. Stix* (no. 64). As with his earlier plans, Lewis had intended the second St. Louis trip to be short, and by December the couple returned to Windsor after a brief side-trip to Washington to see their friend the poet and playwright Archibald MacLeish, Librarian of Congress from 1939 to 1944. Unable to secure semi-permanent accommodations, the Lewises lived at the Prince Edward Hotel in downtown Windsor for several months, and for a short time also they appear to have stayed at the home of Garnet and Marion Trowell, on Ouellette Avenue.[72]

When Lewis returned to Windsor he had the promise of only one major portrait commission, that of the wife of the Hon. Paul Martin (1903-1992), the Liberal member of Parliament for Essex who had been appointed parliamentary secretary to Prime Minister Mackenzie King in 1943, having served on the staff of Assumption College from 1931 to 1935.[73] The commission was initiated in the summer of 1944 at Paul Martin's request, and was confirmed by October 1944.[74] Lewis began *Portrait of Mrs. Paul Martin* (1945; no. 89) in the late fall of 1944 and continued to work on the portrait into February 1945. Paul Martin had agreed that he would do his best to help Lewis find other clients.[75]

Lewis made several studies for the Martin portrait, but the only known one is *Three O'Clock* (1944; no. 68), a study representing the second of two compositional options that Lewis presented to the Martins before beginning the canvas; the first, which was used for the final painting, was vertical in format. This choice enabled Lewis to concentrate on achieving a greater sense of formality, and also had the advantage of giving special emphasis to Mrs. Martin's head, which Lewis considered beautifully shaped.[76] The second pose was a more intimate, domestic, showing Mrs. Martin resting on a sofa.

The portrait was painted when Mrs. Martin was a young woman of about twenty-five years of age; after nearly half a century, the sitter still clearly recalls hearing Lewis express his strong political opinions, and also remembers his fractious personality.[77] From her remarks regarding his character—he was, in her recollection, a "complete sinner, a cynic with no ideals," and "degraded everything and everyone"[78]—we can assume that the sessions were no more enjoyable to her (and the painter) than they had been to Lisa Sainsbury and Mary McLean. She found that sitting for her portrait was a challenging task; at one point, Lewis asked her "to smile up to her ears", an exaggerated expression she was not prepared to assume in the presence of so hostile a witness.[79] The larger-than-usual likeness captures Mrs. Martin's hesitancy quite effectively; her tenseness in the presence of the hypercritical and sarcastic Lewis is evident. As with the Sainsbury and McLean portraits, Eleanor Martin, clad in a full-length royal-blue dress with a white-lace square-necked collar, confronts the viewer head-on. Lewis further enriched his colour scheme by placing his subject in a soft lime-green chair against a turquoise background. The sitter's slender figure and powdered white skin are the focus of attention, but these notes of elegance and leisured ease are undercut by the stiffly parted hair, the nervously clenched fingers, the bow-shaped red lips and the wide, staring eyes. The effect is at once hypnotic and distracting; the sitter seems to be in a state of inward-looking reverie, instead of returning the painter's piercing gaze.

Although complications over the payment for this work ensued,[80] Paul Martin remained genuinely impressed with the portrait and wrote Lewis a detailed and laudatory account of his impressions of it:

> What a magnificent portrait!... I do want you to know how I feel about this treasured possession.... It is evident even to one like myself that Nell has been painted by a great painter. I wish some great critic were at hand. He would use superlatives to describe what you have done. My examination, if my glances be so termed, have yielded hidden qualities and have brought to light characteristic traits which only you, apart from my own reactional knowledge, have seen in my wife—and you have put these on a canvas for everyone to see. I know that each day will bring added proof of the genius which is yours.
>
> To say that we are pleased with the painting is an understatement. We are happy that it is done, honoured to have it, and we will ever be proud to know that it was executed by so great a man.[81]

ALTHOUGH LEWIS HAD HOPED that the Martin portrait would lead to other commissions, it failed to do so, and his subsequent involvement with Windsor society was limited to a few public lectures. The city's artistic community was only in its formative stages in the early 1940s,[82] although the Local Council of Women and the Fakir Art Club had been actively promoting the arts since the late 1920s, and out of these two organizations the Windsor Art Association had grown in 1936. It was not until October 1943, however, that a public art gallery, then known as the Willistead Art Gallery (now the Art Gallery of Windsor), was established.[83] Needless to say, the number of working artists was much smaller than it was in Toronto, and there was no

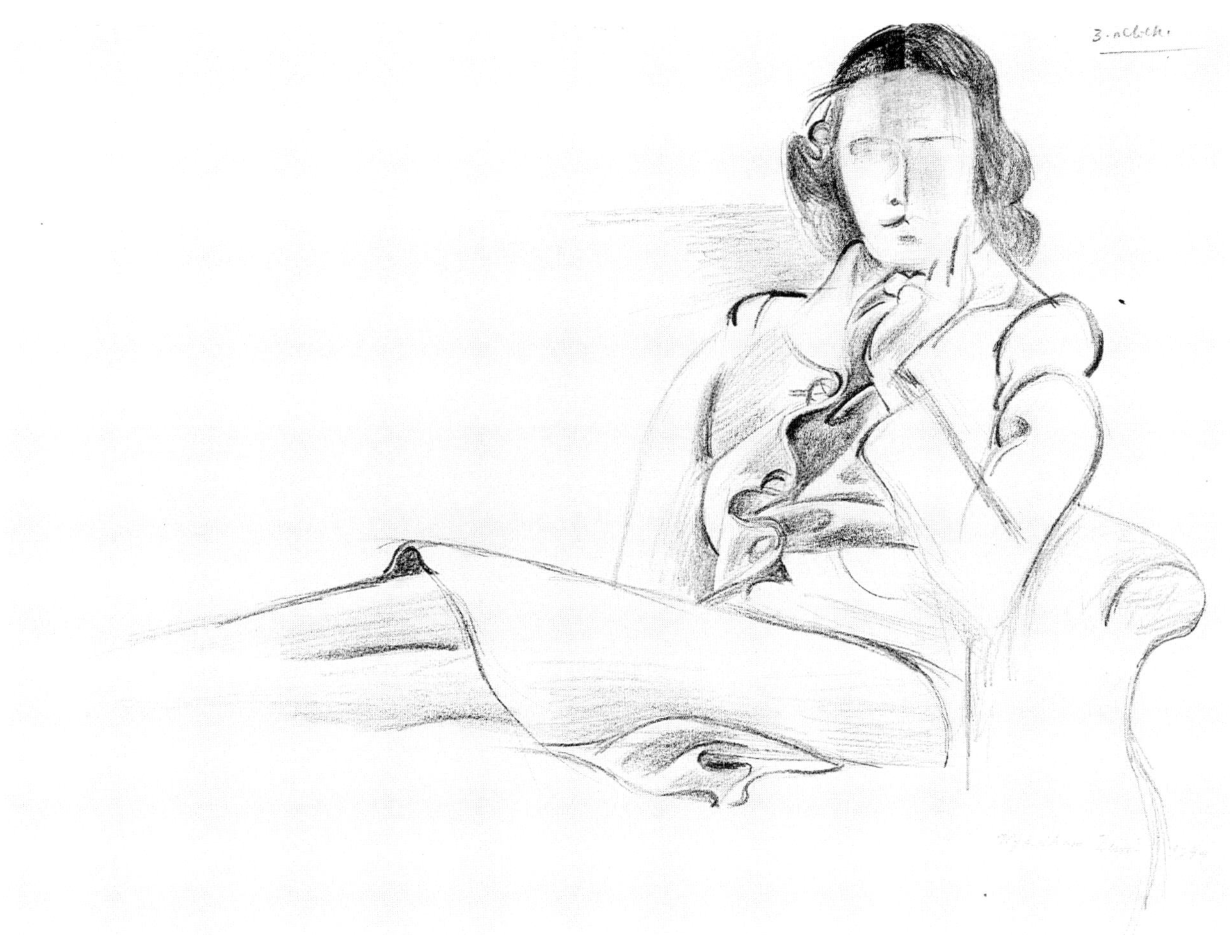

No. 68 *Three O'Clock*, 1944, black chalk on paper (27.5 x 38.0 cm), M 1053. Lent anonymously.

commercial gallery that showed contemporary work, a deficiency Lewis had noted soon after his arrival in the spring of 1943 in a letter to his former dealer, Douglas Duncan: "The only thing this place lacks is Duncan! Why doesn't Charles Street cross Ouellette instead of Yonge.... Why don't you come and have a look at Windsor? You might prefer it to Toronto."[84]

Lewis's involvement with the Windsor Art Association, based at Willistead Manor, in the old, élite neighbourhood of Walkerville, was minimal. On 4 February 1945 he was asked by the association's secretary, Daphne Hein, to be the speaker at a members' tea, which coincided with the opening of the exhibition featuring three Montreal women painters, Prudence Heward, Anne Savage and Ethel Seath. The gallery, then housed in a single, modest exhibition room in Willistead Manor (fig. 38), held monthly exhibitions (except during the summer), and hosted some important travelling shows, such as the annuals of the Canadian Society of Painters in Watercolour, the Canadian Society of Painter-Etchers and Engravers, and the Royal Canadian Academy, and individual touring surveys like *Contemporary British Painting, British War Art, The F.B. Housser Memorial Collection* and *Polish Painting*. With a few exceptions, these exhibitions would not have been much different from the kind of show Lewis could have seen in Toronto, had he been so inclined.

The Willistead Art Gallery's principal commitment was to the exhibiting of contemporary Canadian art and, time and resources permitting, of the works of local and international artists—and in that order of priority. This mandate perhaps explains why no offer to mount a show of Lewis's paintings and drawings was forthcoming. Such critical commentary as was published was limited to a weekly column in the *Windsor Daily Star*, which covered not only visual art but also music and literature. Lewis's talk to the Windsor Art Association was briefly mentioned twice in this column (the second mention being an apology for confusing Wyndham Lewis the writer and painter with D.B. Wyndham Lewis the British humourist).[85]

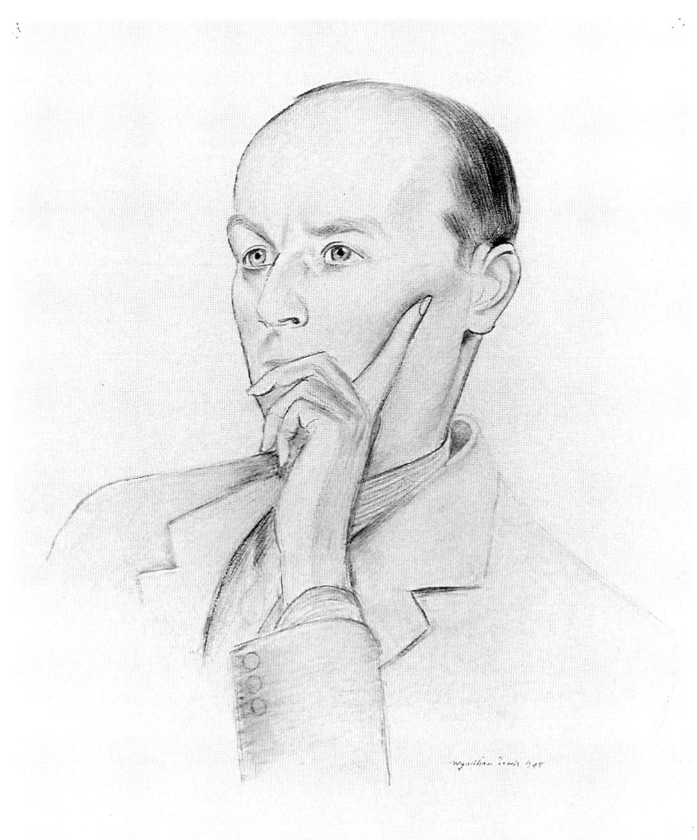

Fig. 39 *Portrait of William R. Valentiner,* 1945, coloured chalks (42.5 x 34 cm), M 1063. Present whereabouts unknown (ownership indicated in Michel, *Wyndham Lewis...,* as Estate of the late W.R. Valentiner). Photograph: Detroit Institute of Arts, Detroit, Michigan.

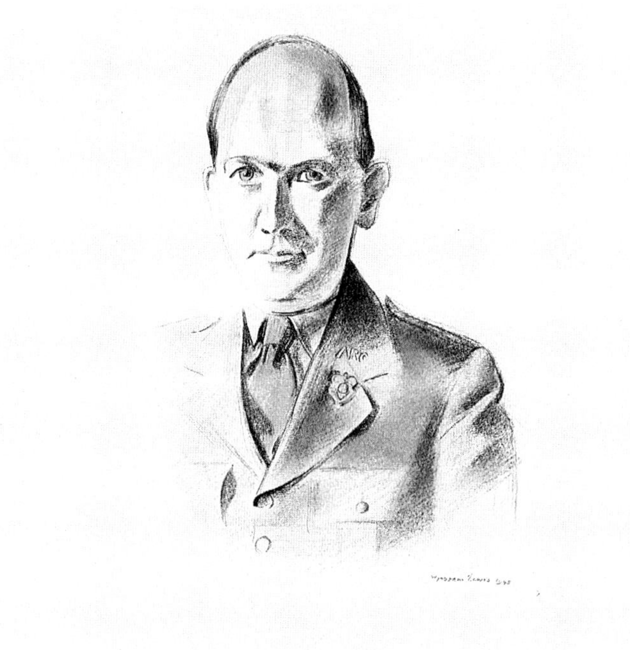

No. 87 *Portrait of John S. Newberry [Jr.],* 1945, coloured chalks on brown paper (50.0 x 38.0 cm), M 1061. The Museum of Modern Art, New York, gift of Detroit Institute of Arts.

Opposite page:
No. 86 *Portrait of John S. Newberry Jr.,* 1945, coloured chalks on paper (57.2 x 41.9 cm), M 1060. Detroit Institute of Arts, Detroit, Michigan, bequest of John S. Newberry Jr., 1965.

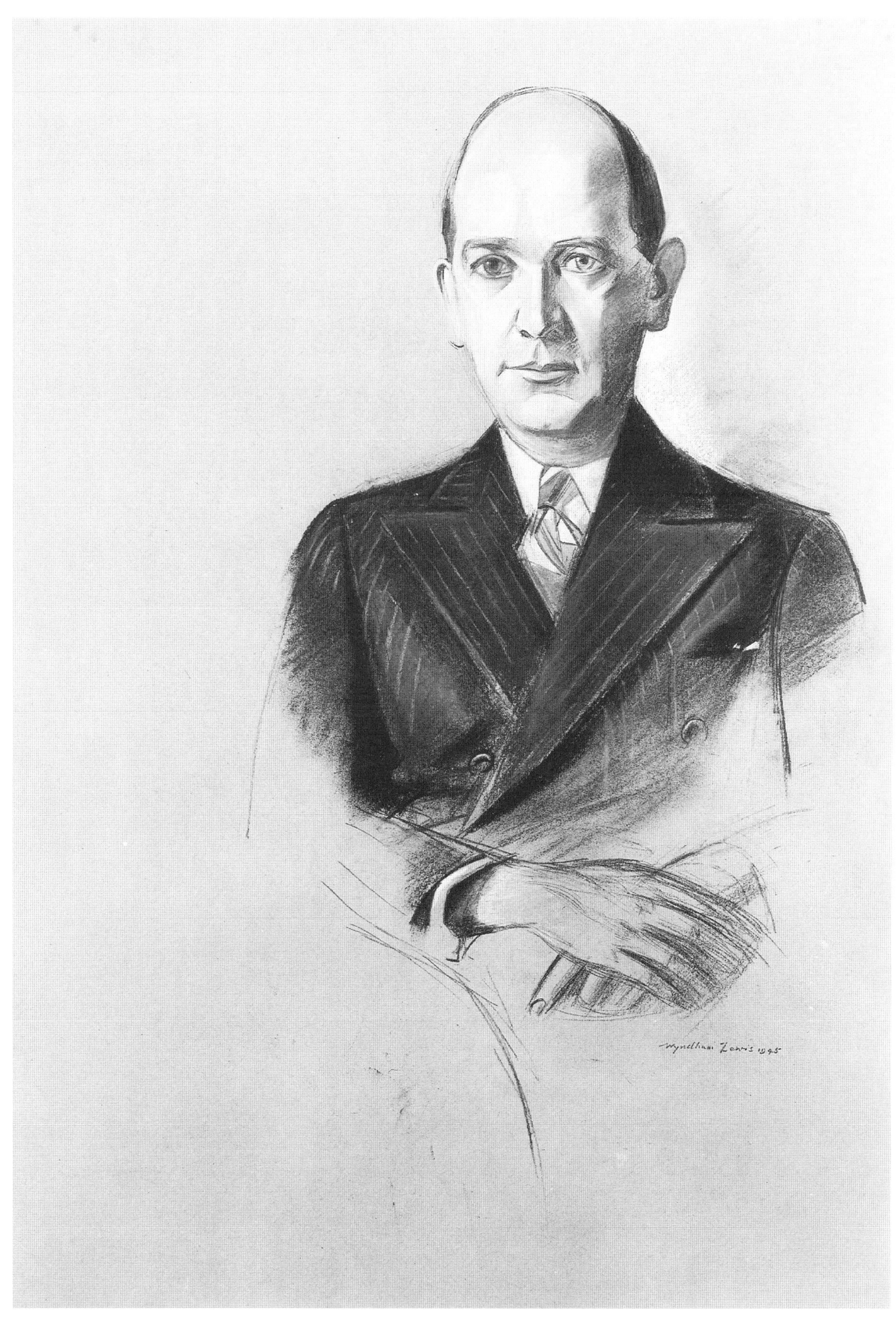
Wyndham Lewis 1945

While Windsor could not boast a vibrant art scene during the early 1940s, Detroit, across the river, being much larger and more prosperous, offered several outlets for Lewis's creative energies, as well as useful contacts. In 1945 he made a chalk portrait of William R. Valentiner (fig. 39), then director of the Detroit Institute of Arts, whom Lewis likely met on the occasion of his November 1943 lecture on the "Frontiers of Art."[86] Probably in the spring of 1945, Lewis drew two chalk portraits of John Stoughton Newberry, one in business attire, the other in American Red Cross uniform (nos. 86-87). The latter portrait records Newberry's service as assistant field director in the American Red Cross, with which he remained on domestic duty until the end of the war; the former was probably executed at the sitter's residence in Grosse Point Farms, Michigan.[87] A native of Detroit whose father was a pioneer lumber merchant and industrialist, Newberry played an influential role in the development of the Detroit Institute of Arts. A graduate of Harvard College in 1933 and the Courtauld Institute, London in 1935, and a collector of modern prints and drawings, he was appointed honorary curator of the Department of Prints and Drawings of the D.I.A., and in 1946 became curator of Graphic Arts. From 1939 to 1963 he served the gallery as leader of the Friends of Modern Art and trustee of the Founders' Society. Despite his power and influence, however, Newberry was unable or unwilling to supply Lewis with further commissions or arrange for the purchase of his work by the D.I.A.

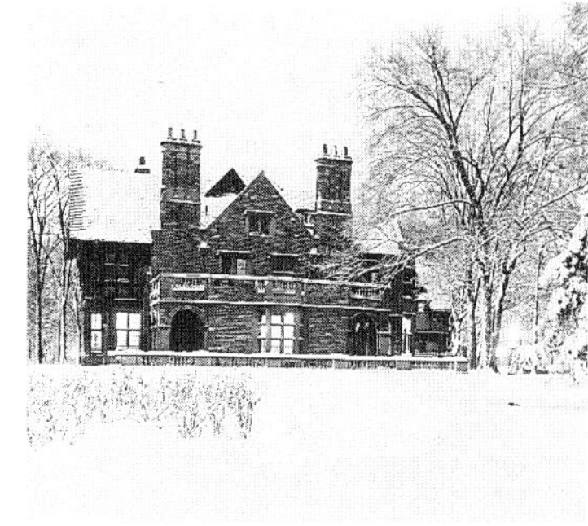

Fig. 38 Willistead Manor, Willistead Park, Windsor, c. 1965 (location of Art Gallery of Windsor until 1974). Photograph: Art Gallery of Windsor.

ALSO IN 1945, as the global conflict was drawing to the close with the promise of an Allied victory, Lewis turned his attention once more to wartime themes. In a lecture given at the University of Michigan, Ann Arbor, on 7 March, and at Michigan State University in East Lansing on 9 March, he compared the views of Ernest Hemingway and Leo Tolstoy on the topic of war.[88] However, in the last of his Canadian lectures, delivered on 14 March 1944 at the Rankin Hotel, Chatham, (a small southwestern Ontario city to the northeast of Windsor), he once more tackled the problem of how to define beauty and ugliness in art. As in his Assumption College lectures, Lewis was concerned with the use of subjective terminology in evaluating the success of a work of art:

> There is nothing in the world that is more productive of misunderstanding than the concept of BEAUTY. The artist, in the nature of things[,] stands at the very centre of this controversy.... A notorious cause of misunderstanding is that people think that a picture (an image) is identified with life (with the original of the image). They look at a painting of a landscape and say "it is pretty" or, "it is ugly", and they think that these two acts of valuation are identical. They regard the landscape, and the painting of the landscape, as upon the same footing, as objects external to themselves.... The paint, or clay, is not an equivalent. The medium as we call it (the paint, or the chalk or the clay) is itself an object in nature: and its beauty—or the reverse—is a different beauty to that of the other object selected for transcription.... The problem of beauty is so difficult, not because it is intrinsically difficult—but because questions of beauty and ugliness, attractiveness and unattractiveness, emotionally, play such an important role in human life.[89]

THAT LEWIS WAS ABLE to contemplate matters of aesthetics in the face of his own impending unemployment and insolvency is a testimony to his iron nerve and professionalism. The façade cracked, however, when his last portrait commission in the United States ended in failure. E.P. Richardson of the Detroit Institute of Arts explained to Jeffrey Meyers that his institution was unable to help Lewis, having "absolutely no money for purchases":

> We were dependent on gifts. Nothing was more out of fashion than a modern English artist in those days and people thoroughly disliked Lewis' work. At the end of his stay, Dr. Valentiner, the director of the museum, persuaded young Mrs. Henry Ford II to have her portrait done by Lewis in colored chalks, hoping that her example would lead to other commissions. When the portrait was done, the Fords had some friends and the Lewises together for an evening to see the portrait. Lewis came into my office early the next morning in great agitation. 'It was a complete failure. Nothing could be more so. There is nothing to do but get out—go somewhere.' Where? He was penniless. The job

> at Assumption was over. Could I raise some money to get them to Ottawa? Malcolm MacDonald was governor-general [i.e. British High Commissioner] and an old friend, who would see Lewis cared for until he could get home and make a fresh start.
>
> I had a hard time finding enough money to pay the Lewises' trainfare to Ottawa. I know Lewis thought I should have found more but I had put in all I could afford my self to make up what I gave him. That was the last of Wyndham Lewis in Detroit and in our lives.[90]

Having become totally frustrated by his inability to find steady employment and in fear of the future, Lewis in May 1945 moved his base of operations to Ottawa, where he and his wife remained for the next two months. It is not known why they took this step, but, as E.P. Richardson noted, Lewis's friend Malcolm MacDonald was there to assist him in his pursuit of portrait commissions and loans. The difficulties the Lewises experienced in locating an available apartment in Ottawa resulted in their being forced to book a room in the expensive Lord Elgin Hotel—the last of their dubious "royal" (or at least "aristocratic") addresses in Canada—until the war ended.[91] To his chagrin, Lewis found that options and opportunities were even scarcer in Ottawa than elsewhere,[92] and consequently he had to rely almost entirely on the generosity and forbearance of the British High Commissioner, to whom he owed the commission for his sole official wartime painting, *A Canadian War Factory*. Their friendship extended far beyond the complex trans-Atlantic negotiations for this work, ranging from their correspondence and the advice given by MacDonald to Lewis on his essay "Canadian Nature and Its Painters", to the diplomat's absorption, after the war, of Lewis's debt of six years' back rent on his London studio and apartment.[93] MacDonald also shared Lewis's interest in the Canadian sub-Arctic and Arctic regions, as manifested by his book *Down North* (Toronto, 1945), the dustjacket of which reproduces a painting by A.Y. Jackson of a radium mine on Great Bear Lake. Yet MacDonald's love of Canada had grown in spite of an initial reluctance to accept his post, which he had phrased in terms similar to Lewis's at the outset of his own removal from England to the New World: "But you are condemning me to exile", he had said to Winston Churchill on hearing of his appointment in February 1941, "All the lights will be on in Ottawa and I shall yearn for the dark of London."[94] Soon enough MacDonald would be rhapsodizing about the Northern Lights.

As a tribute to his benefactor, Lewis executed a portrait of MacDonald shortly before his own return to London (1945; no. 90). Although probably unfinished, as is suggested by the sketchy treatment of the sitter's clothing and of his lower lip, this drawing is an extremely sensitive rendering of an intelligent face. *Portrait of Malcolm MacDonald* provides ample insight into the character of this sympathetic and patient gentleman, especially through the rendering of the sitter's eyes, the treatment of which contrasts sharply with the monocular, minimalist vision Lewis accorded to Marshall McLuhan. At a time when the artist was beginning to be confronted with the spectre of his own imminent blindness, such concentration on the organ of sight is an index of the degree to which he admired, identified with, and perhaps envied this "exiled" but reconciled compatriot.

During the first week of August 1945 Lewis and his wife, having borrowed $725 from MacDonald for their fare home, sailed for England on the *Strathden*, the first passenger ship out of Canada, returning to their flat in London's Notting Hill. There the "lonely old volcano" would remain, blind after 1949 but still untiringly active and unregenerately the Outsider and the Enemy, until his death in March 1957.

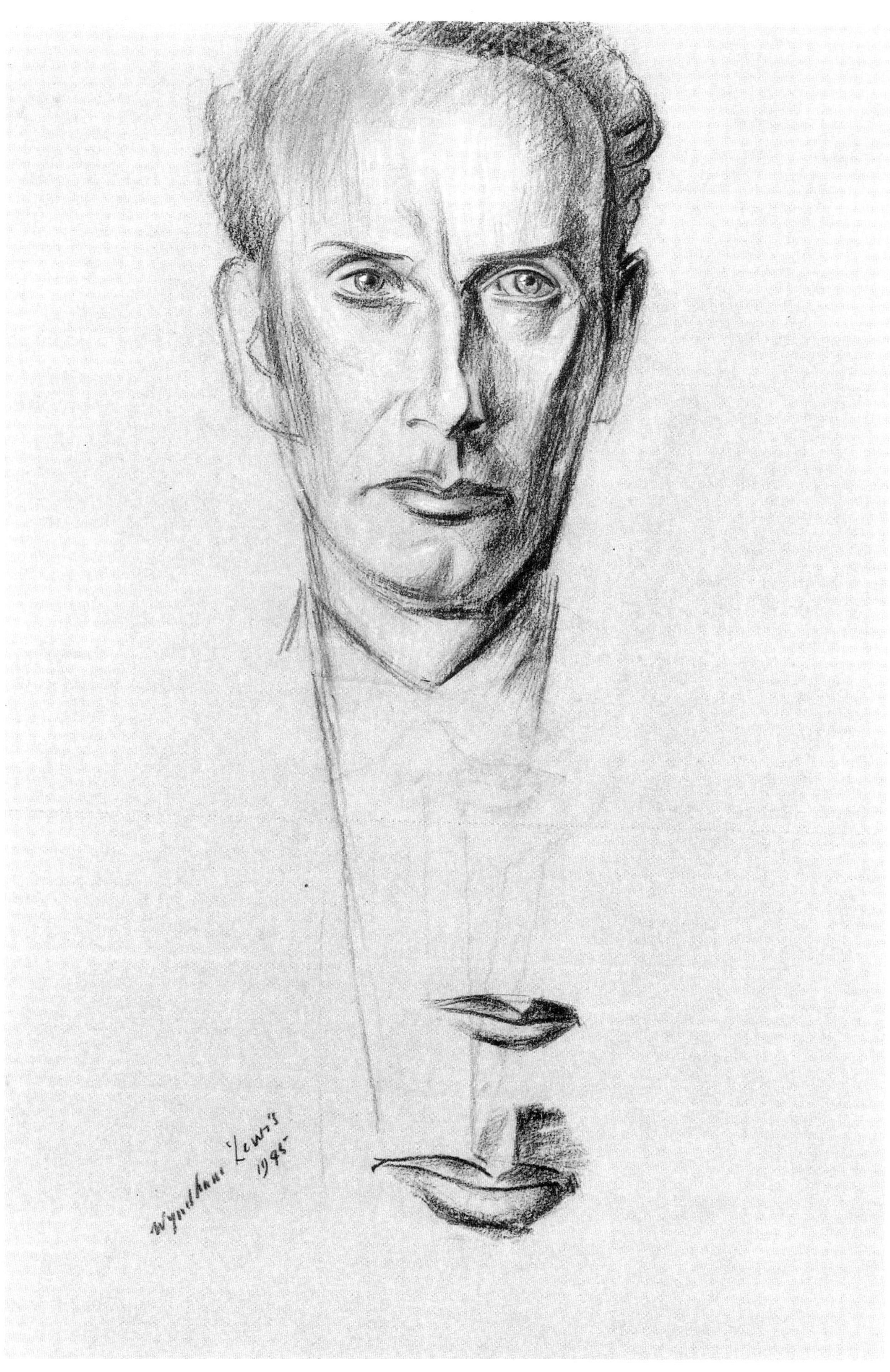
Wyndham Lewis
1945

Conclusion

"*Outsidedness* is to be where the light is."
—Wyndham Lewis, *Rude Assignment* (1950).

Opposite page:
No. 90 *Portrait of Malcolm MacDonald,* 1945, coloured chalks on paper (36.4 x 26.6 cm), M 1072. National Portrait Gallery, London, England.

MALCOLM MACDONALD WAS AMONG the few people Lewis met in Canada with whom he did not end up in serious conflict. Hesitant as he was to admit his fondness for anyone, Lewis did express as well some affection for a few non-threatening individuals like Father Stan Murphy and Douglas Duncan. That he missed Duncan's company after moving to Windsor in 1943 is suggested by this joking admonition on a note appended to a change-of-address form: "Listen big boy. If you don't write more often I shall have you excommunicated."[1]

Such rare expressions of affection for people close to him show a private, emotional side of Lewis that he rarely revealed, and then only in gruff, tough-guy terms. Although he would have hesitated to reveal this more tender and amicable aspect in public, especially to potential enemies, to do so in private, and under controlled circumstances, was clearly a personal need. His time in Canada had much of the tenor of his earlier years in Britain, during which he hungered for ad-mission into the inner circles of high society and the artistic élite, only to reject them once he had succeeded in achieving his goal. Despite Lewis's persistent claim to have been *persona non grata* during his North American exile, the extensive range of contacts available to him in Toronto gives the lie to his complaints about being marginalized and made to feel like a total outsider. As his biographer Jeffrey Meyers has observed, "If his career in Canada was a failure, I think it was the result of a rather perverse determination to make it so."[2]

Lewis's preoccupation with his own sense of isolation and constant feeling of being on the outside characterized his entire life and career. The image he had cultivated, that of "the Enemy," can be dated to the Vorticist era (though one assumes that he must have adopted it as far back as his days at Rugby School). Lewis had launched his reputation by taking on the Italian Futurists and their leader, Marinetti, in *Blast* and elsewhere, then engaged in a running battle with the Bloomsbury group and their supporters in London during the early 'teens, renewing the conflict in 1930 with the publication of *The Apes of God,* in which he also lampooned his former friends the Sitwell siblings and the poet Stephen Spender. He would go on to antagonize the British Left and Right alike in *The Art of Being Ruled* (1926) and subsequent political books and pamphlets; to denounce the time-obsession of Ezra Pound, James Joyce, Marcel Proust and Gertrude Stein in *Time and Western Man* (1927); to anatomize the "youth cult" in *The Doom of Youth* (1932); to attack the inflated reputations of such influential figures as Ernest Hemingway, Virginia Woolf and James Joyce in *Men Without Art* (1934); and, in his last decade, to respond to George Orwell's irresponsible description of him as a pro-Stalinist in his 1952 counterblast, *The Writer and the Absolute.* As B.W. Powe explains,

> He became the Enemy in order to know the enemy. His essays, novels, polemics, poems and plays form a single inquiry into the murderous currents of the mass-age. But for him to find the enemies of life, he had to devise a way of seeing them. He made a method. Which is: characterize the atmosphere of your time, consciously exaggerate objects of attention so that they become grotesque and therefore laughable. (Laughter insures a measure of distance.) Confront how we exist in cultural-political arenas and our lack of awareness of that environment's impact. Only a slave dances to the jerk of the invisible strings. Only a slave lines up to be slaughtered without asking why.[3]

Jeffrey Meyers attempted to set Lewis's famous quarrelsomeness and iconoclasm in the context of his opposition to the "Time-philosophy" of the modernist movement in and of which he was both an leading player and a lone adversary:

> Lewis took the central unifying symbol of all aspects of contemporary thought that he opposed: romanticism, impressionism, relativism, subjectivity, and the Freudian emphasis on the unconscious. He rejected these tendencies more for aesthetic than for philosophical reasons, and felt these false and sloppy habits of thought were inimical to serious art. This could be created only through classicism, rational thought, pure style, objective presentation and, in the plastic arts, hard line and clear contour.[4]

Lewis "wanted to be liberated from all associations and restraints, and felt he could forge ahead only after he had dropped the intellectual ballast of the past."[5] If progress meant rejecting former friends and colleagues, neglecting parental duties and repudiating ancestral allegiances, so be it; the original prophet of the Global Village and the advocate of world government as a guarantor of universal peace saw no contradiction in making enemies in order to retain his independence as the Enemy. Nor did his wartime retirement to a foreign country in which he expected to be welcomed on his own merits induce a change of heart or an alteration of behaviour: Lewis would not cease to be Lewis for anyone.

That Lewis willingly and wittingly assumed the role of the Outsider is evident in practically every move he made in Canada, but, he assured Marshall McLuhan, the blame for his isolation lay not with himself but with the size of the pond in which he sought to play the large fish. "In a small community where everybody knows everybody else, and one is an outsider, intrigues of the most moronic kind are bound to blow up...." As if by way of demonstrating the very pettiness against which he raged, he then insisted that his would-be benefactor would "stop posing as a friend and 'admirer' of Mr. Lewis, either in this locality or in areas to the south."[6]

For Lewis, the true artist must be both a genius and an enemy of society—an index of the extent to which, despite his protests to the contrary, he was a product and exemplar of the modernist ethos. A long list of painters, writers and thinkers adopted this oppositional, *poète maudit* persona, including such nineteenth-century figures as Lord Byron, Edgar Allan Poe, Charles Baudelaire and, perhaps most significantly, James McNeill Whistler, whose *The Gentle Art of Making Enemies* delighted Lewis.[7] Marshall McLuhan insisted that, despite his association with post-Romantic modernism,

> Lewis's theory of art and communication is a traditional one. The hero, the genius, is a god-intoxicated man. He communes with the noumenal world. And the contrast of this knowledge with the misery of the human condition constitutes his dementia or madness.... The hero, in short, is, as such, a type of mania from above and a type of misery as well as of the grandeur of the human condition.... If "the world of the 'pure present' of the Classical Ages is obviously the world that is born and dies every moment," it is clear that it is such a world that Lewis seeks to arrest in his paintings (and novels).[8]

In many ways, being on the outside was for Lewis a pre-requisite for the sustenance of creative activity and perhaps even of existence itself. The Creation Myth and Crucifixion series and related imaginative pictures, produced when Lewis was at the most depressed of his emotional states in Canada, attests to the power and inner strength that he could find in times of personal distress. It is interesting to note that those periods when Lewis was the most content with his lot, such as his year-long residence in Windsor, did not result in any significant artistic production, save for such occasional works as *Portrait of the Artist's Wife* and *Landscape* (also known as *Creation Myth*).

In retrospect, Lewis's Canadian sojourn can be seen as a valuable if chastening experience, not only for the protagonist of this (mis)adventure but for critics and art historians, thanks to the ways in which it helped to define his shifting position *vis-à-vis* the modernist tradition, and also for the very important reason that the ordeal of finding himself a has-been in the New World fundamentally shook up a number of his conservative beliefs and caused him to question certain ingrained assumptions. One of these was his unrealistic (though understandable) expectation that his stature as a major British artist, writer and intellectual would accord him the respect and deference that he had come to think of as his due—despite the drastic waning of his international reputation. By remaining in North America for this extensive period, Lewis was forced to confront his very pronounced Englishness, with all its attendant biases, class complexes and presumptions, and to realize how much more British he was than North American, despite his Canadian and American roots. His alienness—and sense of alienation—were brought home to him when, as Marshall McLuhan recalled, he heard his own extremely English accent on a recording.[9] Lewis made his own observations on this matter when he commented, "It is far easier (experience seems to me to show) to bring an American to England, than to transplant an Englishman to America."[10] But he was liberal-minded enough to recognize, and acknowledge, that the dislocation had wrenched him out of his shell and exposed himself to an awareness that, in the modern age of mass communications and unlimited mobility, it was impossible to remain a Little Englander or a desert islander. "If I were asked what my prolonged stay in America has brought me of a tangible sort," he remarked in an unpublished essay, "I should answer that it has taught me a great deal about Europe, of which I was ignorant before I lived on this side of the Atlantic. I am now a much greater authority upon European affairs than I was before I left Europe."[11] Even more positively, he could reflect, on his return to England, that "For my own part—ensuing upon travel in 'those United States' which never seemed to have an end—it will influence everything I think and write henceforth. It has tended to transform me from a good European to an excellent internationalist."[12] No Canadian reading these words can fail to regret that Lewis did not acknowledge that his Canadian experience and acqaintances—in particular his mutually stimulating relationship with Marshall McLuhan—had a similarly revelatory and transformative effect.

The decline that is evident in Lewis's production of imaginative works after his move to Windsor can partly be explained by the fact that a division of attention, between writing and artmaking, is observable elsewhere in his career. As many commentators have suggested had Lewis devoted all his time and energies to working in one medium, one discipline, he would have produced considerably more of a creative and lasting nature than he did.

Although his pictorial output during the Windsor year is small, this comparatively tranquil interlude provided Lewis with the opportunity to research and write major sections of perhaps the most important nonfiction work of his later life, *America and Cosmic Man* (London and Brussels, 1948). This book, which had a profound impact on McLuhan, who described it in a letter to Ezra Pound as "an H-bomb let off in the desert",[13] raises many of the questions that Lewis asked of himself during the war and immediately after. In addition, it reveals how significantly altered were his opinions on race, politics and culture in the aftermath of his disillusionment with the excesses of the far right, as epitomized by Hitlerism, which, like Orwell, he had come to see as being different from Stalinism only in insignificant details. The basis of this self-examination and re-evaluation of society stemmed from his exposure to North American realities, but in particular from the Toronto period of personal crisis, which he subjected to close analysis both in his imaginative works and in his contemporaneous and subsequent writings (most clinically in *Self Condemned*).

Lewis saw his role in Canada as that of advancing the understanding and appreciation of the Anglosaxon heritage (in its greater, non-racial sense). What he discovered, however, was that the North American experience forced him to turn the question back onto himself: who was Lewis, this Canadian-born inveterate Englishman-in-exile? Where, on what grounds, and for what, did he stand? *America and Cosmic Man* is an appropriate example of this switch in viewpoints, enabling him to study aspects of North American society and culture and to relate them to his own global concerns, such as the attainment of a permanent armistice and the shutting down of the arms race, the emergence of the United States as a world leader, and the dissolution of nationalities and nationalisms in the postwar era—an idealistic vision which current events in Europe have rendered both prophetic and perhaps hopelessly naive.

The differences between North America and Britain may seem obvious to us now, but during World War II Canada was still considered by England to be essentially a raw and immature clone or offspring of itself—a loyal and obedient colony, albeit nominally independent thanks to the Statute of Westminster, enacted by the British Parliament in 1931 to recognize the autonomy of the British Dominions. Lewis came to Canada burdened with this familiar delusion. Once in this country, however, he discovered that it differed very greatly from England and from Europe, not only in its social structure, its ethnic makeup, the nature of its institutions, and its concept of nationhood, but in its in some ways perverse attachment to the vast, rugged, outwardly inhospitable vistas of the North, which he learned about through A.Y. Jackson and the paintings of the Group of Seven, and from such books as Bruce Hutchison's *The Unknown Country* (1942) and Malcolm MacDonald's aforementioned *Down North*. Lewis's published and unpublished comments on the Canadian character and the forces that shaped it had their counterparts, of course, in the observations of earlier British immigrants and visitors such as Susanna Moodie, in her *Roughing it in the Bush*, and by the many military topographers and explorers who depicted Canadian geography in watercolours and words. Nonetheless, no British observer before or perhaps after him, with the possible exception of his West Coast contemporary Malcolm Lowry, has exhibited the breadth of interest or perspective that Lewis did, bridging his interests in art and literature with equally intensive considerations of politics, history, philosophy and social issues.

Perhaps one of the most enduringly crucial ideas that Lewis explored during his Canadian years was that of the future role of mass electronic communications, as represented by television, radio and the telephone. The telecommunications media have become so absorbed into our everyday lives that we take their all-pervasive, transformative presence for granted, rather than regarding them as unique technical phenomena, as they once were viewed. Lewis's insightful prediction that the proliferation of such devices would render both the written word and visual art—easel painting in particular—next to redundant is, in many ways, an anticipation of the theories of Marshall McLuhan, who in 1962 declared that "Television has completely altered our attitude toward space. We are no longer content with pictorial space, with a merely visual abstract, uniformly patterned, enclosed space. Instead, we are tending toward sculptural space."[14] Lewis's preoccupations also foreshadow present-day artistic and critical concerns, as does his insistence that art must reflect and respond to the concerns of contemporary society.[15] (At the same time, however, he continued to warn against artists becoming implicated in the political turmoils of the passing moment rather than dedicating themselves to the demands and obligations of their ancient calling.) Lewis's forecasts of the diminishing role of abstraction in art were not to be borne out, however, at least for several decades. On the other hand, his questioning of the idea of progress as a necessary and inevitable good anticipated a debate that was central in the west during the 1960s, coming to a head during the Vietnam war.

Had Lewis not cast his lot with North America in 1939, he may never have been capable of so acute a scrutiny of the times in which he lived as he delivered himself of in *America and Cosmic Man* and *Self Condemned*. Whether Lewis was right in all his observations is not so relevant as the fact that he continued to hold his own as a major modern thinker and as a mirror of the complexity and contradictions of the war and immediate postwar years. It is to such figures that we, with contemporary eyes, look back to gain perspective on how our own experiences compare and contrast with those of the recent and remote past.

Although Lewis did not leave much of an impression on the artistic community of Windsor (or indeed of Toronto), he is perhaps the most important, internationally recognized artist to have lived and worked in southwestern Ontario to date. His brief tenure at Assumption College left only a limited legacy, and despite the fact that he had virtually no impact on Windsor's cultural growth, the work that Lewis began to research and draught during and immediately after his stay still has considerable resonance.

It is also interesting to note that, in formulating his proposals for global harmony and co-operation, Lewis argued that Canada should join the United States—a concept that takes on an ironic shading in the light of the North American Free Trade Agreement, not to mention Canada's endless constitutional wranglings, the obstacles being thrown in the way of achieving a European confederation, the elusiveness of a peace settlement in the Middle East, and the chaos resulting from the breaking apart of the former Soviet empire.

On the matter of the role of the artist in modern post-industrial society, Lewis was perceptive in foreseeing the future of the state's increasing involvement in both the promotion and the institutionalizing of culture. Although he might have approved of the forming of The Canada Council and its provincial and municipal counterparts to assist artists and promote cultural awareness, Lewis was suspicious of governmentally driven agencies that demanded the silencing of critical voices in exchange for financial security.[16] His vociferously expressed ambivalence about matters that appear either to have been resolved long ago, or of which the intelligentsia are hesitant to speak, remains salutory in a time of officially prescribed political correctitude, self-imposed censorship, and the surrender of artistic integrity to the dictatorship of the marketplace. So, of course, does his challenge to the complacency, philistinism and chauvinism that he saw as standing in the way of Canada's national maturation.

Lewis's primary allegiance was to the rights and freedoms of the individual imagination. His unwavering dedication to this fundamental force is the principal reason why he and his diverse, sometimes difficult, sometimes unwielding, sometimes disturbing works continue to be read, studied, analysed, argued over and—as we hope this exhibition will give ample occasion for—enjoyed to this day.

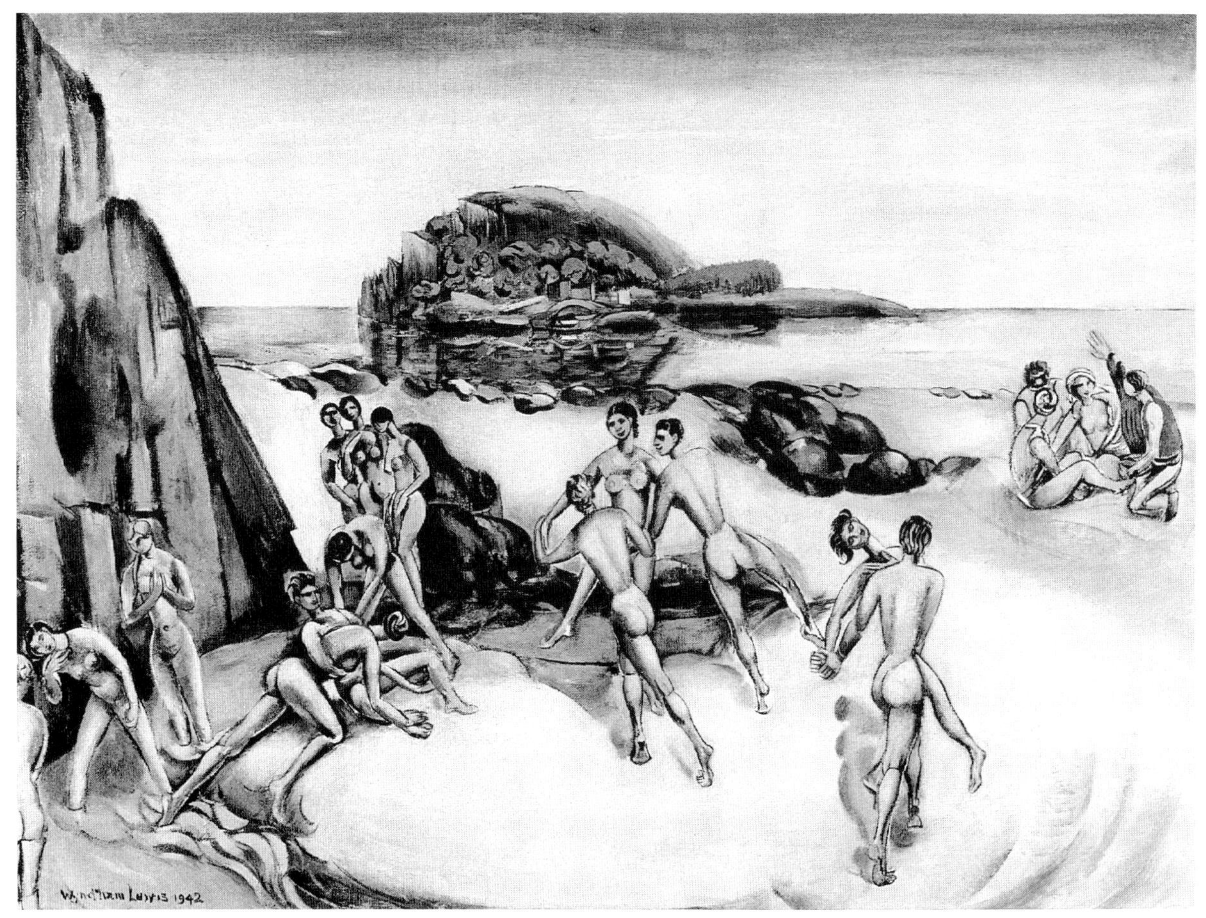

No. 48 *The Island*, 1942, oil on canvas (56.0 x 78.5 cm), M P104. Santa Barbara Museum of Art. (Reproduced in colour on back cover.)

"Magical Presences in a Magic Place": From *Homage to Etty* to *The Island*

ROBERT STACEY

"Spy out what's half-there, the page under the page,
Never demand the integral, never completion:
Always what is fragmentary, the presage...."
— Wyndham Lewis, *One-Way Song* (1933).

IN A DRAUGHT OF A LETTER dated 1 July 1942, an embittered and embattled Wyndham Lewis, writing from his "twenty-five feet by twelve" bunker in the Tudor Hotel, made a direct appeal for support to his principal Toronto patron, J.S. McLean. Although his first object was to secure funds to pay for his return passage to England, a more pressing concern was his immediate survival:

> You are the only person in Ontario, now that Vincent Massey has left, who is interested in art of an intelligent type who has a comprehensive collection. I have worked some time in this country now: and work *in* a country belongs to it in some measure. There is an oil painting down at the Picture Loan I should like you to have a look at: a subject-picture, on the lines of some of the watercolours and drawings you have seen. I have told [Douglas] Duncan if you like it to let you have it for anything he sees fit. He knows my circumstances: I owe two months rent at this hotel and the months of July and August are going to be fearfully painful and difficult.

Evidently feeling that the tone of this *cri de coeur* was not quite right, Lewis scratched out the paragraph and began anew: "A largish oil painting of mine is at the Picture-loan which I would like you to see. I worked on it a long time; it is the best I have done here. Further, there is a new set of drawings; these from life. You could pick [what] you liked of them to liquidate our last year's debt. And if you like the oil I have told Duncan to let you have it for whatever he sees fit."[1]

The "largish oil painting", which the artist described in a deleted passage in this letter as a "piece of inventive picture making", is his cryptic oil-on-canvas *The Island*, completed in 1942 and arguably his last masterpiece. Despite his urgent plea to McLean, the picture did not find its way into this enlightened entrepreneur's private or corporate collection, remaining instead in the hands of Lewis's long-suffering dealer, Douglas M. Duncan, the proprietor of the Picture Loan Gallery, then the most advanced such facility in Toronto. Whether Duncan—the model for the cruelly caricatured Cedric Furbish in Lewis's semi-autobiographical novel, *Self Condemned*—purchased the work from the painter or accepted it in repayment of his several debts to him is unrecorded; a generous benefactor but a disorganized businessman, "DMD" sometimes failed to distinguish between his own collection and the pictures that belonged to the artists he represented and supported. The subsequent fate of *The Island* is related in the penultimate section of this essay.

That so signal an achievement as this virtually unknown but important canvas should have received so little critical attention, either during the artist's lifetime or thereafter, is less surprising when the almost total obscurity suffered by most of Lewis's *oeuvre* of the first half of the 1940s is considered. Charles Handley-Read, who reproduced only one watercolour from the North American period in his 1951 monograph, *The Art of Wyndham Lewis*—*Allégresse Aquatique*, of 1941 (no. 31)—provides a hint as to one cause of this neglect: "The large body of work then produced is now widely distributed among private collectors, Colleges, Museums and Art Galleries. Very few examples have so far been seen in England."[2] Secondly, there has been a tendency to dismiss Lewis's production from the years of his Canadian "exile" on the strength of his own vituperative comments about these five frustrating years. Although Jane Farringon toes the standard line about his "disastrous sojourn in America and Canada" being artistically fallow, she does, however, acknowledge that "Imaginative work from this period becomes even more fantastic and introspective."[3] And it is the"imaginative work"—a singular and particular component of it—that concerns us here.

In his second volume of autobiography, *Rude Assignment*, Lewis himself alludes to this aspect of his output and to its internal cohesiveness, remarking that, "In a large and fairly homogeneous group produced in 1941-2 and the paintings and drawings, done between 1934 and 1938 (the major part seen in a one-man show at the Leicester Galleries, London [in December 1937]) I have varied between realist fantasies and semi-abstraction. The satiric realism of 'Beach Babies', and the semi-abstract '[One of the] Stations of the Dead'[1933; M P50],...or 'Stage Scene' [i.e. *Players upon a Stage* (1936-37; M P69)], both appeared in the same exhibition."[4] The difference is that the 1941-42 series is characterized by what could be described as "lyrical" rather than, or as well as, "satiric," the governing tenor the privately fanciful or the imaginative rather than the realistic. In these hermetic works this most political of writers exercised his artist's license to draw and paint according to the dictates of the imagination rather than of the conscience or the didactic tendency that drove his journalism and much of his fiction. In an era in which art that is not political (or at least "politically correct") is proscribed as frivolous and irresponsible, such independence seems doubly courageous and salutory, especially considering the illiberal, con-formist climate in which it made its stand.

In *Wyndham Lewis: Paintings and Drawings*, Walter Michel writes that the drawings of the 1940s, and in particular those he designates the "Toronto drawings,"

> present us with another of the several worlds of Lewis's creatures. Unprogrammable in style and fanciful in theme, they continue to ignore the general current of painting of the day. Light in texture, they remind, within Lewis's *oeuvre*, not so much of the twenties and thirties as of the period before World War I. To be sure, they do not court the abstract with the assurance—which now seems youthful—of that work, but revive its innocence and sense of serious play, transmuted by thirty years of living and working. They are contemplative rather than exuberant, games of the mind, hardly conscious of stylistic categories.[5]

Michel goes on to emphasize the quality of volition and willpower that these otherwise random-seeming visual mind-games manifest:

> To the freedom of the hand and mind, which could at random make a great picture of a witch or a figure falling from a horse, everything was possible. A group of drawings of 1941-2 introduces new and diverse variations on a theme Lewis had drawn many times before: nudes and bathers. They range from a charming, sensuous cycle (inspired by a collection of paintings by [William] Etty, in the house of a Toronto industrialist) to *Allégresse Aquatique* and the two drawings that are on pl. 161, works that are among Lewis's greatest.
>
> His imagination is now more vivid, and lighter and deeper than it had ever been. *Allégresse Aquatique* is grey, blue and green, dotted with red heads of swimmers, like corks bobbing upon the water. But, with its enigmatic and playful figures and setting in a place where the earth and the sky almost touch, it is also a microcosm. Here, as in the two drawings on pl. 161, the spatial arrangement is a key to the meaning. *Bathing Women* [no. 29], by the easy grace with which its two bathers fit into a landscape that enfolds them, conveys a feeling of harmony between man and nature; and *Two Women on a Beach* [no. 30] takes this idea further, fusing its figures in the setting.[6]

Not mentioned here by Michel, though surely included by him in this description, is Lewis's *The Island* (no. 48)—the culmination, artistically if not chronologically, of the Toronto "cycle."

Before I proceed to an examination of these rarely seen and still more infrequently discussed pictures, I would like to establish, if possible, the identify of the unnamed "Toronto industrialist" whose collection provided Lewis with the *donné* for these magically real (and really magical) images. As is so often the case with Lewis mysteries, a combination of the deductive and inductive methods is called for, the evidence being circumstantial and often conflicting, and the solution by no means conclusive. That Lewis intended matters to be so is entirely in keeping with what we know about his character, and with his philosophy of art.

ON 3 JUNE 1941 Lewis received an encouraging note from J.S. McLean, who that year had commissioned four portraits from the artist, including one of himself, the latter for hanging at the head office of his privately owned firm, Canada Packers Ltd. (see nos. 2, 4-5). As none of these likenesses was considered, at the time, to be particularly successful, McLean perhaps had designs of palming off the resolute non-flatterer on a fellow victim, as the letter suggests:

> I have another prospective subject for you, in the person of Sir James Dunn.Sir James is a Canadian who has spent most of the last 20 or 30 years in England. His business is finance, and in some way he seems to have control of the Algoma Steel Corporation at Sault Ste. Marie, Ontario.

> About two weeks ago he telephoned me to ask whether he might have a look at the Portrait. I, of course, said 'yes' and he accordingly came to the Office. After looking at the Portrait he stated:—
>
> That he was thinking of having a Portrait done.
>
> That he was familiar with your reputation as a Painter and with your books, and he would like to discuss with you the matter of doing a portrait for him.[7]

McLean advised Lewis that he could reach Dunn at the Toronto offices of the Algoma Steel Corp., at 25 King St. W., in the Canadian Bank of Commerce tower. Lewis quickly replied, expressing his delight at hearing of "Sir James Dunn's visit":

> It was exceedingly good news that Sir James Dunn is interested in the portrait and would like something done himself; and I have to thank you for your kindness in showing him the picture and, I am sure, encouraging him in his desire to try his luck in the sitter's chair. Augustus John was very friendly with Dunn and his family (I seem to remember that they were neighbours in Hampshire). I will immediately write him at the address you mention. I will let you know what happens.[8]

No doubt Lewis did a little homework before taking up McLean's suggestion. He would have discovered from the available references that Dunn—described even before his death in 1956 as "The last of the millionaires"—was born in 1874 at St. Peter's Village, Bathurst, New Brunswick; was educated at Dalhousie University, Halifax; and, after being admitted to the bar and joining the Montreal legal firm of J.M. Greenshields in 1900, and becoming a member of the Montreal Stock Exchange in 1902, set up the London office of the American stock promoter, F.S. Pearson, in 1905. There, he quickly achieved prominence as a financier, arbitrageur and underwriter of Canadian utilities and industries. (As Lewis remarked in an undated essay, "Canada *exports* business talent, as can be seen in the case of Lord Beaverbrook and Sir James Dunn. It does not seem to import anything of that kind."[9]) Dunn's wartime services to his adoptive country earned him a baronetcy in 1921, and in 1926 he crowned his success by marrying his second wife, Irene, Lady Queensberry. In 1935, with an assist from C.D. Howe among other powerful friends, he became president, chairman and owner of the then-bankrupt Algoma Steel Company, based in Sault Ste. Marie, Ontario, and set about putting the firm on a sound business footing. The outbreak of hostilities in 1939 brought him back to his native North America, and from then until his death in 1956 he divided his time between "the Soo," Toronto, New York, and his two summer residences in New Brunswick.

Dunn's rise to prominence had been interrupted by a number of serious setbacks, the first of which had occurred in 1913, when his business partner, Louis Fischer, defaulted and fled England, leaving behind enormous debts and damaging Dunn's credit in the City of London. This disaster forced him to disperse the large art collection that he had built up at the urging of an older Canadian connoisseur, Sir William Van Horne. Through Knoedlers, the New York dealer, he disposed of fourteen old and modern masters, including a Holbein, a Memling, a Bronzino, a Gainsborough, three Goyas, a Ruysdael, and an El Greco. Dunn also sold several paintings to Henry Clay Frick, among them the top half of Manet's *The Bullfight*, which the artist had cut in two after its return from the Paris Salon in 1864. Dunn's biographer and one-time business partner, Max Aitken, Lord Beaverbrook, a fellow New Brunswicker who, too, had made good in England, sympathized with his loss:

> I know what sadness overwhelmed him as he took down from the walls of his home one after another of these pictures he treasured. But it was never his way to grieve over what could not be remedied. While he dispersed that wonderful first collection, James Dunn resolved that one day he would buy even finer pictures. His fancy turned for a time to the work of contemporary artists, and at the end of the war he began once more to buy.
>
> In the early days of his financial recovery after the Fischer default, his first choice may have been a picture named "Dorelia" painted by Augustus John....
>
> Another artist to benefit from Dunn's lavish patronage was Sir William Orpen, who was directed to paint seventeen portraits of famous politicians and generals attending the Versailles Peace Conference....
>
> Then came a period when Dunn bought many of Sir Alfred Munning's pictures. This phase was short-lived, because Dunn met [Walter] Sickert and was immediately drawn to this brilliant man....

By 1932 in the depth of the depression,...Sickert was in low estate, for few people could afford to buy paintings.

Dunn, anxious to help so distinguished an artist,...agreed to buy twelve paintings. Dunn could choose the subjects himself. He wanted twelve portraits of his friends.... There was to be one portrait of Lord Greenwood, one of Lord Castlerosse, and three of James, one of Christofor, then his secretary and afterwards his third wife [and, following the death of Dunn, the wife of Lord Beaverbrook], and one of me....[10]

Wyndham Lewis had been preceded by John and Orpen at the Slade School of Art, and he knew Sickert well through his participation in the 1911 and 1912 exhibitions of the Camden Town Group; although their estimation of one another waxed and waned, Lewis did not forget that the senior artist had called him "the greatest portrait painter of this, or any other, time."[11] As is recorded in *Blasting and Bombardiering*, it was Orpen who, during a chance meeting at Cassell in 1917, had first given Lewis the idea of escaping from the trenches by becoming an official war artist. This "salvation" had been made possible by the recommendation of the London art critic P.G. Konody, then acting as advisor to the head of the Canadian War Records Office, Lord Beaverbrook, who would go on to purchase his *The Mud Clinic* of 1937 and subsequently present it to the Beaverbrook Art Gallery. As we shall see, Beaverbrook, *via* Dunn, had an indirect influence on the direction Lewis's non-commissioned, imaginative work was to take in the early1940s.

"James's love of pictures certainly extended to a love of being portrayed", Beaverbrook somewhat caustically observed of his boyhood friend. Dunn "enjoyed contacts with painters and admired their special talents. Conversations with artists always fascinated him. And these diversions gave him relief from the stresses and strains of his eventful and exciting business activities."[12] Beaverbrook had played a key role in steering Dunn toward certain artists and schools of art after his friend had resumed collecting, but regretted that he "never took an interest in Canadian painters."[13] Instead, besides the twentieth- and eighteenth-century British artists he favoured, he was advised by "the Beaver" to pick up works of the then-unfashionable Victorian school, which today form the core of the Sir James Dunn Foundation behest to the Beaverbrook Art Gallery, Fredericton, latterly augmented with the acquisitions in this area by Lord and Lady Beaverbrook themselves.[14]

In June 1941 Lewis wrote to Dunn, explaining that he was doing so on J.S. McLean's suggestion, and that the portrait prospect "sounds very interesting."[15] Replying a week later, Dunn remarked that he had "very impressed" by the artists's "very direct portrait of Stanley McLean", and promised that "if I can see my way to afford (in these days when taxes take everything) having a portrait painted I will ask you to do it."[16] Unwilling to leave matters hanging, Lewis wrote on 4 July to assure Dunn that "what I want is to be at work, and I am satisfied with much more modest sums than an artist is accustomed to expect in England. I am not so well known on this side of the water as the other. To be specific, I will paint a portrait for anything from 700 to 1000 dollars."[17] Lewis was prepared to give up his Toronto flat and move to Montreal if necessary to carry out the commission, but although Dunn replied with a request that Lewis pay him a visit at his Toronto office, no immediate order to begin work was given. Beleaguered by continuing problems at Algoma Steel, Dunn suffered an attack of coronary thrombosis at the end of July 1941 while staying at the house of a business friend, J.P. Bickell.[18] He was closely attended in his illness by his secretary, Miss Marcia Christophorides, who took over effective control of Dunn's affairs until he recuperated (and, a year later, became the third wife of her employer). Thus it was with Christofor, as she was called, that Lewis dealt when, at the end of the first week of August 1941, he tried to contact Dunn, and it was she who outlined to him Sir James's plan of an advertisement for Algoma Steel. Writing to this potential patron in what was clearly desperation, Lewis bluntly explained that

> there is a wolf at the door, which has to be kept away. If very soon I dont shoo it away, it will devour me. I do not have to tell you how, even in his home town, an artist is always apt to have a wolf on his doorstep. But we are in Canada—in the midst of an economic blizzard!
>
> As to a portrait, or portrait-sketch, I *might* do something that pleased you very much. I should like to try. I have had some luck that way.... — But as to the other proposal, I am *quite certain* that I could do a striking poster of your works, that would be of use on the business side. Should we pursue that certainty first, and when you feel in the mood I could try my hand at the portrait afterwards?

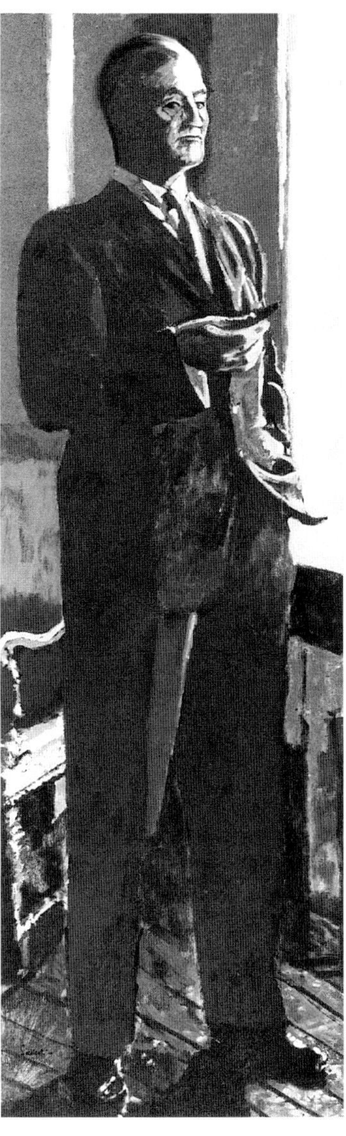

Fig. 40 Walter Richard Sickert (1860-1942): *Sir James Dunn, Bart*, 1934, oil on canvas (118.6 x 61.3 cm). The Beaverbrook Canadian Foundation, the Beaverbrook Art Gallery, Fredericton, N.B.

> I should actually greatly enjoy, for a change, to do something big and bold and striking: and to translate into pictorial terms, in a way to arrest the eye, the power and bustle of a great plant, would be a highly congenial task.
>
> A big group of the executive body of the plant—done boldly and with the required *bravura*—...would also be a work into which one could put a great deal of stuff: conceived as a great-poster-like decoration which would not suffer from reproductions, if necessary upon a mammoth scale.... You dont want some tame, conventional, design....[19]

Perhaps Lewis had in mind something along the lines of the kind of "poster-ish" work he associated with Tom Thomson and the Group of Seven, which he was coming to know through his friendship with A.Y. Jackson. For Lewis, the "mushroom city of Toronto", like its fictive evil twin, Momaco, was basically "vast mining camp"—a bigger, more pretentious version of such industrial frontier towns as Sault Ste. Marie, Sudbury, Kirkland Lake, Timmins or Cobalt, and all its "hundred...millionaires" were connected in some way with the mineral-extraction, refining and manufacturing industries. His almost abject willingness to do pictorial publicity for Dunn may have stemmed not only from impecunity but from his desire to see for himself "the northland"—the subject of his projected autobiographical novel, *Hill 100* (in whose synopsis the above-quoted phrases appear).[20] Both objects, at any rate, were thwarted: no "poster" of, and no visit to, the Algoma Steel works at the Soo seem to have resulted from this overture. As so often happened with Lewis, the "certainty" proved to be nothing of the kind. The "something big and bold and striking" that would eventually come his way was *A Canadian War Factory* (see no. 57), an assignment for which he was recommended to Sir Kenneth Clark by Canadian's High Commissioner in London, Vincent Massey. Ironically, it was the chapter in *America I Presume* (1940) mocking Hart House, the University of Toronto men's facility erected by the Massey family, that had led (or so Lewis believed) to his being shunned by both the high society and the intelligentsia of the city to which the expiry of his U.S. visa had forced him to return. Hence his difficulty in scaring up portrait commissions and the importance of contacts like McLean and Dunn.

The next move in Lewis's campaign was to secure a sitting with Sir James himself (and perhaps as well, his correspondence hints, with the alluring Miss Christophorides). In the second week of September 1941, arrangements were made for Lewis to take the train to Dunn's birthplace, Bathurst, a lumbering, mining, shipbuilding and seaside resort town in northern New Brunswick. A few miles outside of town, Lord Beaverbrook informs us, Dunn maintained a summer establishment "modestly called Dunn's Camp, although the property actually covered more than 10,000 acres, bought from the Provincial Government.... In the woods, he built a substantial house in the Canadian style...looking out upon an long and deep lake." Although "Life at the Camp was very far from fulfilling Dunn's ideal of gracious living,...[n]othing seemed to work properly," and "The food was not good", nonetheless, "Dunn's Camp was a place of friendship, good company, excellent drink and stimulating conversation."[21]

No fan of "primitive" conditions, never an outdoor sketcher, and rarely given to descriptions of local colour, Lewis left few hints as to his reaction to these half-wild, half-tame surroundings. "The landscape of the Maritimes", he declared in his 1946 essay, "Nature's Place in Canadian Culture", "...is scarcely teeming with figures. I have never seen so lonely looking an inhabited place as Bathurst and its neighbourhood."[22] His response was more politic in a letter he sent to his hostess on his return to Toronto: "Brief as my stay was I enjoyed the peace of the woods and the little lake...."[23] In other correspondence, however, he was less complimentary about the trip and its abortive outcome:

> I went down to the Maritimes to the sumptuous 'home' of the magnate to paint there the magnate (if he was well enough) but primarily the manager [a Mr. Rahilly], who was visiting him. But the magnate had a doctor in attendance: and the doctor, after a day or so, said he mustn't sit. The manager hadn't arrived yet. Then the secretary [i.e. Miss Christophorides] informed me that the magnate (who had had a breakdown) was 'trying to run before he could walk' and could not sit for about a month.... So far I have got no elucidation from the bedside of the ailing magnate back in the Maritimes. *And* I have spent a hell of a lot of money on making myself respectable—a new suit, and all other requisites of attire for personal attendance upon the great ones of this bloody earth! (This quite apart from canvases, paints, travelling expenses).[24]

Thus it was that Lewis failed to round out to fifteen the total number of likenesses of himself that Dunn commissioned in his lifetime—a figure that included three from the 1920s and '30s by Augustus John, two from the 1930s by Walter Sickert (fig. 40), and three by Lewis's *bête noire,* Salvator Dalí, painted between 1948 and 1955.

As it happened, it was the lure of another portrait commission that caused Lewis's abrupt departure from Bathurst for Toronto.[25] He was sent packing with the advice that he contact "another big shot": Mitchell Hepburn, the premier of Ontario from 1932 to 1942, whose official portrait Sir James wished to procure as a gift to the province. "Mitch" Hepburn had supported Dunn in his controversial bid for control of Algoma Steel in 1934, and in 1939 had provided the struggling firm with a government subsidy; thus the portrait—had it materialized—would have amounted to a return for favours received. Back in Toronto by late September, Lewis embarked on yet another frantic paper-chase as he strove in vain to track down and arrange a sitting with the elusive politician, who was then in Ottawa for a federal conference.[26] During the next month he tried to set up an appointment for Hepburn to visit his studio to look at his pictures, but nothing appears to have come of this final grasp at a retreating chimera. That same month of October 1941 saw Lewis being diagnosed by an eye-specialist as suffering from glaucoma, and doomed to go blind within six months unless he submitted to an eye operation, or at least underwent major dental work if his rotting teeth turned out to be the cause of the trouble. But, as Lewis himself constantly reminded his correspondents, he lacked the money to pay his rent and the grocer's bills, so the necessary surgery was put off. (At any rate, the total blindness that descended in 1951 was caused not by dental but by a cerebral tumour pressing on the optic nerve, a condition first diagnosed in 1945.)

And so ended yet another of Lewis's portrait farces. Small wonder, then, that the disgruntled painter did not add Dunn's name to those of J.S. McLean and Douglas Duncan as the sole patrons of the fine arts in 1940s Toronto.[27] But it seems that out of this tragicomedy of bad communications and missed connections indirectly came an expected reward, in the form of a revived interest in the human figure in the landscape, and in the unrestrained play of the imagination's inner gaze. The results of this renewal, Lewis claimed in his July 1942 letter to McLean, were "from life", but there is no evidence that he drew or painted from the nude model during his Toronto sojourn. Lewis could have sat in on a life class at the Ontario College of Art, of course, or sketched in a fellow artist's studio, but of such atypical activities we have no record. He may have meant by this remark that his ultimate "model," in the other sense of the word, was the *académie* as practised a century before at the Royal Academy Schools. For as we have seen, part of the remarkable series of works that came from this inward-turning was, again to quote Walter Michel, "inspired by a collection of paintings by Etty, in the house of a Toronto industrialist".

This person definitely was not J.S. McLean, who owned no Ettys, although he purchased several of the drawings in Lewis's "Toronto" cycle.[28] The most likely candidate, however, for the unnamed collector is Sir James Dunn, who in November 1933 purchased, from the London dealer R.E.A. Wilson,[29] six oil paintings by the nineteenth-century British painter of academic and allegorical nudes and historical and mythological subjects, William Etty (1787-1849): *Study (Nude),* dated to the late 1820s (fig. 41), *Nude — Half-Length* (c. 1830-35), *Seated Nude* (c. 1830-35; fig. 42), *The Flower Girl* (c. 1834-40), *By the Shore* (c. 1835-40; fig. 43), and *The Bather* (c. 1835-40; fig. 44). These are now in the Beaverbrook Art Gallery, having been donated through the Sir James Dunn Foundation after their owner's death, or, in the case of *Nude Study—Half Length,* through Lord Beaverbrook, who had been given the work by Dunn.[30] Where (and indeed if) Lewis saw these paintings remains uncertain; Dunn may have had them with him at his Toronto office or hotel suite; or possibly even at his New Brunswick "camp," where their perceived lubriciousness would have elicited less censorious comment than in a big-city drawing-room or public gallery. At the very least, Lewis could have seen the works in photographic form. It is hard to conceive of an artlover like Dunn not taking the opportunity to show his collection, in some form or other, to a painter and critic of such renown and discernment as Wyndham Lewis.

Although, on the surface, the dissimilarities between Etty and Lewis seem more salient than the similarities, there are interesting parallels in their careers, their circumstances, and their aesthetics. A hint of approval of the old rebel against academic prudery can be gleaned from this aside in a review by Lewis of the 1921 Royal Academy show: "There is also a sprinkling of nudes—descreet, compared with similar wares at the Salon, rather flashy, fleshy photographs if compared with the allurement of a Kirchner or the charm of an Etty."[31] Lewis may not have

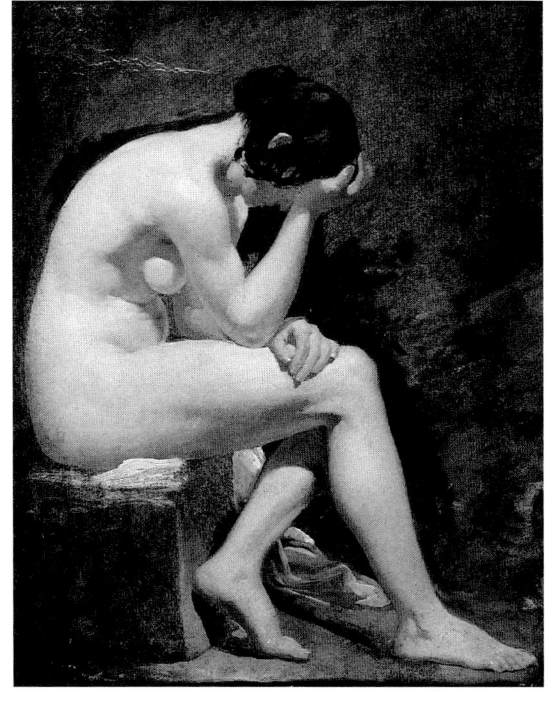

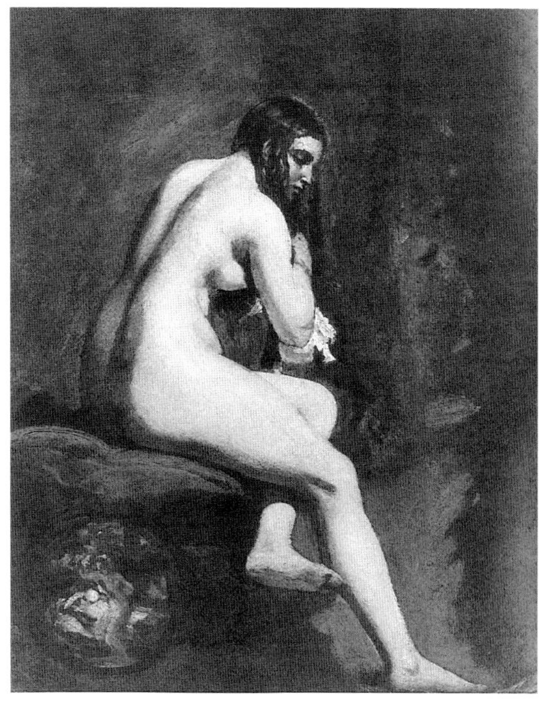

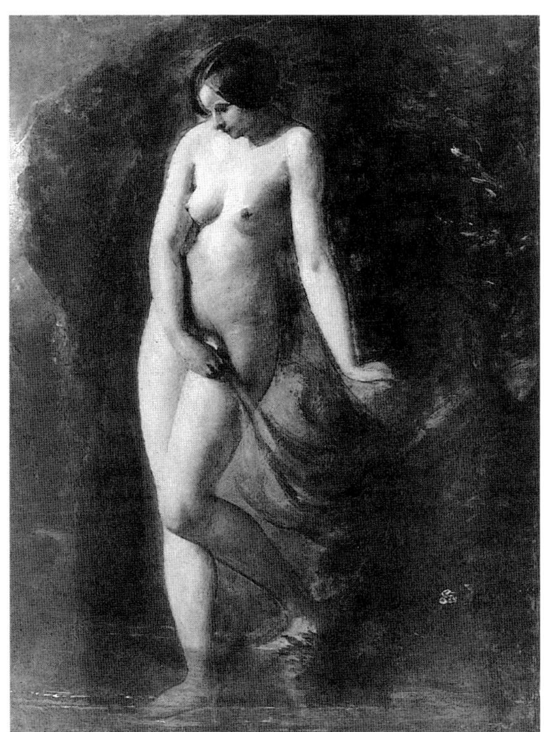

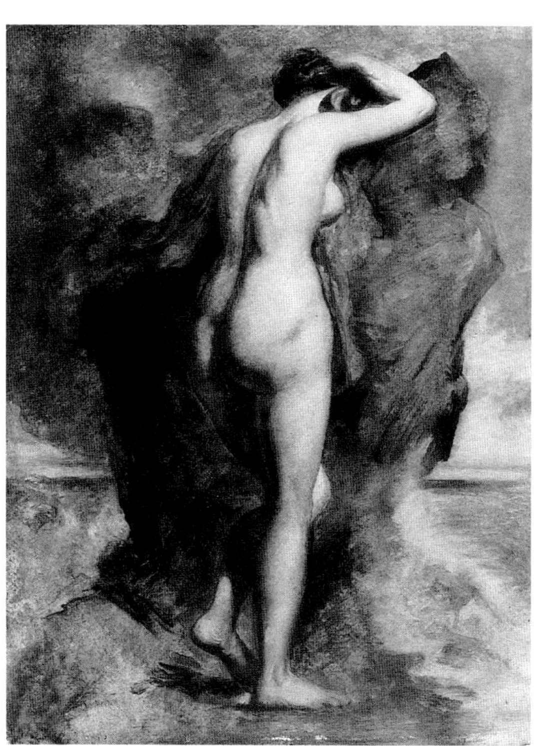

Clockwise from top left:
Fig. 41 William Etty (1787-1849): *Study (Nude)*, late 1820's oil on paper (56.5 x 44.5). Fig. 42 William Etty: *Seated Nude*, c. 1830-35, oil on paperboard laid down on panel (60.0 x 47.3 cm). Fig. 43 William Etty: *By the Shore*, c. 1835-40, oil on paperboard (63.8 x 48.6 cm). Fig. 44 William Etty: *The Bather*, c. 1835-40, oil on paperboard laid down on panel (68.0 x 51.8 cm). All, gift of the Sir James Dunn Foundation, The Beaverbrook Art Gallery, Fredericton, N.B.

shared the enthusiasm of his critic-friend William Gaunt for the then-disparaged Pre-Raphaelites, but he probably would have endorsed his description of "stout little William Etty of the voluptuous nudes, with an odd and exceptional streak of genius"[32]—a genius Delacroix had been one of the first foreign artists to recognize.

The closest of the affinities between Etty and Lewis lies in their joint fixation on the infinite variety of the forms, shapes and tones of the human body (for preference, the female) in its naked, unadorned state, whether in action or in repose—and also on their shared affinity with the sea (though neither could be construed as marine painters *per se*). Both were "externalists," interested in the physical appearance of things and little concerned with the inner workings of the corpus. Accordingly, both had perfected a mode of rendering the flesh that emphasised externality, sheen and reflectivity (as in the depiction of bronze and steel armour and armaments, and of limbs that seem to possess the metallic qualities of medieval soldiery or of modern machines)—the principal difference in their treatments being that Etty's take on his subject matter was "hot" and Lewis's "cold." Both were more interested in the creation of various mental states in the viewer by visual means than in the exact, scientific replication of natural appearances. Both suffered significant neglect, especially and most hurtfully in mid-career. (A French art historian has described Etty, in words that could be applied to Lewis, as "one of those painters whose stature is difficult to appreciate, because few English artists, beneath the surface of an apparently successful career, have been more fundamentally at variance with their time and country...."[33]) Both were obsessed by the "oceanic," and found fertile ground in the implicit conflict or concert between the littoral figure (solitary or grouped) and the wave-plied foreshore. And both were forced to depend on patrons with whose *mores* and values they were in sharp conflict, yet who alone could sustain them in their many hours of need. Lewis in his impoverished exile had to rely on the capricious largesse of plutocrats, aristocrats and bureaucrats; Dennis Farr tells us that "Even after Etty had established a reputation, many of his exhibition pieces were not commissioned works. A few of the nobility and landed gentry patronised him, but his main source of income derived from professional men, merchants and latterly, industrialists."[34]

Thanks to his abhorrence of Victorianism and all it stood for, the much-censored Lewis would have found grounds for admiration of Etty in his defiant stand against the prurient disapproval of the critics who decried the sensuality and candour—not to mention the frequent "sketchiness"—of his nudes. This would have been especially true of those canvases and panels that celebrated the human flesh without benefit of mythological, religious or narrational trappings. The two artists had a further bond in their joint predicament as neglected geniuses who had been passed over in their own lifetimes and whose future status was far from assured. At the time that Lewis stumbled upon the "Toronto industrialist's" private cache of Ettys, he himself was in the ebb of his reputation and fully aware of having been written off by the British and American art establishments, and of being virtually invisible in what he took to be the philistine backwater of Toronto. Etty's stock had languished in obscurity since his death; in 1933, when R.E.A. Wilson mounted the sale of paintings from which Sir James Dunn purchased the bulk of his collection of works by this artist, the anonymous author of the catalogue's "Note on the Artist" bluntly stated that, although "it is possible to see in Etty a basis for Corot and Courbet, no less than for Renoir, much less than anything personifying the taste of his own age and country,"

> Now, he is forgotten. No one has made an effort to preserve him, even as a curiosity born out of time. His paintings, for all their superb wizardly, are unfashionable and unmarketable in America. To the devotees of the period from Ingres to Cézanne—those, of course, from whom all judgments come—he is less than a name, unknown. Mrs. [Virginia] Woolf might make a perfect study of him; a frail and rather pathetic little man, a provincial and a lonely, wandering in the streets of London, blue and violet in the light of their new gas lamps, thinking of Diana, Leander and Endymion, with their lovely names.[35]

This passage would surely have struck a responsive chord in Lewis, reminding him of his own ill-treatment at the hands of Roger Fry and the Bloomsburyites. Had he not discovered that he, too, was "unmarketable in America"? Lewis would have been aware of the modernist prejudice against Etty as a purveyor of soiled maidens and "dollies on the dias" for the titillation of rich vulgarians in their studies and billiard-rooms over cigars and brandy. After all, even at the nadir of his critical reputation, Etty was much sought-after within a certain pleasure-loving set on either side of the Atlantic—yes, even among the "opulent methodists" of the "ugly teetotal

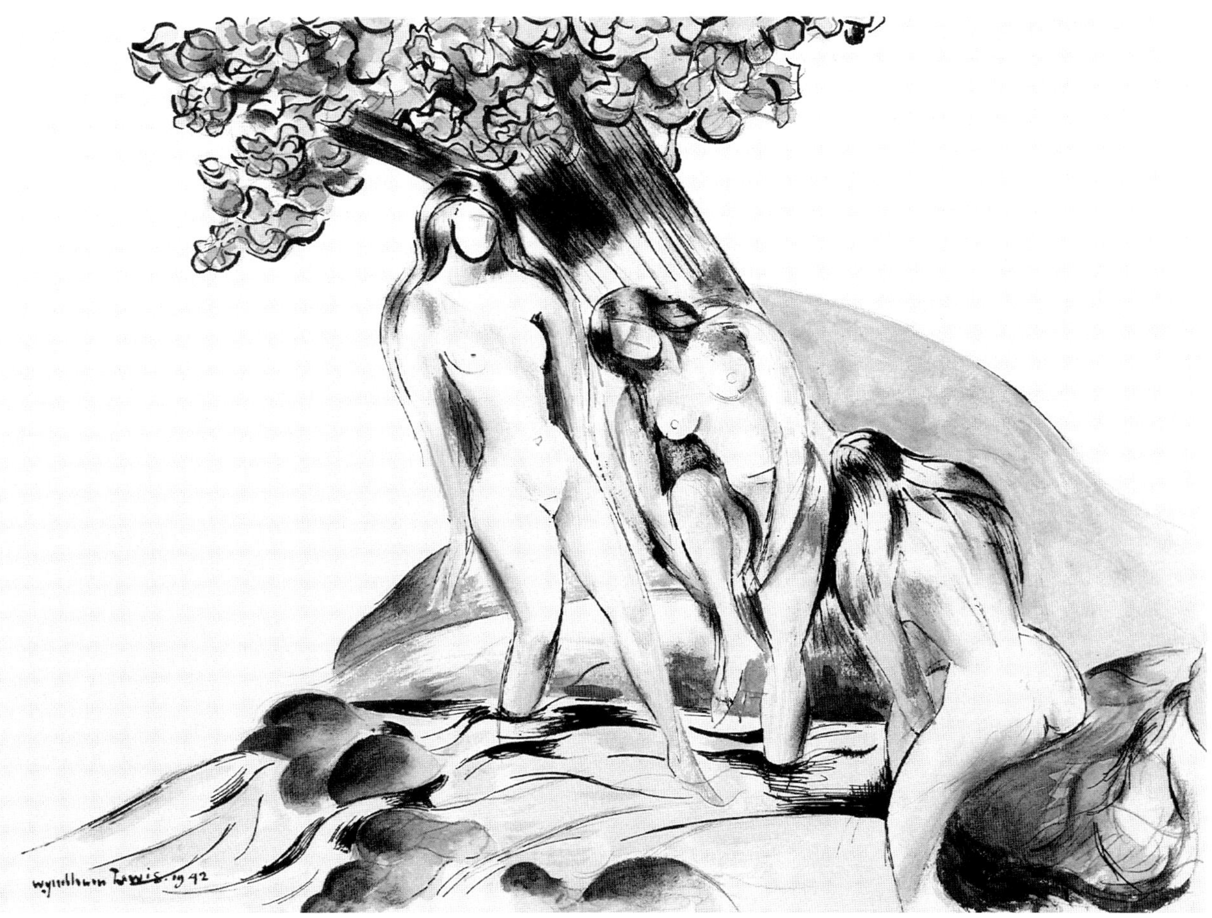

No. 46. *Homage to Etty*, 1942, pen-and-ink, graphite and watercolour on paper (25.4 x 41.8 cm), M 994. National Gallery of Canada, Ottawa. (Reproduced in colour on page 122.)

Baal", Toronto. Despite the gap of years and sensibility, a reviewer of that city in 1950 could spot the underlying similarity between these two solitaries, describing Lewis's "charming Homage to Etty" as "three nudes which for all the difference in the styles of Etty and his admirer have an odd relationship."[36]

All of Sir James Dunn's Etty canvases date from what Dennis Farr denominates the artist's 'heroic period' , which extended from 1825 to around 1840, and which reveals the profound influence on his development of his European grand tour of 1821-23.[37] In Italy he had especially admired and copied the works of Veronese and Titian; in Paris, he made a "memorial" of a "glorious Water-nymph of Rubens", *Les Sirènes*, and copied Giorgione's *Fête Champêtre* at the Louvre.[38] In terms of composition, subject matter and general atmosphere, the Dunn-owned Ettys that bear the closest comparison to Lewis's "homages"—including and especially the eponymous *Homage to Etty* (no. 46)—are *The Bather, By the Shore,* and, to a lesser extent, *Seated Nude* and *Study (Nude). The Bather* has been described as follows: "The figure, shown stepping gingerly into a stream, her right leg in the water, her left on the bank, resembles in terms of its subject a number of other 'bathers' by the artist, notably *The Fairy of the Fountain* (Tate Gallery), ...and *Musidora* (Tate Gallery)...." Although the landscape appears to have been a later addition by another hand, "the attitude of the figure, conducive to its present setting, does allow for the possibility that Etty did have the subject of a 'bather' or 'nymph' in mind when he sketched out the study and that it may date from the early 1840s, when Etty's output of such pieces was especially prolific."[39] The pose of the figure in *By the Shore,* according to this commentator,

> has been freely adapted from two well-known classical statues. The attitude of the legs, bent at the knee, is based on the Venus de Medici (Uffizi, Florence) while the upraised arm is reminiscent of the celestial Venus (Uffizi, Florence.)...
>
> The present study is in many ways typical of the way in which Etty's studies were adapted, after his death, by the addition of props and scenery, to encompass narrative elements. The intention, in this case, was clearly to depict the character of Andromeda by the addition of the rock and shoreline.... Rather than Andromeda, the Beaverbrook study, in its original form, must have more closely resembled the study in Etty's 1850 sale with a far more prosaic title: 'A female standing, her hands raised to arrange her hair.'[40]

Writing of Etty's *The Deluge* (also titled *Reclining Female Nude*) of c. 1835-45, in the Victoria and Albert Museum, Gill Saunders sees this "rather puzzling picture, perhaps referring to women's sexuality as a cause of the Flood, as of the Fall", as belonging "to a great series of pictures in the nineteenth century associating the naked woman with water as a symbol of her sensuality. A transitional element between earth and air, water was, for the ancients, a female principle symbolizing birth and fertility, hence the mythology of Venus (goddess of the sea) rising from the waves"[41]—and, by implication, drawing mankind back down into the generative flux. That Lewis, too, accepted this conceptual association is suggested by his recurrent use of sea imagery and his lifelong preoccupation, as both painter and writer, with the bond that still exists between human beings and the watery medium from which the species primordially sprang.

NOWHERE IN LEWIS'S VOLUMINOUS WRITINGS have I been able to find a direct allusion to any specific "source" or impetus for the suite of works on paper under study. In introducing the 1941-42 drawings, Walter Michel states that "with one or two exceptions..., the titles [were] provided by Lewis, either spontaneously or when requested by Mr Duncan to do so."[42] In fact, the inscription on the original mount of one of the most important drawings of the series, *Homage to Etty*, is in Douglas Duncan's hand.[43] But there is still the strong possibility that Lewis supplied Duncan with this allusive title, just as he did for such related early-1940s pictures as *"...And Wilderness were Paradise enow", Allégresse Aquatique, Marine Fiesta, Centaur Observing a Group of Girls, Pool of Amazons, and Sunset in Paradise.*

The titles of such works as *Bathing Women* and *Bathing Scene* (1945; no. 88) support the suggestion that the cycle—a term I believe I am justified in using—did not "begin" in 1941, but rather was resumed after a hiatus, and that, as with so many other of Lewis's serial compositions, it can be traced to a much earlier phase of his career. Similarly, the Creation Myths of the 1940s seem to be grafts from seedlings planted as early as 1912, the date of his first two *Creations*

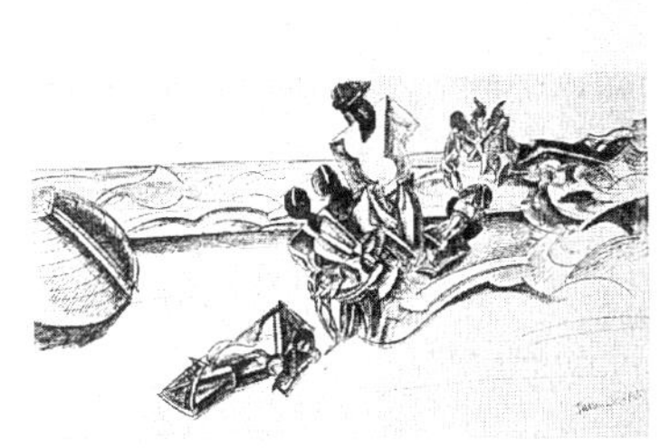

Fig. 45 *A Shore Scene*, 1920, pencil, pen and ink, wash (28.5 x 45.5 cm), M 421. National Gallery of Art, Wellington, New Zealand.

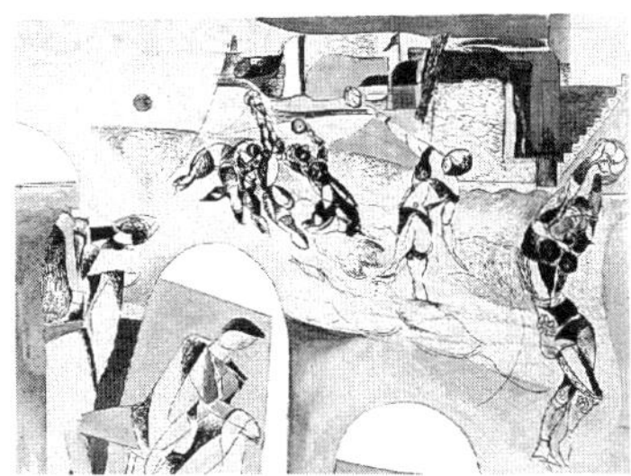

Fig. 46 *Beach Scene*, 1929, pen-and-ink and watercolour washes, gouache, on light-grey paper (31.0 x 42.5 cm), M 645. Private collection.

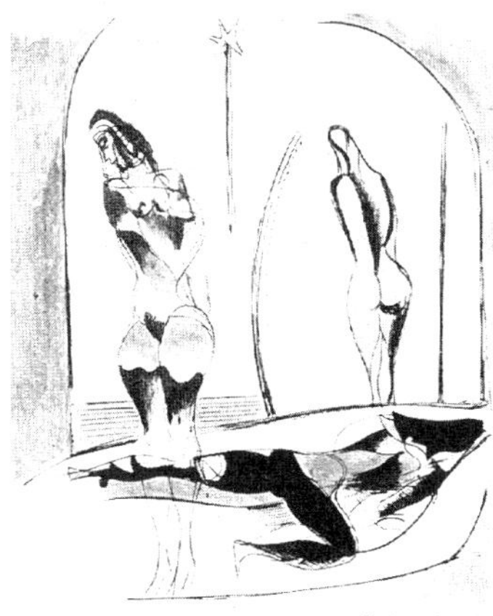

Fig. 47 *Sea Cave*, 1938, pen-and-ink, watercolour wash (24.0 x 19.0 cm), M 921. Private collection.

(M P2, M 46) and his long-lost *Kermesse* (M P4) of the same year, which Lewis had originally also titled *Creation* (it appearing to depict "a violent release of energy like the creative Life-force in Bergson's philosophy"[44]). And *Small Crucifixion Series, III* (no. 25) and *Small Crucifixion Series, IV* (M 983), both from 1941, can likewise be seen as recapitulating the stance of the male figure in *Man and Woman* (M 75), yet another work of 1912. Thus we find Lewis drawing semi-abstracted bathers as far back as 1909 and continuing to explore the figure/landscape motif with such pictures as *Sunset Among Michaelangelos* (c. 1912; M 88), *At the Seaside* (1913; M 123), the three *Bathers*, of 1919-20 (M 362-364), *Figures at a Beach House* (1919-20; M 368), *A Shore Scene* (1920; fig. 45), *Archimedes Reconnoitring the Enemy Fleet* (1922; M 519), *Beach Scene* (c. 1929; fig. 46); *Two Beach Babies* (1933; P 53), the two *Bathers*, of 1938 (M 898-899), *Bathing Scene* (1938; M 900), and *Sea Cave* (1938; fig. 47). Furthermore, by virtue of their aquatic/maritime character and subject matter, *Abstract: Harbour* (1930; M 676), *Boats in Port* (1933; M 788), *Nordic Beach* (1933-36; M P55), *Sunset-Atlas* (1934; M 847), *Harbour* (1936; M P59), *Landscape with Northmen* (1936-37; M P66), *Newfoundland* of 1936-37 (no. 1), *The Armada* (1937; M P70), and *Hamlet and Horatio: Gargoyles*, of 1941 (no. 14) all have at least a generic kinship with the beach and bathing images of the 1910s, 1920s and 1930s. Ezra Pound had anticipated this reprising and refiguring tendency as early as 1919, when he reviewed the one-man exhibition *Guns* at the Goupil Gallery: "Another property of Mr. Lewis' work is its 'partialness.' I mean that every series of the three series of Lewis' drawings I have seen appears to be the beginning of some exposition which might go on indefinitely for the rest of the artist's life."[45]

"In the spectacular erotic or dance encounters" of 1919-20, writes Walter Michel, "the imagination is free and inventive as it had been before the war. *A Shore Scene*[,] the most elaborate composition in ink of the period, takes these elements and builds them into one of Lewis's greatest drawings. Forms never seen before, composed into clusters like the flowers of a tropical fruit, rise from the main diagonal.... The tiny group in the background would still be a fascinating composition if it were blown up to a large size, but here this inventive power is thrown away on figures two inches high."[46] This enrichment of background and middle-ground was to be revived in *The Island*.

Beach Scene is part of a set of four coloured drawings on athletic themes commissioned by Lord Inchcape in 1929, its companion pieces being *Boxing at Juan-les-Pins* (M 646), *Wrestling* (M 654), and a reworking of *The Pole Jump* of 1919 (M 344). Michel calls these "'story-telling' pictures", which "show him succeeding, seemingly at will, in what in the war pictures had still been the exception: the transformation of any realistic scene into a magical performance.... It was the acquisition of this new power of imbuing the simplest reality with a deep visual meaning which allowed Lewis, in his subsequent development, to dispense with the more literary devices of surrealism."[47] *Beach Scene*, Michel continues,

> is one of Lewis's few paintings of figures in a detailed landscape. The liveliness of the composition results from the interaction of the figures with a spatial motif of three bands (sand, water and sky) radiating out, like spokes of a wheel, from a hub which may be imagined near the top of the right-hand edge. The ball players, undulating within a wedge whose point is the sun, link the three zones and, by their diverse balances, assert a gravitational flux which energizes the picture. The lines of the landscape, in turn, partition the figures so that they seem to be opposing something human and wilful against an indifferent nature.
>
> All three pictures, through nothing more than the physical arrangement of figures, produce a meaning that is metaphysical.[48]

The most obvious common denominator in all these diverse works is the artist's preoccupation with the "vast planetary abstraction of the OCEAN", with the ports, ships and seafarers he blessed in the first number of *Blast*, and with the history of nautical exploration and discovery that, for Lewis, was the chief claim to glory of the islanded "English race", whose "Character is based on the Sea."[49] The "open-mindedness and tolerance" of the Anglo-Saxon, he contended at the height of World War II, was that of "the man who has a footing in every land, and whose 'homeland' is really the ocean...."[50] The Canadian novelist Sheila Watson has rightly pointed out that sea-imagery runs throughout his entire literary as well as visual production:

> Oddly enough Lewis's work began, some time before 1909, among the rocks and stone hamlets of Finnestre. "My literary career," he recalled in *Rude Assignment*, "began in France.... What I started to do in Brittany I have been developing ever since."...
>
> It was here on the rocky border of the sea that Lewis reached, as he recalled in

one of his stories, a system of early dreams which he had considered effaced.

In the stories which he began to publish, when he returned to London in 1909, the sea is there.... What was dream came to the surface later in the drawings and paintings which followed the experiences of war. It appeared in *The Surrender of Barcelona* (1936 [M P61]), now in the Tate Gallery, and is a dominant presence in *The Armada* (1937 [M P70]), in the Vancouver Art Gallery collection....

The sea is so much a part of Lewis's paintings that it almost escapes notice....[51]

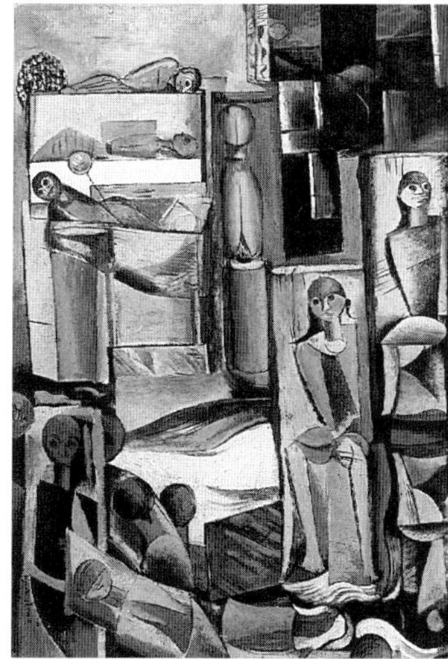

Fig. 48 *The Mud Clinic*, 1937, oil on canvas (85.1 x 59.1), M P70. Gift of the Second Beaverbrook Foundation, The Beaverbrook Art Gallery, Fredericton, N.B.

The son of an amateur yachtsman whose American-born father had married into a family of Upper Canadian Great Lakes grain-shippers, Lewis was a lifelong haunter of coastlines and borders, in preference to interiors and heartlands. Wherever he happened to find himself in the restless decades that followed his birth on board the *Wanda*, off Amherst, Nova Scotia, he seemed always to be longing for the opposite shore: when in Europe, his gaze was bent on America or North Africa, when in America, on Europe, Asia, or beyond.

In December 1911, at the *First Exhibition of the Camden Town Group*, Lewis was represented by *Port de Mer* [M P1], a "largish canvas" which "represented two sprawling figures of Normandy fishermen, in mustard yellows and browns...."[52] This now-lost work, bought from the show by Augustus John, was typical of his earliest paintings, which, in the words of Jeffrey Meyers, "were of fishermen and fishwives in the Norman and Breton ports.... Lewis was powerfully attracted to the violent energy of these people, and in 'Les Saltimbanques' [1909] likened them to 'corrosive lavas that illuminate before they destroy the object in their path.' This description of a circus troupe in Quimperlé [on the south coast of Brittany], who symbolize the neglected artist, was probably influenced by Picasso's 'blue period' paintings of elongated acrobats on a deserted beach."[53]

Lewis announced his retirement as an art critic in 1951, some forty years after the appearance of "Les Saltimbanques", in the form of an essay which he punningly titled "The Sea-Mists of Winter."[54] (I say "punningly" because what Lewis could "see," as a result of the cranial pharnygeoma that would eventually kill him, was "the veil of moisture like a sea-mist"—"atmospheric opacities"— that had fallen before his inner eye, rather than in outside nature. His fate invited an identification with such earlier blind visionaries as Homer and Milton.) In between these enclosing dates, there had flowed a constant stream of "marine fiestas," littoral scenes and island vistas. In the early 1940s, when Lewis considered himself to have become becalmed and cast away on a wintry desert isle in the midst of the lost continent of presumptive America, his imagination constructed not only "places of exile" out of "inhabited places",[55] but havens of arrival and homecoming out of uninhabited or marginal ones on the borders between sea and land and sky, and between time and space.

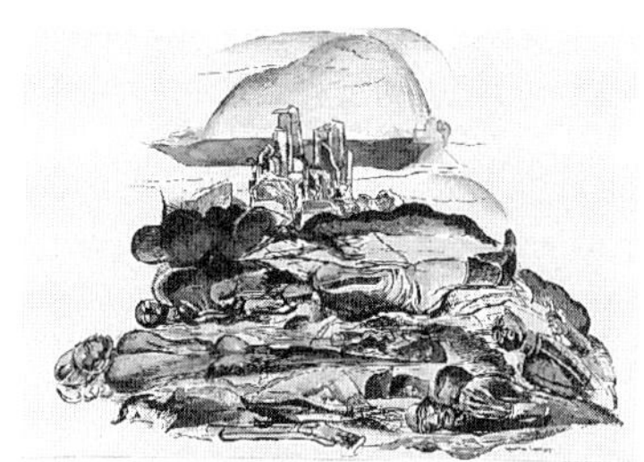

No. 14 *Lebensraum I: The Battlefield*, 1941, pen-and-ink, watercolour and graphite on paper (29,0 x 40.5 cm), M 976. Art Gallery of Ontario, Toronto.

It is unlikely that any exact correlation can be made between the beaches of the 1940s' Bathers sequence and such actual sandy shorelines as Lewis might have trod during his North American half-decade: for instance, at Sag Harbour, on Long Island, where he spent the summer of 1940;[56] on Lake Ontario west or east of Toronto; on the south side of the Toronto Islands (known, locally, as "The Island"); or along the ocean-front at Bathurst, N.B. While any of these places could have provided an impetus or an idea, if not an actual foreground or background, the spaces in which the swimmers and sunbathers dance and wrestle, snooze and wash themselves are as abstracted and generalized as in Etty's maritime nudes.

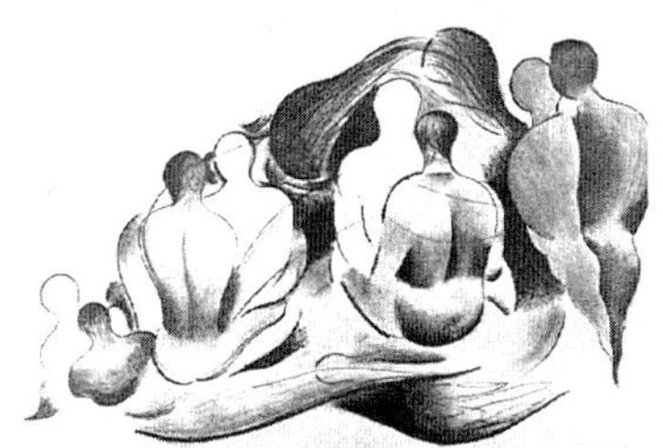

Fig. 49 *Athletes*, 1920, chalk (33.7 x 49.5 cm), M 383. Private Collection.

Walter Michel divides Lewis's compositions of the 1940s into two main groups, subclassified as follows: "Creation Myths" and Tragedies; and Fantasies and Visions, Bathers and Actors. With its "ovals within ovals," the unclassifiable *The Sage Meditating upon the Life of Flesh and Blood,* of 1941 (no. 18), may also belong to the "general category" of the Creation Myths.[57] We are exclusively concerned here with what, for convenience, I have designated the Bathers series, but so numerous are the overlappings that non-inclusive demarcations among these subsets are not possible. Sheila Watson has drawn our attention to the inner coherence of the imaginative compositions of this period, which she sees as falling into the wartime allegories, the Creation Myths, the Bathers, and the Crucifixion Series. In her view, two works, *Four Figure Composition* (1938; M P81) and *What the Sea is Like at Night* (1949; M 1104),

> link two other pictures painted in Toronto to the "Creation Myth" series: *Allégresse Aquatique*...and *Jehovah the Thunderer* [1941; no. 20].... Other pictures in the [Douglas] Duncan collection, *The Island..., Marine Fiesta* [1942; see fig. 52], and *Two Women on a Beach,* watercolour and crayon on the same blue paper as that used for *Creation Myth: Maternal Figure* [1941-42; no. 28], belong to the same world of fluid forms.

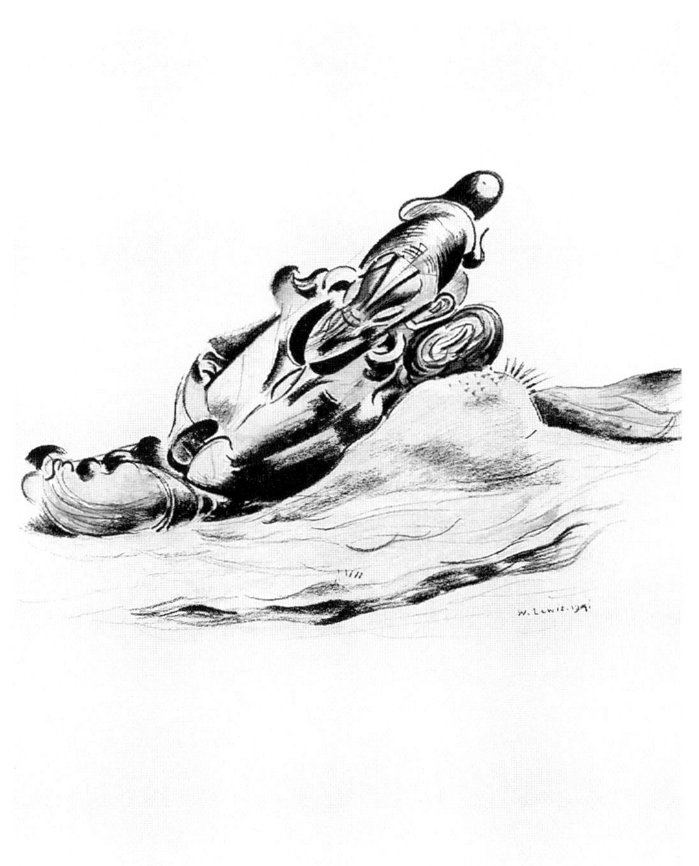

No. 18 "...*And Wilderness were Paradise enow*", 1941, black chalk, and watercolour on paper (42.5 x 32.0 cm), M 965. Private Collection.

> Eric Newton, speaking of the surrealist aspect of Lewis's work, observed in 1951 that perhaps Lewis had not created quite enough specimens of what he and Charles Handley-Read called "imaginative composition" as distinct from his paintings of the 1914-18 war and from his paintings and drawings from life "to furnish a classifiable world with its own fauna and flora." Mr. Newton was alluding specifically to the world of the "ball-headed creatures that inhabit the 'Mud Clinic'," [1937; fig. 48].... Even if this questionable presupposition with its equivalent classification were granted, it should be remembered that the "ball-headed creatures" appear in some of the pictures painted in 1941 and 1942....
>
> In two of the Toronto watercolour and ink pictures—*Lebensraum [I]: The Battlefield* [1941; no. 14] and *Allégresse Aquatique*—these figures may be seen in landscapes which include details of Lewis's immediate environment. In the first they lie like a blood-sacrifice with their rifles and helmets at the base of a distant group of small skyscrapers. In the second they sport and make love in a wide stream below a red barn. Both are related to *The Inferno* [1937; M P72]....[58]

Watson argues that "In form and mood" the pictures in the Crucifixion Series "belong with the 'Creation Myth' series", a common theme being that of death, transfiguration, and possible rebirth, though not necessarily in recognizable human form. I am not sure on what authority Watson ascribes *Allégresse Aquatique* to the Creation Myths, which Lewis defined as fantasies "of the worlds moving round together in a chaotic corner of creation. The idea of *Creation* [1927; M 628] is always a beginning of a spontaneous growth."[59] The work alluded to "shows the fertilization of an earth spirit in a corner of a world of cloudy and watery spaces in which float huge marine shapes."[60] If *Allégresse* can indeed be linked with this group, then "...*And Wilderness were Paradise enow*", also of 1941 (no. 18), likewise belongs in both the Creation Myths and Bathers camps, since it possesses evolving organic (perhaps sexual) forms in a sand-duned marine landscape.[61]

Watson correctly identifies as a common factor the frequent use of the cheap blue paper that Lewis purchased at his neighbourhood drugstore. Another is the artist's preference for such equally inexpensive media as conté crayon, graphite, pen-and-ink and chalks, which he overlaid with dabs and washes of bright watercolour (red, green and blue prevailing), and highlit with touches of gouache and Chinese white. The result is a play of alternating areas of transparency and opacity, monochrome backgrounds and brilliant outbursts of primary colour, with even the occasional concession to impasto. The animal, vegetable and mineral forms that sprawl and crawl across the picture plane retain the clearly defined outlines of the earlier abstractions and portrait drawings, but the shapes are rounded and fluid rather than angular and static, their sometimes intermingling volumes being suggested by discrete passages of shading—a technique datable to the *Athletes* of 1920 (fig. 49), but which came to the fore in the following decade. New, however, is the stylization of the female body into a mannikinish hybrid with exaggeratedly long legs, high hips and wasp waists—as likely a sardonic comment on 1940s fashion models as the graphic (in both senses) wish-fulfilments of a domesticated ex-womanizer trapped in a Toronto winter.

"It is unfortunate", a critic wrote in 1978, "that the rigour of the Vorticist work has tended to overshadow the contribution Lewis made to English painting with his exhibition at the Leicester Galleries in December 1937. The sea-change in Lewis's attitude to 'sham-culture outfits' which we find in *The Revenge for Love* is mirrored in the almost unexpected flow and geometrical relaxation of the oils painted between 1932 and 1938."[62] In these canvases, the faceless, "ball-headed," anatomically identical figures, whether vertically or horizontally disposed, are meant to signify types rather than individuals, puppets rather than people: tamed bodies, increasingly tired tyros who can be manipulated by slogans, military bands, crowd-masters, the hectoring rhetoric of dictators and radio demagogues, to follow whom is ultimately fatal. But whereas, in *Inferno, Lebensraum I: The Battlefield, Dragon's Teeth* (1941; no. 9), *Supplicating Figures* (1941; no. 23), *Small Crucifixion Series, I* (1941; no. 24) and *Jehovah the Thunderer*, recumbency implies death and dissolution, horizontality in the Bathers pictures is an index of luxurious ease and regenerative contact with land and sea. And yet these opposing states impinge and interpenetrate, sometimes within the same work: in *Inferno*, Walter Michel tells us, "the vertical and horizontal panels in red and grey separate the two worlds which they superimpose".[63] Lewis himself had described these works in 1937 as representing "a world of shapes locked in eternal conflict" and "a world of shapes prone in the relaxations of an uneasy sensuality which is also eternal." He further suggested that "they are in some sort of series, from the 'Stations of the Dead' to 'Inferno'...."[64] There seems little doubt that this "series" continued after his departure from England, and that the tactic of superimposition or juxtaposition of opposite and conflicting states obtains throughout the entire Bathers sequence.

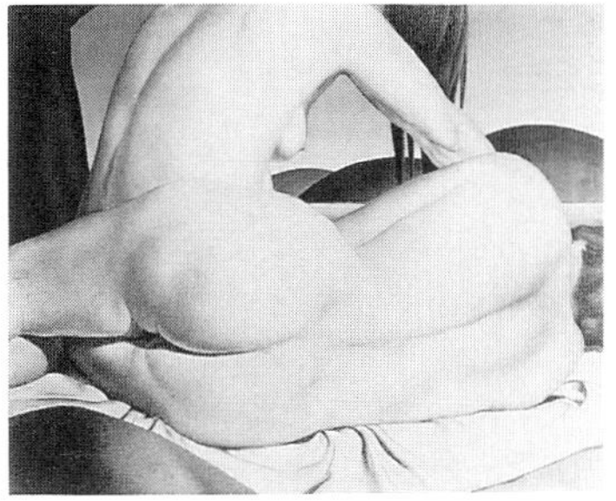

Fig. 50 Bertram Brooker (1888-1955): *Figures in a Landscape,* 1931, oil on canvas (60.9 x 76.2 cm). Private collection.

Despite Lewis's having put into the mouth of the protagonist of his semi-autobiographical *kunstleroman* of 1918, *Tarr*, the polemic that "Anything living, quick and changing, is bad art, always; naked men and women are the worst art of all, because there are fewer semi-dead things about them",[65] and his confession that, while at the Slade (1898-1901), during what Dennis Farr has called its Tonksian "golden age", he preferred to smoke and read the newspaper than perform his duties as *massier* (which included posing the model for the morning's session), his earliest works are highly competent life drawings. He fell away from this discipline during the brief epoch of Vorticism, but the horrific sights he had witnessed as a gunnery officer in World War I compelled him to return to the unsparing depiction of his own species—a resolution that continued, after the Armistice, with his black-crayon, watercolour and gouache nudes of 1919. From here on, he drew and painted fanciful figurative compositions for his own private enjoyment; his portraits were for posterity and (he vainly hoped) for profit.

Although Lewis, like Etty, may subsequently have relied more and more on his own imagination and memory in the rendering of human figures, he never abandoned the motif itself, and in fact published his intention to return to it with a vengeance shortly before his flight to Canada. In a rather tongue-in-cheek piece written for the British picture-magazine *Lilliput*, illustrated with cartoons by Walter Trier (the originals of which are now in the Trier Collection, Art Gallery of Ontario), he attributed the "sudden fading out of the Nude" from current London and Paris exhibitions to the "jealousy" of the wives of the picture-buyers. This sad state of affairs he proposed to "test...out during the next twelve months" by mounting "an exhibition of nothing but Nudes, of the utmost attractiveness." On a more sober note, he argued that "What we lose, as a civilized society, if we banish the Nude altogether from the scene, is obvious. We are not only denying reality—for we are all of us *really* nude people, not persons in Paris fashions or in sports jackets and flannel trousers: we are cutting off from the artist a tract of beauty in which some of the greatest artists have more particularly excelled."[66]

However serious his threat to "throw down this beautiful gauntlet, and thus challenge the interfering matriarch" may have been, Lewis made good his promise in a private rather than public manner when the winds of a new war had blown him to midland Canada. Perhaps it was the very unlikelihood of an exhibition exclusively devoted to nudes being accepted in the "sanctimonious ice-box" of Toronto that sparked Lewis's desire to put on so contentious a show. Only a decade intervened, after all, between 1941, when this unrealized idea first caught fire, and the publication of Bertram Brooker's landmark essay, "Nudes and Prudes", written in answer to (among other provocations) the banning of his own *Figures in a Landscape* (fig. 50) from the 1931 exhibition of the Ontario Society of Artists at the Art Gallery of Toronto, on the grounds that it might shock school-children and their teachers, and the furore caused by the displaying of John Wentworth Russell's allegedly lewd *A Modern Fantasy* at the Canadian National Exhibition in 1927.[67]

And yet, though not in good odour among the city's few collectors and the numerous guardians of public morality, the genre had a healthy share of home-grown practitioners in the period immediately before Lewis' arrival. Nudes might not be marketable, but they could be shown, thanks to the receptiveness of the artists who juried the annual group exhibitions of the various art societies then flourishing. The only condition of admission—other than quality—was that paintings conform to certain contextual norms and conventions which hindsight reveals to be twentieth-century variants on the rules and formulae that had rendered Victorian academic nudes acceptable even to the more liberal-minded clergy and the royal family. The enforced

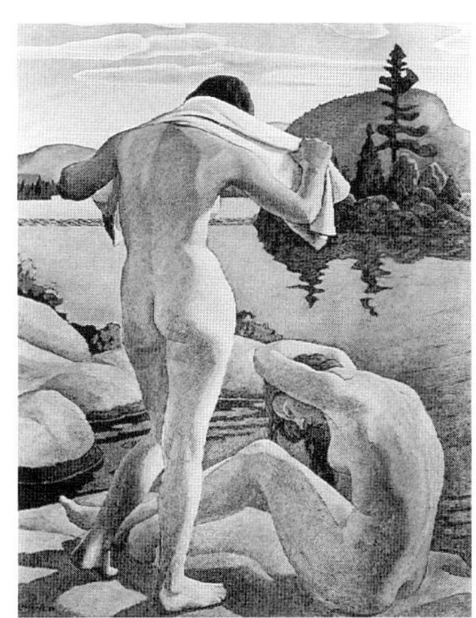

Fig. 51 Edwin Holgate (1892-1977): *By the lake* or *Bathers in Landscape*, 1934, oil on canvas (dimensions unknown) Destroyed by the artist.

sobriety and seriousness of wartime, more than a new repressiveness or a loss of artistic nerve, accounted for the reduction of submissions of nudes to the shows, but they could still be seen on occasion.

Nor can Lewis's failure to find buyers for his own fanciful figure studies in Toronto be ascribed to hostility either to himself or to his manner. Opportunities to exhibit were perhaps fewer than he was accustomed to, but nonetheless existed; for whatever reason, in the five years of his stay in Canada he showed only a handful of pictures, three of them *(Bathing Women, Marine Fiesta* and *Allégresse Aquatique)* being from the Bathers cycle. Had he heeded Douglas Duncan's advice and accepted his willingness to intercede on his behalf, he undoubtedly would have attracted a much wider audience. More extensive exhibiting and its concomitant, exposure to others artists, would have opened his eyes to the fact that the nude was far from "dying out." (What would kill it, as Lewis predicted elsewhere, was the advent of Abstract Expressionism.)

Sadly, despite having had frequent occasions on which to see the work of contemporary Canadian artists in Toronto, Montreal, Ottawa, and subsequently in Windsor, Lewis seems to have been unaware of the resurgence of the figurative tradition across the country, and of the development of a national sub-species of the classic bathers theme: the outdoor nude, as exemplified by Brooker's *Figures in a Landscape* of 1931 (fig. 50) and Edwin Holgate's *By the Lake* (or *Bathers in Landscape*) of 1934 (fig. 51).[68] This extension of the idiom to embrace local scenery and regional references was a feature of American as well as Canadian painting in the 1930s and early '40s. For Lewis, however, the very idea of exposing the artist, much less the undraped model, to the savagery of the northern climate and the bites of the insatiable blackfly would have been too outlandish to contemplate. Relying almost entirely from his imagination, the "laughing observer" first invented his universe—"a world that will never be seen anywhere but in pictures" —and then populated it with "provisional beings." As far as "Canadian nature and its painters" were concerned, he preferred to conceive of the country's "empty" spaces as being wholly denuded of the human presence, as in so many Group of Seven paintings—a misconception or distortion of reality which the Canadian Group of Painters had banded together in 1933 to disprove.

Whatever the stimulus that triggered the Toronto "set" may have been, Lewis's use of that collective term implies a coherence, hence even a sequence, and perhaps even a narrative, the climax (though not the conclusion) of which is *The Island*. Lewis was, after all, a novelist who in the late 1930s had acquired a mastery of plot and characterization that before had eluded him in his deliberately static and savagely satirical fictions. However, if the cycle—a designation implying a return to origins, a circular, rotating movement—does have a story-line, it is resistant to a literal or literary reading. Although any ordering of individual works must remain conjectural, the Toronto Bathers pictures do seem to fall into two overlapping sections. A linking constant is that of figures-in-the-landscape, emphasis always being on the former. "The imagery of bathing figures in the landscape", observes Margaret Werth, "is another current in the pastoral tradition. Visual representations of 'bathers' reproduced the myth of the natural body, the body-in-nature, with the shepherds and gods—the traditional pastoral and mythic components that lent pastoral its narrative structure—filtered out."[69]

The first of two Toronto Bathers sequences, chronologically speaking, consists of coloured chalk, pastel, watercolour and ink drawings of nude figures (most of them, if not all, female) by the seaside or on a lakeshore, often with beach-umbrellas: *Two Women on a Beach, Bathing Women, Allégresse Aquatique*, the undated (but probably 1941-42) *Sunset in Paradise* (no. 96), and *Nude Panel* of 1942 (no. 32). In these works, the figures are somewhat more schematically abstracted than their counterparts in the second part of the set, as can be seen by a comparison of *Allégresse Aquatique* and *Homage to Etty*. In the former watercolour, and similarly in the tripartite *Nude Panel,* the swimmers, waders, tanners and lovers (or wrestlers?) seem to merge rhythmically with the water and the land; their own outlines are vibrant and wavelike, in keeping with the title (*"allégresse"* being a French feminine noun whose English translations are "joy, cheerfulness, elation"). The lounger in the surf, second from left, resembles one of Henry Moore's monumental reclining bronze nudes; his or her posture is close to that of the recumbent male turning his massive back to us in *Sunset in Paradise*. There may be allusions to Renaissance and later paintings and sculpture in several other individual figures and groupings—for instance, the seated sibyl on the far right; the embracing pair immediately to her left, who remind us of innumerable images of feigned struggle between coy nymphs and lusty satyrs; the odalisque in the lower centre; or the wide-shouldered, thick-thighed woman hiking up her skirts to wade into the water in the upper middle-left.

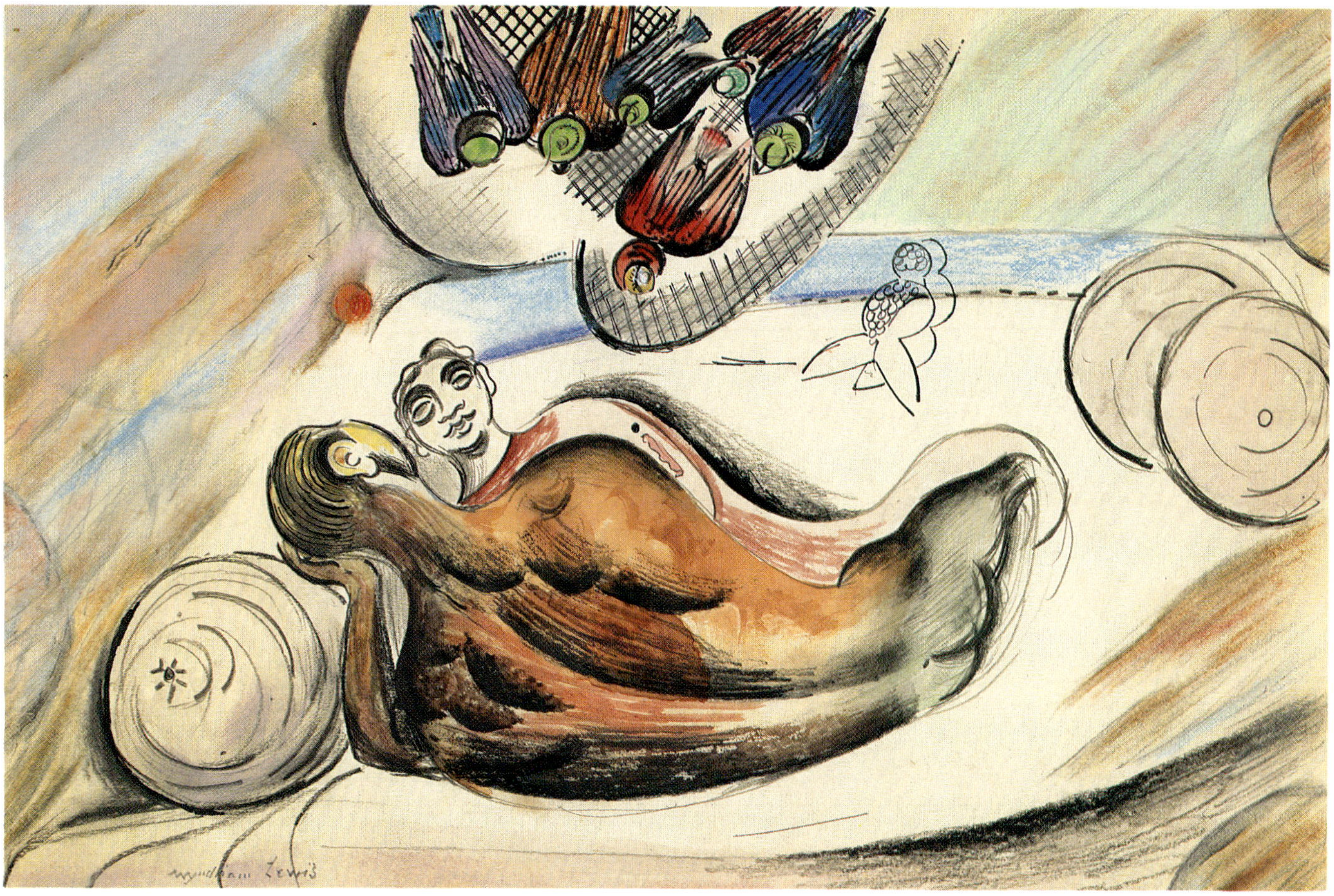

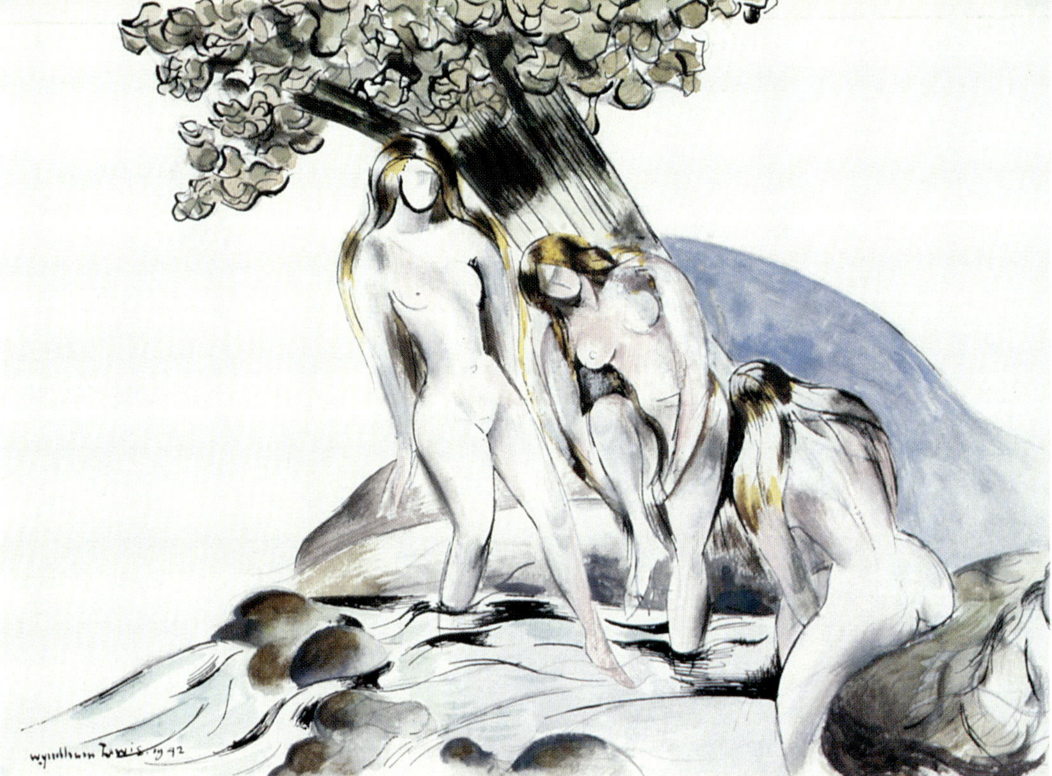

No. 96 *Sunset in Paradise,* n.d. (c. 1940s), pen-and-ink, coloured chalks, watercolour, gouache (20.5 x 30.5 cm), M 1124. Herbert F. Johnson Museum of Art, Cornell University, Ithaca, New York.

No. 46 *Homage to Etty,* 1942, pen-and-ink, graphite and watercolour on paper (25.4 x 41.8 cm), M 994. National Gallery of Canada, Ottawa.

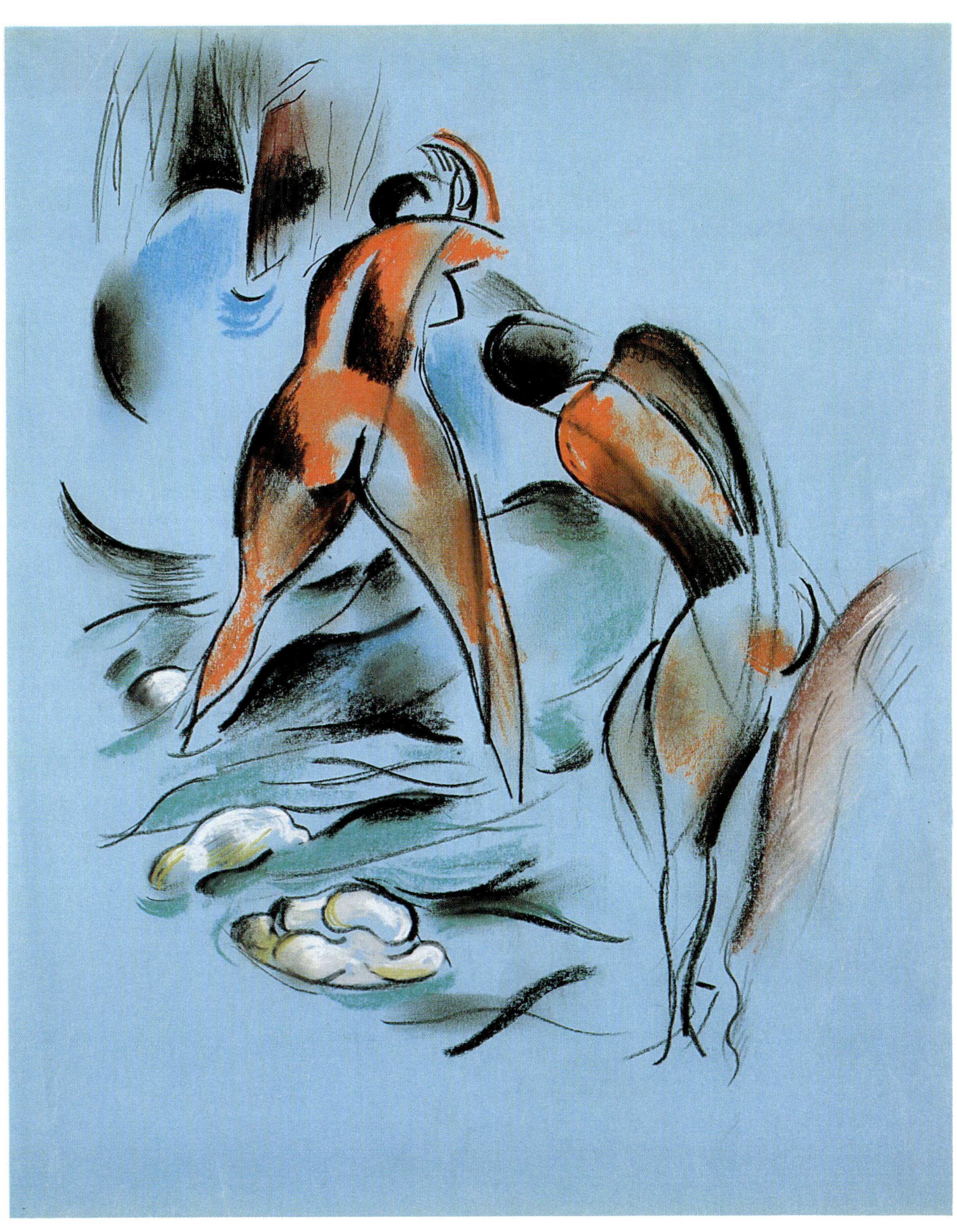

No. 29 *Bathing Women*, 1941-42, watercolour on paper (30.5 x 26.5 cm), M 986.
Private collection.

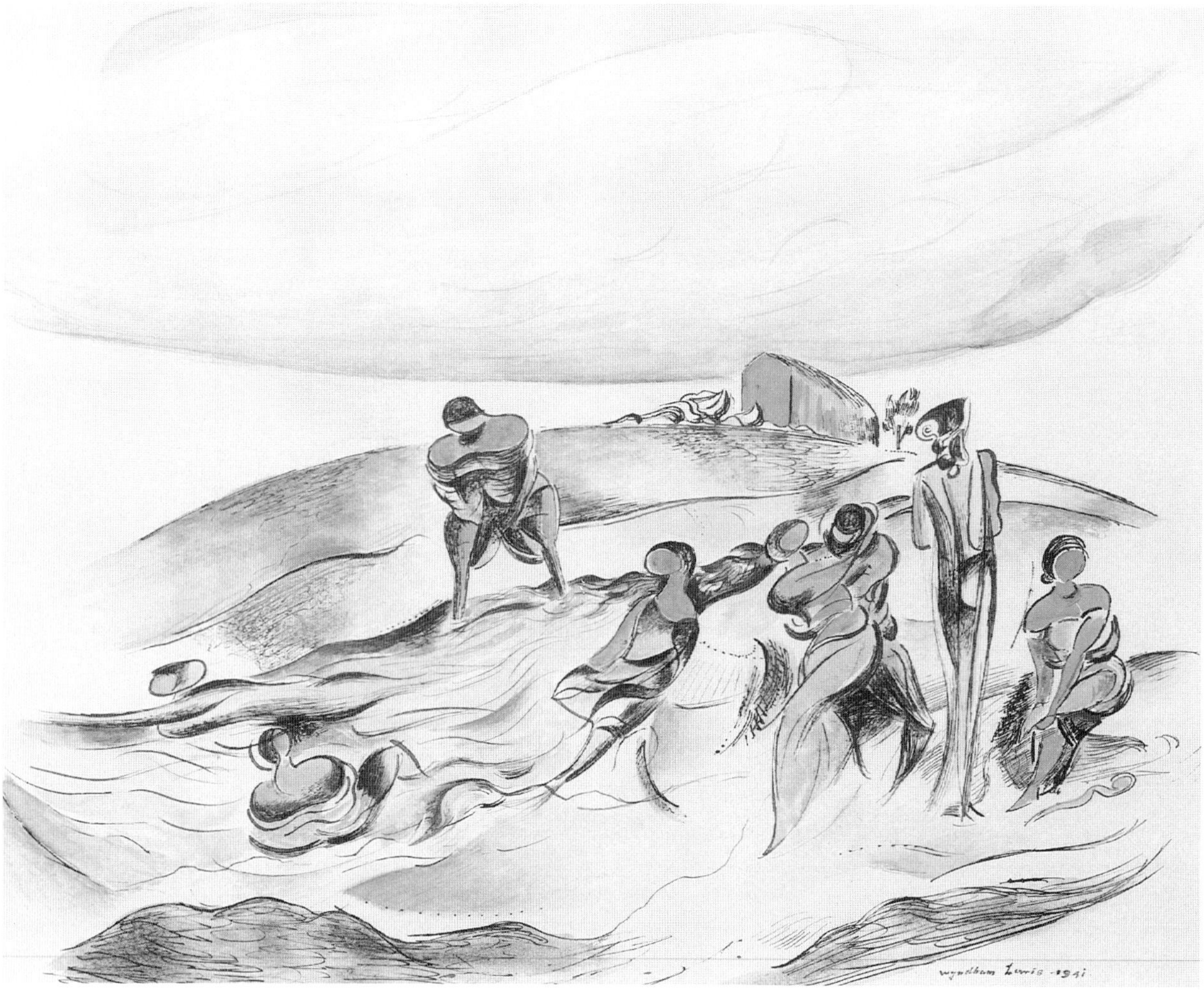

No. 31 *Allégresse Aquatique,* 1941, watercolour on paper (31.8 x 44.5 cm), M 1071. Art Gallery of Ontario, Toronto.

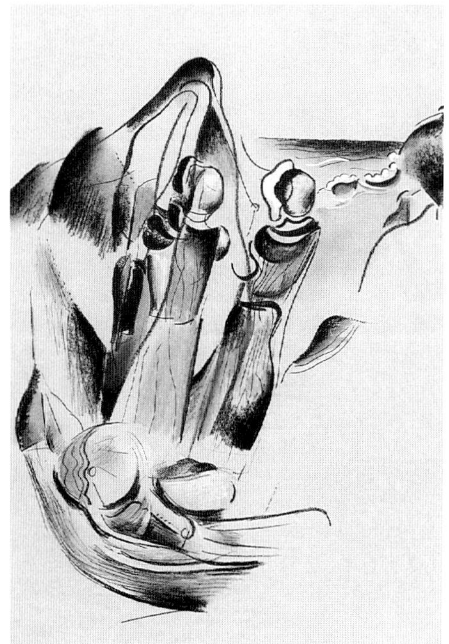

No. 30 *Two Women on a Beach,* 1941, pastel on blue paper (40.5 x 28.5 cm), M 991. National Gallery of Canada, Ottawa.

Sunset in Paradise (the title of which may be a take-off on tour-biz adspeak) presents an amorous twosome on a beach being visited by a flock of six dovelike cherubs, of whose descent the lovers—reminiscent of the happy couples in Etruscan tomb sculptures—seem blissfully oblivious. They may be modern-day incarnations of a triumphant Venus and a disarmed Mars, but, like their sun-worshipping counterparts elsewhere in this group, these lovers are inhabitants of the here and now, to live fully in which is to be in very heaven. Overall, there is a sense of spontaneity about the compositions that indicates neither deliberate referencing of older art, nor calculated innovation; rather, one feels, Lewis is simply (although nothing was ever simple with Lewis) letting his pen or brush take him, as Klee playfully prescribed, on a walk along the seacoast, as it were, of Bohemia.

In the second, more mystifying half of this cluster of images, all dating from 1942—*Centaur Observing a Group of Girls* (no. 43), *A Party of Girls* (no. 44), *Pool of the Amazons* (no. 45), *Marine Fiesta* (fig. 52), *Homage to Etty*, and *Bathers* (no. 47)—a subtle but arresting transformation has taken place. It is as though we had wandered inland from the lazy day of the beach, aim-lessly following a stream until we stumble on a primal, timeless scene: for here are Diana and her naked huntresses, and all the dangers that their espial implies. We are caught short: what is going on here? Everything seemed so blissfully ordinary, back there on the strand—and now it's all be-come strange, and strangely threatening. Whether or not they are meant to be taken for immortals or votaries of a goddess, these new nude bathers are rendered with more anatomical exactitude than their earlier counterparts, and their forms possess an almost Etty-like substantiality. Rather than cavorting on the shore, these alternately naiad-like and Amazonian females are depicted stepping into or out of, or seated and standing by, a pool or brook, sometimes upon a grassy bank or knoll, and usually against the backdrop of a single, Samuel Palmer-esque tree or a leafy glade (which also appears in the top part of *Nude Panel* [no. 39], as a counterbalance to the parasol in the lower-right).

Given Lewis's obsession with the "Time-cult," a metaphorical reading of the watercourse that flows through most of the pictures as a symbol of temporality, oblivion or Heraclitean/Bergsonian flux is hard to avoid. Might the "sage" in his 1941 watercolour, *The Sage Meditating upon Flesh and Blood*, with its water-borne bodies, be none other than the Ephesian metaphysician and relativist himself? In *Time and Western Man*, Lewis characterized Heraclitus as "the first celebrated Western protagonist of the Flux and nothing but the Flux":

> For him it was insupportably real: he was known to the Ancient World as 'the weeping philosopher,' because, in believing that there was nothing but dissolution and vanishing away, so that the river into which you step is never twice the same river, but always a different one, and you yourself of yesterday are as far away to-day, and as much scattered and changed, as are the waters of yesterday's river, he was rendered very gloomy.... He could scarcely be said, from that point of view, to be a man of a 'pure Present,' although standing conspicuously for the Classical Age.[70]

Lewis nonetheless saw Heraclitus's world-view as being closer to the artist's than was that of the Platonist philosophers, for Heraclitus, like Shakespeare and the Greek tragedians, "owned" the "melancholy presentiment of the truth" which it is the artist's curse and duty to communicate, whereas "The platonists were busy...with happier pictures. The artist's truth is in this way the deeper and more terrible. His classical tragic task of providing a *catharsis*—his diabolical role of getting as near to destruction and terror as it is possible without impairing the organism—requires of him a very different disposition to that of the philosopher."[71]

The outwardly idyllic nature of Lewis's watery images thus takes on a rather sinister or elegaic cast if, as one suspects, the bathers' stream is meant to signify the same flow that Heraclitus identified as the element which fire, the basic principle of life, changes into before turning into earth, and then back into fire, in the endless cycle of transformation. The denial of individuality that Heraclitus saw as a precondition of harmony with the world was antithetical to Lewis's belief in the sanctity of the individual self, its essential isolation, and the superiority of human consciousness to mindless, inert matter and the dim awareness of the lower animals. Yet the anonymous, crowding figures he arranges, tableau-like, in Heraclitean landscapes and seascapes, are unindividuated—faceless, like dummies, or blankly masked. Are they human or divine, Edenic or post-apocalyptic? Are they comments on the nature of nature, or on the nature of art? As if in answer, Marshall McLuhan asserts that "Lewis has made plain what he considers to be the relation between the artist and nature. He holds the traditional view of imitation as working in the way that nature works, so that art is another nature.... It is, naturally, in relation

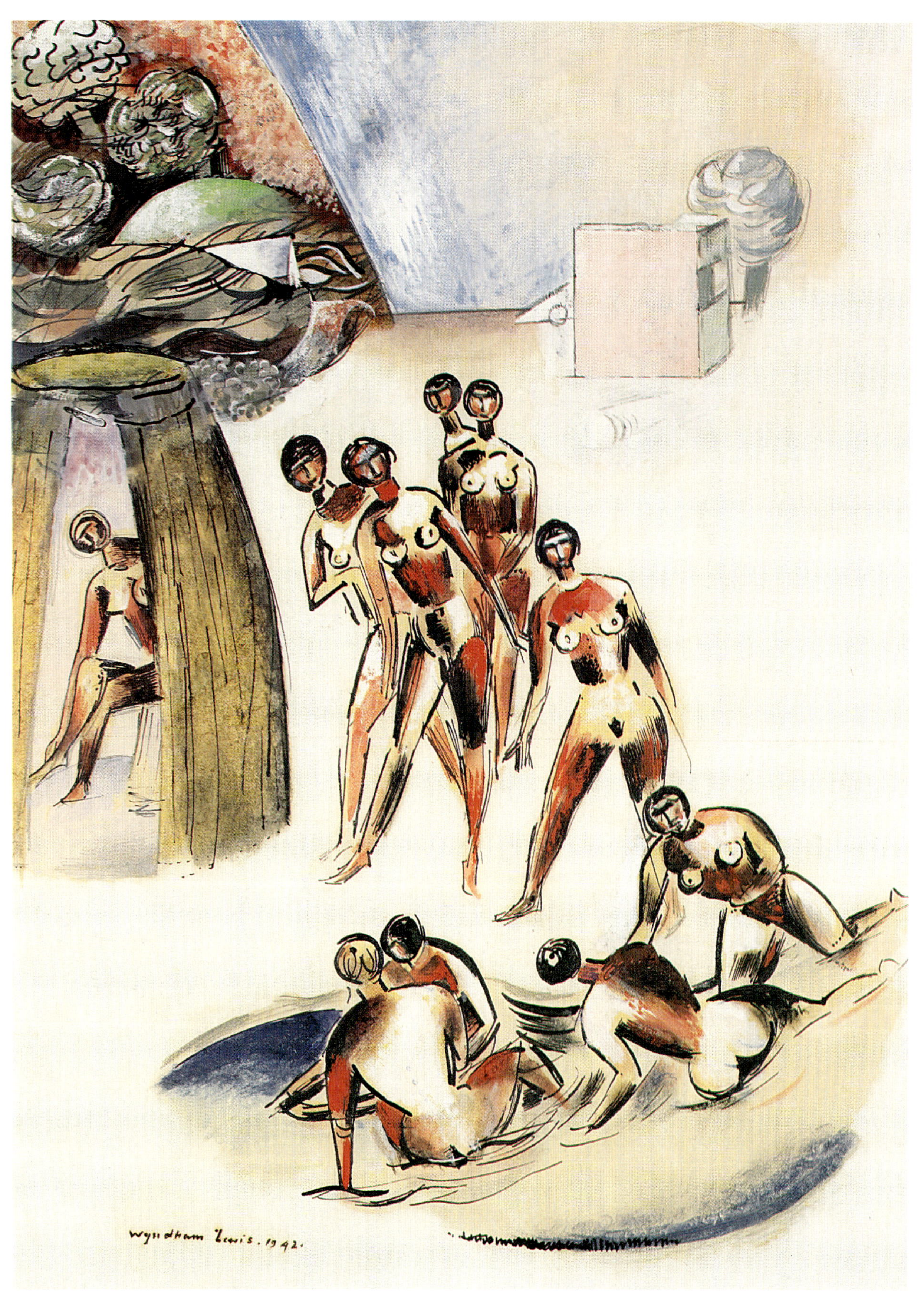
Wyndham Lewis. 1942.

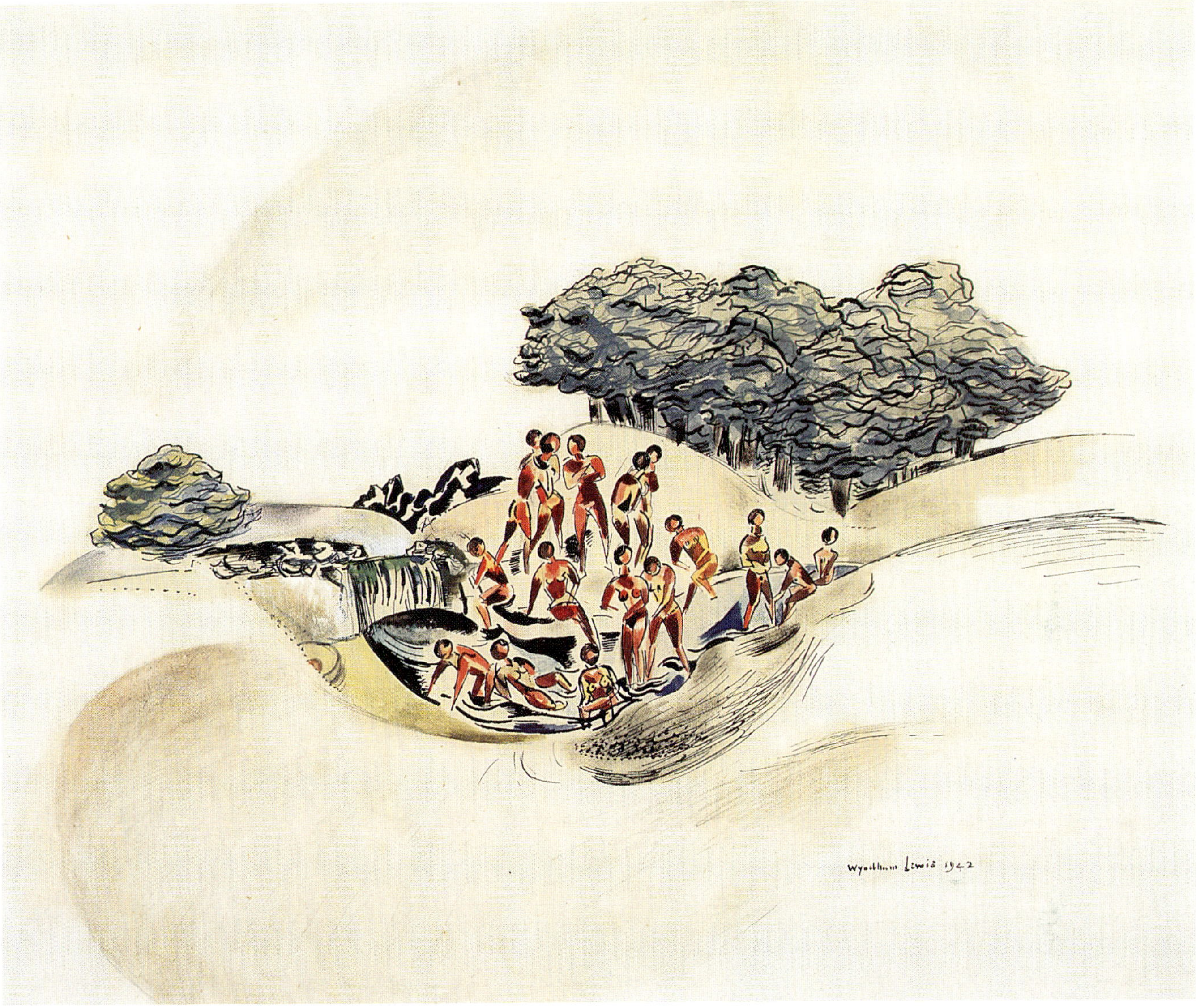

No. 45 *Pool of the Amazons,* 1942, pen-and-ink and watercolour on paper (35.5 x 45.5 cm), M 1003. Collection of Mark McLean, Toronto.

Opposite page:
No. 44 *A Party of Girls,* 1942, pen-and-ink and watercolour on paper (35.5 x 25.5 cm), M 1000. Collection of Mark McLean, Toronto.

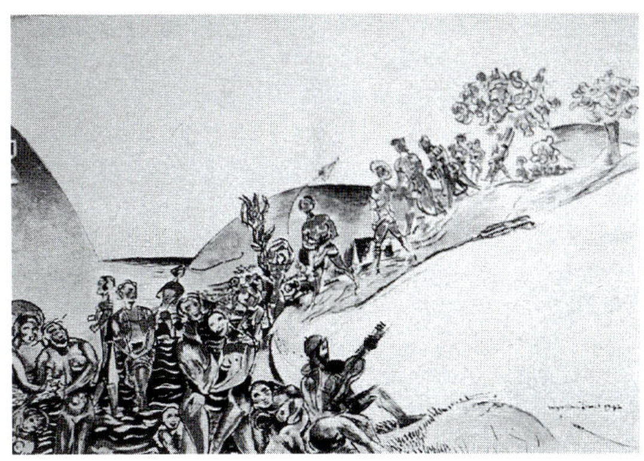

Fig. 52 *Marine Fiesta,* 1942, pen-and-ink, watercolour (30.5 x 45.5 cm), M 996. Present whereabouts unknown.

to the artist's operating in the way that nature works that brings Lewis to a direct statement of his notion of the vortex." He then quotes Lewis's statement in *Wyndham Lewis the Artist* that "the finest artists...are those men who are so trained and sensitized that they have a perpetually renewed power of doing what Nature does, only doing it with all the beauty of accident, without the certain futility that accident implies." And, McLuhan concludes, "it is presumably the view of Lewis that the role of the artist in society is to energise it by establishing such intellectually purified images of the entelechy of nature. The alternative mode is the swoon upon death, the conatural merging of the indiscriminate flux of life, the reflexive feeling and expressing of one's time. It is Lewis's constant theme that the art of our time has chosen the second mode and that its Mona Lisa appeal is to the death swoon."[72]

"Intellectually purified images" or no, the abstracted landscapes of *Homage to Etty* and its companions may well have a sexual component or subtext. In the former work, Thomas Dilworth writes,

> Trees grow vertically. This one, on a slant, is phallic, descending from pubic foliage towards a feminine pool, complete with lip, beneath its mons Venus. The pool of the Amazons is also a vulval declivity between a tufted, arboreal mons, with a grove for pubic hair. Cf. also *Bathers* (1942). Considered this way, the image evokes the mating of Sky Father and Mother Earth in the pagan vegetation-religions Lewis knew about from a) discussions with T.S. Eliot, b) from reading James Frazer's *The Golden Bough*. The "phallus of god" would be a sort of variation on the "hand (with extended fore-and-middle fingers) of God" pointing down, out of a cloud in Christian iconography.[73]

But the rite-of-spring savagery of Lewis's earlier treatments of sexuality has been replaced in at least part of the Bathers cycle by a kind of benign bemusement. The Chagall-like dreaminess of these earthily ethereal visions is at complete variance with the boredom, rage, apprehension and petulance that are assumed to have been Lewis's prevailing moods while in Canada. Airy though they are, the swimmers, waders and dancers give weight to the notion that they were invoked to perform a private function: to provide relief, release, acceptance of an otherwise impossible situation. The furnace-room episodes of *Self Condemned* come to mind when one contemplates these pictures and imagines the shivering artist trying to warm his chilblained fingers before their living fire.

> Paul Edwards argues that Lewis's "withdrawal into domesticity" at the Tudor Hotel was accompanied by a withdrawal into the recesses of the imagination. Many of the pictures that Lewis produced during this period are celebrations of the creative power of the imagination—exuberant 'creation myths' balancing white paper and brilliant but delicate washes in strange forms virtually unprecedented in his art. Lewis, whose eyesight was beginning to suffer from the effects of the tumour that would lead to blindness in 1951, was no longer the linear master of the early twenties. Indeed, some of his draughtsmanship was beginning to look decidedly uncertain, but his power of invention was as fertile as ever. This can be seen in the works he produced as a direct personal response to the war, such as the two *Lebensraum* drawings.[74]

I would argue that such "responses" include the work that does not directly allude to the global conflict but which may have been created in reaction to it, as well as to the artist's trying personal circumstances.

The male sexual-fantasy aspect of the 1940s Bathers drawings is undeniable; virtually all the figures (with the exceptions of the lover in *Sunset in Paradise* and the bearded troubadour at the lower centre of *Marine Fiesta*) are female, the great majority of them being unclad. The artist's implicit voyeurism is made explicit in *Centaur Observing a Group of Girls*; then again, in *Party of Girls*, the watcher hiding behind a tree is female. As with his 1912 drawing, *Eighteenth Century Amazons* (M 55) and the now-unlocated *Amazons* (M 30), exhibited at the Second Post-Impressionist Exhibition in October 1912, the title of *Pool of the Amazons* informs us that we are in the presence of the warrior women of Greek myth who were supposed to have dwelt near the Ther-midon River, on the coast of the Euxine Sea, and in the Caucasus mountains, where they formed a state from which men were excluded. Lewis's antipathy to what Fredric Jameson has labelled "the essentially collective dynamism of feminism or homosexual militancy"[75] is notorious, so some commentary on these "aberrations" may here be intended. ("Amazon" has been interpreted as signifying "breastless," because Amazon girl children had their right breasts cut off so as not to interfere with their bow-arms, but Lewis's heroines do not appear to be so disfigured.) Being neither all-horse nor all-men, Centaurs, if not Centauresses (of which Lewis

Opposite page:
No. 32 *Nude Panel*, 1942, graphite and watercolour on paper (35.5 x 25.5 cm), M 999. Collection of Mark McLean, Toronto.

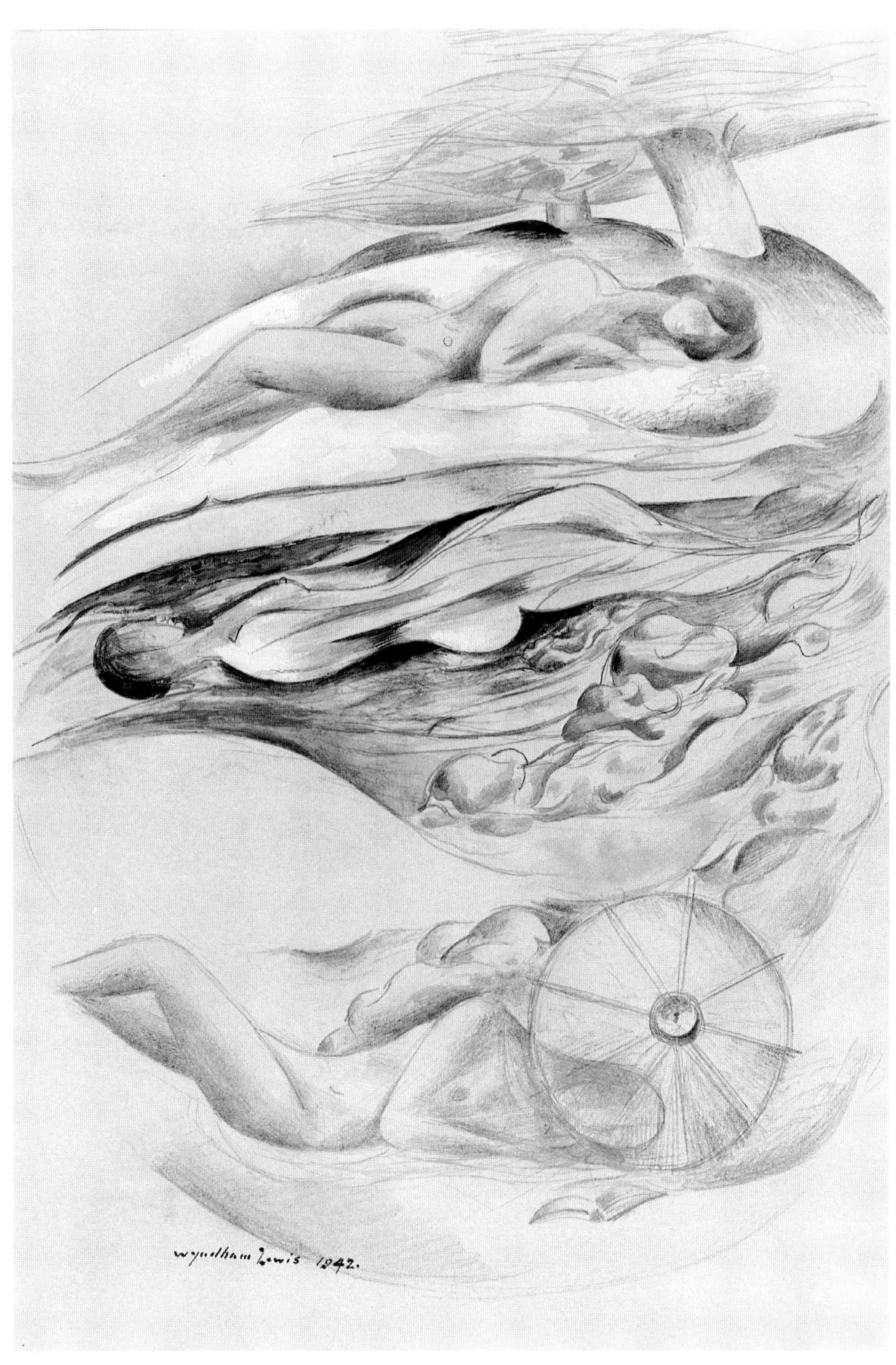
wyndham Lewis 1942.

drew two images in 1912), were doubly ostracized from both civilized society and the company of Amazons. But these wild and savage creatures, whom it took a Heracles finally to subdue, were later thought of as peaceful followers of Dionysus and Eros. The most famous of the Centaurs, Chiron, was renowned for his knowledge of medicine, music and shooting, taught mankind the use of plants and medicinal herbs, and instructed Achilles, Aeneas, Asclepius, Heracles, Jason and Peleus in the polite arts. In Lewis's *Centauress* of 1912 (M 41), Jane Farrington sees "A fragile mythological creature confronted by the harsh and threatening forms of the modern industrial world."[76] In the timeless present of the 1942 watercolour, the muscular Centaur spying on three Amazon-like beauties is perhaps more threatening than threatened.

The mildly risqué theme of "mythological creatures" (fauns and satyrs, or that unfortunate mortal, Actaeon, more often than centaurs), caught in the act of ogling nymphs, sylphs and maidens, has been a popular one in art at least since the Renaissance: witness Watteau's *Nymphe et Satyr* (c. 1714; Musée du Louvre), Arnold Böcklin's *Diana, von Faunen belauscht* (1877; Kunstmuseum, Düsseldorf), Franz von Stuck's *Quellnymphe, von Faunen belauscht* (1911; private collection, U.S.A.), to cite but three examples. The faun peeking from behind a tree at a recumbent Venus or Diana in *Sleeping Nymph Surprised by Satyrs*, formerly attributed to Nicolas Poussin (n.d.; National Gallery, London; a larger version, in the Kunsthaus, Zürich, is dated c. 1632), is positioned so like the centaur in Lewis's watercolour as to invite speculation that here is yet another case of homage-paying or parody.

Of this second sub-group, the work that is closest in composition and feeling to *The Island* (which includes all of these components except the tree) is *Bathers*; present in both is the near-vertical stone cliff on the far left, with the shallow rivulet curving about its base, in which several of the figures bathe. Michel describes this watercolour as being "Similar" to the canvas; it is, in fact, the nearest thing to a preparatory study of any of the pictures in the entire cycle, for none of which have any sketches come to light. Nor do these finished drawings betray the hesitations, rubbings-out and re-startings typical of preliminary investigations of a subject.

A useful comparison can be made between *Pool of the Amazons, Homage to Etty* and *Bathers* and Henri Matisse's 1909 watercolour, *Composition II*, otherwise known as *Demoiselles à la Riviére* (Pushkin Museum of Fine Arts, Moscow; fig. 54). John O'Brian sees this arrangement of five nude female figures assuming various attitudes in or beside a stream as exhibiting "the modernist play with depth and recession—the river and the waterfall seem to be both coming at you and retreating—that Lewis was clearly having fun with in his Bathers pictures" some thirty years hence.[77] The difference is that while the Lewis watercolours, though obviously related to *The Island*, are finished, self-contained works in its own right, the loosely drawn *Composition II* was literally made on spec', being the second of two sketches sent by the artist to the Russian collector Sergei Shchuskin, on 12 March 1909, to pressure him into granting Matisse a commission to paint full-sized stairwell decorations for his house—the result being the three decorative panels of 1909, 1910 and 1916-17, respectively: *Dance II, Music*, and *Bathers by a Stream*. Matisse described the latter canvas, then still in gestation, as "a scene of repose: some people reclining on the grass, chatting or daydreaming. I shall obtain this by the simplest and most reduced means: those which permit the painter pertinently to express all his interior vision."[78] This was precisely the license that Lewis was reclaiming in his late imaginative pictures.

There is both a willed and an "automatist" quality to most if not all of the dozen-odd erotic reveries in the two Bathers series. Michel quotes from a letter Lewis wrote to Augustus John in 1949, "which reflects some of his thoughts about this sort of subject. He lists a number of small compositions he thinks John should undertake"—among them, "for luck...a composition of 10 nude girls bathing in—oh a forest stream":

> Two scenes are to be conjured up with eyes closed, and painted 'naively': John forcing a couple of Scotch lassies up a Normandy cliff-face ('à la Rowlandson'), and John and Lewis at Bayeux, c. 1908, entertaining a band of gypsies. Finally, with eyes opened again, but now turned inward, the painter was to render 'whatever comes into your head—man or monster, witch on broomstick, or any shapes it amuses you to paint. I mean what is disrespectfully called doodling. It could not be that if you did it.'...

Michel continues:

> In Lewis's *oeuvre* as we have encountered it so far—except perhaps for the drawings antedating 1909-10—the *mind* has played a role not envisaged in these prescriptions. But in the remaining drawings of 1942, and those of subsequent years,

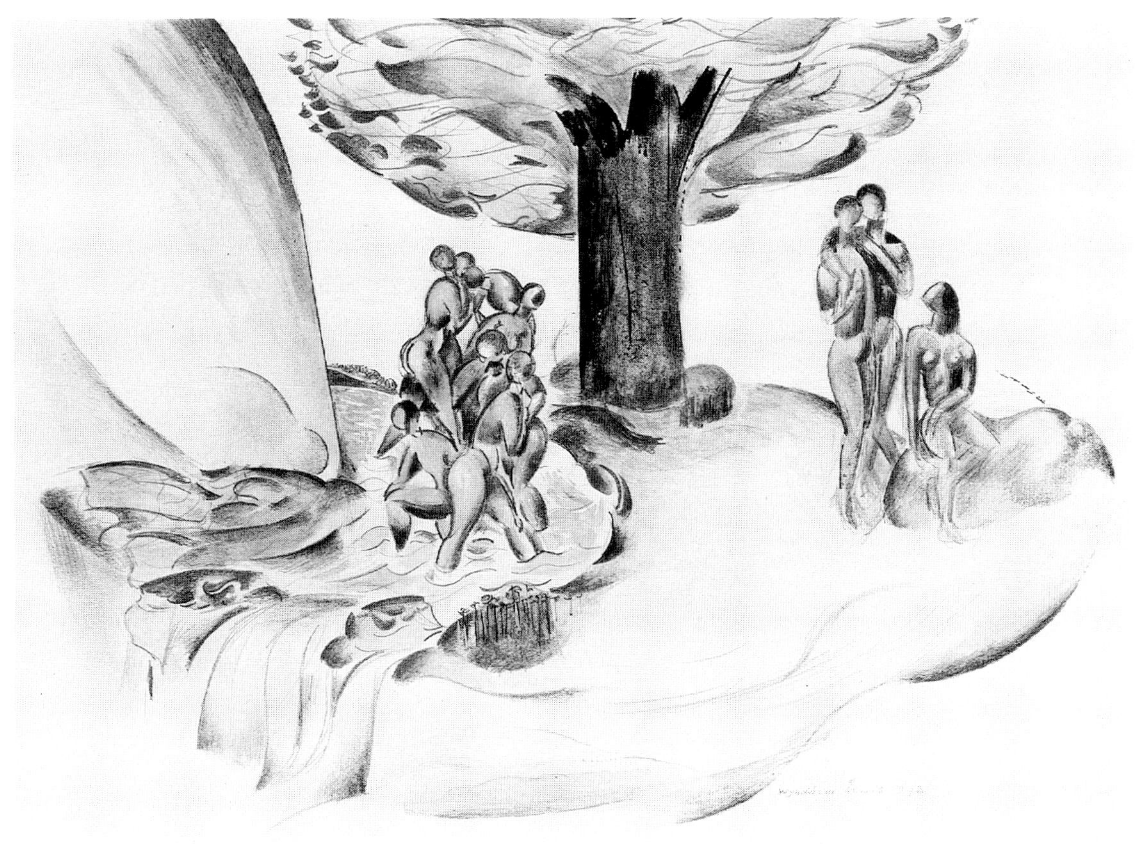

No. 47 *Bathers,* 1942, graphite and watercolour on paper (25.5 x 38.0 cm), M 992. The Board of Trustees of the Victoria and Albert Museum, London.

No. 43 *Centaur Observing a Group of Girls,* 1942, graphite, pen-and-ink, watercolour and wash on paper (45.0 x 30.0 cm), Private collection.

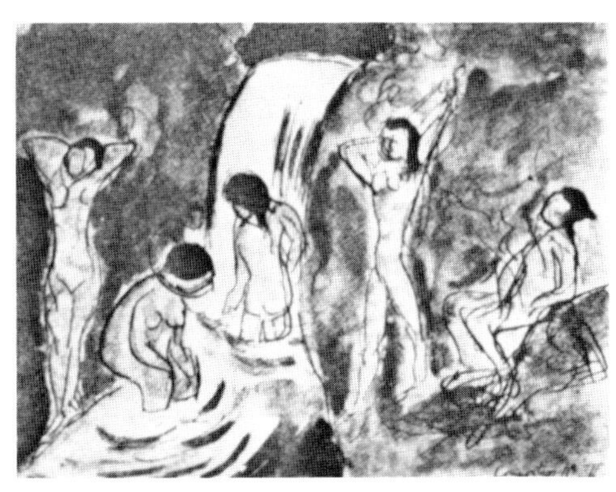

No. 54 Henri Matisse (1869-1954): *Composition No. II,* 1909, watercolour (21.9 x 29.5 cm), The Pushkin Museum of Fine Arts, Moscow.

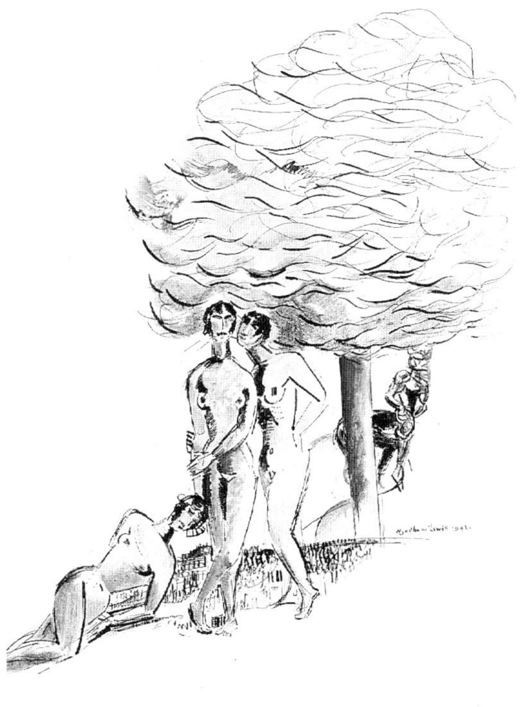

> we shall see nude girls bathing, animals and, if not darts players, children playing and actors. We shall find much that was yielded by the eye, closed, conjuring up visions, or turned inward, producing fantasies.[79]

This is exactly the posture of the idealized painter in Lewis's *The Mind of the Artist, About to Make a Picture* (no. 41), a symbolic self-portrait of 1942. Although the prone watercolourist ruminates over an open book, his eyes appear to be closed. We may infer from this that, for Lewis, literary sources and inspirations were as valid as pictorial ones: it is the creative process of the painter, acting in concert with the viewer's receptive imagination, that "translates" the words on the page into an image—in this case, the seascape floating above the dreaming picture-maker's head.

Of all the visions summoned by Lewis in his ocular twilight, the dark fantasy that is *The Island* is at once the most schematic and most enigmatic. By rights so complete an invention should have formed his farewell to exile and its seasonal discontents, but this at once radiant and ominous work sprang from his brush during the worst of the war years, 1942. Why as much as how it did so, under such trying circumstances, still resists an answer. What there is to be seen in this picture is all can we state with any degree of certainty; the meaning of the work—if indeed there is any, beyond the ontology of paint itself—remains, and must remain, elusive. This fact should not prevent us, however, from confronting the enigma and consulting our memories, imaginations and powers of reasoning in search of clues as to what exactly Lewis is saying to us, and why, whatever its intended purport, *The Island* was, is, and will continue to be at once so compelling and so mysterious.

"What are we and what are you? What do you do with us when we pass across that water. What is that place over there? These are the things we want to know."

—Wyndham Lewis, *The Childermass* (1928).

We don't know—to an agonizing degree we are not allowed to know—what it is all about.... The more it all changes, the more it is the same.

— I.A. Richards, "A Talk on 'The Childermass'", broadcast on the B.B.C. *Third Programme*, 10 March 1952.

ANTICIPATING BY NEARLY HALF A CENTURY Marshall McLuhan's theory of the dissolution of individual identity by the spread of mass electronic media Wyndham Lewis announced in the first number of *Blast* that

> The human form still runs, like a wave, through the texture or body of existence, and therefore of art.
>
> But just as the old form of egotism is no longer fit for such conditions as now prevail, so the isolated human figure of most ancient Art is an anachronism.
>
> THE ACTUAL HUMAN BODY BECOMES OF LESS IMPORTANCE EVERY DAY. It now, literally, EXISTS much less.[80]

In his *Blast*-inspired *Counterblast,* first published in 1954 and reissued in typographically and textually expanded form in 1969, McLuhan, still struggling with the revelation that "The instantaneous global coverage of radio-TV make the city form meaningless, functionless," came up with a phrase that could be a description of the hybrid genre of *The Island:* "a kind of interior landscape of the mind." Such a construct "includes more than one space in its space and more than one time in its time. It's a simultaneous order such as music readily offers." In contrast, "A merely visual landscape...can offer only one space at one time."[81] Also in 1954, the Canadian-born Hugh Kenner, who had been put on to Lewis by McLuhan, observed:

> It is a Wyndham Lewis axiom that we cannot see what is before our eyes: "The Present can only be revealed to people when it has become Yesterday"; in fact, "There is no Present—there is Past and Future, and there is Art." Hence "The production of a work of art is, I believe, strictly the work of a visionary.... If you say that creative art is a spell, a talisman, an incantation—that it is *magic*, in short, there, too, I believe you would be correctly describing it." So the artist is a man at war with Time, inhabiting the invisible point between Past and Future.[82]

The artist who cleaves to this truth, Kenner contends, is one of "the elect who gather their energies into the invisible Present, between Past and Future and outside of Time."[83]

Never again was Wyndham Lewis so to muster his forces in the creation of a work of timeless art than in his multi-layered, densely allegorical canvas of 1942, *The Island,* his own terse account of which appears in the letter to J.S. McLean quoted at the beginning of this essay.[84] For decades, however, this masterful work went unexhibited, unpublished, and undiscussed. To make matters worse, except for that one epistolary mention (which may never have found its way into the final draught of the letter in which it appears), Lewis is silent about the last—and least-known—major imaginative picture of his life.

Like the Bathers that immediately precede and are contemporary with it, *The Island* has been ignored by commentators on Lewis's work, largely because of its having remained in North America rather than finding a home in a British public or private collection. Walter Michel merely indicated in his published inventory that the painting had been "Seen by the author at the late Mr Douglas Duncan's Picture Loan Society in Toronto."[85] For some reason, *The Island* was not among the items borrowed from Duncan by Victoria College, University of Toronto, for its *Wyndham Lewis* exhibition of February 1950—presumably because the show was confined to drawings and watercolours. It was, however, one of the nine oils included in the *Wyndham Lewis* memorial exhibition held at the Santa Barbara Museum of Art in August-September 1957, which came about through the intercession of the ex-Torontonian Hugh Kenner, then associate professor in the English Department of Santa Barbara College of the University of California. Duncan later loaned *The Island* to the Lewis retrospective organized by the art gallery at Toronto's York University in November 1964, along with eight works on paper of the same period. *The Island* remained in his possession (or at least keeping) up to his death in 1968, and then in the hands of his estate until Duncan's sister, Frances Barwick, had it and four other works air-freighted to England in response to a request from Anne Lewis.[86] Omar Pound recalls that Mrs. Lewis "kept [it] hidden away. She didn't like it and in the late '60s [i.e. early 1970s] gave it to me. That is the only history (provenance) I know."[87] When Dr. Pound left England for the United States in 1980, he sold the canvas to John Martin, proprietor of Black Sparrow Press, then based in Santa Barbara, California, who in turn sold it to the Santa Barbara Museum of Art in 1986 on moving to Santa Rosa.

Discussing the work, Omar Pound perceives "an odd connection with it to *The Pole Vault* (1919?), rather than the more Dantesquan *[One of the] Stations of the Dead,* etc. Beyond that I find...that it is *so* remote from WL's other works. 'Playing while the world destroys itself' is how I see *Pole Vault* and *The Island* but that is a very personal (Swiftian?) view of the 2 paintings." He also suggests that "*Human Age* images may well be in it!"[88] John Martin, on the other hand, sees *The Island* as "lovely and luminous" and "a beautiful and important oil and in many ways the culmination of Lewis's Canadian period."[89] Walter Michel (who does not wish to be quoted directly) goes even further: for him, *The Island* is one of the important pictures of the century, quite the equivalent of one of Cézanne's large Bathers.[90]

Although Walter Michel included a cropped black-and-white reproduction of the painting, as seen at Douglas Duncan's, in *Wyndham Lewis: Paintings and Drawings*, but it was not until 1984, that *The Island* was reproduced in its entirety and in colour—appropriately enough, in *Blast*, No. 3, edited by Seamus Cooney for Black Sparrow. Cooney's commentary on the painting notes that it is "Akin to such drawings as *Bathers*, 1942..., or *Allégresse Aquatique*, 1941...", and quotes Michel's remark about the Etty-inspired nudes and bathers of 1941-42. "Something of the air of an earthly paradise," he continues,

> inheres in this scene of bathing, wrestling, dancing, and conversing groups of nudes, with the couple at lower right seemingly engaged in amorous play. But the contrasting group in right middleground, clothed unlike the others and spatially isolated from them, seem different in being absorbed in something other than the here-and-now, intently listening to the narrator's account—presumeably of the island in the background towards which he is gesturing. Paul Edwards suggested in a letter that this island (its importance emphasized by Lewis's picture title) is to be read as a reminiscence of Böcklin's *Die Toteninsel (The Island of the Dead)*—5 versions dating from the 1880s). That Lewis knew this painting is confirmed by a reference to it in *Tarr*, and the island in the present work does markedly resemble Böcklin's, at least in its left half. If the allusion is accepted, the topic of the listening group's preoccupied interest can readily be divined.[91]

The *Tarr* reference is to the fourth chapter of the American edition of Lewis's 1918 novel (substantially revised by the author in 1928), in which appears the following thumbnail sketch of the "studio or salon" of Bertha Lunken, the protagonist's German mistress/fiancée: "It was a complete Bourgeois-Bohemian interior. Green silk cloth and cushions of various vegetable and mineral shades covered everything, in mildewy blight. The cold, repulsive shades of Islands of the Dead, gigantic cypresses, grottoes of teutonic nymphs, had invaded this dwelling."[92]

Lewis had come to suspect all art and literary "scenes," whether in Paris, Berlin or London, and including the ones with which he was formerly associated, because more likely to produce bogus, second-hand Utopias, revamped "bourgeois Victorian vistas", than the lonely outposts and seaports of the ex-combatant in exile, the underground man come up for air. As Sheila Watson notes, it became "obvious" after World War I that "the 'underground' was not necessarily the germinating place of new and delicate forces, or even the place for casting pictorial spells 'intended to attract the architectural shells that were lacking...'. He had already observed in The Cave of the Golden Calf how the 'underground' could become the rallying point for previous modes of awareness."[93] For Lewis the herd mentality of the avant-garde was as bent on proving that "the independent and individual life is not worthwhile" as the psychoanalysts who were hounding the human mind from every cell of the organism until at last it "plunges into the unconscious where Dr. Freud like a sort of mephistophelian Dr. Caligari is waiting" for it —and hanging on the wall of his waiting-room, no doubt, would be a reproduction of *Die Toteninsel*. Thus it was, Watson contends, that "As 'underground' Lewis rejected Böcklin's *Isle of the Dead*. At every point he resisted the conscious withdrawal of the painter into a private and subterranean world."[94] But what, then, of the "imaginative compositions" so designated by Charles Handley-Read as a new development in his art of the 1930s and '40s?

In celebrating *Figures in the Air* (1927; M 635)—visions and vistas of the future—rather than underground and underworld creatures—throwbacks of the past, "herds of submen,"— Lewis was waging his campaign against anthropomorphism, "back to Nature", "savage stuff", the "trek of the Imagination" of the Present that gets stuck in "the first region" it strikes, "the Savage time" so beloved of "Chelsea artists" of every nationality and stripe. After all, "The artist goes back to the fish. The few centuries that separate him from the savage are a mere flea-bite to the distance his memory must stretch if it is to strike the primeval slime of creation." An artist, he stated, "can Interpret, or he can Create. There is for him...the alternative of the Receptive attitude, or of the Active and Creative one." [95] In choosing the active and creative one, Lewis would seem to be rejecting the meditative and the still, but this is not the case. Nor, I think, does a rejection of what Böcklin and his admirers "stands for" obviate the possibility of a "hard-edged" painter's acceptance of certain aspects of his painting that speak, in however foreign an accent, to the innate faculty of invention and the primitive will to create. The *Island of the Dead* allusion may constitute only a small and background aspect of *The Island*, but it bears scrutiny because Lewis put it there and because he rarely did anything without calculated intention—even when releasing his mind into the authority of the imagination.

Critical estimations of the Swiss painter Arnold Böcklin (1827-1901) have risen and fallen as frequently as the international stock market. His "great fame is attested to by the enormous number of writings published on him around the turn of the century.... It seems as though everyone who ever know Böcklin published their reminiscences between 1895 and 1915, when his reputation was at its height...."[96] Though reviled by the early Modernist painters, he retained a posthumous popularity with writers and composers, especially those with an inclination to the mystical and the occult, such as August Strindberg, Sergei Rachmaninoff and Max Reger. In 1907 Strindberg had flanked the proscenium arch of his newly opened Intimate Theatre with copies of *The Island of the Dead* for the première production of his play *The Ghost Sonata*—his intent being to suggest that "this world of wandering ghosts is nothing better than a limbo land, a prelude to the true life, which is death. The finale of *The Ghost Sonata* spells it out,...the set disappears, leaving nothing remaining but Böcklin's painting.... At one time, Strindberg even considered having a quotation from Revelation made visible in letters of fire above the paint-ing."[97] Lewis might have heard about this *coup de théâtre* from the Swedish playwright's second wife, Frida Strindberg, the proprietor of London's Cave of the Golden Calf cabaret theatre club, for which, in 1912, he had painted abstract screens, wall-panels and a drop-curtain—the set-piece being his long-lost *Kermesse*.

Among more sceptical witnesses, however, Böcklin's classicizing romanticism had come to be associated as much with the sentimental as with the irrational. This "injustice" causes the earnestly idealistic heroine of E.M. Forster's 1910 novel, *Howards End*, to exclaim,

> "Yes, yes. The German is always on the lookout for beauty.... My blood boils, when I listen to the tasteful contempt of the average islander for things Teutonic, whether they're Böcklin or my veterinary surgeon. 'Oh, Böcklin', they say, 'he strains after beauty, he peoples Nature with gods too consciously!' Of course Böcklin strains, because he wants something—beauty and all the other intangible gifts that are floating about the world. So his landscapes don't come off, and [Benjamin W.] Leader's do."[98]

The tendency of lumping this Swiss painter with the German Romantic School helps to explain his eclipse during and immediately after World War I. Then, in the 1920s and '30s, as Lewis would have been aware, the Surrealists adopted Böcklin, along with the French and Belgian Symbolists with whom he sometimes is allied, as an unconscious progenitor, thanks to the bizarre, onieric nature of his best paintings. Modernists, however, continued to revile him as an exemplar of *fin-de-siècle* decadence, doubly suspicious because of his obsession with Norse and classical mythology and the cult of the Wagnerian hero and heroine, which had so strong an appeal to the Nazi leadership—including, and especially, Adolf Hitler.[99] It was not until the late 1960s, with the revival of interest in the Symbolists and their precursors, that Böcklin's critical rehabilitation began and serious study of his work got underway.

The title assigned to all five of the recorded versions of *Die Toteninsel* (fig. 55), executed between 1880 and 1886, was not the artist's own, but rather was supplied by an art dealer, Fritz Gurlitt, who had seen only the third version; as far as the artist was concerned, this work was merely a *"Bild zum Träumen"*—that is, "a picture for dreaming about" or "a painting to dream on." As such, it is analogous to his *Villa on the Shore,* which also exists in a number of versions painted between 1863 and 1865.[100]

Despite the fact that, as Rolf Andree lamented in 1971, "Böcklin's art has always been found unintelligible outside Switzerland and Germany, and in this he shares the fate of his contemporaries known as the 'German-Romans'", during his heyday his paintings "exerted their influence even in reproductions and helped the painter achieve a dubious popularity."[101] *The Island of the Dead* in particular was frequently published in print form, in artbooks, in art journals, and in the popular media. The so-called "Hitler" version of 1883 was featured in the popular monthly *Masters in Art* series monograph on Böcklin in March 1906, with the following letterpress:

> "In the spring of 1880," writes Baron von Ostini, "Böcklin completed that work which contains the very essence of his art, and with which his name is so indissolubly linked that when we hear him spoken of we at once think of his great 'Island of Death.' No other painted landscape is so profoundly impressive; no other is so original in its conception, nor so moving in its strange beauty."
>
> Towards the shores of a lonely island a boat draws near. Across its bow rests a coffin decked with flowers, beside which stands the white-robed figure of the dead. "A few more strokes of the oars and the goal will be reached—the rocky island with its dark cypress-trees. Within the steep sides of the rock are many chambers of the dead. He who now approaches will not be alone, for even as he is not the first, so will he not be the last to be rowed across the still waters to the island of death."[102]

This monograph also reproduced *Die Toteninsel's* less familiar companion piece, *Das Lebeninsel (The Island of Life)*, painted in Zurich in 1888 (fig. 56). In some respects, *The Island of Life* is more closely comparable to Lewis's *The Island* than is *The Island of the Dead*, as the description accompanying the *Masters of Art* plate suggests:

> Upon a fairy isle crowned with slender poplars and tropical palms, happy mortals are seen dancing hand in hand upon the green turf. A summer sky smiles above them, and in the clear water beneath, their forms reflected in its glassy surface, strange beings from some imaginary realm swim gracefully around the rocky shores, while swans float leisurely upon the tranquil sea. All is light and sunshine in this happy spot which forms a striking contrast to the mysterious sadness, the solemn peace, of 'The Island of the Dead.'"[103]

In the foreground of both *Die Lebensinsel* and its companion, *Die Gefilde der Seligen*, also known as *Insel der Seligen* (1877), a naked woman is being "ferried" to the Isle of the Blessed on the back of a centaur. The shape of the isolated land-mass in Lewis's *The Island* is closer, at any rate, to that of *The Island of Life* than to that of *The Island of the Dead*—high at the centre, low at the right, rather than being, as in all five versions of the latter painting, high at both ends, with a declivity in the middle out of which tall cypresses spire. According to Carlo Böcklin, the castle of Alfonso of Aragon, on the volcanic island of Ischia, in the Gulf of Naples (fig. 57), which his father had visited for the first time in 1879, returning again in 1890, was the topographical model for *Die Toteninsel*. However, as Rolf Andree advises, the profusion of other possible "sources," and the license taken by Böcklin in contriving his variations on his theme, show "how irrelevant the original locations are with Böcklin, and how fruitless it is to try to track them down."[104]

Although I may appear to be pedantically belabouring the point in stressing this hypothetical Böcklin-Lewis connection, my reason for doing so is not to insist on direct parallels or influences, but to suggest that *Die Toteninsel* and *The Island* (and works like them) have a generic relationship *in kind*—a kinship which lies in the nature of their authors' philosophies of art and artmaking. Literary and musical inspirations for *The Island of the Dead* seem to be at least as pertinent as geographical ones, Böcklin being of the opinion that poetry (for instance, Torquato Tasso's Crusader epic, *Jerusalem Delivered*—specifically, the episode in which the enchantress Armida inveigles Rinaldo to her island of illusions, which is altered to a soul's death-journey in *Die Toteninsel*), offered painting qualities that had been lost to art with the advent of photography. Lewis in his turn contended that the public had been "vulgarized and demoralized by [the] camera and a hundred other devices."[105] For Böcklin, as for Lewis, a picture ought to be lyrical, poetical, fantasy-enhancing, and should create symbols of the joys and struggles of human existence through the depiction of emotion-charged moments. Such moments could be epical or mythic, but, again like Lewis, Böcklin leavened them with satire and humour, debunking even as he exalted. Both painting and poetry, in his view, came from the same source, *Empfindung* (i.e. feeling or sensation).[106] *The Isle of the Dead* serves, then, not so much to invoke its various antecedents and inspirations, which are many, as to instill in the viewer, by purely visual means, a tragic or heroic mood: in short, to *communicate* something.

Although Böcklin differed from Lewis in pantheistically revering Nature, he was at one with him in finding its manifestations "both beautiful and terrible, and symbolized this complexity in his work." Like Lewis, too, he "reproved other artists for being too cerebral, too concerned with theory rather than the simple act of making art.... Despite his Gymnasium education and academic training, he lamented the emphasis placed on thought at the expense of feeling."[107] Both artists were further allied in insisting on the potency of paint to suggest moods and liberate the creative imagination. This romantic article of faith held that a private image could become, in passing from the painter's mind to the canvas, a collective symbol of a power that might be liberating or terrifying—or both. Lewis's latter-day rejection of the emotional neutrality (and, he would argue, the moral negativity) of formalism, abstractionism, "extremism," and faddish "mannerism" of all kinds in art, in favour of the unfashionable humanism he espoused in *The Demon of Progress in the Arts*, can be seen as a defence of true feeling in an age when the "absurd things which are happening in the visual arts...are what must happen when art becomes totally disconnected from society, when it no longer has any direct function in life, and can only exist as the plaything of the intellect."[108]

Yet, despite such similarities in their ways of seeking, Böcklin had but limited appeal for Lewis, as is suggested by the fact that he linked him with Hegel, the German philosopher for whom he entertained even less of a regard than he had for his former idol, Nietzche. "Philosophers", Lewis huffed, "have from time to time decorated the imposing architectures of their systems with aesthetics as a building is embellished with wall-painting.... But you get the feeling from listening to the metaphysician, while he discourses of art, that you would not pay much heed to what he thought of an individual work of art. You would know that Hegel's taste in painting would probably be Böcklin: and his conclusions on the subject of aesthetics."[109] On the other hand, Lewis later would state that, though "Delacroix and Géricault are great romantics, ...Burne-Jones, Böcklin and Turner have them beat...."[110]—presumably as romantics.

Lewis could hardly have found Böcklin's uneasy mélange of melancholy, nostalgia, jocundity, prurience and morbidity much to his taste. In combination, such qualities were identified with what was, for him, the ultimate Teutonic "type," as represented by the failed painter Otto Kriesler, the villain/victim of *Tarr*, who suffers from "a homesickness for his early self." In his 1951

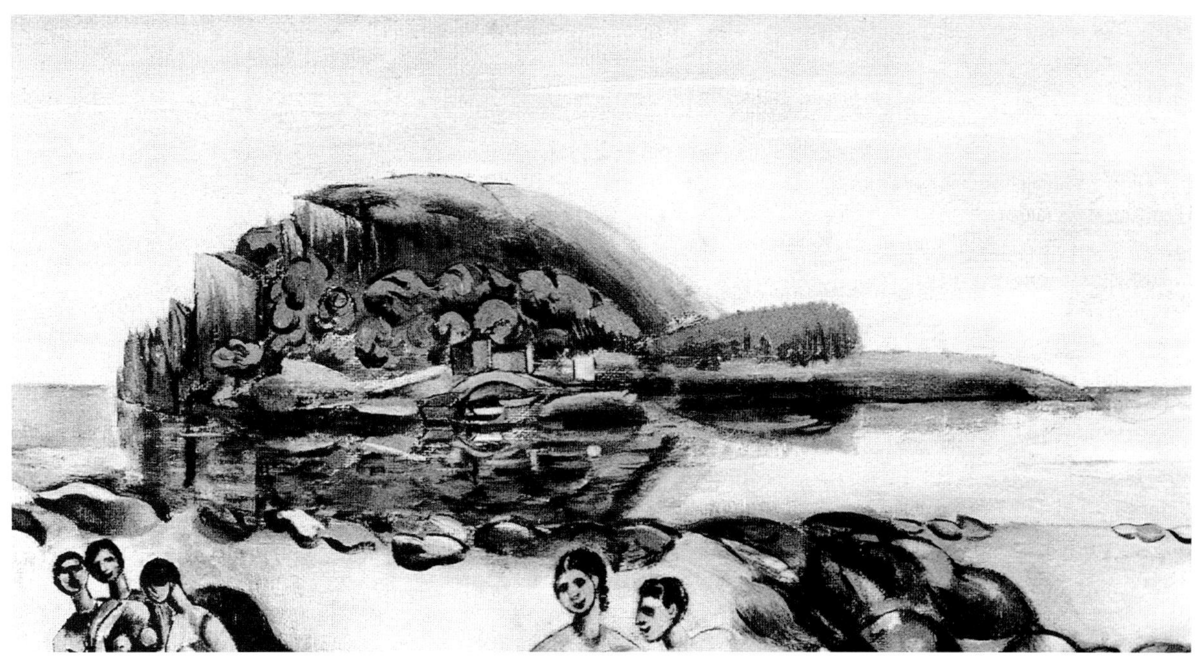

No. 48 *The Island* (detail; reproduced in colour on back cover).

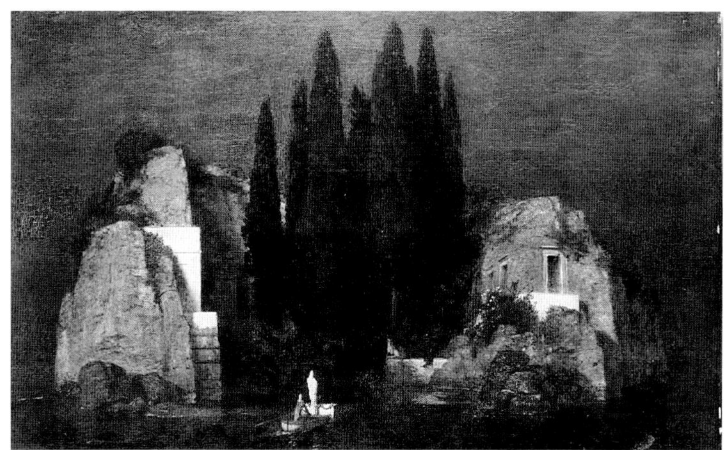

Fig. 55 Arnold Böcklin(1827-1901): *Die Toteninsel (The Island of the Dead),* 1880, oil on wood (73.6 x 121.9 cm). Metropolitan Museum of Art, New York, Reisinger Fund, 1926 (26.90).

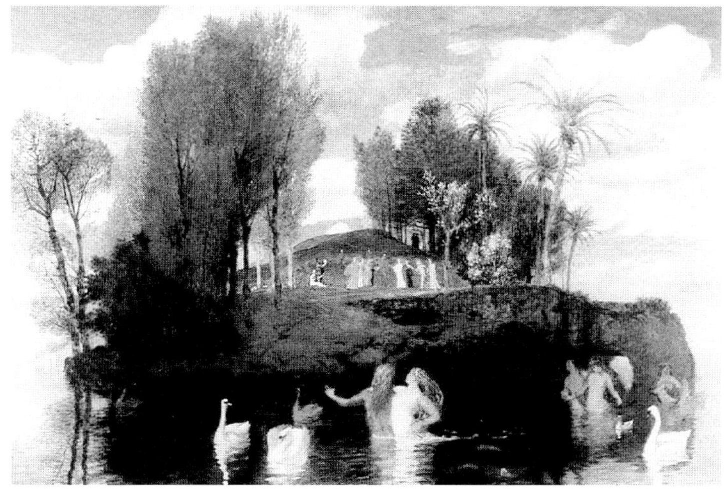

Fig. 56 Arnold Böcklin: *Die Lebensinsel (The Island of Life),* 1888, oil (94.0 x 140.0 cm). Kunstmuseum, Basel.

paper, "Böcklin now?", Georg Schmidt proposed that the Pre-Raphaelites were England's "burden" in the same way that Böcklin was Switzerland's. Sentimental though his "realism" may be, however, Böcklin's converse anti-naturalism in matters of composition and colouring would perhaps have appealed to Lewis, that great hater of the photographic aping of external appearances. As Rolf Andree remarks, "The essence of *The Island of the Dead* is not trueness to nature, but the bringing together of differing impressions from nature to create a whole that will awaken in the viewer a mood of withdrawal and dissociation from the world."[111] This, certainly, was Lewis's own mood in the early 1940s, when, languishing in self-condemned exile, he began to entertain serious doubts not only about his own survival but of that of western civilization. The apocalyptic or eschatological atmosphere of *The Island* is thus perhaps attributable to the artist's feelings of despair in the face of so much failure—his own and the systems and philosophies in which he had invested so much often misguided energy and faith. And yet, like *Die Toteninsel*, the work testifies to the painter's unshakable belief in the permanence of art in the face of change and decay.

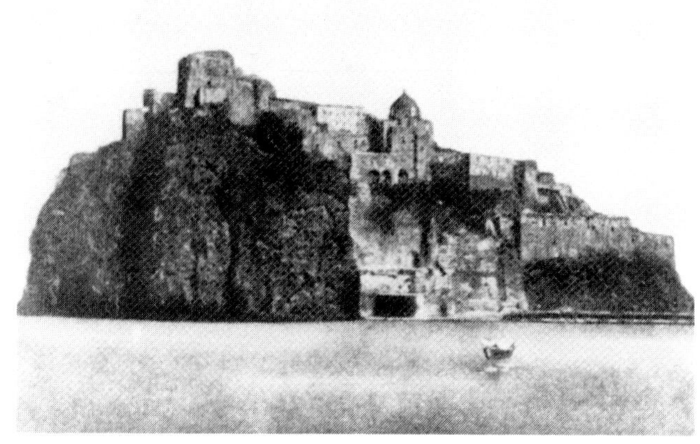

Fig. 57 The island of Ischia, Italy

In "Sirens", the follow-up to an article on Ischia entitled "The Island of Typhoëus" (which appeared in the February 1909 issue of Ford Madox Ford's *The English Review*), Norman Douglas, describing the god Pan as "the personification of the midday hush, of that which can be felt", added that "The Swiss painter Boecklin, whose Gothic exuberance often ran on lines antithetical to what we call Hellenic serenity, has yet divined the psychology of the matter in 'Das Schweigen im Walde'—the shudder that attunes the mind to receive chimerical impressions, the *silence that creates....*"[112] The "first law" of Lewis's pictures, Hugh Kenner contends, is that they are "quiet.... Theirs is a static world, supernally emptied of sound.... Lewis... presents us with pictures which are *about* their necessary condition of silence and immobility."[113] One of the functions of this silence is to induce a creatively receptive state in the viewer: that is, "a visual dream." (The eponymous hero of Robert Musil's 1906 novel, *Young Torless,* inquires, "What's this sudden silence that's like a language we can't hear?" For Lewis, art was a silent language that we can see.)

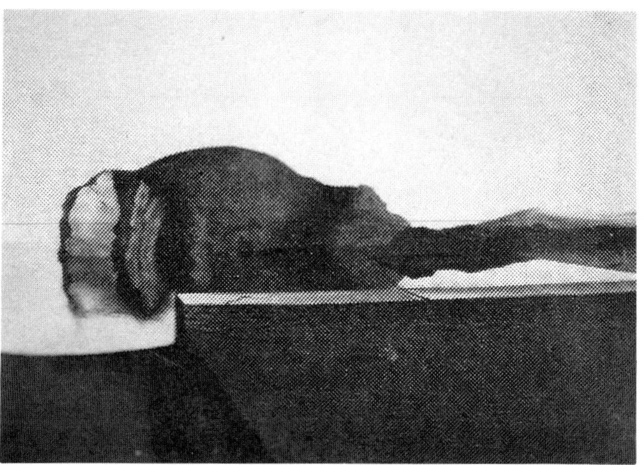

Fig. 58 Salvador Dali (1904-1989): *The True Picture of the Isle of the Dead by Arnold Böcklin at the Hour of the Angelus* (detail), 1932, oil on canvas (77.5 x 64.5 cm). Von der Heydt-Museum, Wuppertal.

More recently, Lewis had enjoyed William Gaunt's groundbreaking study of Romantic painting, *Bandits in a Landscape*, which the author had sent him in 1937. In the chapter on Léopold Robert ("an innocent and hard-working Swiss painter, whom Fate selected to enact in reality the drama of which others wrote", i.e. by committing suicide, in 1835), Lewis might have noted the fact that "A collector in Neufchâtel...expressly commissioned *A Scene of Despair on the Isle of Ischia*."[114] Unfortunately, this work—a figure painting—is not reproduced in the book. Several of the plates may, however, have found their devious way into *The Island:* for instance, Joseph Vernet's *The Bathers* (i.e. *Les Beigneurs: Matin)* (see fig. 59), or Francesco Guardi's *The Island in the Lagoon*, of c. 1770 (private collection, Milan).

Gaunt's chapter on "Guardi and the Haunted Lagoons" may similarly have revived Lewis's memory of a sinister Guardi *caprice, Il Ridotto (The Parlour)*, seen by him at the Museo Correr in Ca'Rezzonico during his trip to Venice with Nancy Cunard in 1922. The opening chapter of his satiric novel *The Vulgar Streak*, completed on Long Island in 1941, begins with a description of this painting, "alive with passion and intrigue", a colour-photogravure of which is found hanging in a Venetian shop-window by the failed artist and passer of counterfeit money, Vincent Penhale, who later recalls the picture when he is arrested by the Italian police.[115] Gaunt explains that the name applied to Guardi's "pictures of pure intention", which could also describe Lewis's exercises in "inventive picture making" (though for these the term used by Goya, *capricho*, may be more appropriate),

> is the description of the license granted to a painter, whereby he was released from the necessity of giving a faithful record of an existing view and could arrange a number of subjects according to his own fancy.... The method has something in common with

> the present-day 'surrealism,' which produces surprise by the incongruous assortment of objects; of familiar things seen in unfamiliar surroundings. The deep-seated impressions of everyday existence gain in emphasis when set free; and thus Guardi in his *caprices* conveys the poignant effect of the final spit of land where the void begins, where domes and towers fall into inanity, and a shore life of fishermen and beachcombers pursues a ragged and dream-like course.[116]

Itself a kind of serious *caprice* or Helvetian *capricho*, Böcklin's *The Island of the Dead* is, in Edward Lucie-Smith's analysis, "a 'synthetic' picture, in a fully Symbolist sense. It does not depict nature as it actually exists, but brings together various impressions received by the mind of the artist, to create a new and different world, governed by his own subjective mood. In this case, the mood is one of withdrawal, of rejection of reality."[117] Lewis, another advocate of the "synthetic" treatment of reality, and a believer in the primacy of the "super-real" over both the mundanely real and the speciously surreal, argued in 1944 for "the role of art as *expression*—as *language*", declaring that "The *visual arts*—where the expressional imagery is more *direct* than in other—is A LANGUAGE"—in fact, "*a handwritten* language too". This visual (but silent) language "discourses *about* the features of the objective universe", but is "*not* a technique for producing a facsimile of the visible world...." Art is "*not* an imitation of a natural object, or a scene in nature", but "a magic *sign*—a few brush strokes—that transports us to a mountain or to an ocean."[118] In another lecture of 1944, Lewis put into capitals his proclamation that "VISION is THE POWER OF SEEING WHAT is NOT THERE."[119]

Of course, in creating a pictorial "there" out of "what is not there," to quote or borrow from a familiar work by another artist, whether dead or alive, famous or infamous, does not require an unqualified admiration of that source, merely a belief in its usefulness as a starting-point. For all we know, Lewis may have found confirmation of his doubts about the rebarbative romantic tendencies of modern German art in the tributes paid to the Swiss neo-classicist Böcklin by such Expressionists as Lovis Corinth, Max Slevogt, Emile Nolde and the expatriate Russian, Wassily Kandinsky, who to him were all, to a greater or lesser degree, questionable. Perhaps of similar doubtfulness to him, then, would have been the Böcklin homages, allusions or parodies of such Surrealists as Max Ernst, Giorgio di Chirico and Salvador Dali, whom Lewis variously condemned as "mercenaries" and political and pictorial "reactionaries" (although he also expressed grudging respect for di Chirico's architectural fantasies).

In a somewhat self-contradictory fashion, Lewis had trained his gunsights on the Surrealists in 1931, rejecting the "dogmatic subjectivism which would manipulate objective truth, of necessity, in favour of some version of the private world of the isolated mind", on the grounds that "all reality is a merging, in one degree or another, of the external and the internal, that all reality, to some extent, is one reality saturated with the imagination." The true art of the imagination—that is, "All art worth the name"—is "already super-real."[120] Despite his dismissal of such "subjective" dogmas as Freudianism, Dada and Surrealism, Lewis nonetheless believed in the importance of the artist having freedom to draw upon every available source and resource, including dreams and nightmares—not only his own, but those of key precursors. Meryl Secrest makes the interesting point that

> Dali's symbolism may be based securely on his own obsessions, but it goes without saying that his works, and those of the Surrealists in general, were the honourable descendants of a long tradition. Henry Fuseli (1741-1825), the Swiss-born painter who lived in England and, as professor of painting at the Royal Academy, taught such important pupils as Etty, Constable and Landseer, was a fantasist whose distortions and stylizations, most evident in his famous exploration of the irrational, *The Nightmare* (1782), gave him a permanent place in the surrealist pantheon. Another was Arnold Böcklin..., the major Swiss painter of the nineteenth century, whose landscapes of heightened imagery and menace were widely appreciated and imitated. His best-known work, *The Isle of the Dead*..., is as haunting as a dream image and was to have an enormous influence on Dali. He painted an extended study of the work, and made frequent references to the painting's surreal fountain and menacing cypresses in his own work.[121]

In arguing the case of "Super-nature versus Super-real" in 1939, Lewis insisted that Surrealism "is in effect a sly return to old forms of painting, and not the most desirable at that"; thus "Meissonier and Böcklin are the avowed masters of Dali",[122] who had been engaged in writing an extended study of the latter artist throughout the decade. Yet in painting *The Island,* this inveterate anti-Surrealist may conceivably have had in mind not only *The Island of the Dead* but Dali's 1932 canvas, *The True Picture of the Isle of the Dead by Arnold Böcklin at the Hour of the Angelus* (fig. 58)—a work which, when shown to him by its owner, Baron von der Heydt, made a strong impression on Adolf Hitler, and which he would recast in 1944-45 as *Giant Flying Demi-Tasse with Incomprehensible Appendage Five Miles Long* (private collection, Basel). The humpbacked silhouette of the island in *The True Picture...* indicates that Dali intended to depict Böcklin's original inspiration as he himself had seen it, the castellated outline corresponding much more nearly to the actual shape of the volcanic Ischia, as viewed from a dis-tance, than to the saddle-shaped form of *Die Toteninsel.* The same can be said of the island in Lewis's painting of that title, which also lacks the dark grove of cypres-ses towering from the declivity at the centre of all five versions of the Death-Isle.

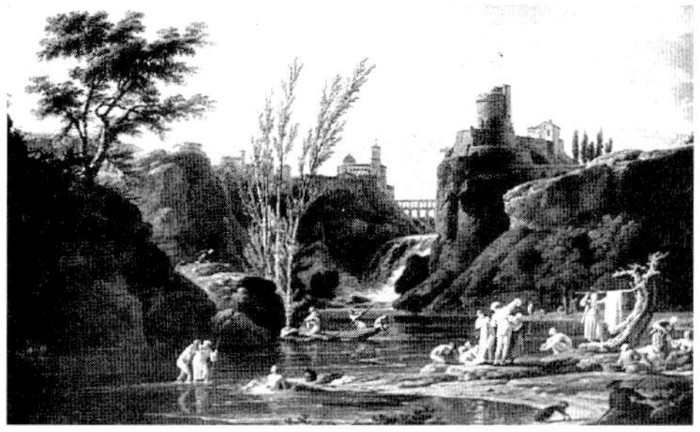

Fig. 59 Joseph Vernet (1714-1789): *Beigneuses: Le Matin*, oil on canvas (98.0 x 162.0 cm). Musée du Louvre, Paris. (One of four canvases commissioned by Mme. du Barry depicting the times of day.)

The basically pyramidal composition of *The Island* falls into three main parts: the island in the central background, eerily reflected in the mirror-like water; the throng of animated bathers and athletes in the left and central foreground and middle-ground; and the small group of reposeful conversants off to the far right. As in so many of Lewis's Bathers pictures of all periods, the attractant to the larger assemblage of figures is water: in this case, a purling stream at the foot of a sheer cliff and, just to its right and possibly feeding it, a small pool. Wading, bathing, dancing, running, watching, wrestling, or perhaps engaged in "amorous play", these creatures are, again, exclusively female; for all we know, they may be Maenads, or Amazons. As elsewhere in the Bathers sequence, the element of struggle suggested by the couples locked in embraces, dance-positions or wrestling-holds (it is hard to tell which) seems like a throwback to the manic grapplings of the *Wild Body* stories (published in 1927 but most dating from 1909 to 1917); to the *Combat* drawings of 1914 (M 161-162); and to "the series of pen drawings of pen drawings of pin-head figures strutting about in an anonymous landscape performing their own instinctive rituals" which Lewis intended to depict "phases of a combat or courtship in the insect world.'"[123] But the prevailing ambience of the lower-left quarter of *The Island* is that of the placid William Etty nudes which elicited the 1941-42 homages. (The waders in the brook, like those of *Homage to Etty, Pool of Amazons* and *Bathers,* also evince a knowledge on Lewis's part of Böcklin's *Nymphe an der Quelle,* painted in two versions in 1854 and 1855, both of which depict a nymph bathing her limbs at the foot of a small waterfall.)

A patriotic observer with an exile's acuity of vision, Nikolaus Pevsner was convinced that "The Nude, in spite of William Etty, has been a rarity in English painting over centuries—and is now. One need only compare in one's mind the Royal Academy and the Paris Salon." This phenomenon he attributes to the fact that "the English have nothing of the Italian, the Mediterranean confidence in the body. It may be said that Puritanism has driven it out...."[124] The comparative scarcity of nudes in British (and, by extension, in Canadian) art adds to the unusualness of Lewis's Toronto-period experiments with the subject. An extraordinary precedent for such works as *Pool of the Amazons, Bathers* and *The Island,* in particular, is *The Maiden's Haunt,* by the itinerant English painter Julius Caesar Ibbetson (1759-1817) (fig. 60), of which John Sunderland has written: "Ibbetson's bland pastoral landscape genre is here enlivened...by the presence of a female bathing party. Such quasi-mythological paintings were common in French and Netherlandish painting of the seventeenth and eighteenth centuries, but very rare in England. An unexpected example is Gainsborough's freely painted *Diana and Actaeon* in the royal collection."[125] Yet another is the same painter's late, unfinished *Nymph at the Bath* (Tate Gallery, London), the figure of which is based on an Antique design also used by Adriaen de Vries.[126]

The arrival in England of Titian's *Diana and her Nymphs Surprised by Actaeon* and *Diana Discovering the Pregnancy of Callisto* (both c. 1559; National Gallery of Scotland), formerly part of the Orléans Gallery, which had come into the hands of the Bridgewater family after the French Revolution, had created some havoc in the minds of British artists then unfamiliar with such "Baroque" treatments of Ovidian mythology. One of these was Thomas Stothard (1755-1834), among whose collection at his decease were such tellingly titled works as *The Diana Sleeping, Diana and Nymphs Bathing, Surprised by Satyrs, Nymphs Bathing, Birth of Venus, Bacchanalia,* and *Figures in a Waterfall,* and whose memorial exhibition at the British Institution in 1841 included *The Bath of Diana* and *Diana Sleeping.*

However, the fashion for classical nudes-in-a-landscape did not continue without interruption in England. William Etty's torch was passed on to his student, William Edward Frost, who painted and exhibited classical subjects into the 1860s, as did a number of other minor artists, but the genre had been proscribed by the Pre-Raphaelites, whose Brotherhood was formed in 1849, the year of Etty's death. Ruskin's horror of the unclothed female alone had a further dampening effect, one that lasted for several decades. However, after mid-century a counter-reaction set in, the fundamental cause of which was, in the words of Christopher Wood, "a dissatisfaction with Pre-Raphaelitism, coupled with a desire to renew contact with the traditions of European art.... The 1860s were a period of intense artistic ferment, out of which emerged many different directions in English art. The classical movement was one of these. The aesthetic movement, which developed at the same time, was inevitably highly eclectic, and took many different forms."[127] The Victorian and Edwardian Parnasseans—Lord Leighton, Sir Lawrence Alma-Tadema, Sir Edward Poynter, Albert Joseph Moore, Solomon J. Solomon, John William Waterhouse—legitimized the revival of the Renaissance and Mannerist bather subject by placing nude and semi-nude figures (goddesses, athletes, Greek and Roman maidens) in classical, mythological and literary settings, mixing historicism, eroticism and exoticism in ways that foreshadowed the tactics and topics of the Symbolists—as did such Aesthetic Movement leaders as Sir Edward Burne-Jones and Walter Crane. Crane's *The Renaissance of Venus* (1877; Tate Gallery, London) combines several of the ingredients Lewis used in *The Island:* nude nymphs (on the shore of Cythera), the dark silhouette of a mountainous island looming on the horizon. Lewis may sincerely have hated such pictures, but they were part of the culture out of which he emerged and against which he shaped his own career, in opposition to the Royal Academy, where the "classicists" continued to find a home well into the modern era.

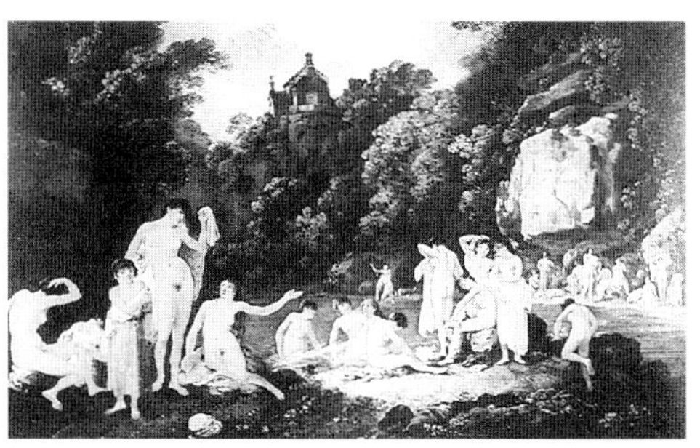

Fig. 60 Julius Caesar Ibbetson (1759-1817: *The Maiden's Haunt* 1804, oil on panel (37.5 x 48.3 cm). Victoria and Albert Museum, London.

More recent and germane antecedents for late-Lewis bathers, beach-babies and Amazons, such as those of Puvis de Chavannes (the master inventor of the genre), Paul Cézanne, Paul Signac, Paul Seurat, Edmond Aman-Jean, Auguste Renoir, Paul Gauguin, Maurice Denis, André Derain, Otto Friesz, Henri Matisse, Robert Delaunay, Erich Heckel and, in the United States, Childe Hassam, Maurice Prendergast, and Arthur B. Davies, come readily to mind. The post-Romantic modernist bathers mode can be said to begin with Cézanne (dubbed by Lewis "a heaven-sent idiot, the essential painter"),[128] who painted over 200 treatments of the subject, culminating in his *Grandes Baigneuses* series of 1890-1906 (fig. 61), which in turn led to so many radical developments—perhaps most notably Picasso's *Demoiselles d'Avignon* of 1907. But, Dore Ashton reminds us, such early, romantic canvases as *Bathers on the Rock* (Chrysler Museum at Norfolk, Virginia) "illustrate Cézanne's admiration for the work and ideas of Delacroix."[129] And Delacroix, it should be remembered, was a great admirer of William Etty.

Although he was later to dismiss Matisse as being "best at a very circumscribed, thin, gay, and pretty cleverly arranged effect", in 1919 Lewis had declared him to be "certainly as good a painter as any working in Paris today. He possesses more vitality than Picasso; and he appears to have more stability...."[130] Of all his numerous treatments of nude bathers, picnickers and dancers cavorting in Attic (or at least Riviera) settings with Bergsonian *élan vital,* Matisse's huge 1906 canvas, *Le Bonheur de vivre* (fig. 62), seems compositionally closest to *The Island,* despite the fact that its mood, as the title indicates, is entirely more cheerful and unambiguous than that of the latter painting.[131] Although the "golden age" ambience of *The Joy of Life* has its closest analogies with such immediate precursors as Matisse's own *Luxe, calme et volupté* of 1904, Puvis de Chavanne's *L'Eté* of 1873, Cézanne's *Trois baigneuses* of c. 1879-80, Derain's *L'Age d'or* of c.1903, and Signac's *Le Temps d'harmonie* of 1905 (themselves lineal descendents of Giovanni Bellini's *Feast of the Gods,* Titian's *Bacchanal* and *Concert champêtre,* Agostino Caracci's *Recicipio Amore* and Ingres's *Golden Age)*, John Jacobus proposes that "A further revealing juxtaposition can be made with Edvard Munch's figure paintings, dating back as far as 1890, which show a totally different, pessimistic and despairing attitude toward the earthly paradise."[132] This attitude was shared, of course, by Lewis, whose chronic pessimism was exacerbated by the outbreak and dragging on of the Second World War. And yet there is pictorial evidence from the early 1940s that suggests a mature reconciliation with "life," if not with the forces that had rendered his own existence so fraught with difficulty, that could hardly have been expected under the circumstances. Unless, that is, those very circumstances were responsible for this late blooming into equanimity.

Perhaps surprisingly, it is Picasso, more than any other contemporary artist, who has the closest affinity to the new-old Lewis of the Bathers and *The Island*, despite the antipathy of the latter painter for the former. The event that brought these two figures together, in art if not in life, was the *Picasso: Forty Years of his Art* exhibition, organized in 1939 by Albert Barr for the

Museum of Modern Art, New York. The catalogue of this retrospective, which Lewis had savagely reviewed in the spring of 1940, reproduced such examples of his contributions to the *baigneuse* tradition as his 1918 and 1922 pencil drawings, *Bathers* and *Women by the Sea*, his 1921 tempera on wood, *Four Classic Figures*, and his 1923 canvas, *By the Sea*. In his largely pejorative critique, however, Lewis focused on *The Race* (1922), in which "one sees a couple of foully bloated females, masquerading in Greek costume, disporting themselves on a beach."[133] Lewis's own series of fleet-footed, light-bodied Bathers, started within a year of the review, can be seen as a kind of pre-emptive strike against his Spanish contemporary in the "'back to nature' crusade" that he had been leading in Europe until "interrupted, but [which] after the war will be resumed."[134]

Lewis's dismissal of Picasso as "this protean Jack-in-the-box among painters" notwithstanding, there is an extraordinary similarity between *The Island* and the aforementioned *Bathers*, of 1918 (fig. 63), described in the MOMA catalogue as being not only one of the finest drawings of his "'classic' period", but "one of the most elaborate of all Picasso's figure compositions. The distortions and elegant simplifications are obviously influenced by the art of Ingres."[135] *Bathers* corresponds so closely in compositional structure to Lewis's painting—graceful foreground and middle-ground figures, cliff on the left, obscurely defined island in the background—as to indicate either direct influence (conscious or unconscious), commentary, parody, or a desire to outdo. There are also striking parallels between the embracing or grappling couple in Lewis's *Allégresse Aquatique* and the similarly positioned pair (both female, one turning away from her wooer to regard the viewer) in the Picasso drawing; and between the seated, long-tressed woman with her back to us on the left side of *Homage to Etty* and the large figure looking over her shoulder on the left side of *Bathers*.

Lewis's professed indifference in art history is yet another of his half-serious, half-jocular claims to being "a man without a past" that must be taken with several shakes of salt. Separated as he was in Toronto from the kinds of "sources" upon which he relied for material, including and especially his library and clipping-files, it was natural that he should have made up the loss by drawing from his private image-bank while working on these pieces of "inventive picture making." Nor was this habit a late development; isolation and incipient eye-trouble merely accelerated the process. The practice of what came to be known, during the 1970s and '80s, as "appropriation" was but one of many foreshadowings of postmodernism that critics have retrospectively detected in the militantly modernist programme of the "Great London Vortex." Reed Way Dasenbrock contends that the Vorticists' "aim of imitation"

> is the construction of a parallel or equivalence between the past and the present. This view clashes with the modern sense that imitation produces derivatives that cannot be equivalents. But the Vorticist notion is the traditional one, closer to the notion of imitation found in the Renaissance. Petrarch, for instance, defines proper creative imitation precisely as a mode of attaining equivalence.... The notion of imitation as the creation of a family resemblance implicity makes Petrarchan (or Humanist) imitation a mode of canon formation....
>
> Petrarch's example of weak or excessively faithful imitation is painting, but a notion of imitation close to his begins to operate in painting in France in the nineteenth century...in the art of Edouard Manet. Just as Petrarch at his extreme included lines of Arnaut Daniel, Dante, Cavalcanti, and Cino da Pistoia in a poem, Manet in his paintings of the early 1860s...appropriated figures from paintings by Velasquez, Raphael, Watteau, and others, also at least partially with the aim of defining a canon.... Like Petrarch, Manet provides the pattern for a new kind of painting, though few subsequent painters attained equivalence with their model as clearly as he did in *Le Déjeuner sur l'Herbe* and *Olympia.*
>
> Imitation in the service of making things new, thus, is an ideal both of Renaissance literature and French modernist painting before it becomes the ideal of Vorticism.... The Vorticists, moreover, were aware of and drawing upon these predecessors.... The Vorticist artists' fashioning of new art out of old would have been unthinkable without the models of Manet, and, in more oblique ways, Cézanne and Gauguin.[136]

Lewis himself confessed to having begged the question of "Why *abstract* paintings", offering instead, "Why not variations on Manet, Gainsborough, Raphael...?"[137] In view of such a position and such antecedents, it is perhaps not surprising that *The Island* should also contain yet another "imitation" of a nineteenth-century painter: Manet himself, an artist about whom Lewis had somewhat mixed feelings, the favourable ones outweighing, however, the unfavour-

Fig. 61 Paul Cézanne (1839-1906): *Grand baigneurs (Large Bathers)*, c. 1896-97, lithograph on paper (48.1 x 62.9 cm). National Gallery of Canada, Ottawa.

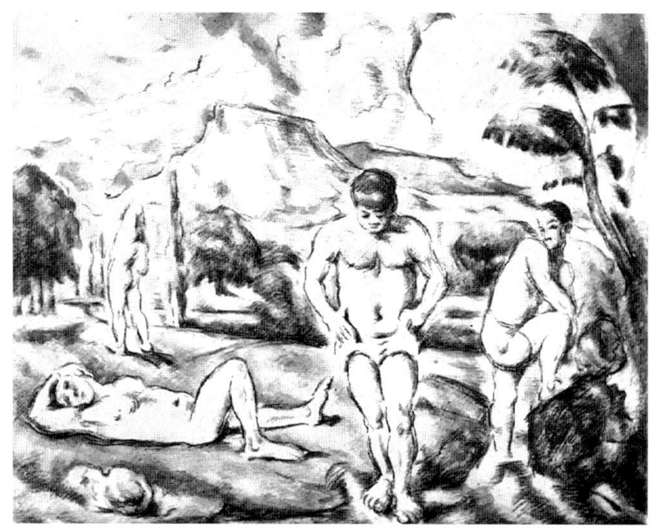

Fig. 62 Henri Matisse (1869-1954): *Bonheur de vivre*, 1905-06, oil on canvas (174.1 x 238.1 cm). Barnes Foundation, Merion Station, Pennsylvania.

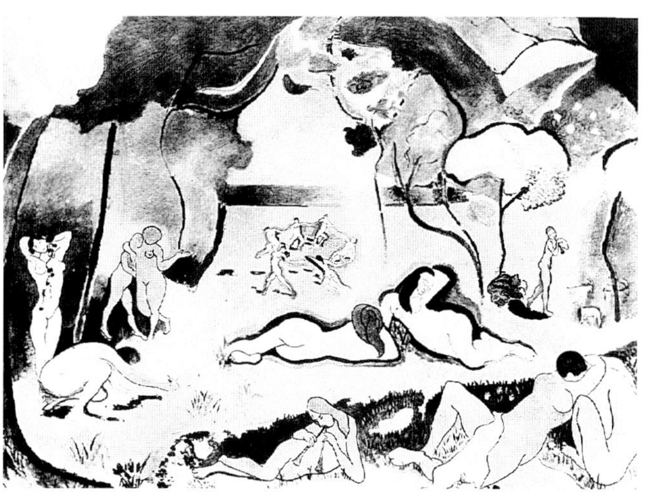

Fig. 63 Pablo Picasso (1881-1973): *Bathers*, 1918, graphite (23.2 x 31.1 cm). Fogg Art Museum, Cambridge, Mass., Paul J. Sachs Collection.

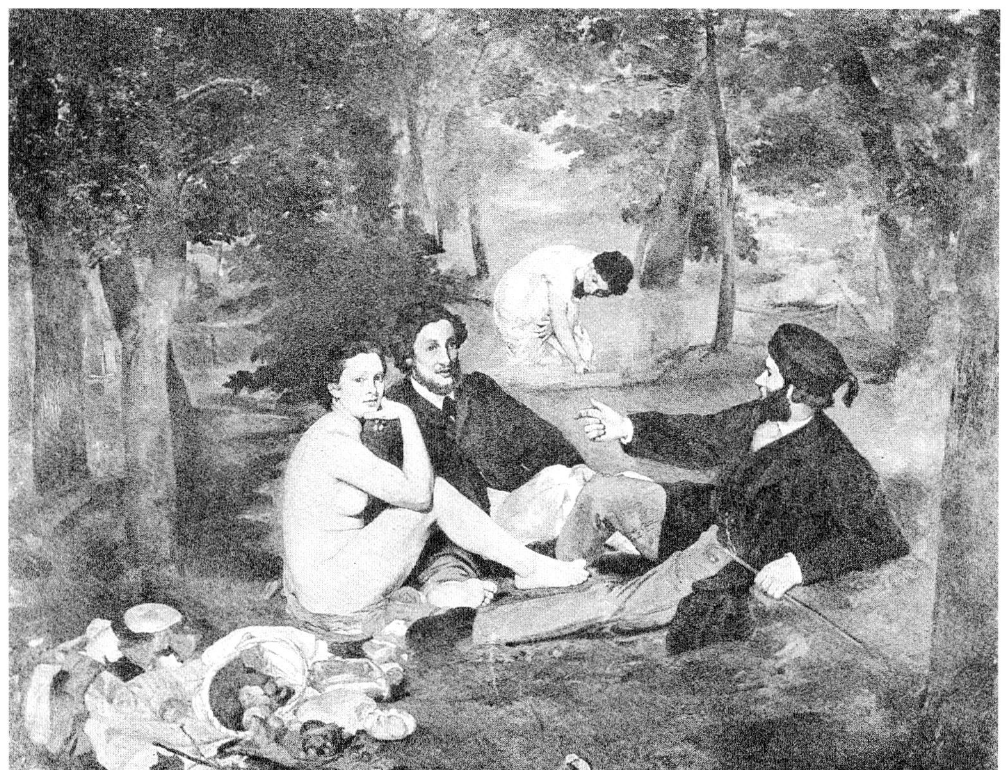

Fig. 65 Giorgione (1477/78-1510): *Fête Champêtre*, 1508, oil on canvas (110.0 x 138.0 cm). Musée du Louvre, Paris.

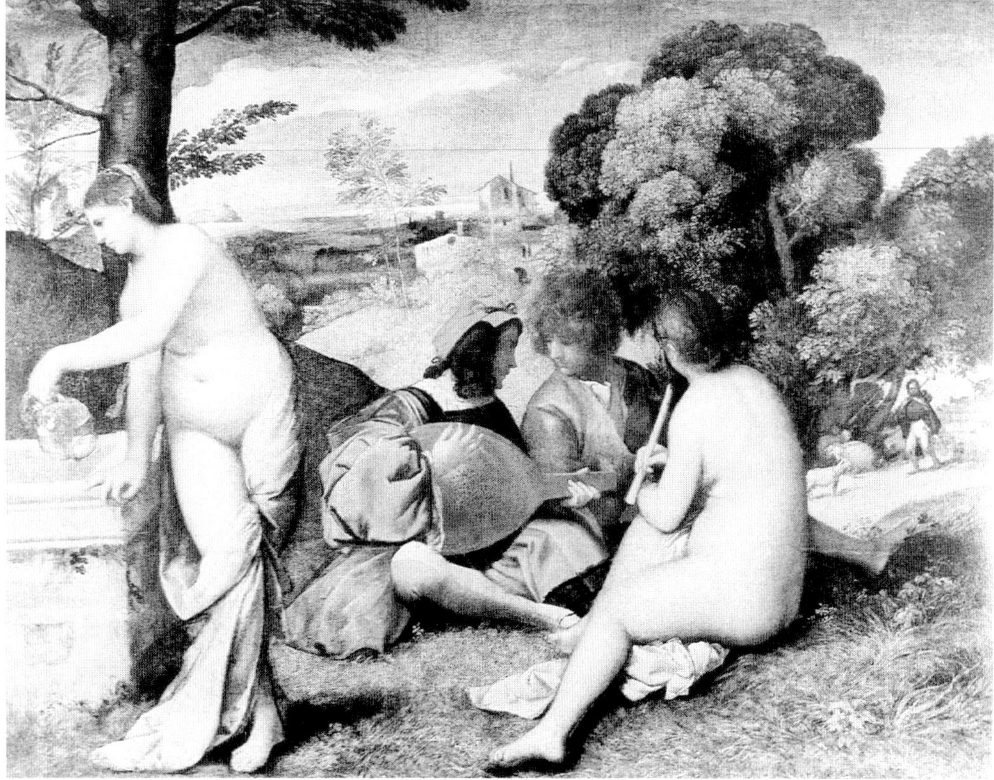

Fig. 64 Edouard Manet (1832-1883): *Le Déjeuner sur l'herbe*, 1863, oil on canvas (208.0 x 264.5 cm). Musée d'Orsay, Paris.

able. (He insisted, for instance, that Manet, though regarded by André Malraux as "the *first* of a new kind of artist," was, in fact, "a great traditionalist, setting up Velasquez as a model, in opposition to the vulgarity and bad painting of the Salons."[138]) As Seamus Cooney observes, separated from the revellers commanding central stage in *The Island* is a small group of figures (no. 48: detail), to one of whom the others appear to be intently listening; close observation reveals that they are posed more or less like the picnickers in Manet's *Le Déjeuner sur l'herbe* of 1863 (fig. 64), the original title of which, incidentally, was *Le Bain*.

This once-scandalous treatment of an intimate colloquy among decidedly contemporary representatives of Culture and Nature, or of the City and the Country, has been elevated to the status of the first and quintessential Modernist painting: an answer to Baudelaire's call of 1845 for the depiction of the heroism of *"la vie moderne."* And yet, as Marcia Pointon has observed, *Le Déjeuner* goes against the grain of Modernism by introducing "the transgressive tendency of allegory." Or rather, it "makes out a space which is neither social nor allegorical but which is between the social and the allegorical; it is a space where there are no meanings, only the signs of absent meanings."[139]

Defiantly new and original though it may be, Manet's painting is full of references to, if not reverential of, older and other art. And just as it possesses a "capacity for transformation, for appropriation, and for inversion", so it offers up a rich bounty of antecedents and quotations. "Source spotting", Pointon comments,

> has been a major industry among Manet scholars. Interpretations o*f Le Déjeuner sur l'herbe* include the ingenious tooth-comb of Mauner...at one extreme who argues—by reference to the many iconographic models identifiable—that the painting constitutes a philosophical meditation upon the binary opposition between the material and the spiritual. Mauner takes for granted the most fundamental of oppositions—that constituted by gender; the opposition that he identifies as the pivot for the painting's meaning, an opposition between the material and the spiritual, as well as the terms which that opposition take, are grounded in the very issue of gender which goes unnoticed in his elaborate interpretation. On the other hand there is Hanson who sees it as a painting of modern life and stresses the parallels in lithography and other contemporary popular imagery.[140]

The two most frequently cited iconographical models for the painting's main group are a sixteenth-century engraving by Marcantonio Raimondi after Raphael's *The Judgement of Paris,* and Giorgione's *Fête* or *Concert Champêtre*, tentatively dated 1510 (fig. 65).[141] Manet himself is said to have identified the latter work as his main source in referring to the copy that he (like William Etty before him) had made of it in the Louvre. Hanson reminds us that "The monumental nude figure in *Déjeuner sur l'herbe* was preceded in Manet's *oeuvre* by a copy of Titian's *Venus of Urbino* ...and a small series of nudes in landscape settings which culminated in *The Surprised Nymph* of 1861...." These studies, she argues, "are heavily dependent on old master sources for both themes and motifs.... The painting known as *The Surprised Nymph* shows only a nude woman in the woods and thus displays no over subject matter connections." However, when Manet sent the painting to Russia in 1871, it included the figure of a satyr, and bore the title of *Nymph and Satyr.* "Both the use of this figure which gives the figure an anecdotal element, and its remov-al which deprives the picture of explanation or justification, are steps in Manet's own development toward the presentation of the modern nude."[142]

If, as one writer has suggested, Manet "makes a nature out of culture",[143] it might be argued that Lewis makes a culture out of nature. Manet was described by Paul Jamot in 1932 as *"grand artiste qui situe la réalité dans l'irréel"* (a great artist who places reality in unreality).[144] Lewis insisted that it was the artist's obligation to "put something new in the world", rather than merely to accept and enjoy and replicate what already exists (hence his hatred of Impressionism and Post-Impressionism). "The artist's function", he wrote, "is to create—to make something, and *not to make something pretty,* as dowagers, dreamers, and dealers here suppose"[145] The raw materials that go into this literal act of creation can include, however, things that have already been created by others. Whether or not the appropriative process is a conscious one, or the histories of the stolen goods are known to the artist, is irrelevant; what matters is that something new has been made to enter and renew the world. Nor, as we shall see, did Lewis regard as contradictory his insistence that another task of the artist was to reduce the sheer "quantity" of "things" that are in nature.

In the sub-group in the upper middle-right of *The Island*, Lewis both follows and departs from Manet: there are four figures (as in Giorgione's *Fête Champêtre*), rather than three, and three of them, including the (male?) figure on the left—an echo of the naked muse/prostitute in the left foreground of *Le Déjeuner*—are clad. The sole naked figure, positioned third from left, is also the only manifestly female member of the party. Absent (or perhaps now part of the group) is the shift-wearing bather/wood-nymph wading up to her knees in the shallow background pool of the Manet canvas—a disruptively hovering presence who in a sense has been replaced, in Lewis's painting, by the island itself. The male figure on the far right now gestures upward, rather than at the object of his (and the viewer's) voyeuristic regard. Do these changes point to an illustration of the Cartesian mind/body split, the huddling interlocutors on the right of *The Island* being intended to exemplify the intellect or the spirit, the naked fun-lovers gambolling to left and centre standing for the carnal and the emotional? If this is the case, could the solitary unclad figure be meant to represent a convert from the passing joys of the flesh to the enduring passions of the mind, which Lewis considered to be an exclusively masculine province? In other words, is Lewis *rewriting* the "plot" of *Le Déjeuner sur l'herbe* to conform with his own ethical and philosophical position?

The dominance and centrality of the conversing men in *Le Déjeuner* (the woman clearly being excluded from their dialogue) has led Marcia Pointon to posit that the picture "addresses the fundamental question of narrative for pictorial art and it addresses the question in relation to subjectivity. *Whose story is it?* might be a suitable sub-title and the answer has to be, of course, the viewer's." However, "The many narratives constructed around *Le Déjeuner sur l'herbe* in words and in images testify to this impulse to demystify by explication, a process that can only be achieved through furthering the narrative movement towards some kind of closure."[146] But could it not be argued that the *real* "narrative" in any work of art is the artist's investigation of the world, and that the viewer is an onlooker who participates in the "story" by engaging with it imaginatively?

One of the objects of the painter's search, Lewis believed, is to refertilize "extinct modes", to authenticate "interesting new and specifically scientific notions", and to give "a new bit of life" to dead artists, as Picasso had done to El Greco. But—again with reference to Picasso—"To dash uneasily from one seemingly personal mode to another may be a diagnostic" of a "highly sensitive but non-centralized talent".[147] In invoking Manet's flawed masterpiece, Lewis, recapitulating Cézanne, anticipated Picasso's own immersion in it, which first manifested itself in his 1949 oil, *Le Déjeuner sur l'herbe* (Musée Picasso, Paris), began anew in 1954 with four drawings closely after the original, and then took the form of a concerted project, the last of his series of interpretations of old masters, executed between August 1959 and July 1962.[148]

The contemplative, almost pastoral tone given to *The Island* by the symposium-like *Déjeuner* interlude offsets the frenetic action in the foreground; it may be significant that this small, isolated cluster of humanity is physically closer to the island across the water than are the agitated creatures on the upper beach. Closer to Dis?—or closer to Paradise? Does the strait between the foreshore and the island represent the waters of generation? Or, alternately, Lethe or the Styx? For, as the German art historian Harald Keller remarks, "It has been too glibly proposed that in Giorgione's *Concert champêtre*...the ideal solution is discovered: a free Renaissance society which has found its form of expression with the aid of Antique prototypes. But the two nude figures are demigoddesses, and the picture itself seems more like an image of death—a memorial for a young friend too early dead."[149]

The analogical complexity of *The Island* brings us back to one of the fore-sources of the whole Bathers sequence, Lewis's *Creation Myth No. 1* (1933), which Hugh Kenner has anatomized as follows: "an abstract, classical world to the right is balanced by the dream-world of the flesh to the left: hooded female figures posed in a corridor labelled 'Athanaton' (Immortality)."[150] Is the same division to be discerned in *The Island?* Certainly repose and tranquility, on the right, are balanced against frantic (or at least antic) motion (and emotion), on the left, with the spectre of death hovering on the horizon like an all-too-real mirage. But can we be sure that Lewis is following Böcklin's—or, for that matter, Giorgione's—allegorical formula to the letter? It may not be coincidental that in the background of Lewis's *Lebensraum I: The Battlefield,* painted the year before, rises a mountainous island (again separated from the main by a narrow strait of water), which is similar in contour to that of *The Island.* The shape recurs in 1942's *The Three Beggars* (no. 52), in which the propped-up mendicants—outcast from the city below them on the right—contemplate, on the left, the coffin or sarcophagus of a fallen comrade who appears

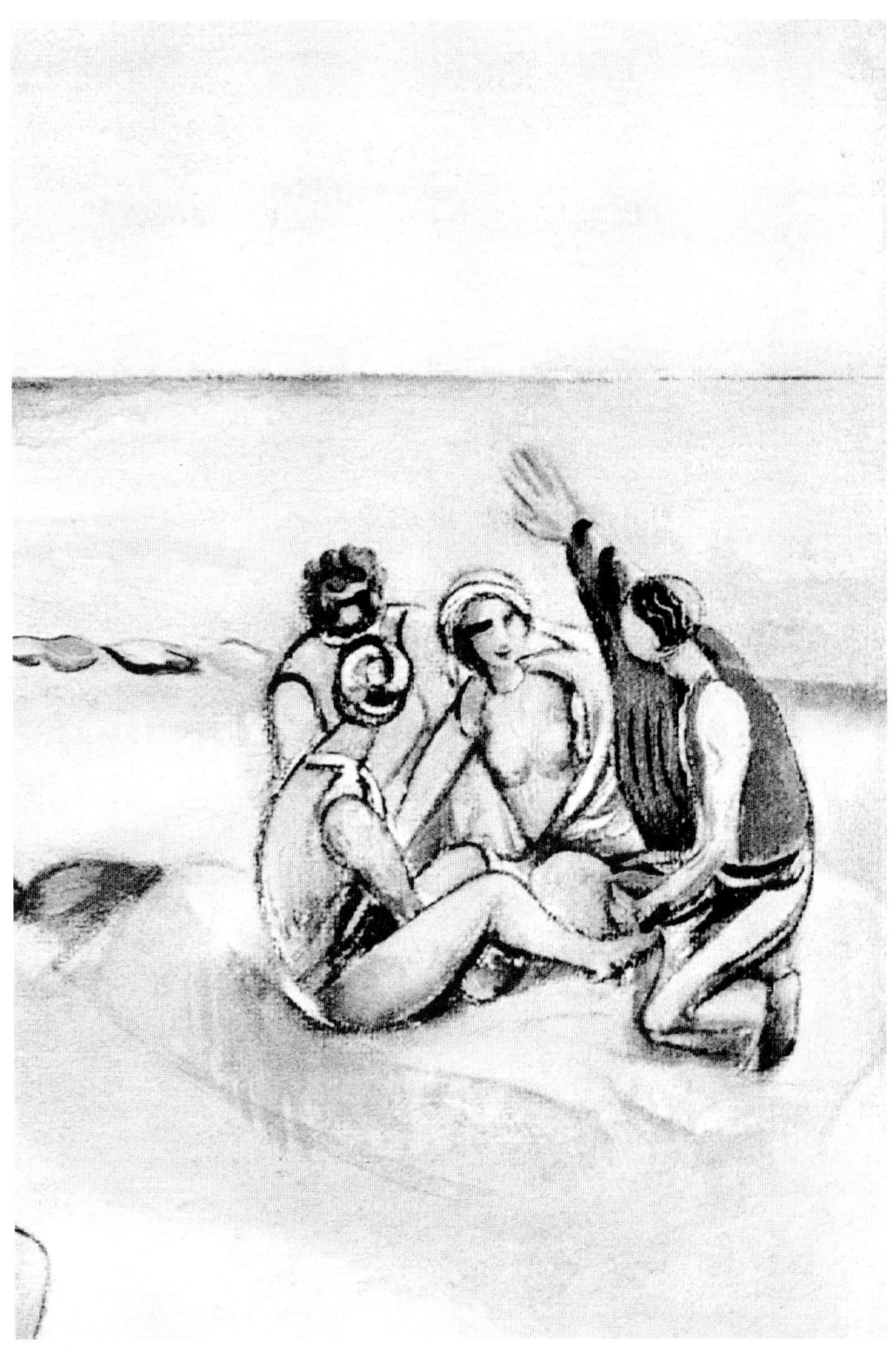

No. 48 *The Island* (detail).

to be struggling to arise from the grave. In *Lebensraum I,* as in *Dragon's Teeth,* the prostrate figures, which hark back to the slain victims in Goya's *Bury them and keep quiet* and *All this and more* etchings, from the *Disasters of War* series of 1810-20 (published in 1863), are recently dead; in *The Island,* they may have died and been reborn in a heavenly or hesperidean afterlife—in which case the speaker at the far left is conceivably pointing to the fallen world they but lately escaped in dying.

Are we, then, in the presence of seraphs? Possibly, but the bathing beauties on the foreshore—especially those splashing in the stream in the far left, who, if anything, recall the ochre-coloured figures of women, three standing, one seated, in Matisse's above-mentioned monumental canvas of 1916-17, *Bathers by a Stream* (Art Institute of Chicago)—do not jibe in form or function with Lewis's anti-Miltonic concept of angels, as laid out in his dystopian *Human Age* trilogy. In the eyes of Fredric Jameson,

> Lewis's angels, as befits this essentially conservative or reactionary thinker, are, not surprisingly, sexless and project an attempt to imagine a life liberated from sex and desire.... To imagine angels is therefore here an impossible attempt to imagine a world beyond sex.... Sex is...but the most concentrated expression of everything which repels the angelic mind about human nature: of the intensely personal, passionate, grappling nature of human desires and longings and of human involvements.

The nether/neverland of *The Childermass* and its sequels is "a world without women or sex, into which the latter are systematically introduced...."[151] The "libidinal Utopia" of the two Bathers series and *The Island* is therefore a reversal of this trilogy's para- or parallel universe, on the delineation of which Lewis would expend his last creative energies: all female, all manifestly sexual, but whether living or dead, damned or saved we have no way of knowing. It may be significant that the clothed male figures in *The Island* are absorbed in some serious discourse which causes them to turn their backs on the unindividuated "beach babies" frolicking and fighting in the sand, and which induces all the interlocutors but the principal orator himself to disregard the entity on which he appears to be expounding. His gesture evokes a line from *The Childermass:* "The sort of existence we are contemplating in the Paradise over there can only mean *personal* existence, that I'm sure you will agree, since mere *individual* existence would not be worth troubling about, would it?" On the other hand, the speaker of these word is that bombastic bully, The Bailiff—hardly a figure with whom to conjure heavenly visions.[152]

That angelic beings as well as witches, supernatural creatures and mythic beasts were on Lewis's mind during the early 1940s is evident not only from the divebombing dove/cherubs of *Sunset in Paradise* but from a drawing entitled *Angel* (no. 95), which might have been torn from a Fuseli or Blake sketchbook: armed with small, finlike wings, this sinuously inflected figure seems bent on transforming itself into the letter "S." In the chapter lampooning Hart House in *America I Presume,* Lewis poked particular fun at Will Ogilvie's chapel murals, with their "hundreds of horrid little angels, all with the same face, like strings of quintuplets [see fig. 13]. Like that Johnny Blake, that kind of thing. Spooky and ugly. Hope I don't go to heaven if it looks like that."[153] *His* angels would be quite the opposite—as would his heaven.

Wherever in or out of the world *The Island* may be situated, its predominant rock-browns, sand-yellows and water-greys give it an overall sombreness, at least in contrast to the high-keyed Bathers watercolours, chalks and pastels. Lewis has been uncharacteristically sparing in his palette, as a result of which the rare areas of brighter hue—the thin band of cerulean sky at the very top of the canvas, the apple-green jersey of the seated figure on the far right, the darker emeralds of the trees on the island and, standing out from it, the crimson of the small building on the far shore, which forms the apex of the compositional triangle and thus acts as a focal-point—are muted by the prevailing tonalities. And yet the mood produced in the viewer by this chromatic reticence is not necessarily one of corresponding gloom or dread; other responses are possible, and no doubt were anticipated by the artist. One's reactions, rather, are conditioned by the interpretations one brings to the work, and by the private images, feelings and memories it evokes at the time it is being contemplated.

But if there is no "programme" operating here, no secret pictorial agenda or authorial ulterior motive, the temptation to interpret *The Island* according to the language and iconography of Symbolism, brought up to date by wartime overtones, is nonetheless increased by the many references in Lewis's correspondence and writings to the loaded theme of islands and their corollary, isolation. In 1940, for example, he employed the term metaphorically to describe the condition of the abstract artist who has "purged natural forms entirely of their organic or natural references", the "main difficulty" of which choice "is that it is as if you were living upon a small island, all the few trees, rocks and fauna of which you knew by heart. You can get terribly sick of the same old hypostatized tree, or the same little platonic brook."[154] In a 1941 letter to his publisher Lorne Pierce, he of laid out the theme of his *Anglosaxony: A League that Works:*

> More and more it becomes apparent that we the island-nations, with our sea-power, will be the *outsiders,* in the coming years: I mean that of the big power-groups that are in process of formation, we are the inhabitants or controllers of the great ocean wastes, *outside* the old continental nucleus.... We shall subdue the land-citadel in the end.[155]

But for the re-born naturalist in art, the island state was not invariably a sign of solipsism, but rather the index of a sound geography of self: thus, in a 1942 lecture on "Public Spirit and Egotistic Mind", Lewis contrasted "The man of the Lone-Wolf class," for whom "Life is a chaos, in which it is his business to subsist upon as favourable terms as possible", and "The other type of person, who does regard himself as self-contained, a complete island", who, thanks to the confidence given by this sense of integrity and wholeness, "will impart his information to others: to the public, or to others around him".[156] For Lewis, the exemplar of this anti-Lone Wolf spirit was none other than the Enemy himself, the inveterate warrior against warfare who could proclaim, "I belong to the *public* class, not to the *private* class"—his selfless and thankless devotion to the public interest being, he believed, the source of so many of his difficulties.

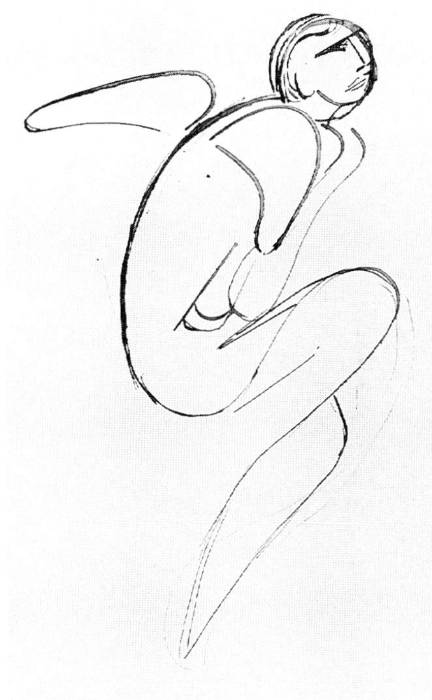

No. 95 *Angel,* n.d. (c. 1940s), pen-and-ink on paper (12.0 x 9.5 cm), M 1106. Herbert F. Johnson Museum of Art, Cornell University, Ithaca, New York.

In other instances, the island symbol, for Lewis, is national rather than individual in scope: hence "bodies surrounded by water"—Blitz-battered England being the handiest example—stand, in certain lights, for insularity, cultural and otherwise. And yet their status as islanders, he had stated in *Blast,* was what had forced the British to conquer the seas and explore the globe, English, in the process, becoming the closest thing Earth has to a universal language. While lauding "The Arabs of the Atlantic", Lewis in 1914 also blessed "England, industrial island machine, pyramidal", and declared, "This island must be contrasted with the bleak waves."[157] Islands can epitomize peace and calm amid storm and stress; alternatively, they represent the redoubts of besieged defenders of a cause, an ideal or a movement. The negative connotations of the isolate state, to so cosmopolitan a person as Lewis, reluctantly reduced to the status of a powerless and platformless private individual, are suggested in a letter he wrote from Toronto at the end of 1942: "Being here is much the same as if one were in Baffin Land."[158] The following January he complained to the novelist Naomi Mitchison, "I am marooned on a lakeshore in Upper Canada,"—an experience that qualified him, he joked, for a position as "Keeper...for some tumble-down old bombed-out lighthouse" back in Britain.[159] The coming of summer and renewed creativity did not improve his outlook, as can be seen from this comment in a letter to Geoffrey Grigson: "I am *really* marooned on this island-continent, with the Pacific on one side of me and the Atlantic on the other."[160] Two years later, though he was happier in Windsor than in Toronto, he could still write to a correspondent that "...I am here with my wife (in a border-city) strictly speaking because I am marooned here—upon a vast, densely populated island."[161]

On public occasions, however, the island trope could take on alternately negative and positive connotations, being associated on the one hand with "a stupid nationalism and growling isolation: as if we were Neanderthal Man rather than Twentieth Century Man" (against which he opposed a proto-McLuhanesque globalism),[162] and on the other with a desireable state of retirement from the confusions and compromises of modern life. In Lewis's notes for his lecture on the theme of "ordering nature," which he delivered in St. Louis in February 1944, he came out on the side of the latter vision:

> Nature is, as you know, a chaos.
> It is a chaos of sound. And it is a visual chaos.
> All art, of any description, is the *creation of an island of order*—
> in the midst of this chaos.
>
> In nature there is *too much of everything*
> So first of all the artist *reduces the quantity.*[163]

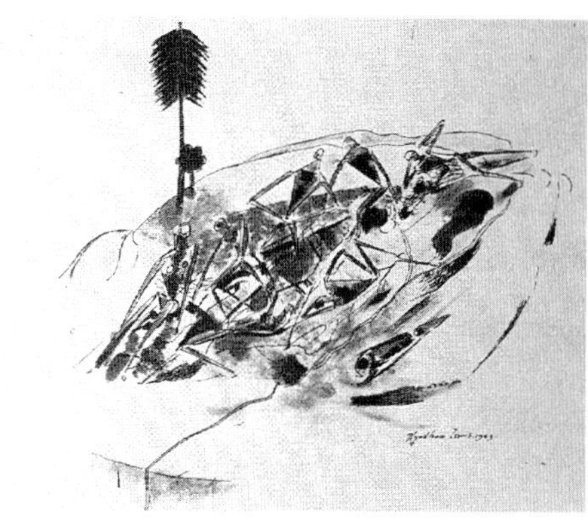

Fig. 67 *Women*, 1949, pen-and-ink, watercolour (27.5 x 35.5 cm), M 1105. Private collection.

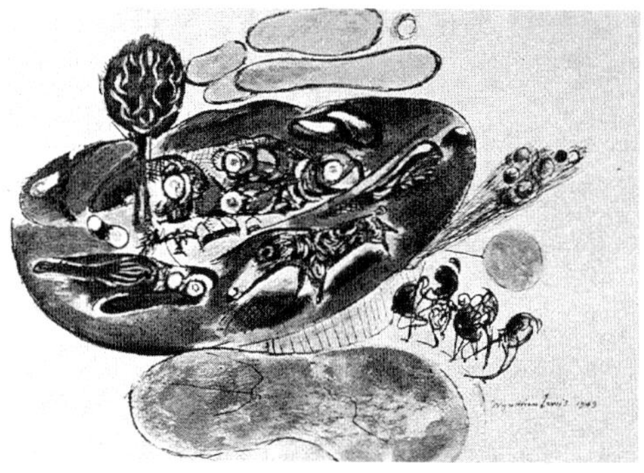

Fig. 68 *Fantasy*, 1949, pen-and-ink, wash, gouache (22.0 x 34.5 cm), M 1096. Private collection.

Lewis concluded another, undated talk with the statement that "In the time at my disposal I have said what I can to create a little bridge, between the mainland of the initiated and *the island of art*."[164]

But if art could create an "island of order" for Lewis, it also exacted an exorbitant cost: the sense of desertion and desolation suffered by the self-described "talented intruder." In Canada, and especially in that hinterland backwater, Toronto, Lewis felt doubly cut off from what he deemed the "real" world—in actuality, the pre-war literary and artistic London that recharged his creative batteries and nourished his imagination. Ironically, it was the Eurocentric Lewis's cultural colonialism, manifested in his refusal to seek out or associate with the younger and more advanced artists, writers and thinkers of a foreign, provincial city he insisted was bereft of them, that transformed this self-proclaimed exile into that very island, "entire of itself," which John Donne was too certain no man can truly be.

The question then arises as to whether the island of the painting of that title is meant to exemplify the artist's own beleaguered situation in Canada (or indeed in the larger context of America); or whether, conversely, its presence is merely to serve as a compositional foil to the mainland on which his paradoxical figures enact their rites and rituals. Or again, did Lewis intend us to read it as standing for one of the three *loci* of Dante's *Divine Comedy*—a triad to which he often alludes in his writings, and which structure he roughly emulated in the *Human Age* trilogy ("completed" in 1955, the fourth and final part being left unfinished), in which Purgatory is Third City and Hell, Metapolis? After returning to England in August 1945, however, Lewis personally distinguished only between the *Paradiso* of the creative imagination and the *Purga-torio* of day-to-day existence: "If Paris could be described as my Paradise", he wrote in his previously quoted "Vita of Mr. Wyndham Lewis" (a Dantean title, surely), "London is my Purgatory—I have no Hell—no artist has a Hell." Though Toronto, for Lewis, came close.

The fictional Momaco, or at least the microcosmic "prison" of the Hotel Blundell, was, of course, a kind of Inferno for the self-condemned protagonist, Dr. René Harding, and for his depressive wife, until its destruction by fire "resulted in their coming out of their seclusion into a more normal existence." The "first of the new friends made by René" after the conflagration is a recent emigré from Scotland, Professor Ian McKenzie —loosely based on Marshall McLuhan, whom Lewis met in Windsor in July 1943—and with this acquaintance came the end of "these years of numbness" and the breaking of the white, wintry "silence" that had immured them. Lewis couches this release in the following Crusoe-esque terms: "A rough parallel to this would be the case of a man who had been wrecked upon a desert island and never spoken to for many years, until at last a ship anchored off the coast of the island, and the castaway found himself speaking once more.... At the end of his conversation with McKenzie, René was in the situation of the awakened dreamer."[165]

In Lewis's case, salvation came in the late summer of 1942, several months *before* the Tudor Hotel fire of February 1943, with the unexpected knocking on his door by Fr. Stanley Murphy, who had sought out the recluse in order to extend an invitation to deliver the Christian Culture Series lectures in Windsor the following January. Because they antedate the Windsor era, however, the Toronto Drawings and *The Island* can only be said to anticipate the comparative idyll that was the aptly named Assumption. Yet this awakening from the nightmare also broke the reverie that produced the extraordinary cycle of imaginative pictures which appears to have grown, at least in part, out of an act of homage to William Etty, and which came to unexpected fruition in *The Island*.

On reflection, then, what Lewis acerbically referred to as his "Tudor period" turns out to be an interlude of concentrated creativity and artistic if not personal fulfilment. So implausible and unpredicted is this late flourishing that Walter Michel could write, "the period, miraculously, gave rise to a number of drawings which constitute the fourth of the major surges of visual activity which stand out in Lewis's career.... That, from the shabby and lonely hotel room at the Tudor, there should have come the brilliant watercolours of 1941-2, is remarkable." Then he stands back and qualifies the statement:

> But it had been similar with the earlier periods of concentrated painting: the 1912-13 experimental work, that of the years after World War I and the paintings of the thirties were all done in seclusion. Perhaps, for his best work, Lewis required extensive periods

> of solitude, which, due to his irrepressible interest in the affairs around him, might have to be to some extent enforced. Solitude, in fact isolation, was one thing that Toronto could offer. In this vacuum, oblivious for a few hours of his surroundings, Lewis produced images that are among the most imaginative and gayest of his career. This deeply moving spectacle, the mind of the artist turning into itself to find a brightness that existed nowhere outside, is symbolized in several of these drawings, most literally in *The Mind of the Artist, About to Make a Picture.*[166]

NOT UNTIL THE END OF THE WAR did Lewis return—and then only briefly—to the bather theme, his idiom once again being that of lyric and/or satiric fantasy. Several motifs of the first half of the Toronto Bathers sequence reappear in a number of works that coincide with Lewis's last year in Windsor, his long-deferred departure from Canada, and his return to war-weary England: the above-cited *Bathing Scene* of 1945, *Negro Heaven* (1946; M 1081), *Fantasia* (1947; M 1083) and *Women* (M 1105), dated 1949, but, according Mrs. Lewis, "begun in the early forties." In these pictures, Walter Michel sees Lewis being

> as unpredictable as ever.... Two of the pictures are mildly satirical: *Fantasia*, with its mermaid, giraffe and a number of Victorian-looking gentlemen—one in polite conversation with a nude woman bather, another carrying an umbrella—and *Negro Heaven*, playground of the resurrected, enjoying paradisial bliss. In these and others there is much visual wit. For example, in *Bathing Scene* the cloud at the top consists of a dozen blue curls, filled with red and heightened with a white gouache highlight; the water is four green wavy lines, heavily underlined in opaque white; and the cliff at the left, two lines terminating in emptiness. The bathers are lively toys, schematic as the setting; extravagantly, those at the top are surrounded by green, wavy aurioles.[167]

A Colloquy (1946; fig. 66), in which three skeletally limbed but bulbous-torsoed, ball-headed beach-creatures impassively regard a decapitated fourth lying at their feet, may be another meditation on the folly of those who idly play while civilization burns. This disturbing drawing's closest parallels in Lewis's wartime *oeuvre* are *Lebensraum I: The Battlefield* and its horrific sequel, *Lebensraum II: The Empty Tunic* (1941-42; M 988). In *Women* (fig. 67) Lewis has reverted to the spikier anatomy of the 1910s, populating his hillside with insectlike stick-beings seemingly in mortal combat under a sword-limbed palm (or pine?)—a late irruption, perhaps, of the misogynistic strain so blessedly absent from the bulk of the decade's meditations on the female form. On the other hand, another pen-and-ink and watercolour of 1949 (fig. 68), the phantasmagorical *Fantasy* (which calls to mind Walt Disney as much as it does Chagall), introduces a mood of reconciliation in the place of disharmony and despair: the supine forms in a placid pastoral landscape seem to lie together, and may even be lovers, lolling in the shade of another of Lewis's flame-foliaged trees. But is that a bull advancing upon them? And are the figures in the foreground dancing—or fighting?

As ever with Lewis, all interpretations are provisional, all hypotheses subject to revision. We can never be sure exactly where we are with this artist, only that he has taken us somewhere that no-one before has travelled. This knowing unknowableness is consistent with his chosen role as village explainer-*cum*-caped enigma. Lewis not only enjoyed assuming an enigmatic persona, he believed that all true art must defy rational explanation and reduction to formulaic equations. At the same time, however, every work of art worthy of attention is required to make sense on its own terms and according to its own internal logic—hence Lewis's rejection of the forced, hybrid, hothouse flowers of Surrealism. Instead, he seems to have been making a case for a more volitional form of engagement with the inner and outer realms, which involved not just the power but the empowerment of the imagination. Geoffrey Grigson perceived that "A common element in most of Lewis's preferred things, a common absence in things he disliked, is the wonderful, which is in part the wonderfulness of the thing built and dared and by the imagination. You could say of Lewis, violent that he seemed, that he walked in the temples of the highest human order and calmness and believed in permanence."[168]

Lewis's search, renewed in the late 1930s and early 1940s after a decade of wandering in a desert of forking political paths and mirages taken for oases, was for a way of integrating the rational, the irrational, the liminal, and the subliminal. This pursuit of the miraculous through the objective had a perhaps ironic correlative in his absconded father's determination, as expressed in a self-published essay baldly entitled "Imagination", "not to confine myself exclusively to the

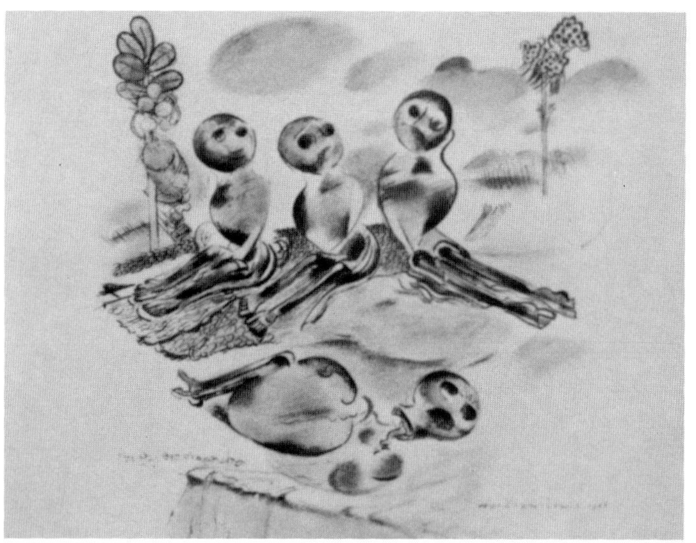

Fig. 66 *A Colloquy,* 1946, pen-and-ink, coloured chalk (25.5 x 33 cm), M 1080. Private collection.

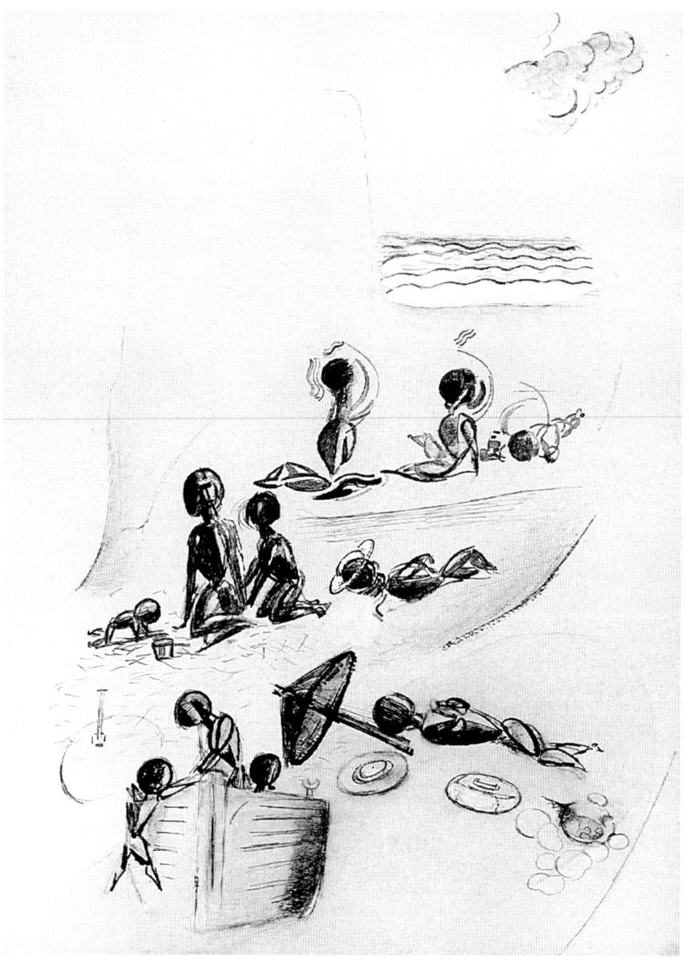

No. 88 *Bathing Scene,* 1945, pen-and-ink, black chalk, watercolour, wash, and gouache on paper (37.5 x 33.0 cm). Private collection.

ideal, the handling of which requires a tangibility which is found only in contrast with the real", but to compare "the relative influences of two great opposing elements, the *real* and the *unreal*, on the ups and downs of life."[169] In his defence of the reality of the imagination against the combined forces of Victorian puritanism, rationalism, materialism and orthodox religiosity, Charles E. Lewis (the "essay-writing bum" of his son's unsparing thumbnail portrait) asserted that "Its mission is not to tantalize but to comfort; and in this respect its fancies are not all mythical reasonless phantoms to be despised and repelled, but kind, ever thoughtful, and faithful friends, whose virtues, unhappily, we are too prone to imbibe in the spirit and falsify in the flesh."[170] This yachtsman-*flâneur*, who would pursue his restless fancy at the expense of his abandoned wife and child, typically reverted to nautical terminology when attempting to define the imaginative faculty: "It is a sublime subject to think about, but a puzzling one to handle, and difficult and guideless in its immensity.—Its horizon is ever receding—indeed, its scope is boundless, and as the very means by which we seek to compass it are those by which it is inflated, so does its beauty beguile and its elasticity bewilder. But while it cannot be described, nor measured, nor confined, it blends in reason only when associated with what is real."[171] The year before the birth of his only son (who would perpetuate the errant father's marital and parental irresponsibility), the senior Lewis ventured that, while artists "are highest in the art of portraying pathetic scenes in life," the "grandest achievement of the greatest painter can only be suggestive." It is the viewer's corresponding ability to "make it admirable" that "renders those sublime touches of Art a mutual success—not alone an exclusive honor to one, but a general triumph in which the humblest may claim participation."[172]

A century and more after the publication of these too-optimistic words, the freedom to imagine is again being challenged on a multitude of fronts, a recurrent phenomenon in history which the younger Lewis had studied and assailed, moving from the prophets and profiteers of war and the censorship that attends it, to the growing power of the mass media to enforce conformity and deaden both thought and feeling. It is a matter of conjecture whether, reading his father's idealistic apologia, as he may well have done in writing the "autobiographical fragment" of around 1940 in which he analyzed the character of this champion of the "do-nothing mode", Wyndham Lewis agreed with its gist or rejected the paternal flight into fancy as a romantic escape from real experience. But in Charles E. Lewis's insistence that Time is the final Enemy, and Imagination its only combatant, he must have found a fore-echo of his own philosophy of life and work:

> Reality is the wreck of Imagination; and we see the evidences, all too sad and true, that Time has cast upon the shore. To a great extent, this is inevitable. We are all drifting in that rocky *portage* which, looming in a black barrier against the sky, betokens at once the end and the origin of the turbid waters of life. Well, let it come in the gradual progress of events; and why I raise my voice is to expostulate with that mad seamanship which, crowding on all sail and steaming directly for the land, precipitates catastrophe.[173]

Here, then, is a prototype of Wyndham Lewis the lonely prophet—and of Lewis the idealizing realist who, Prospero-like, conjured up *The Island* as if to defy fate, history, the very sea-mists that soon were to enshroud his vision.

In his art if not in his prose, Lewis's operative ethos was that of the Keats whose definition of Negative Capability nicely characterizes the ideal viewer of the Toronto Drawings and *The Island:* one who is "capable of being in uncertainties, mysteries, doubts, without any irritable reaching after fact and reason", and thus one who can be admitted to "the Penetralium of mystery". When, discontented with "half-knowledge", we demand to be informed just who these nameless, faceless figures are and what they are meant to represent, what the island signifies and where on (or off) Earth it might be located, we must remember that the artist himself may not have been absolutely certain about such matters, and that he painted (and wrote) in order to find out for himself, his "conclusions" being the process of discovery rather than the discovery of the process. In Hugh Kenner's words, "The picture, if not a statement about the subject's appearance, is a meditation on the subject's nature, a meditation conducted by the hand."[174]

"What kind of reality do such beings have?" Kenner then proceeds to ask of Lewis's "race of visually logical beings" who people the abstractions of the 1930s and, as we have seen, the imaginative works the 1940s as well. "For we come, as so often in the visual or verbal Lewis universe, to a question like a question of metaphysics, and an interesting question, not a trivial one.... What kind of reality have these?... They have all the same kind of reality, which is—there seems to be no other word—*magical*."[175] Seeking to define the *"magical"* kind of reality that

Lewis "made of outlines" which, "always in evidence," do not so much bound the forms as constitute them, Kenner again warns us not to mistake these "outlined shapes" for "a surface in some 'real' world", but rather to see the paint as simply "an area of colour, like Cézanne's areas of colour." Yet, he continues,

> the paint as such seems not to interest Lewis; impasto is rare. The canvas before us is not a place where impingements of pigment have occurred, as in Abstract Expressionism, nor where a skill as empty as accident has left its record, as at the Royal Academy; instead, like the wall of Lascaux, it is where the icons are. The cave-painters' painted bulls, and painted deer are the closest analogy we are likely to find: magical presences in a magic place.[176]

Having sketched the lineaments of this place and its presences, Kenner still must inquire into the *actions* of these temporally frozen creatures:: "What are they doing, in these 'magical' pictures, whatever they may be?" His answer is both equivocal and categorical: "Waiting, existing, the way a thing exists within the logic of the picture-space."[177] This space is "A world with its own laws,...which are not disclosed, presented as though we knew what those laws were....":

> As we look at these pictures of an unreal, real world, strange configurations stir, 'massive as laws', in response to knowledge we normally do not know we possess. The paradigm of coherence provided, for instance, by a title (useful to the gallery manager and a comfort to the viewer) bids us acknowledge a purely visual rightness we can recognize but not easily discuss.... [T]he same is true of cave-paintings, in the presence of which we recognize our itch to 'explain.' Framing our anthropological hypotheses, we acknowledge an *order* which we formulate as a question so that we can try out answers. Once the investigator has an answer that fits the question, he is appeased so long as he ignores the elusive fact that it was not the picture that asked the question but he. Pictures do not ask, they confront.... The discursive mind is determined that something other than the picture shall explain the picture: something perhaps no less puzzling than the picture, but better adapted to discursive categories.
>
> This fact should put us on the alert, as should the obscure need that is appeased by a title.[178]

And yet the "itch to 'explain'" must be scratched; suggestive titles and ambiguous subject matter *do* beguile and tease us; confronted with a conundrum, the inquiring mind seeks to know. Another way of putting it is that drawings and paintings challenge us to complete the inventive act of their authors by stretching our faculties to comprehend their meanings—meanings which are simultaneously plural and singular. After all, Lewis did not expect his viewers merely to be passive observers; he demanded, and still demands, that they participate actively—that is to say, democratically—in the intellectual and emotional bargaining session that is communication. Either we take up that challenge (which in fact is a kind of back-handed invitation) or, as too many have done in the past, refuse it—to our loss. The process of discovery will be circular and continuous rather than conclusive and determinate. For even in defying interpretation, the Bathers cycle and its consummation, *The Island*, lead us back to all art's starting-point: those myths of creation out of which Lewis's "creation myths, tragic images, crucifixions and light-hearted fantasies" alike are born.

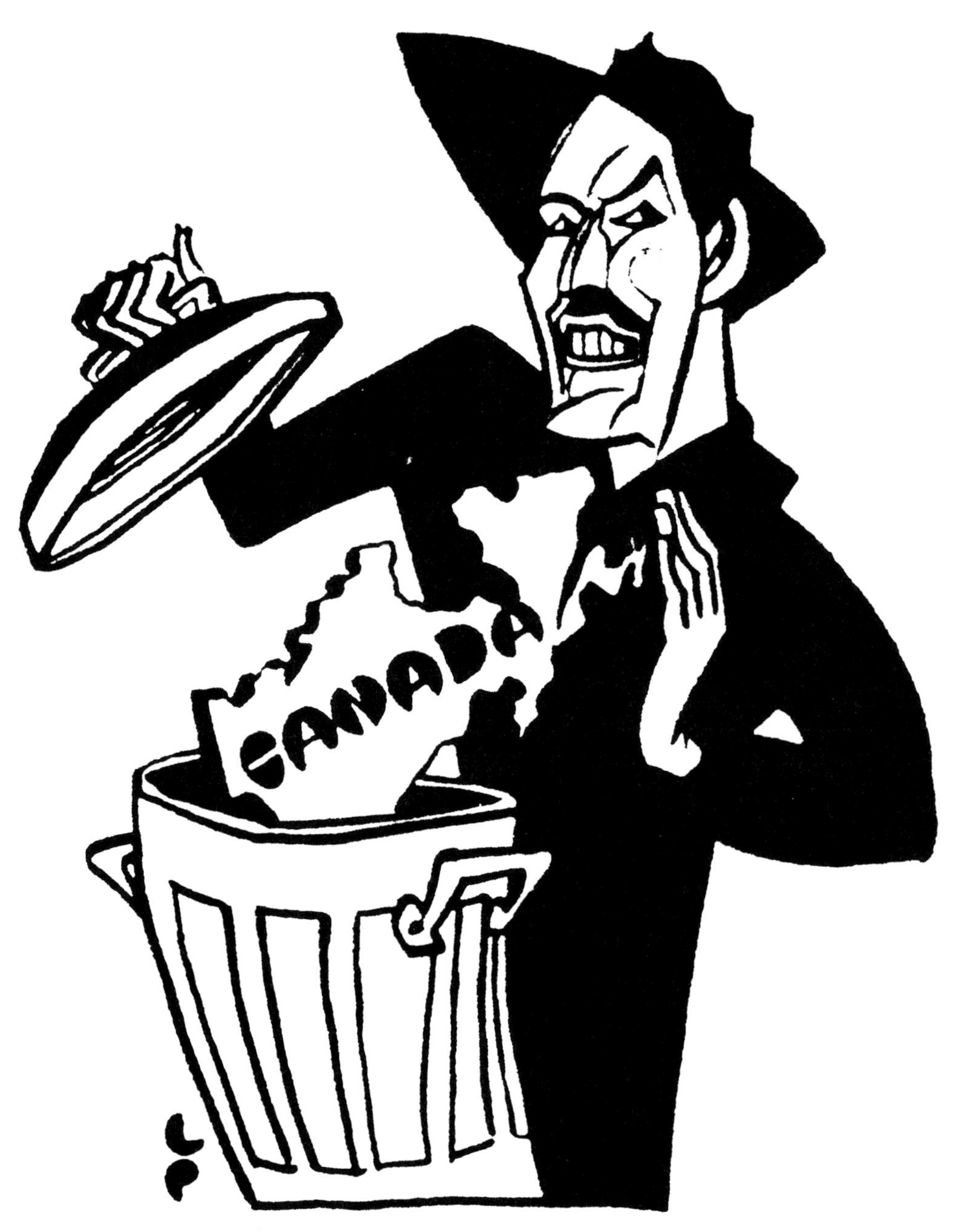

Fig. 69 Lewis Parker, Lewis: *"the most parochial nationette on earth"*, *Maclean's Magazine* 76 (August 24 1963).

Out of Canada: Wyndham Lewis's North American Writings

THOMAS DILWORTH

MODERNISM IN THE ARTS IS APOCALYPTIC. It is a revelation of the most important cultural transformation in modern western history. Wyndham Lewis is one of the literary Four Horsemen of this apocalypse, trailing, in the estimation of posterity, James Joyce, T. S. Eliot, and Ezra Pound. By crossing the Atlantic in 1939, Lewis brought Canada into the history of literary modernism. After finishing his novel *The Vulgar Streak* in New York State, he moved to Ontario, where he produced most of his North American writing. He wrote essays for a Canadian magazine and worked on three books of political analysis. And his experience in Toronto and Windsor became the basis of a new novel, *Self Condemned*, which he finished after his return to England.

Socially and as a writer, Lewis was hampered by his chosen role as satirist. It made him "the enemy," as he called himself, of socially comfortable establishments. In *The Apes of God* (1930), for example, he antagonized the leftist, sexually ambiguous arts establishment in London. As a consequence, he was despised as a person and ignored as a painter and writer. This reaction brought his malice to a boil. In his writing, he found it difficult to purify rage through technique. Satire is seldom, if ever, "pure" art; it tends to sacrifice aesthetic values to ulterior, ideological motives. Lewis's writings do that; they are vehicles for war. As a writer, then, his life-long inner battle was between angry egoism and technical mastery—a battle that technical mastery never conclusively won. Lewis brought his personal struggle with him to Canada, where it acquired new dimensions that would lead, in *Self Condemned,* to an impressive resolution.

He came pursued by furies. One was his reputation as a fascist sympathizer; throughout the fashionably Marxist 1930s, Lewis was far from being what we now would call "politically correct." In his book *Hitler* (1930), he criticized the Versailles Treaty, which had led to the oppression of Germany, and naively praised Hitler and his party, which had not yet taken power. In the mid-thirties he wrote two peace pamphlets against adopting a warlike attitude towards Germany. In 1939 Lewis tried to alter his public image with an anti-Nazi book, *The Hitler Cult and How it Will End.* Unfortunately, the outbreak of war made his critique of fascism seem irrelevant.

Another fury was an innate tendency towards paranoia. One evening in Windsor, Ontario, while out walking his dog, Lewis was overcome by panic and rushed in to Father J. Stanley Murphy, of Assumption College, literally to hide, convinced that political agents were following him.[1] (Psychologically, fear underlies and fuels anger.)

Furies drive people into exile. And during Lewis's stay in Toronto, he was in exile—unable to find enough work to alleviate poverty, ignored by the academic establishment, virtually friendless. This was largely his own fault. He was very cool, suspicious, and inclined always to launch a pre-emptive strike. But it was also the fault of the establishment, which, after all, took offence. In spite of personal discomfort and alienation, however, he was able to write political commentary that is dispassionate and generous, and *Self Condemned,* which contains the most profound and challenging "criticism of life" that he ever achieved in a novel.

AFTER HIS ARRIVAL in Quebec, Lewis passed through Toronto and then lived for some months in Buffalo, New York. Before returning to Toronto to live, he wrote *America I Presume* (1940)—the title evokes Stanley's famous remark to Livingstone. The book is a fictionalized travelogue in which Lewis adopts the persona of Major Archibald Cocoran, touring the States to lecture on killing a tiger. While he travels, he records his observations of American culture. Lewis stayed longest in Buffalo, which he gives the fictional name Nineveh so that he can accuse its wealthy citizens of snobbery without fear of reprisal. Other American cities, at which accusations are not leveled, have their own names, including New York and Boston, both of which he praises highly. Lewis sees as American characteristics nervous instability, sloth (except for New Yorkers), vainglory, pragmatism, kindness, natural courteousness (especially among the poor), and a "manly openness" unique among nations.[2] Americans, he says, have the "highest standard of good fellowship in the world."[3]

But before he finishes, he makes what is, in retrospect, a tactical error. In Chapter Sixteen, he slights "unlovely" Toronto and indulges in prolonged mockery of Hart House, the male student's union of the University of Toronto, which he calls Brunswick Hall, after a nearby street. The Warden of this "towering gothic pile" is based on the actual Warden of Hart House, an effete English bachelor named Burgon Bickersteth. His fictional counterpart, called Brandleboyes, has a homoerotic fascination for naked athletes and likes to spend his summers with the Hitler Youth. "This man was mad about a building," writes Lewis, "and *what* a building."[4]

After a light supper on the terrace, the Warden takes Lewis's protagonist on tour, first into an "immense, empty, stony, dark, echoing hall," which "apparently served no purpose...except to convey immensity."[5] This is the Great Hall, its panelled walls decorated with the armorial shields of the world's universities. The tour continues through a reading room, picture gallery, tiny chapel, and handball courts. Then they come to the swimming pool, where naked young men disport themselves. Lewis writes,

> Now for the first time I said to myself, I was fully in America (though it was only Canada). I had got into the bowels of this New World: this deceptive continent. It was not just hot dogs and hamburgers, skyscrapers and G Men. Walt Whitman was more fundamental to America than they were. I had, in this machine of a country, got down to the *Leaves of Grass*.... I had got—and I saw that I had got—into a *classless* universe.... These were the genitals of Hellenic statuary. These were the movements and attitudes of the early gods of Europe, nearer than us to the dream of the Golden Age.... This was the overheated incubator of the American Idea.[6]

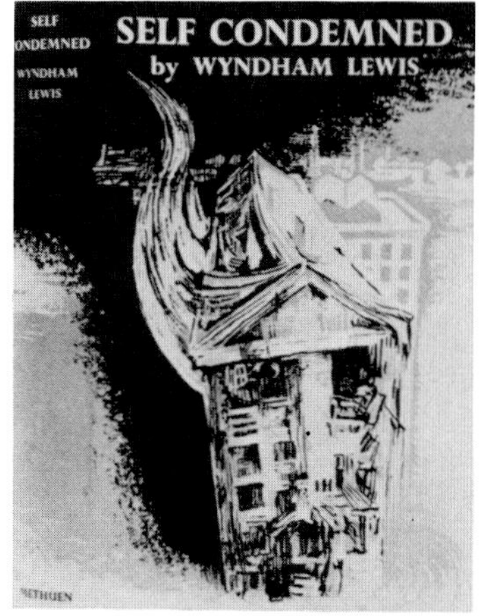

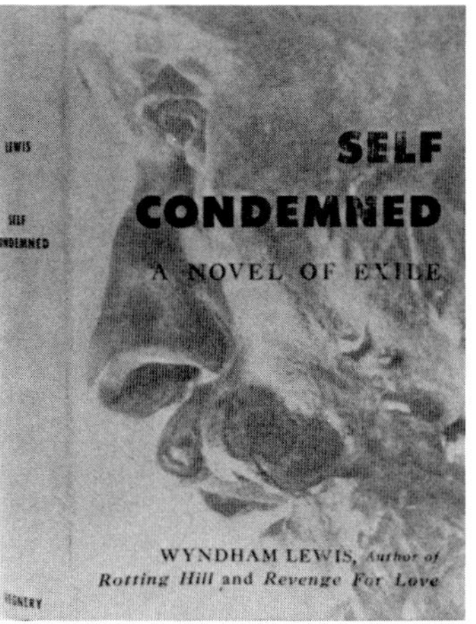

After exclaiming, "What a place for Socrates," the Lewis persona notices the Warden becoming friendlier, touching his arm. The tour continues through the basketball court, over the inward-sloping circular track, into the theatre, and then to the private guest rooms upstairs, and concludes with the exhausted protagonist's escape. He never discovers what the building actually is. When he describes it to his wife, she exclaims, "It is like the Arabian Nights.... It is staggering! It is like the pyramids. It is more than the skyscrapers and the waterfalls. It is a cataract of young bodies. Why it is a dynamic club the size of the Crystal Palace. It is breathtaking."[7]

Toronto was not amused. Jeffrey Meyers, Lewis's biographer, thinks that Lewis's treatment of the Warden is what gave offence.[8] But what Toronto really resented was the mockery of a building so beloved of the city's English and anglophile establishment. Even after the foundation of Massey College, Hart House remains the chief symbol of the University of Toronto's once-plausible pretension to being the Oxford of the North.[9] To call the Great Hall "absurd," to ridicule the architectural centrepiece of the campus and the city—this was unforgivable. To cast erotic aspersions on Toronto's young manhood, and to mention their genitals—this was unspeakable. Soon after the book appeared, Lewis returned to Toronto, took up residence at the Tudor Hotel, and was ignored by the élite of the city.

IN THE FOUR MONTHS before he returned to Canada, Lewis wrote *The Vulgar Streak*, a novel set in Italy and England. He had planned it before crossing the Atlantic but wrote it entirely between June and October of 1941, in a borrowed summer house on Long Island. It is Lewis's shortest novel, and technically impressive in that it lacks the blatant authorial intrusions and shifts between viewpoints that mar his other works. Yet it is technically flawed, and in a way that demonstrates the chronic inability of Lewis to achieve objectivity in fiction. In *The Vulgar Streak* he criticizes the English class-system, the spiritually vacuous man of action, and the banking system. Unfortunately, these subjects have little to do with one another and are not adequately rooted in the action of the novel.

The protagonist, Vincent Penhale, is lower-class in origin but has learned to speak and behave as a member of the upper class. For a year he has been passing counterfeit money, which, he later explains, is no worse than the "fraudulent and oppressively administered currency" of banks.[10] The novel begins in Venice, a city built on imperialism and banking and therefore symbolic of the corruption at the heart of European civilization. (Vincent shares all but one of the letters of his first name with "Venice.") In the ancient city, he meets and seduces an upper-middle-class woman. She becomes pregnant, they marry, and Vincent comes genuinely to love her. His love inspires him to cease passing false banknotes. One evening the counterfeiter, his former supplier, summons him to say that he has killed an intruder. Vincent helps dispose of the body. Shortly after, both are arrested and Vincent's working-class past is disclosed in the papers. He tells the truth about his life to his pregnant wife, who collapses and, three days later, dies of a haemorrhage. After a final, friendly conversation with a faithful upper-class friend, who is a Catholic convert, Vincent hangs himself. (I mention the friend's Catholicism because an important theme of Lewis's next novel is the antithesis between Catholicism and nihilism—a theme latent but undeveloped here.)

Throughout the novel Vincent rails didactically against "the class religion" of England.[11] Immediately before his suicide, he tells his friend that, instead of pretending to be upper-class, he should have become a revolutionary or, "something better still," he should have realized how meaningless the class-system is and merely forgotten about it.[12]

He has supposedly been unable to realize this because of the tragic flaw he confesses to his friend: "My main trouble," he says, "is that I am all made up of *action.*"[13] This had been the diagnosis of a psychiatrist earlier in the novel. Vincent sees this characteristic as having its archetypes in Hitler and Mussolini. Vincent decides that his disastrous life consequently corresponds to the fate of Europe. "I have proved," he says, "upon my little personal stage, that force is barren," that "in ... action-for-action's-sake nothing can be achieved."[14] The problem with all this is that the Vincent we read about is simply not a man of action. During the six months covered by the novel, he does nothing on his own initiative other than seduce a woman and hang himself.

Moreover, Vincent is a sympathetic figure, unlike the archetypal fascist men of action. The seduction of his future wife coincides with the Munich Conference, when Hitler seduced Chamberlain, the British prime minister, into allowing the dismemberment of Czechoslovakia. But Vincent then falls in love with his wife, gives up crime, and is revealed to be sardonically intelligent, sensitive, and socially and personally conscientious. He is too good to generate the novel Lewis wants; and Lewis is not a good enough novelist to stop insisting on what he wants. Vincent's self-criticism is merely Lewis straining to join what he himself, as authorial god, has put asunder. Vincent's goodness generates sympathy in the reader, which makes this novel appealing and easy to read, but it undermines the novel's symbolism and denies aesthetic significance to much of his didactic talk.

The Vulgar Streak was published in London in September 1941, in a small edition that was partly destroyed in a bombing raid. It was not published or distributed in North America because U.S. and Canadian publishers thought its criticism of the class-system would undermine England in time of war. Their refusal to publish was unfortunate for Lewis but is not one of the catastrophes of literary history. Although *The Vulgar Streak* has most of the requirements of a successful novel, its technical failures render it aesthetically–like its interesting and enjoyable protagonist—suicidal.

AFTER FINISHING *The Vulgar Streak,* Lewis moved to Toronto, where he established several friendly contacts. One was Lome Pierce, the director of Ryerson Press, who asked him in 1941 to write a short book on democracy and its present danger. Lewis complied and the result was *Anglosaxony: a League that Works* (1941), a seventy-five-page booklet that is now virtually unobtainable. Intending it as "a practical book for just now," he wrote it quickly in a rambling, easy-to-read editorial style meant for popular consumption. [15] His purpose in *Anglosaxony* is to define, by comparison, democracy and fascism. He makes a personal declaration of allegiance to democracy–another attempt to put to rest the fury occasioned by his supposed fascist sympathies. Because of his antipathy towards Joseph Stalin, he writes,

> I have not been spared the epithet "fascist." But fascism—once I understood it—left me colder than communism. The latter at least pretended, at the start, to have something to do with helping the helpless.... It does start from the human being and his suffering. Whereas fascism glorifies bloodshed and preaches that man should model himself upon the wolf....[16]

Because the subject involved him personally, he had thought long and hard about it and has some interesting things to say.

The basic reality underlying politics is, he contends, psychology. The democrat and the fascist are not primarily adherents to political theory; they are basic human types. Many an American policeman or businessman is a fascist in this sense. So are many communists. Any nationalist is to some degree a fascist, no matter how liberal his ideology, since he favours his nation over others. Any authoritarian is fascist. In contrast, nature's democrats are open, easy-going, inclined to live and let live. They are universalists, not favouring their own class, race, or nation over others. Democrats are, he says, gentlemen. The book is entitled *Anglosaxony* because Lewis argues that Anglosaxons in England and North America tend to be universalists and, therefore, democrats.[17] The war-fueled chauvinism of this contention—tell it to the Irish or the American Indian—is the only serious fault in the book.

Lewis traces the beginning of fascism from Darwin's theory of the struggle for survival, which Nietzsche translated into the struggle for power. The first human embodiment of what would become political fascism is the Futurist propagandist Marinetti, whom Mussolini had recently honoured as the father of fascism. Lewis remembers Marinetti in London before the previous war as "a little living geyser of a man, popping and detonating like a clockwork figure."[18] He and his Futurists entourage admired speed (the racing car, the airplane), power (the locomotive), and youth (themselves). Lewis recalls leading a gang to one of Marinetti's lectures in order to shout him down–behaviour which itself resembles that of the fascists.

According to the psychological distinction he makes in this booklet, Lewis was one of nature's fascists. He had been the *führer* of Vorticism–a movement deeply indebted to Marinetti's Futurists–and the author of the catalogues of denunciation in the issues of *Blast* (1914-15). The youthful Lewis had been a great devotee of Nietzsche, although he repudiated the German philosopher in later life. His sexual life had been a continuous *blitzkrieg,* devoid of emotional depth or moral compunction. He had been childish and, as every parent knows, children are fascists.

In *Anglosaxony,* he concludes that democracy is more practical than fascism because democracy lets people alone. It is not a political philosophy which, like fascism or communism, tortures human nature into shapes and attitudes–those of angel, superman, or hero–that cannot be held for long. Fascism, in particular, hates the human average–the very thing Lewis, in his Nietzschean youth, disparaged as "the herd."

Lewis was not, in this book, being hypocritical. All people are inclined to attack negative traits in others which, unacknowledged, belong to themselves. Moreover, at the age of fifty-nine, Lewis was not now, if he ever had been, simply an emotional fascist. Under the pressure of two decades of intense disapproval and disregard, this wild child of the English avant-garde had grown up. After having lost his struggle for preeminence in literary-artistic London, he found there was no longer, for him, much occasion or advantage to the exercise of fascist egoism. If this was true in London, it was truer in Toronto, where he had no choice but to look beyond the ego for meaning.

He says, rightly, that fascism and communism are religions in which people worship and serve the state. In contrast democracy is not a religion but it does arise from and remain attached to one. For Lewis, "our kind of democracy has no reality independent of Christianity," from which it emerges like a carving in a bas-relief. This is so even "if Christianity in the case of nine out of ten democrats is apparently dead and forgotten."[19] When a reader for Ryerson Press objected to this passage in manuscript, Lewis defended it in a letter to Lorne Pierce:

> I do not say here that Democracy *is* Christianity. All I say is that it would never have existed as we know it without Christianity, and that it has survived the decay of religion. It is almost all that there is left of Christianity: but revealed religion and ethics are not one and the same thing, as your reader seems to believe.[20]

Lewis saw human rights as fundamental to democracy and believed that "all 'rights' must and only can derive from God."[21]

Lewis was upset when *Anglosaxony* was not reviewed. He informed Pierce that he suspected the opposition of "idealists" (Marxists) for whom "democracy" was synonymous with "injustice." He also suggested that the book was not reviewed because he "did not exactly hit it off with the intellectuals of Toronto," which is "probably not a good place to be an intellectual in." Pierce had to reassure him that there was no organized opposition. Lewis also suspected the Canadian inclination to devalue all things Canadian, including books published here. He admonished Pierce, "if you cannot break this attitude, you will never have any artists or writers."[22]

DURING HIS DARK YEARS in Toronto, Lewis continued his political analysis. He was assembling material for a book on the origin of American liberties—material which may have been lost in the Tudor Hotel fire.[23] Since he had been researching American history, he was invited to lecture on the subject in November and December of 1943 at Assumption College in Windsor. He delivered the twelve Heywood Broun Memorial Lectures on "the Concept of Liberty from the Founding Fathers of the USA till Now." After the war, he reworked these lectures for publication as the first 150 pages of *America and Cosmic Man* (1948). This book is disunified but genuinely prophetic. It sees the United States as the prototype of world-wide union involving the abolition of individual nation states. The U.S.A. is, he argues, a new kind of country, "the first entire cosmopolis" destined "to produce the first of a new species of man"—a species not divided by class, race, religion or nationhood.[24]

In words that probably inspired Marshall McLuhan's phrase "the global village," Lewis says that, through telephone communications and air transportation, "the earth has become one big village." Consequently, the existence of "plural sovereignty" is "a little farcical."[25] Until national sovereignty is abolished, there can be no lasting peace. What Lewis liked most about the United States was its freedom from the cultural constraints of national and racial identity. He experienced this freedom most fully in New York, where "you are *in the world,* instead of just in a nation."[26]

Lewis claims that America is not so much a territory as the psychology of a people gathered to be free and willing to fight for brotherhood. He does, however, have critical reservations. He dislikes the "uniformity" that the melting-pot produces. Nonconformity is the essence of free-dom; standardization diminishes it. Lewis complains that "anything comes to be denounced as 'un-American' which does not respond with a zealot 'Yes!' to some fiat of government." This trait he sees as identical to the patriotic docility of Nazi Germany.[27]

Lewis is well aware of American national egoism, its economic imperialism and sense of "manifest destiny." This "Americanism" is, he says, a state-religion founded after the Civil War, with the president as high priest. But it is not, he thinks, the heart of American identity and will not last.

He then analyzes the characters of recent presidents and traces the tension between Republican and Democrat to two founding fathers: the conservative Alexander Hamilton, who distrusted the mob; and the eccentric, anarchic Thomas Jefferson, steeped in radical French ideas. Lewis clearly identifies with Hamilton, a man of exceptional integrity who repeatedly proclaimed that the best form of government was monarchy, even though he knew that doing so made him unpopular. Though no monarchist, Lewis, too, had made himself unpopular through political advocacy.

In his way, Lewis had come to love the United States, "a wonderful country."[28] In slightly disconcerting terms, he says that "this is what Heaven must be like—agreeably inhuman, naturally; a rootless, irresponsible city...but where everything is superficially fraternal."[29]

Unlike the U.S.A., for Lewis Canada is not analogous to heaven or a prelude to the new world order. He writes,

> there is the most impassable race-barrier separating the English-Canadians and the French-Canadians; on the English side this is interpreted as indicative of a racial superiority, enjoyed by themselves *vis-à-vis* the "Peasoups." The fact that a majority of French-Canadians have Indian blood does not improve their chances of social equality with the Nordic Blonds; and catholicism is a peculiarly unpopular religion with the latter-day Puritans of this isolated and backward country.[30]

These observations about English-Canadian prejudice were accurate, but Lewis was also venting indignation over his treatment by Toronto's WASP establishment. He was himself part Indian—as he had recently learned from his relatives in Toronto and New York State—and he respected the Catholic Church.

WHILE IN CANADA, Lewis wrote five articles for publication. Four of them appeared in *Saturday Night,* two in 1941, two in 1942. They are beautifully written and thoughtful. In the first, he discusses the surprising bravery of English civilians during the Blitz and places their behaviour in fascinating historical perspective.[31] He reminds the reader that "total war" is not new and that it has generally been a series of sieges rather than battles. He adds that, historically, it has been the Spanish civilian who has been the toughest at withstanding sieges and was nearly the despair of Napoleon. In his second article, Lewis traces the English bravery to its sources.[32] One of these is an obsessive "code of emotional suppression" that forbids the exhibition of "what it regards as a degrading fearfulness." Another, deriving from Protestantism, is a sense of personal responsibility and resistance to authoritarianism. Yet another is a sporting sense that considers success ignominious and prefers a lost cause—which is why the English hate war: it is a game that must be won and so goes against their nature. In his third article, Lewis comments on the paradox that assurance of ultimate victory slackens resolve, while bad news stiffens it.[33]

His fourth article is a minor, literary counterpart to his published admiration for the paintings by the Group of Seven.[34] He praises Morley Callaghan's stories in *Now that April's Here* as "replete with a message of human tolerance and love" and reminding us of peace after anguish and reconciliation after conflict, so that "we are back in a world from which we have strayed in which the final appeal is not to the ego, in which men know they are not gods, nor yet cunning machines in a Behaviourist, or Fascist, nightmare."[35] Callaghan's stories are chiefly an occasion for Lewis to express his own relief and hope. It is an extraordinary revelation of his new, or underlying, humanism. John Reid, an aspiring Canadian writer who had met Lewis in London, rightly says this was "a Lewis no one had seen before"—a man whose endurance of intense loneliness had made possible this uncharacteristic appreciation of peace and love.[36]

Lewis wrote another article he intended to publish but for some reason did not. In it, he offers Canadians advice that is as friendly as he can make it and is nearly as timely now as it was when he draughted it:

> Canada should give more care to making itself agreeable and gracious, in its intercourse with strangers.... One feels that in "upper Canada"—Anglosaxon Canada—there is a sort of pride in being repellent, rather than attractive, to the stranger within-the-gate. What the Canadian of these parts tells you is that the social organism to which he belongs is "snooty": or, he will say, "more English than the English." And he seems in an odd way pleased about it.... But the problem of being attractive has never been present to Canadians, I think, because of the great isolation in which they have lived. And the isolation of Ontario has in the nature of things been greater even than that of French Canada. Yet if Canada is ever to blossom out into a sizeable country...it would be no use at all to [be] all Gallic charm at one end, and all titanic Western beauty at the other, while remaining smug, drab and snooty in the middle.[37]

FINISHED IN 1952 and published in 1954, *Self Condemned* draws heavily on Lewis's experience in Canada. He probably began writing it during his years in Toronto. To reporters at the scene of the Tudor Hotel fire, he listed among his lost property "a novel in manuscript."[38] For reasons already discussed (in endnote 23), it is possible that this manuscript was not burned and likely that it was far from being a finished novel. It may have been an early version of the first half of *Self Condemned*. This is suggested by Lewis in a two-page typescript, which was completed for publicity purposes in December 1943. In it, he claims to have "on the stocks a large narrative book, the scene of which is laid in Canada—in the city of Momaco," which, he says, he intends to postpone publishing, since only books bearing on the war should be published during the war.[39] A more likely reason for delay would have been the fragmentary nature of the manuscript—probably the material in notebooks which John Reid recalls Lewis keeping in Toronto and from which passages were later incorporated into the finished novel.[40] Because this novel about Canada was conceived of and probably partly written in Canada, by the bearer of a Canadian passport, it has some claim to be considered a work of Canadian literature.

The protagonist of the novel is René Harding, an Englishman with a French mother (just as Lewis himself had a French-Canadian grandmother). He resigns his history professorship in an English university because he objects to history being a recounting of the criminal activities of kings and governments. By emphasizing their misbehaviour, history implies that it is important, and therefore perpetuates it, while ignoring the more significant achievements of artists and scientists. René says goodbye to relatives and friends and, shortly before war is declared, leaves with his wife for Canada. They settle in "Momaco," a city whose name was suggested by the west-Toronto suburb of Mimico, though Lewis sets his imaginary city at the eastern end of Lake Ontario.[41] Because of its location and because they are several times mentioned together as Canadian cities, Momaco cannot be Toronto. But Momaco is based on Toronto before postwar immigration gave it broad cultural vitality. The Hardings hate this "bush city," which is "so ugly and so devoid of all character as of any trace of charm, that it was disagreeable to walk about in."[42] On Sundays it becomes a sort of absolute void, "the Intense Inane."[43] René's attempts to find employment in Momaco are vain, and he and his wife endure poverty, sheltering for three years and three months in a twelve by twenty-five foot room in the Hotel Blundell, modeled on the Tudor Hotel on Sherbourne St. There they grow closer than ever before in their marriage. One night the hotel burns down, under suspicious circumstances, and a tea-leaf-reading manageress named McAffie, with whom they were friendly, is murdered by the arsonist who torched the

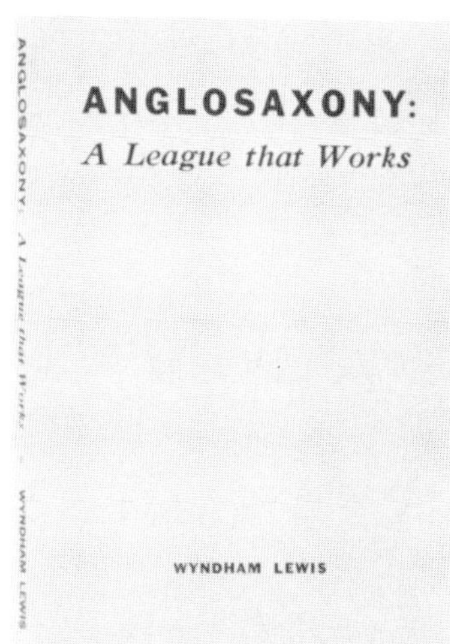

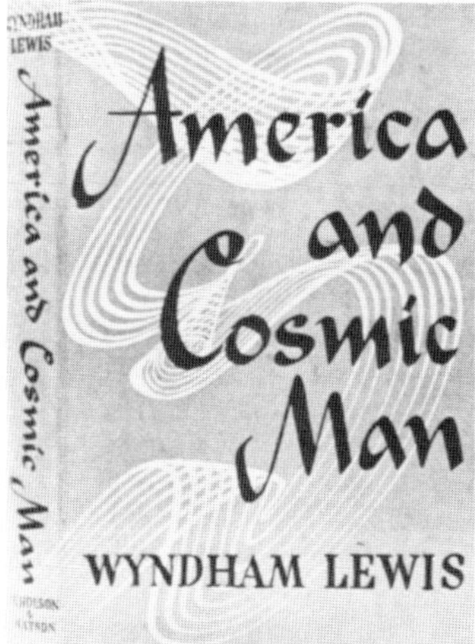

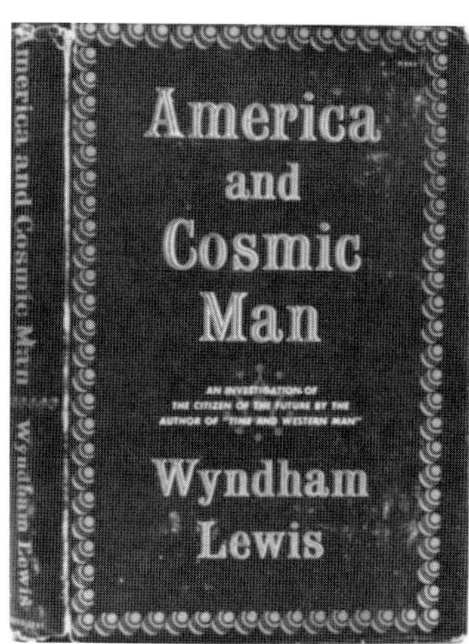

building. Afterwards, René obtains an academic appointment at the University of Momaco. This depresses his wife, who thinks it means they will live there indefinitely. Desperate in her hatred of the city and because of the new tension between herself and her husband, she commits suicide. This causes René to have a breakdown. He goes to rest for three months at a Catholic seminary called the College of the Sacred Heart at Niagara, where he gives two lectures a week. After considering becoming a Catholic, he recovers, returns to Momaco, and then moves south to take a position at a prestigious American university. But he has lost his intellectual and existential integrity. He is, in an image that recalls the icy ruin of the burned out hotel, "a glacial shell of a man."[44]

Some of the characters in the novel are commemorative of Canadians Lewis knew. The hotel employee McAffie, called "Affie," memorializes a manageress of whom the Lewises were fond and who died in the Tudor Hotel fire. The arsonist who murders her is named Martin, probably after the prominent Windsorite Paul Martin, with whom Lewis had argued about the commission for a portrait of his wife. René's best friend in Toronto is a philosophy professor named McKenzie, possibly meant to recall Marshall McLuhan, whom Lewis knew as a professor of English at St. Louis and Windsor. The College of the Sacred Heart is Assumption College, which would later become the University of Windsor. There, Lewis was friendly with the Basilian priests who ran the college. They were probably the most benign group he had ever known: "bold and intimate, very comradely."[45] Certainly they were the only group in Canada who made him feel welcome.

Among them he was closest to Father Stan Murphy, founder of Assumption's Christian Culture Series, who in the summer of 1942 had sought out Lewis to invite him to lecture at Assumption (see fig. 35). In the novel, Murphy is the college registrar, Father Moody, "very kind and pleasant...rosy-faced...his eyes, blazing with childish benevolence...his temples flushing a rich joyous pink."[46] Also at the College is "tall, slightly sinister-looking" Father O'Shea, a professor of philosophy—which, for him, "began and ended with St Thomas Aquinas." This was Father Edwin Garvey, an aggressive and dominant figure at the college and in the labour movement in Windsor. To the end of his teaching career, philosophy consisted for Garvey of Aquinas and Jacques Maritain, who lectured at Assumption in 1943. The librarian, Father McAuliffe, who cooks in his room and gives René gin, was Father Ed Lee, a popular professor of English and devotee of James Joyce. And finally, French-Canadian Father Lemoine—"small,...unlike their aggressive Irish faces his was gentle and self-effacing": this was gentle Father Lebel, who became the first president of the University of Windsor.[47]

To anyone who knew them, the priests are recognizable in their fictional counterparts. But Professor McKenzie, a Scottish émigré, bears no resemblance to the eccentric, aggressively intelligent Marshall McLuhan. Harding's wife is not Mrs. Lewis, who disliked Toronto less than her husband did. And, most important, René Harding is not Wyndham Lewis.

But Harding is a Lewis persona. He writes a column for the local paper; Lewis wrote for *Saturday Night.* Harding was, and becomes again, a history professor; Lewis had agreed to go to Assumption College thinking he would be teaching history.[48] Harding's rejection of history corresponds to Lewis's dislike for "time philosophy," as expressed in his best book, *Time and Western Man* (1927). But Harding departs from Lewis's path when he re-enters the academic profession permanently and writes a book expressing hope for the redemption of history in the emergence of a group of supermen, more intelligent, more creative, and less selfish than past world leaders. For Lewis, who rejected Nietzsche's superman in *Anglosaxony* and *America and Cosmic Man,* Harding's late-Nietzscheanism evolutionary hope is a collapse of intelligence.

This, and his capitulation to conventional time-serving, may have symbolic implications for Canada as a whole, since Harding is half-English, half-French—a division symbolized in the contrast between his Christian name and surname. The French name "René" means "born again"; the English "Harding" has negative, deadening connotations. His names suggest that the protagonist's tragic fate consists of his ceasing to be René in order to become entirely Harding. The national analogue to that would be the Anglicization of Canada.

The chief dilemma in the novel is between history-as-a-commemoration-of-immorality, and an alternative to time, unspecified but symbolized by Catholic Christianity. The first hint of this antithesis occurs at the start of the novel when the caretaker who cleans the Hardings' English flat refers first to Hitler, then to Lucifer, as a "nasty ole man". She is Mrs. Harradson, an amusing simpleton, but also a Catholic. That apparently enables her to mutter equal disapproval of the dictator and the evil archangel without concern for the gulf between time and eternity. She can comprehend history but imaginatively transcends it. After the Hardings leave England, Mrs. Harradson dies of a fall during the Blitz—"foul play" is suspected.[49]

She therefore has as her counterpart Affie, the manageress murdered in the Hotel Blundell, in a conflagration symbolic of the war in Europe. In her fortune-telling, Affie seeks to convince people that her perception exceeds the limits of the present. It is a simple trick: she gains purported prescience by reading the tenants' mail. Knowledge of the future is not, of course, time-transcendence. Fortune-telling as an alternative to talking about the past (i.e. history) merely burlesques the novel's true thematic antithesis. Only in death, which associates her with Catholic Mrs. Harradson, does Affie transcend time.

The most emphatic expression of the antithesis between history and something greater than time occurs at mid-novel when the ship bringing the Hardings from England is within sight of Quebec City. The language here evokes the statement of Jesus to Peter that is especially important to Catholics: "Upon this rock in the Greek of the New Testament, *petrus* I will build my church" (Matthew 16:18). Lewis relates:

> This magnificent rock, more impressive than Gibraltar, is a catholic citadel, the importance of which was appreciated by René. As he stared at it, he did not see a colonial battle in the eighteenth century between a handful of French and English troops, he saw instead a magnificent cardinal, assisted by a herd of clerics, celebrating mass, in the Cathedral. He saw the French population multiplying, the English dwindling, and this rock symbolizing catholic power, rather than anything pettily national.

When a fellow passenger says to Harding, "I imagine you are thinking of an Englishman called Wolfe," Harding replies, "You are wrong."[50]

Having rejected history, Harding is at this point close to Lewis, who admired much of what the Catholic Church represented intellectually, morally, and culturally. Lewis also had personal Catholic affinities. His mother had been a non-practising Catholic, though she had had her son baptized. During the First World War, when soldiers were made to go to church services, Lewis used to attend Mass, though only to escape the "imbecile...music and words of those English hymns." Cecil Eustace, the director of the publishing firm of Dent Ltd., who had introduced Lewis to Father Murphy in 1942, had the impression that Lewis was at that time interested in religion and Catholic writers. The four crucifixion pictures drawn and painted by Lewis in 1941 are further evidence of his religious interest. Lewis had long considered Catholicism the only "real religion."[51] More even than the United States, the Catholic Church epitomized the universality that he hoped would characterize the new, nationless world state. His wife became a Catholic after his death, and regretted that Lewis had not—because, as she put it, "I am sure now he would have been happier, as in his own way he was so attached to the Church."[52] But, for all his attachment, he apparently lacked adequate religious faith that was specifically Catholic.

In *Self Condemned,* the positive alternative to history is the timelessness symbolized by Catholicism. The tragedy that leaves René Harding self-condemned is implicit in his choice. He is tempted to become a Catholic at the College of the Sacred Heart, when he experiences prayerful intimacy with God. This vanishes with his recovery from his breakdown. He then decides to go on professionally describing and analyzing the ignominious misdeeds of historical figures. He decides not to remarry. In a sense he decides to marry time and its meaninglessness.

But without religious faith, what else can he do? Illuminating the problem is a discussion near the end of the novel that extends over three weeks between Harding and Professor McKenzie:

> Is not human life too short to have any real values, is it not too hopelessly compromised with the silliness involved in the reproduction of the species, of all the degradations accompanying the association of those of opposite sex to realize off spring? Then the interminable twenty years of growing up...twenty years of learning to be something which turns out to be nothing. In maturity, the destruction of anything which has value by the enormous mass of what has no value. In other words, the problem of problems is to find anything of value intact and undiluted in the vortex of slush and nonsense: to discover any foothold (however small) in the phenomenal chaos, for the ambitious mind: enough that is uncontaminated to make it worth-while to worry about life at all. And as to condemning the slush and nonsense, the pillage and carnage which we have glorified as "history"; why, that throws us back upon the futility of our daily lives, which also have to be condemned.[53]

Like the writing of the postwar French existentialists, this passage states the "problem of problems": without God, and assuming that hedonism is contemptible, what is the value of human life?

Morally and spiritually, René Harding is self-condemned. But the words of the title are not hyphenated. The title reads like a newspaper headline, announcing that the events narrated in the novel condemn the "self." This work is not merely about Harding; it is about the ego and its insistence in regarding itself as autonomous from, and preferable to, God—whom it may or may not believe in. This is the self Lewis condemns.

The novel provides no alternative to the life of the ego, and no solution to the meaninglessness of time for the irreligious. If, objectively and intellectually, religion is the solution, subjectively, without faith, the solution is unavailable to Harding, as it was to Lewis. The great technical achievement of the novel is the restraint with which it clearly expresses the problem without solving it.[54]

Not that this novel is very good, as Jeffrey Meyers implies by calling it Lewis's "greatest novel"[55]—none of Lewis' novels is "great." The later chapters may be the most interesting of Lewis's fictions–the dilemma that faces Harding is an impressive literary achievement—but the novel is not otherwise very impressive. Especially in the early chapters, it is tediously uneconomical, too long by about 150 pages. Its slack economy decreases unity. The novel is sometimes clumsily written, sometimes from a wavering point of view. Some of this technical imperfection may be owing to Lewis's being blind when writing the novel and therefore with only aural access to his text. But there are faults blindness does not excuse. The basic premise of the book, Harding's objection to history, is silly. There is nice symbolism in the hotel being a microcosm of a world caught in the conflagration of war. But Lewis-as-omniscient-narrator repeatedly says that the hotel is "a microcosm"—seven times by my count. Worse, on several pages towards the end he interprets the novel; a better writer would have left interpretation to the reader.

Lewis's experience in the United States made him an internationalist. Canada treated him to an unfriendliness against which he was forced to enlist what values he could muster. These he found in his marriage, in his art, and in a faint but sincere faith that inclined him towards the Catholic Church. There was more for him to Canada than unfriendliness—including the cultural vitality of Quebec, and the benevolence of A. Y. Jackson and of Stan Murphy and the Basilian Fathers of Windsor. But because literature concerns ego-drama, its greatest emotional power comes from unhappiness. And for that, Lewis had to thank Toronto and, of course, himself.

Catalogue of Works

IN THE EXHIBITION

This catalogue is organized chronologically. The letter "M", followed by a number or by "P" and a number, refers to a *catalogue raisonée* number in Walter Michel's *Wyndham Lewis: Paintings and Drawings* (1971). All measurements are in centimetres, height preceding width. For Canadian exhibition histories of the works listed below, see the section of this catalogue entitled "Wyndham Lewis: Canadian Exhibition History." Works with an asterisk after the catalogue number were shown in Windsor (21 November 1992-24 January 1993) only. The Art Gallery of Windsor regrets that, for logistical reasons, No. 35 *Estelle with Kerchiefed Head*, and No. 48 *Bathers*, were withdrawn from the exhibition too late for deletion from this catalogue.

No. 1
NEWFOUNDLAND
1937, Oil on canvas
70.5 x 49.5 cm; (M P67)
Junior Common Room, New College, Oxford, England

No. 2
MATILDA
1940, Black chalk on paper
45.5 x 30.5 cm; (M 959)
Lent anonymously

No. 3
PORTRAIT OF MARY McLEAN
1940-41, Oil on canvas
73.5 x 51.0 cm; (M P100)
Patrick Stewart, Victoria, British Columbia

No. 4
PORTRAIT OF J.S. McLEAN
1941, Oil on canvas
106.0 x 77.0 cm; (M P101)
Mr. and Mrs. Clair Stewart, Caledon East, Ontario

No. 5
PORTRAIT OF MRS. R.J. (LISA) SAINSBURY
1941, Oil on canvas
89.0 x 58.5 cm; (M P103)
National Gallery of Canada, Ottawa,
gift of R.J. Sainsbury, London, 1964

No. 6
PORTRAIT OF DR. LORNE PIERCE
1941, Black and coloured chalks on blue paper
48.5 x 31.0 cm; (M 978)
Beth Pierce Robinson, Kingston, Ontario

No. 7
PORTRAIT OF DOUGLAS LePAN
1941, Black chalk on paper
38.0 x 28.0 cm; (M 107)
Dr. Douglas LePan, Toronto

No. 8
HEAD OF A WOMAN
1941, Black chalk and watercolour wash on paper
46.2 x 32.0 cm; (M 973)
Lent anonymously

No. 9
DRAGON'S TEETH
1941, Watercolour, ink and graphite on paper
35.5 x 25.0 cm; (M 969)
Lent anonymously

No. 10
WITCH ON COW BACK
1941, Coloured chalk and gouache on paper
29.0 x 43.6 cm; (M 985)
National Gallery of Canada, Ottawa,
gift of the Douglas M. Duncan Collection, 1970

No. 11
FIGURE ON HORSEBACK
1941, Black chalk on paper
26.5 x 35.5 cm; (M 970)
Austin/Desmond and Phipps, London, England

No. 12
HORSEMEN
1941, Black chalk on paper
25.5 x 38.0 cm; (M 974)
Walter and Harriet Michel

No. 13
A MAN'S FORM TAKING A FALL FROM A SMALL HORSE
1941, Pen-and-ink, watercolour on paper
29.0 x 45.0 cm; (M 977)
C.J. Fox, London, England

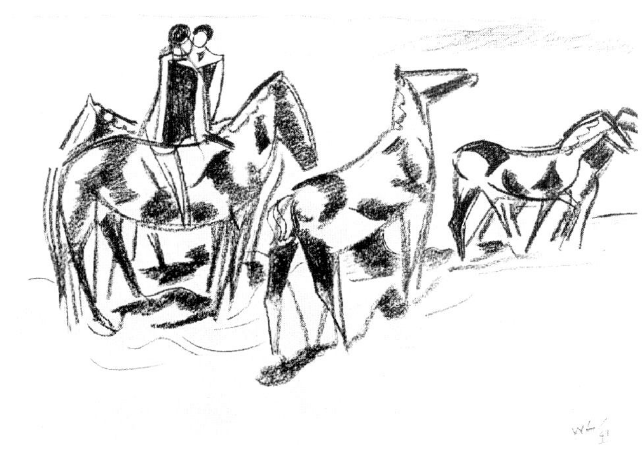

No. 12 *Horsemen*

No. 14
LEBENSRAUM I: THE BATTLEFIELD
1941, Pen-and-ink, watercolour and graphite on paper
29.0 x 40.5 cm; (M 976)
Art Gallery of Ontario, Toronto, purchase, 1941

No. 15
ARMLESS MAN ON STAGE
1941, Black chalk and wash on paper
28.5 x 44.0 cm
Lent anonymously

No. 16
HAMLET AND HORATIO, GARGOYLES
1941, Watercolour, gouache and graphite on paper
45.7 x 31.8 cm; (M 972)
Art Gallery of Ontario, Toronto gift from the
J. S. McLean Collection, by Canada Packers Inc., 1990

No. 17
THE SAGE MEDITATING UPON
THE LIFE OF FLESH AND BLOOD
1941, Graphite, ink and gouache on paper
40.0 x 34.7 cm; (M 979)
Lent anonymously

No. 18
"...AND WILDERNESS WERE PARADISE ENOW"
1941, Black chalk, wash and watercolour on paper
42.5 x 32.0 cm; (M 965)
Lent anonymously

No. 19
JEHOVAH THE THUNDERER
1941, Graphite, ink and watercolour on paper
37.0 x 25.5 cm; (M 975)
Lent anonymously

No. 20
UNTITLED
1941, Crayon, coloured chalks and watercolour on paper
48.0 x 28.0 cm
Mr. and Mrs. Clair Stewart, Caledon East, Ontario

No. 21
ADORATION
1941, Black and white chalk on paper
38.0 x 25.5 cm; (M 963)
Walter and Harriet Michel

No. 22
SUPPLICATING FIGURES
1941; Pen-and-ink and watercolour on paper
29.4 x 45.3 cm; (M 984)
Mark McLean, Toronto

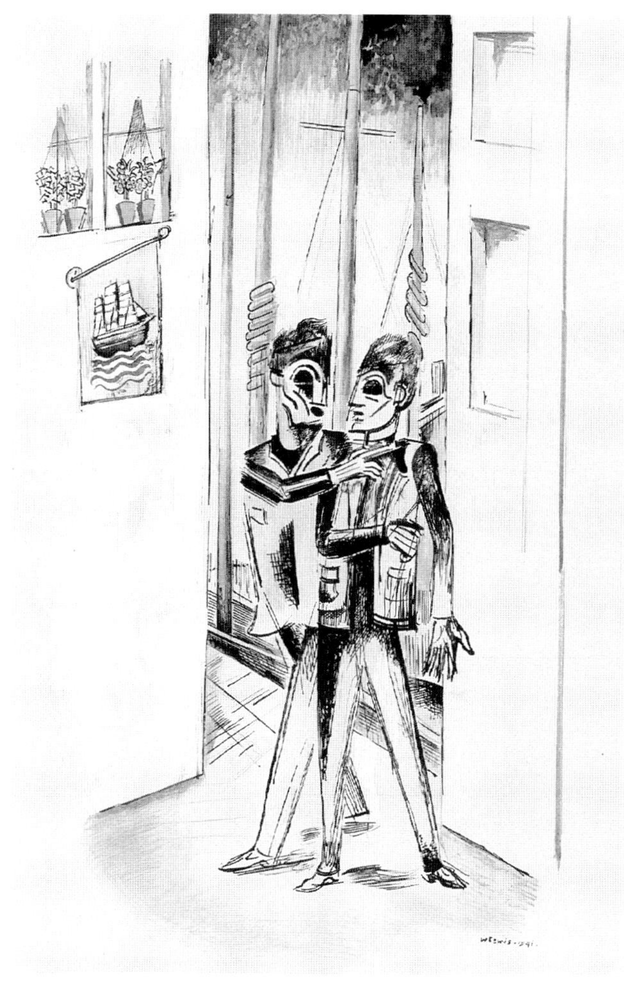

No. 16 *Hamlet and Horatio, Gargoyles*

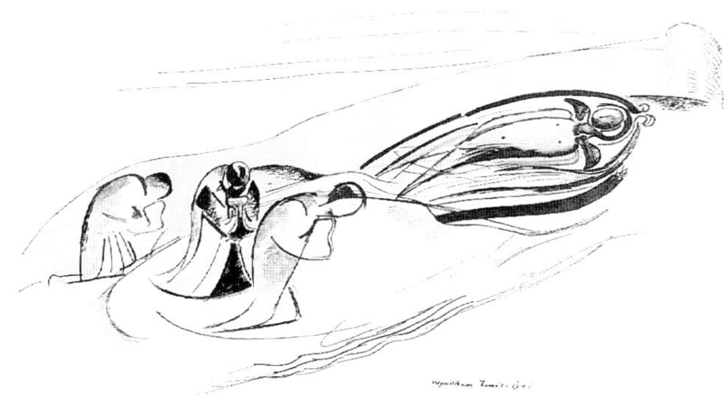

No. 22 *Supplicating Figures*

No. 23
SMALL CRUCIFIXION SERIES, I (OR III)
1941, Graphite, ink and watercolour on paper
35.5 x 25.0 cm; (M 980)
Lent anonymously
Note: an inscription, *verso,* in Douglas Duncan's hand, gives the title as *Small Crucifixion Series, III,* but Michel numbers it *I* of a series of four treatments of this subject.

No. 24
SMALL CRUCIFIXION SERIES, II: PIETÀ
1941, Pen-and-ink and watercolour on paper
33.0 x 25.5 cm; (M 981)
Rodney Milne-Day, London, England

No. 25
SMALL CRUCIFIXION SERIES, III
1941, Graphite, ink and watercolour on paper
36.5 x 25.0 cm; (M 982)
Lent anonymously

No. 26
CREATION MYTH, NO. 17
1941, Charcoal, gouache and graphite on paper
50.2 x 34.9 cm; (M 968)
National Gallery of Canada, Ottawa, gift of
the Douglas M. Duncan Collection, 1970

No. 27
CREATION MYTH: MATERNAL FIGURE
(also known as *Gestation*) 1941
Crayon and coloured chalks on blue paper
34.5 x 29.3 cm (sheet); (M 971)
Lent anonymously

No. 28
CREATION MYTH
1941-42, Pen-and-ink, graphite and watercolour
on paper, 37.0 x 25.5 cm; (M 987)
Walter and Harriet Michel

No. 29
THREE GLADIATORS
1941-42, Pen-and-ink and watercolour on paper
38.0 x 25.0 cm; (M 989)
Lent anonymously

No. 30
BATHING WOMEN
1941-42, Watercolour on paper
30.5 x 26.5 cm; (M 986)
Lent anonymously

No. 31
TWO WOMEN ON A BEACH
1941, Pastel on blue paper
40.5 x 28.5 cm; (M 991)
National Gallery of Canada, Ottawa, gift of
the Douglas M. Duncan Collection, 1970

No. 32
ALLÉGRESSE AQUATIQUE
1941, Watercolour on paper
31.8 x 44.5 cm; (M 1071)
Art Gallery of Ontario, Toronto, purchase, 1941

No. 33
NUDE PANEL
1942, Graphite and watercolour wash on paper
35.5 x 25.5 cm, (M 999)
Mark McLean, Toronto

No. 34
SYBIL [i.e. *SIBYL?*]
1942, Black chalk and watercolour wash on paper
35.0 x 50.0 cm; (M 1019)
Lent anonymously

No. 35
ESTELLE WITH KERCHIEFED HEAD
1942, Graphite, chalk and wash on paper
35.0 x 44.5 cm; (M 1013)
Lent anonymously

No. 36
KERCHIEFED HEAD, LOOKING DOWN
1942, Black chalk on paper
25.5 x 25.5 cm; (M 1025)
Lent anonymously

No. 37
NEW ORLEANS IN TORONTO
1942, Black chalk, graphite and watercolour
on paper, 35.0 x 25.0 cm; (M 1016)
Lent anonymously

No. 38
TURBANED STUDENT
1942, Black chalk on paper
45.5 x 37.5 cm; (M 1020)
Lent anonymously

No. 39
PENSIVE GIRL
1942, Graphite on paper
47.5 x 37.5 cm; (M 1017)
Lent anonymously

No. 40
MOTHER AND CHILD (also known as *Pietà*)
1942, Pen-and-ink and watercolour on paper
38.0 x 23.0 cm; (M 1001)
Lent anonymously

No. 41
PIETÀ (also known as *Madonna and Child*)
1942, Pen-and-ink and wash on paper
38.0 x 24.0 cm; (M 1002)
Herbert F. Johnson Museum of Art, Cornell University, Ithaca, New York, gift of Walter and Harriet Michel

No. 42
MOTHER LOVE
1942, Pen-and-ink, graphite and watercolour wash on paper, 45.5 x 28.5 cm; (M 998)
Lent anonymously

No. 43
THE MIND OF THE ARTIST ABOUT TO MAKE A PICTURE
1942, Pen-and-ink and watercolour on paper
39.5 x 30.5 cm; (M 997)
Lent anonymously

No. 44
CENTAUR OBSERVING A GROUP OF GIRLS
1942, Graphite, pen-and-ink, watercolour and wash on paper, 45.0 x 30.0 cm; (M 993)
Lent anonymously

No. 45
A PARTY OF GIRLS
1942, Pen-and-ink and watercolour on paper
35.5 x 25.5 cm; (M 1000)
Mark McLean, Toronto

No. 46
POOL OF THE AMAZONS
1942, Pen-and-ink and watercolour on paper
35.6 x 44.0 cm; (M 1003)
Mark McLean, Toronto

No. 47
HOMAGE TO ETTY
1942, Pen-and-ink, graphite and watercolour on paper, 25.4 x 41.8 cm; (M 994)
National Gallery of Canada, Ottawa, gift of the Douglas M. Duncan Collection, 1970

No. 48
BATHERS
1942, Graphite and watercolour on paper
25.5 x 38.0 cm; (M 992)
The Board of Trustees of the Victoria and Albert Museum, London, England

No. 49
THE ISLAND
1942, Oil on canvas
56.0 x 78.5 cm; (M P104)
Santa Barbara Museum of Art, Santa Barbara, California, gift of the Women's Board, 1986

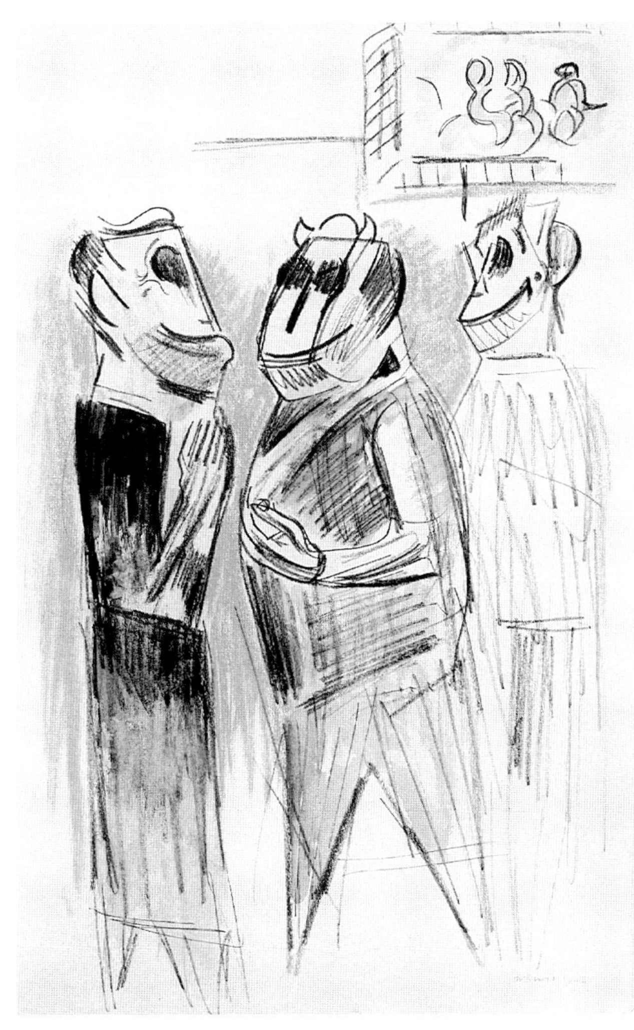

No. 50 *Three Actors*

No. 50
THREE ACTORS
1942, Coloured chalks and watercolour on paper
45.0 x 29.5 cm; (M 1006)
Lent anonymously

No. 51
WITCHES SURPRISED BY DAWN
1942, Black chalk and watercolour on paper
29.0 x 43.0 cm; (M 1008)
John and Helen O'Brian, Vancouver, British Columbia

No. 52
STILL-LIFE: FIGURES IN THE BELLY OF A DUCK
1942, Graphite and watercolour on paper
35.0 x 25.7 cm; (M 1005)
Vancouver Art Gallery, Vancouver, British Columbia, purchase, 1970

No. 53
THE THREE BEGGARS
1942, Pen-and-ink and watercolour on paper, 37.0 x 27.5 cm; (M 1007)
Lent anonymously

No. 54
FIGURE KNITTING
1942, Graphite, coloured chalks and watercolour wash on paper 35.0 x 50.0 cm; (M 1014)
Mercury Gallery, London, England

No. 55
THE BALL OF WOOL
1942, Graphite and wash on paper
34.5 x 25 cm; (M 1009)
Shirley Allen, Ottawa

No. 56
MOTHER AND CHILD, WITH MALE FIGURE
(also known as *Family Group*) 1943
Graphite and coloured chalks on paper
28.0 x 37.5 cm; (M 1023)
Mr. and Mrs. Eric McLuhan, Toronto

No. 57
THE SULLEN EYE
1943, Charcoal on paper
42.5 x 32.5 cm; (M 1029)
Mercury Gallery, London, England

No. 58
A CANADIAN WAR FACTORY
1943, Oil on canvas
114.3 x 85.7 cm; (M P105)
The Tate Gallery, London, England (T00135)

No. 59
WORKMAN
1943, Black chalk on paper
35.5 x 28.0 cm; (M 1033)
Herbert F. Johnson Museum of Art, Cornell University, Ithaca, New York, gift of Walter and Harriet Michel

No. 60
TABLE WITH TRAY AND ARMCHAIRS
1943, Black chalk on paper
13.8 x 19.8 cm; (M 1030)
Herbert F. Johnson Museum of Art, Cornell University, Ithaca, New York, gift of Walter and Harriet Michel

No. 61
TABLE WITH TRAY AND CUPS
1943, Black chalk on paper
35.5 x 48.5 cm; (M 1031)
Lent anonymously

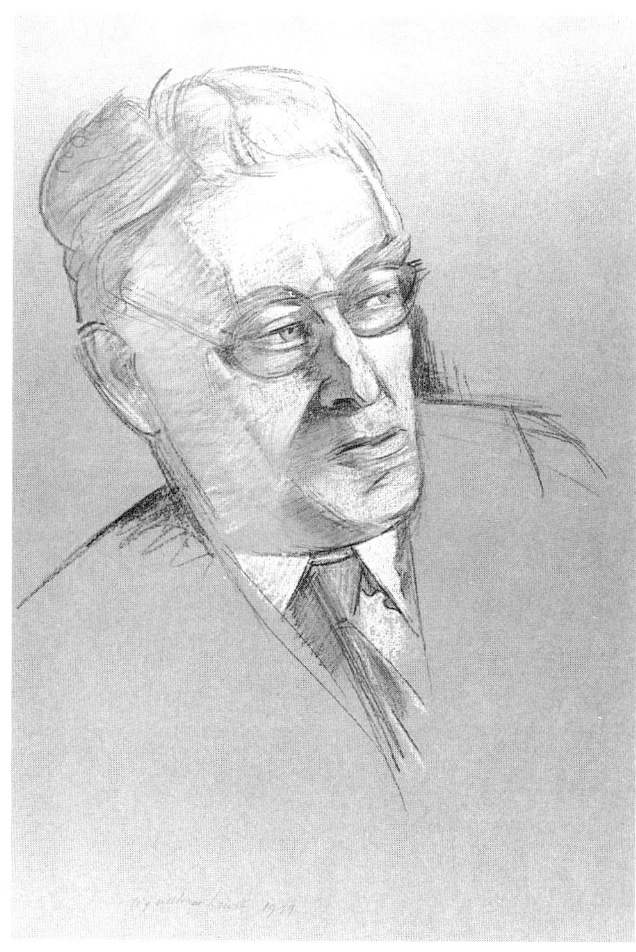

No. 63 *Head of a Canadian*

No. 62
TRAY WITH CUPS
1943, Black chalk on paper
35.5 x 48.5 cm; (M 1032)
Lent anonymously

No. 63
HEAD OF A CANADIAN
1944, Black and coloured chalk on grey paper
45.5 x 30.5 cm; (M 1044)
Herbert F. Johnson Museum of Art, Cornell University, Ithaca, New York, gift of Walter and Harriet Michel

No. 64
PORTRAIT OF MRS. ERNEST W. STIX
1944, Oil on canvas
117.0 x 81.5 cm; (M P110)
Washington University in St. Louis, Gallery of Art, St. Louis, Missouri

No. 65
STUDY FOR PORTRAIT OF DR. ERLANGER
1944, Black chalk and coloured chalks on blue paper
45.0 x 30.0 cm; (M 1038)
Herbert F. Johnson Museum of Art, Cornell University, Ithaca, New York, gift of Walter and Harriet Michel

No. 66
PORTRAIT OF JAMES TAYLOR
1944, Oil on canvas
76.0 x 52.0 cm; (M P111)
James Taylor

No. 67
PORTRAIT OF MARSHALL MCLUHAN
1944, Black chalk on paper
37.5 x 23.5 cm; (M 1046)
Corinne McLuhan, Toronto

No. 68
THREE O'CLOCK
1944, Black chalk on paper
27.5 x 38.0 cm; (M 1053)
Lent anonymously

No. 69
PORTRAIT OF PAULINE BONDY
1944, Black chalk on paper
39.5 x 31.0 cm; (M 1036)
Lent anonymously

No. 70
PORTRAIT OF PAULINE BONDY
1944, Black and coloured chalks on green paper
47.0 x 33.0 cm; (M 1035)
Mary Catherine Lyter, Canoga Park, California

No. 71
PORTRAIT OF A YOUNG LADY (i.e. Pauline Bondy)
1944, Black and coloured chalks on paper
46.5 x 32.0 cm; (M 1049)
Bryan Ferry, West Sussex, England

No. 72
PORTRAIT OF PAULINE BONDY
1944, Oil on canvas
72.5 x 45.5 cm; (M P106)
Pauline Bondy, Toronto

No. 73
PORTRAIT OF THE ARTIST'S WIFE
1944, Black and coloured pencil, black and coloured chalks on paper, 37.5 x 28.0 cm; (M 1048)
Art Gallery of Windsor, Windsor, Ontario, purchased with funds from the Bobs Cogill and Peter Haworth estate and the assistance of the Government of Canada through the Cultural Property Export and Import Act, 1991

No. 74
LANDSCAPE (also known as *Creation Myth*)
1944, Black and coloured chalks over graphite on paper
28.0 x 37.5 cm; (M 1045)
Art Gallery of Windsor, Windsor, Ontario, purchased with funds from the Bobs Cogill and Peter Haworth estate and the assistance of the Government of Canada through the Cultural Property Export and Import Act, 1991

No. 75*
PORTRAIT OF FATHER D. CUSHING
1944, Oil on canvas
66.7 x 61.3 cm; (M P112)
Assumption University, University of Windsor, on permanent loan to the Art Gallery of Windsor

No. 76
PORTRAIT OF FATHER M.J. FERGUSON
1944, Oil on canvas
66.3 x 61.8 cm; (M P113)
Assumption University, University of Windsor, on permanent loan to the Art Gallery of Windsor

No. 77
PORTRAIT OF FATHER FRANK FORSTER
1944, Oil on canvas
67.2 x 61.3 cm; (M P115)
Assumption University, University of Windsor, on permanent loan to the Art Gallery of Windsor

No. 78
PORTRAIT OF FATHER D.L. DILLON
1944, Oil on canvas
65.5 x 60.0 cm; (M P114)
Assumption University, University of Windsor, on permanent loan to the Art Gallery of Windsor

No. 79
PORTRAIT OF FATHER VINCENT L. KENNEDY
1944, Oil on canvas
66.3 x 61.3 cm; (M P116)
Assumption University, University of Windsor, on permanent loan to the Art Gallery of Windsor

No. 80
PORTRAIT OF FATHER ROBERT MCBRADY
1944, Oil on canvas
66.5 x 61.5 cm; (M P117)
Assumption University, University of Windsor, on permanent loan to the Art Gallery of Windsor

No. 81
PORTRAIT OF FATHER THOMAS A. MACDONALD
1944, Oil on canvas
66.3 x 61.8 cm; (M P118)
Assumption University, University of Windsor, on permanent loan to the Art Gallery of Windsor

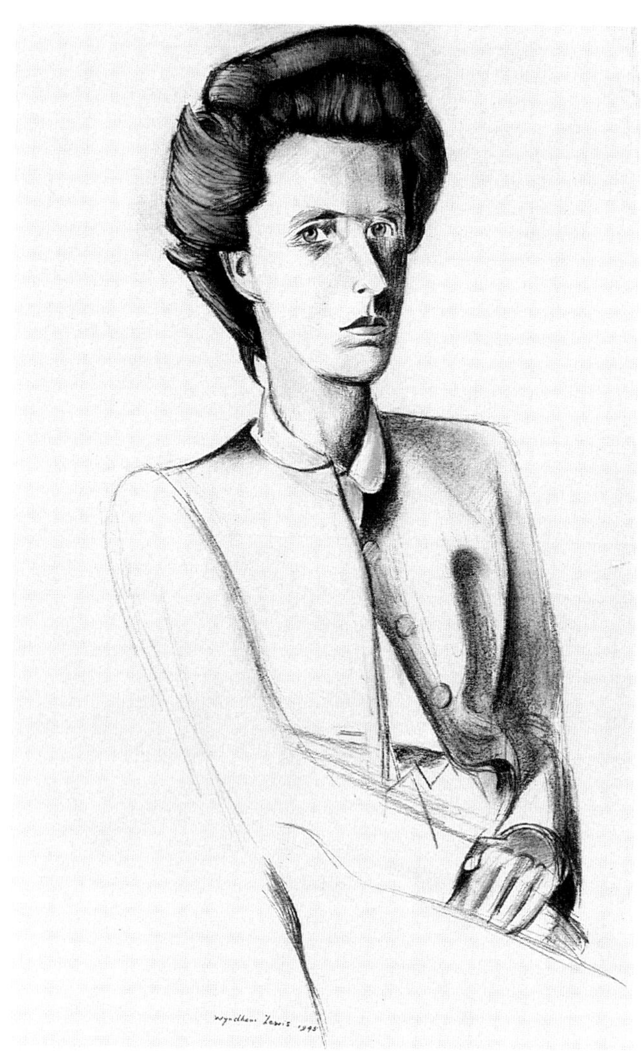

No. 88 *Portrait of Miss X*

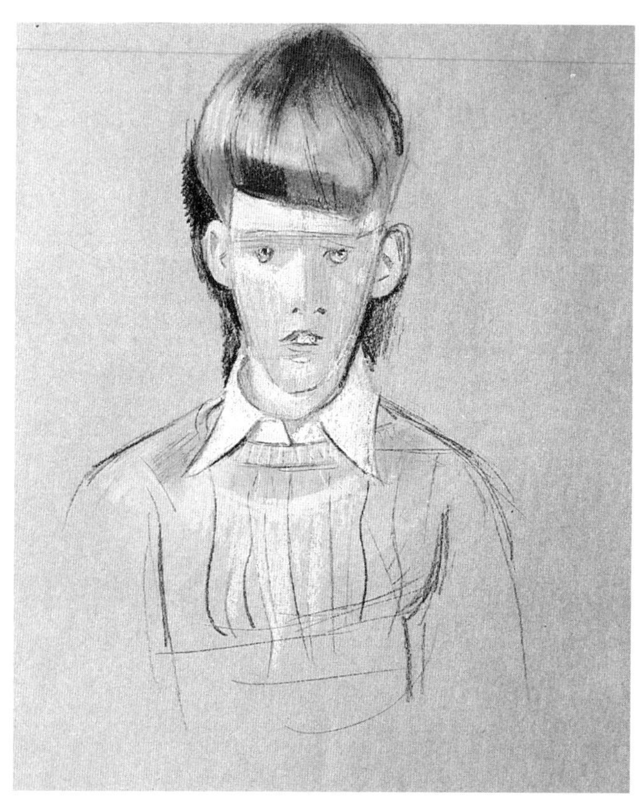

No. 93 *Head of a Boy*

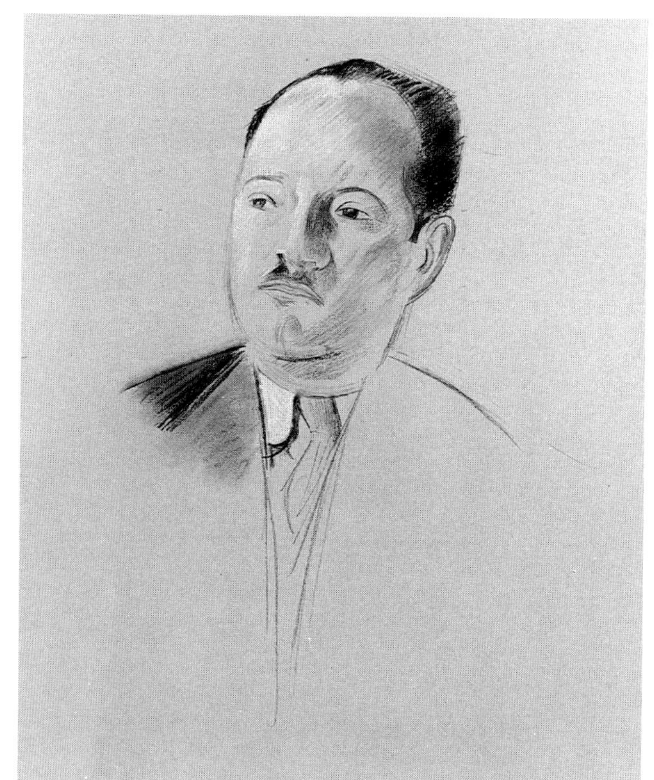

No. 94 *Man's Head*

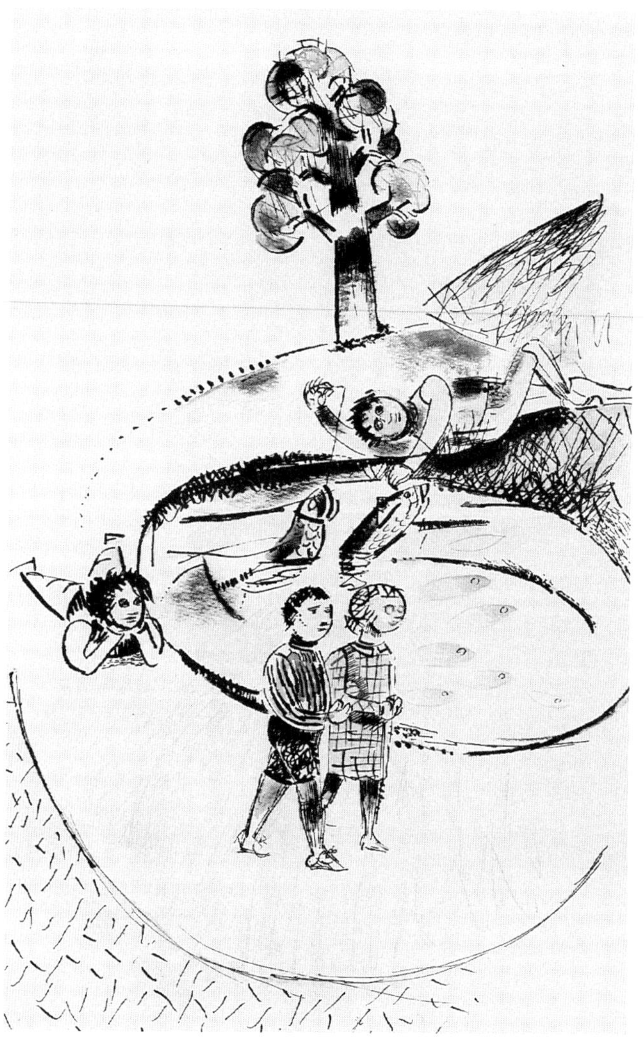

No. 92 *Children Playing*

No. 82
PORTRAIT OF FATHER J.T. MUCKLE
1944, Oil on canvas
66.8 x 61.3 cm; (M P119)
Assumption University, University of Windsor, on permanent loan to the Art Gallery of Windsor

No. 83
PORTRAIT OF ARCHBISHOP DENIS O'CONNOR
1944, Oil on canvas
65.5 x 60.0 cm; (M P120)
Assumption University, University of Windsor, on permanent loan to the Art Gallery of Windsor

No. 84
PORTRAIT OF FATHER WILLIAM G. RODGERS
1944, Oil on canvas
65.5 x 60.0 cm; (M P121)
Assumption University, University of Windsor, on permanent loan to the Art Gallery of Windsor

No. 85
PORTRAIT OF MRS. MARGARET (FELIX) GIOVANELLI
1944, Oil on canvas
63.5 x 41.0 cm; (M P109)
Bryan Ferry, West Sussex, England

No. 86*
PORTRAIT OF JOHN S. NEWBERRY, JR.
1945, Coloured chalks on brown paper
57.2 x 41.9 cm; (M 1060)
The Detroit Institute of Arts, Detroit, Michigan, bequest of John S. Newberry Jr., 1965

No. 87
PORTRAIT OF JOHN S. NEWBERRY, [JR.]
1945, Pastel and conté crayon
50.0 x 38.0 cm; (M 1061)
The Museum of Modern Art, New York, gift of Detroit Institute of Arts

No. 88*
PORTRAIT OF MISS X (i.e. *Edith Ferry*)
1945, Coloured chalks on blue-green paper
46.4 x 29.3 cm; (M 1062)
The Detroit Institute of Arts, Detroit, Michigan, gift of Mrs. Arthur U. Hooper, 1960

No. 89
PORTRAIT OF MRS. PAUL MARTIN
1945, Oil on canvas
114.8 x 71.5 cm; (M P122)
The late the Hon. Paul Martin Sr. and Mrs. Eleanor Martin, Windsor, Ontario

No. 90
PORTRAIT OF MALCOLM MACDONALD
1945, Coloured chalks on paper
36.4 x 26.6 cm; (M 1072)
National Portrait Gallery, London, England

No. 91
BATHING SCENE
1945, Pen-and-ink, black chalk, watercolour, wash, and gouache on paper
37.5 x 33.0 cm; (M 1054)
Lent anonymously

No. 92
CHILDREN PLAYING
1945, Pen-and-ink, graphite and watercolour on paper
37.0 x 22.0 cm; (M 1055)
James H. Winterkorn, Cambridge, England

No. 93
HEAD OF A BOY
n.d. (c.1940-45), Black and coloured chalk on grey paper
35.5 x 30.5 cm; (M 1069)
Herbert F. Johnson Museum of Art, Cornell University, Ithaca, New York, gift of Walter and Harriet Michel

No. 94
MAN'S HEAD
n.d. (c. 1940-45), Coloured chalks on grey paper
43.0 x 34.5 cm; (M 1073)
Herbert F. Johnson Museum of Art, Cornell University, Ithaca, New York, gift of Walter and Harriet Michel

No. 95
SEATED WOMAN
n.d. (c. 1940-45), Black chalk on paper
47.5 x 35.5 cm; (M 1076)
Walter and Harriet Michel

No. 96
HEAD OF ANNE (i.e. *Anne Lewis*)
n.d. (c. 1940-45), Black and coloured chalks on brown paper, 24.5 x 18.5 cm; (M 1065)
Walter and Harriet Michel

No. 97
HANDS
n.d. (c. 1940-45), Black and coloured chalks on green paper, 48.5 x 32.0 cm; (M 1067)
Lent anonymously

No. 98
ANGEL
n.d. (c. 1940s), Pen-and-India ink on paper, 12.0 x 9.5 cm; (M 1106)
Herbert F. Johnson Museum of Art, Cornell University, Ithaca, New York, gift of Walter and Harriet Michel

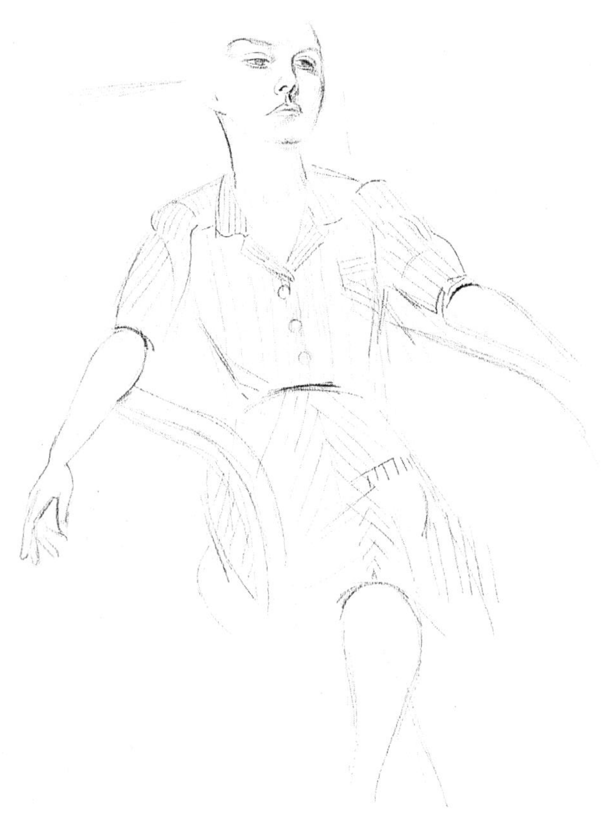

No. 95 *Seated Woman*

No. 99
SUNSET IN PARADISE
n.d (c. 1940s), Pen-and-ink, graphite, watercolour, gouache and coloured chalks on paper, 20.5 x 30.5; (M 1124)
Herbert F. Johnson Museum of Art, Cornell University, Ithaca, New York, gift of Walter and Harriet Michel

No. 100
HANGED MAN AND FIGURES
n.d. (c. 1940s), Pen-and-ink on paper
27.5 x 16.5 cm; (M 1110)
Lent anonymously

No. 101
HANGED MAN AND SOLDIERS' HEADS
n.d (c. 1940s), Pen-on-ink on paper
27.5 x 16.5 cm; (M 1111)
Lent anonymously

BOOKS

No. 102
AMERICA, I PRESUME
New York: Howell, Soskin and Co., 1940
Thomas Fisher Rare Book Library, University of Toronto

No. 103
THE HITLER CULT AND HOW IT WILL END
London: J.M. Dent and Son, 1940
Thomas Fisher Rare Book Library, University of Toronto

No. 104
THE VULGAR STREAK
London: Robert Hale, 1941
Thomas Fisher Rare Book Library, University of Toronto

No. 105
ANGLOSAXONY: A LEAGUE THAT WORKS
Toronto: Ryerson Press, 1941
Thomas Fisher Rare Book Library, University of Toronto

No. 106
SELF CONDEMNED
London: Methuen and Co., 1954
Thomas Fisher Rare Book Library, University of Toronto

No. 107
AMERICA AND COSMIC MAN
London and Brussels: Nicholson and Watson Ltd., 1948
Thomas Fisher Rare Book Library, University of Toronto

MANUSCRIPTS AND ARCHIVAL MATERIALS

No. 108*
Timetable for Assumption College Second Annual Summer School, 1943; Art Gallery of Windsor, Windsor, Ontario

No. 109*
Pamphlet advertising Third Annual Summer School, Assumption College, Windsor, 1944; Art Gallery of Windsor, Windsor, Ontario

No. 110*
Untitled (sketch on the draught of a letter to John Rothenstein, dated 15 July 1942); Pen-and-ink on paper 28.5 x 21.0 cm
Collection of the Department of Rare Books, Cornell University, Ithaca, New York

No. 111*
Wyndham Lewis's Canadian address book, n.d. (c. 1940-45)
Collection of the Department of Rare Books, Cornell University, Ithaca, New York

No. 112*
Pamphlet advertising Christian Culture Series, Assumption College, Windsor, 1944; Collection of the Department of Rare Books, Cornell University, Ithaca, New York

No. 113*
Author/publisher contract agreement, Ryerson Press, n.d. (c. 1941); Collection of the Department of Rare Books, Cornell University, Ithaca, New York

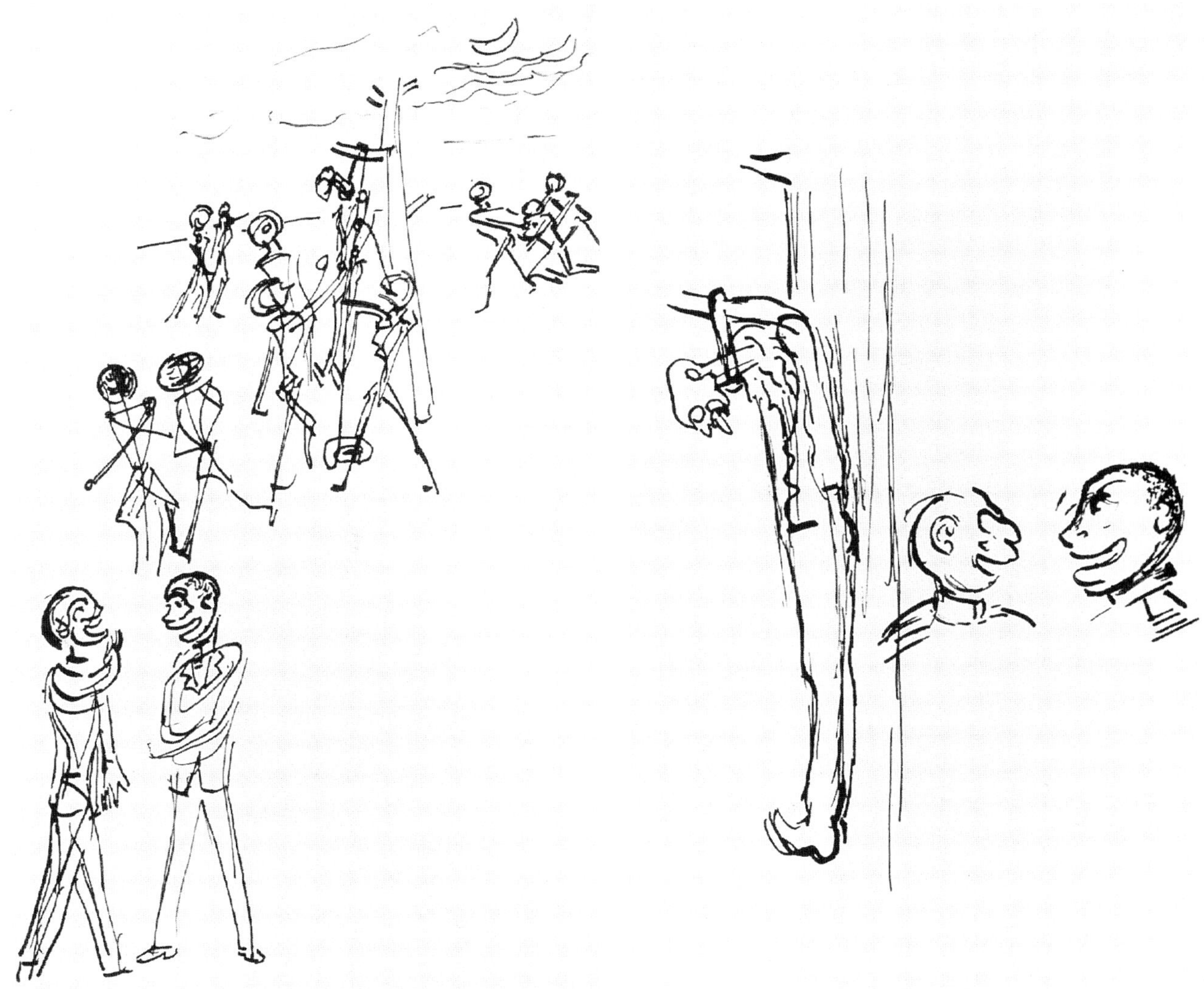

No. 100 *Hanged Man and Figures*

No. 101 *Hanged Man and Soldiers' Heads*

Chronology: 1939-45

1939

2 September: Wyndham and Anne Lewis sail to Canada on the *Empress of Britain.*
12 September: in Toronto, at the King Edward Hotel (37 King St. E.).
5 October-November: in Buffalo, New York, at Stuyvesant Hotel (Elmwood Ave.), working on portrait of Samuel Capen, chancellor of State University of New York at Buffalo, and portraits of family of Charles Abbott.
7 December: publication of *The Hitler Cult* (London: J.M. Dent).
15 December to March 1940: in New York City, at Winthrop Hotel (Lexington and 47th St.) and Tuscany Hotel (120 E. 39th St.).
Late December: in Bethlehem, Connecticut, with American critic Geoffrey Stone.

1940

January: Poetry Society of America dinner with Richard Aldington and Padriac Colum.
25 January: lectures at Harvard University, Cambridge, Mass.: "Satire and Contemporary Poetry"; records *One-Way Song.*
14 February: lectures at Columbia University, New York: "Should American Art Differ From European Art?"
24 April: in New York City, at 81 Irving Place.
12 August: publication of *America, I Presume* (New York: Howell, Soskin & Co.).
14 August: in Sag Harbour, Long Island, New York (Main St.), writing *The Vulgar Streak.*
3 October: in Sag Harbour, Long Island, at The Jermain House.
4 October: "How Would You Expect the English to Behave?", *Saturday Night* (Toronto).
November: expiry of American visa, forcing Lewis's return to Canada.
19 November: in Toronto.
20 November: in Toronto, c/o Thomas Cook and Son, 68 King St. W.
30 November: dinner in Lewis's honour at York Club, Toronto, hosted by J.S. McLean; other guests include Eric Arthur, Charles Comfort, Douglas Duncan, Barker Fairley, John Reid, Carl Schaefer.
November 1940 to April 1941: studio at 22 Grenville St. Toronto.
30 November-3 or 4 December: in Ottawa, Ontario, at Lord Elgin Hotel (100 Elgin St.), "among the civil servants and statesmen", to pursue "war-records" and portrait commissions; requested by H.O. McCurry, director, to give lecture on "The Importance of the Visual Arts" at the National Gallery of Canada.
5 December: back in Toronto.
7 December: W.L. and Anne Lewis move into the Tudor Hotel, Apt. 11A, 559 Sherbourne St., Toronto; describes apartment as "One big room, kitchen and bathroom" (to mid-June 1943).
12 December: broadcasts talk on C.B.C. radio: "Can Democracy be Defined?"

1941

January to December: at the Tudor Hotel, Apt. 11A, Toronto; begins the "Toronto drawings."
10 March: occupies Lawren P. Harris's studio, Studio Building, Severn St., Toronto; friendship with A.Y. Jackson and Keith MacIver.
18 April: unveiling of *Portrait of J.S. McLean* at Canada Packers headquarters, Toronto.
31 May to mid-July: in Montreal, Quebec (studio at 43 Prince Arthur St. West).
6 June 1941: in Ottawa, at Chateau Laurier hotel (1 Rideau St.), to see H.O. McCurry, director, National Gallery of Canada.
30 June: publication of *Anglosaxony: A League That Works* (Toronto: Ryerson Press).
10 August: in Toronto.
September: trip to Bathurst, New Brunswick, staying with Sir James Dunn (also to Halifax, Nova Scotia?).
October: experiences severe eye problems.
15 November: "Reasons Why an Englishman is an Englishman", *Saturday Night.*
8 December: publication of *The Vulgar Streak* (London: Robert Hale Ltd.)
Gives talk at Simpson's Bond Fair, Simpson's department store, Yonge St., Toronto: "Keep Culture Alive."

1942

January to December: living at Hotel Tudor, Apt. 11A, Toronto; continues the "Toronto drawings" and paints *The Island.*
February: writing article, "Is a Canadian Renaissance Likely" (unpublished M.S. Cornell).
13 June: "That 'Now-or-Never' Spirit", *Saturday Night.*
Summer: meets Fr. J. Stanley Murphy, who invites him to lecture at Assumption College, Windsor, Ontario.
10 October: "What Books for Total War?", *Saturday Night.*

1943

January to mid-June: living at Tudor Hotel, Apt. 11A, Toronto.
2 January: lectures at Assumption College, Windsor: "Religious Expression in Contemporary Art

15 February: Tudor Hotel fire; Lewises move briefly to Selby Hotel (592 Sherbourne St.), Toronto.
Early spring: visit to Ottawa, probably to see Malcolm MacDonald in connection with the commissioned painting *A Canadian War Factory*.
Mid-June to end of September: living at Royal Apartments, Apt. 2, 30 Ellis East, Windsor.
June-July: teaches summer school course at Assumption College: "The Philosophical Roots of Modern Art and Literature."
October 1943 to February 1944: living at 1805 Sandwich St. West, Windsor.
7 November to 19 December: Heywood Broun Lecture Series, Assumption College: "The Concept of Liberty in America."
30 November: lectures at Detroit Institute of Arts, Detroit, Michigan: "The Frontiers of Art" or "The Cultural Melting Pot."

1944

February: in St. Louis, Missouri, at Park Plaza Hotel.
18 February: lectures at Wednesday Club, St. Louis.
21 February: lectures at City Art Museum, St. Louis.
29 February: lectures at Arts Club of Chicago: "The Meaning of Ugliness in Rouault, Picasso and Others."
11 April: in St. Louis, Missouri, at Fairmont Hotel (4907 Maryland).
May to July: in St. Louis, at Coronada Hotel.
July-August: in Windsor, Ontario; gives three-week summer course, "The ABC of the Visual Arts." (one lecture entitled "The Nature of Criterion in the Fine Arts.")
October-November: in St. Louis, Mo., at Fairmont Hotel.
November: in Washington, D.C., sees Archibald McLeish, Library of Congress.
December to May 1945: in Windsor, Ontario.

1945

February to April: in Windsor, Ontario, at Prince Edward Hotel.
4 February: lectures at Windsor Art Association.
7 March: lectures at University of Michigan, Ann Arbor: "Hemingway, Tolstoi and War."
9 March: lectures at Michigan State University, East Lansing: "Hemingway, Tolstoi and War."
13 March: in Windsor.
14 March: lectures at Rankin Hotel, Chatham, Ontario: "The Problem of Beauty."
14 May: in Windsor.
Mid-May to July: in Ottawa, at Lord Elgin Hotel; mailing address, as of 19 June, c/o 214 Sparks St., Dominion Bank.
First week of August: sails to England on the *Strathden*.
19 September: living at Flat A, 29 Kensington Gardens Studios, Notting Hill Gate, London W1.

Additional Canadian Dates

18 November 1882: birth of Percy Wyndham Lewis on board the *Wanda*, off Amherst, Nova Scotia; christened in Montreal.
November-December 1917: successfully applies for commission, Canadian War Memorials, London.
31 December 1917: reports to Ypres Battery, Belgium, seconded as war artist.
January 1918: stationed at Canadian Army Headquarters, Vimy Ridge, France.
December 1918: *A Canadian Gun Pit* exhibited in *Canadian War Memorials* exhibition, Royal Academy, London.
February 1919: *Guns*, exhibition of Lewis's war drawings and (lost) oils, Goupil Gallery, London.
April 1919: demobilized.
29 August 1946: "Canadian Nature and its Painters", *The Listener* (London).
Early July 1948: publication of *America and Cosmic Man* (London: Nicholson and Watson).
1950: Canadian passport re-issued.
22 April 1954: publication of *Self Condemned* (London: Methuen & Co. Ltd.).
November 1967: publication of "The Great War: Wyndham Lewis and the Underground Press", *artscanada* (Toronto).
Winter 1968: publication of "Wyndham Lewis in Canada" issue of *Canadian Literature*, ed. George Woodcock.
1971: publication of *Wyndham Lewis in Canada*, edited by George Woodcock (Vancouver: University of British Columbia).

For dates of Lewis exhibitions in Canada, see "Wyndham Lewis: Canadian Exhibition History" in this catalogue. For other Canadian publications, see "Selected Bibliography."

Wyndham Lewis: Canadian Exhibition History

Note: titles given as in published exhibition catalogues and handlists

1919

Canadian War Memorials Exhibition
Anderson Gallery, New York, 10 June-31 July 1919; Canadian National Exhibition, Toronto, August-September 1919; Art Association of Montreal, October-November 1919
    No. 66. *Canadian Gunpit* (loaned by the National Gallery of Canada, Ottawa)

1920

Canadian War Memorials Exhibition, New Series: The Last Phase
Canadian National Exhibition, Toronto, August-September 1920; Art Association of Montreal, September-October 1920
    A Canadian Gun Pit
[*Note:* National Gallery of Canada curatorial files indicate that this work was included in this exhibition, but published reviews in N.G.C. exhibition files do not mention it.]

1924

Second Exhibition of Canadian War Memorials
National Gallery of Canada, Ottawa, 18 January-30 April 1924
    47. *A Canadian Gunpit*

1926

Exhibition of Canadian War Memorials
Art Gallery of Toronto, October 1926
    104. *Canadian Gunpit*

1939

Temporary exhibition of some of the pictures in the British Pavilion, New York World's Fair (arranged by John Rothenstein, opened by Lord Tweedsmuir)
National Gallery of Canada, Ottawa, October 1939
    The Surrender of Barcelona

1941-42

Britain At War
The Museum of Modern Art, New York, May-September 1941; National Gallery of Canada, October 1941; Art Gallery of Toronto, 15 November-14 December 1941; Art Association of Montreal, January 1942; London Public Library and Art Museum, Elsie Perrin Williams Memorial Building, London, Ontario, February 1942
    A Canadian Gun Pit, lent by the National Gallery of Canada, Ottawa

1942

19th Annual Exhibition, Canadian Society of Graphic Art
Art Gallery of Toronto, April 1942
Lent by the Picture Loan Society, Toronto:
    Witch on Cowback
    Bathing Women

15th Annual Exhibition, Canadian Society of Painters in Watercolour
Art Gallery of Toronto, April 1942
Lent by the Picture Loan Society, Toronto:
    Jupiter the Thunderer
    Marine Fiesta

1943

Group exhibition with David Milne, Michael Forster, Ian MacIver, Kathleen Daly, Jack Nichols Picture Loan Society, Toronto, Ontario, January 1943 (opening date: 20 January)
    Lewis mentioned in published review as showing several watercolours

English Paintings Since 1900
London Public Library and Art Museum, Elsie Perrin Williams Memorial Building, London, Ontario, 7 May-12 June 1943
    23. *Lebensraum, the Battlefield*
    24. *Allégresse Aquatique*

1948-49

Contemporary British Drawings
National Gallery of Canada, Ottawa, 1948-49
Lent by Messrs. Reid and Lefevre, London:
    42. *Head from the Casting Shop*

1950

Wyndham Lewis: Drawings and Water Colours
Victoria College, University of Toronto, February 1950
Belonging to the artist:
    Head of a Woman (1941) $100
    Lebensraum II: The Empty Tunic (1941) $60
    And Wilderness Were Paradise Enow (1941) $60
    Crucifixion Series I (1941) $60
    Crucifixion Series III (1941) $60
    A Man's Form Taking a Fall From A Small Horse (1941) $75
    Cat-nap (1942) $90
    New Orleans in Toronto (1942) $60
    Still Life: In the Belly of a Bird (1942) $75
Lent by the Art Gallery of Ontario:
    Allegresse Aquatique (1941)
    Lebensraum I: The Battlefield (1941)
Lent by Douglas Duncan:
    Witch on Cowback (1941) $100
    Two Women on a Beach (1941) $100
    Women Bathing (1941) $90
    Creation Myth: Maternal Figure (1941) $90
    Creation Myth No. 17 (1941) $125
    Jehovah the Thunderer (1941) $125
    Three Martyrs (1941) $100
    Three Gladiators (1941) 90
    Dragon's Teeth: Three Cultures (1941) $90
    Homage to Etty (1942) $90
    Centaur Observing a Group of Girls (1942) $100
    War News (1942) $100
    Marine Fiesta (1942) $125
Lent by Professor [Norman] Endicott:
    Cow (1941) $60
Lent by Mr. J.S. McLean:
    Figure on Horseback (1941) $60
    Witches Surprised by Dawn (1942) $100
    Hamlet and Horatio (1941) $100
    Crucifixion Series: II Pietà (1941) $75
Lent by Mr. John Reid:
    Crucifixion Series IV (1941) $75

Lent by Professor [Marshall] McLuhan:
Family Group (1943) $90

1954
Exhibition of the Beaverbrook Collection of Paintings and Prints and Some Portraits from the Collection of Sir James Dunn, Bart.
The Bonar Law-Bennett Library, The University of New Brunswick, 8-20 November 1954
23. *The Mud Clinic*

1955-57
British Watercolours and Drawings of the Twentieth Century
Organized and circulated by the British Council, Canadian tour, 1955-57 (catalogue introduction by Geoffrey Grigson); tour included showing at Willistead Art Gallery of Windsor, Windsor, Ontario
25. *Red Nude* (1919)
26. *Abstract Design* (1912)
27. *Column Figures* (1921)

1964
Paintings from the Canadian War Memorials
National Gallery of Canada, Ottawa, 26 June-October 1964; Art Gallery of Hamilton, Hamilton, Ontario, November 1964
A Canadian Gun-Pit

Exhibit of Paintings and Books by Wyndham Lewis
York University Art Gallery, Glendon College, York University, Toronto, Ontario, 27 November-30 December 1964
1. *Portrait of Pauline Bondy* (1944)
2. *Portrait of Pauline Bondy* (1944)
3. *Portrait of Marshall McLuhan* (1944)
4. *Portrait Drawing of Jessie Dismorr* (1922)
5. *Head of a Woman* (1941)
6. *Head of a Woman* (Mrs. Lewis) (1941)
7. *Estelle with Kerchiefed Head* (1942)
8. *Figure Knitting* (1942)
9. *Cat-nap* (1942)
10. *War News* (Mrs. Lewis) (1942)
11. *Self-Portrait* (n.d.)
12. *Portrait of Mrs. R.J. Sainsbury* (1941)
13. *Woman, - side face* (1922)
14. *Woman's Head, inclining on one hand* (1919)
15. *Seated Woman* (n.d.)
16. *Thoughtful Women* (probably before 1923)
17. *Seated Woman with Necklace* (c. 1923)
18. *Woman Wearing Hat* (c. 1923)
19. *The Sitwell Brothers* (1923)
20. *Figure on Horseback* (1941)
21. *Crucifixion Series II Pieta* (1941)
22. *Crucifixion Series I* (1941)
23. *Crucifixion Series III* (1941)
24. *Witches Surprised by Dawn* (1942)
25. *Witch on Cowback* (1941)
26. *Figure on Horseback* (1941)
27. *Gargoyles, Horatio & Hamlet* (1941)
28. *Mother and Infant with Male Figure* (1943)
29. *Bathing Women* (1941)
30. *Dragon's Teeth* (1941)
31. *Creation Myth: Maternal Figure* (1941)
32. *And Wildernes Were Paradise* (n.d.)
33. *Lebensraum, No. 2 (Empty Tunic)* (1942)
34. *Still Life - In the Belly of the Bird* (1942)
35. *Homage to Etty* (1942)
36. *A Man's Forms* (1941)
37. *Marine Fiesta* (1942)
38. *Jehovah the Thunderer* (1941)
39. *Two Women on a Beach* (1941)
40. *Centaur Observing a Group of Girls* (1942)
41. *Three Martyrs* (c. 1942)
42. *Creation Myth No. 17* (1941)
43. *The Island* (1942)
44. *The Armada* (1937)
45. *Bull's Head* (1941)
46. *Three Gladiators* (n.d.)
47. *Two Figures* (n.d.)
48. *The No. 2* (c. 1918)
49. *Design for a Box Lid* (1912)
50. *Book Cover Design for "The Enemy"* (1927)
51. *The Battlefield* (1941)
52. *Allégresse Aquatique* (1941)
53. *Reclining Nude* (n.d.)
54. *Nude on a Sofa* (1936)
55. *Post-Jazz* (1913)
56. *Three O'Clock* (1944)
57. *The Duc de Joyeux Sings* (ca. 1922)
58. *The Sea Cave* (1938)
59. *Bathing Scene* (1938)
60. *Fantasy* (1947)
61. *War Drawing* (1918)
62. *Nude Study* (c. 1936)
63. *Study of a Girl* (n.d.)
64. *Timon of Athens Portfolio* (1912)

1966
Windsor Collectors
Willistead Art Gallery of Windsor, Windsor, Ontario, 5 October-10 November 1966
33. *Portrait of Mrs. Martin* (1945)

1967-68
Some Paintings, Drawings and Prints from the Douglas Duncan Collection
Willistead Art Gallery of Windsor, Windsor, Ontario, 4 October-9 November 1967; London Public Library and Art Museum, London, Ontario, 5-27 December 1967; Art Gallery of Hamilton, Hamilton, Ontario, 6 January-22 January 1968
35. *Creation Myth No. 17* (1941)
36. *Marine Fiesta* (1942)

1982
Wyndham Lewis: A Centennial Salute
Art Gallery of Nova Scotia, Halifax, Nova Scotia, 5 August-5 September 1982
1. *A Canadian Gun-Pit* (1918)
2. *The Armada* (1937)
3. *The Mud Clinic* (1937)
4. *Allégresse Aquatique* (1941)
5. *Creation Myth, no. 17* (1941)
6. *Witch on Cowback* (1941)
7. *Lebensraum: The Battlefield* (1941)
8. *Two Women on a Beach* (1941)
9. *Homage to Etty* (1942)
10. *Still Life in the Belly of the Bird* (1942)

1984-87

Preferred Places: A Selection of British Landscape Watercolours from the Permanent Collection of the Art Gallery of Ontario
Exhibition organized and toured by the Art Gallery of Ontario, Toronto, 30 November 1984-6 July 1987; travelled to: Glendon Gallery, York University, Toronto, Ontario, 30 November 1984-13 January 1985; Kitchener/Waterloo Art Gallery, Kitchener, Ontario, 26 February-26 April 1985; Sarnia Public Library and Art Gallery, Sarnia, Ontario, 5 June-6 July 1987

Lebensraum: The Battlefield

1987-88

Twentieth Century British Art from the Collection of the Art Gallery of Ontario
Exhibition organized and toured by the Art Gallery of Ontario, Toronto, 13 August 1987-11 July 1988; travelled to: Art Gallery of Peterborough, Peterborough, Ontario, 13 August-15 September 1987; Rodman Hall Arts Centre, St. Catharines, Ontario, 2 October-1 November 1987; Sarnia Public Library and Art Gallery, Sarnia, Ontario, 11 June-11 July 1988

Allégresse Aquatique

1989

Lest We Forget
London Regional Art and Historical Museums, London, Ontario, 9 September-29 October, 1989; Art Gallery of Hamilton, Hamilton, Ontario; Robert McLaughlin Gallery, Oshawa, Ontario; Agnes Etherington Art Centre, Kingston, Ontario; Confederation Art Centre, Charlottetown, Prince Edward Island; Dalhousie Art Gallery, Halifax, Nova Scotia

37. *A Canadian Gun Pit* (drawing)

1990

Selections from the Canada Packers Gift
Art Gallery of Ontario, Toronto, 2 May-3 June 1990

Hamlet and Horatio, Gargoyles

As is indicated above, under 1939, Lewis exhibited *The Surrender of Barcelona* at the British Pavilion, New York World's Fair, New York City. In January 1944 Marshall McLuhan and Felix Giovanelli mounted an exhibition of books and pictures by Lewis for the Wednesday Club, St. Louis, Missouri. The memorial exhibition *Wyndham Lewis* was held at the Santa Barbara Museum of Art, Santa Barbara, California, in August-September 1957, with loans from several Canadian collections, including those of Douglas Duncan and Norman Endicott.

Selected Bibliography

There are two Lewis bibliographies: Bradford Morrow and Bernard Lafourcade's *A Bibliography of the Writings of Wyndham Lewis* (Santa Barbara, Ca.: Black Sparrow Press, 1978), and Omar S. Pound and Philip Grover's *Wyndham Lewis: A Descriptive Bibliography* (Folkestone: Dawson, 1978); the former includes a section on writings about Lewis up to 1978. The following selected bibliography concentrates on titles published during or after, and/or directly relating to, the period 1939-45, and on specifically Canadian references. Asterisks (*) after titles indicate exhibition catalogues or checklists. "Cornell" stands for Wyndham Lewis Collection, Department of Rare Books, Olin Library, Cornell University, Ithaca, New York. For an alphabetical listing of Lewis manuscript and typescript material in this collection, see Mary F. Daniels, *Wyndham Lewis: A Descriptive Catalogue of the Manuscript Material in the Department of Rare Books Cornell University Library* (Ithaca, New York: Cornell University Library, 1972).

PART I: PUBLICATIONS BY LEWIS

America and Cosmic Man. London and Brussels: Nicholson and Watson, 1948; Garden City, New York: Doubleday & Co., 1949.

America, I Presume. New York: Howell, Soskin and Co. 1940.

Anglosaxony: A League That Works. Toronto: Ryerson Press, 1941.

Blasting and Bombardiering. London: Eyre and Spottiswood, 1937; 2nd edition, London: Calder and Boyars Ltd., 1967; reprinted London: John Calder, 1982.

"Canadian Nature and Its Painters." *The Listener* 36 (Autumn 1946): 267-68.

Creatures of Change and Creatures of Habit: Essays on Art, Literature and Society, 1914-1956. Ed. Paul Edwards. Santa Rosa, California: Black Sparrow Press, 1989.

Enemy Salvoes: Selected Literary Criticism. Ed. with introduction by C.J. Fox, general introduction by C.H. Sisson. New York: Barnes and Noble Books, Harper and Row Publishers Inc., 1976.

The Essential Wyndham Lewis: An Introduction to his Work. Ed. Julian Symons. London: André Deutsch, 1989.

"Hill 100: Outline for an Unwritten Novel." *Wyndham Lewis in Canada,* ed. George Woodcock. Vancouver: University of British Columbia Press, 1971, pp. 90-96.

"How Would You Expect the English to Behave?" *Saturday Night: The Canadian Weekly* 57 (4 October 1941): 18-19.

The Letters of Wyndham Lewis. Ed. W.K. Rose. London: Methuen/ Norfolk, Connecticut: New Directions, 1963.

"The 'Now-or-Never' Spirit." *Saturday Night: The Canadian Weekly* 57 (13 June 1942): 6.

"On Canada", *in Wyndham Lewis in Canada,* ed. George Woodcock. Vancouver: University of British Columbia Press, 1971, pp. 24-29.

"Reasons Why An Englishman Is An Englishman." *Saturday Night: The Canadian Weekly* 57 (15 November 1941): 34b.

The Rôle of Line in Art. London: Corvinus Press, 1941; new edition, with a foreword by Robert Stacey, New York: Privately printed by Cameron McWhirter, 1992.

Rude Assignment: A Narrative of My Career Up-to-date. London: Hutchinson, 1950; new edition, subtitled *An Intellectual Autobiography,* ed. Toby Foshay, Santa Barbara: Black Sparrow Press, 1984.

Self Condemned. London: Methuen and Co., 1954; Chicago: Henry Regnery Co., 1955, new edition, with introduction by Hugh Kenner, 1965; New Canadian Library edition, with introduction by Rowland Smith, Toronto: McClelland and Stewart, 1974; reprint, with afterword by Rowland Smith, and appendix ("Variant Ending to *Self Condemned*), Santa Barbara: Black Sparrow Press, 1983. Holograph and typescript notes, draughts, partial copies, and variant texts for this novel, dating from c. 1940 to 1954, are at Cornell.

A Soldier of Humor and Selected Writings. Ed., with an introduction, by Raymond Rosenthal. New York and Toronto: New American Library, The English Library Ltd., 1966.

Unlucky for Pringle: Unpublished and Other Stories. Edited with an introduction by C.J. Fox and Robert T. Chapman. London: Vision Press, 1973.

The Vulgar Streak. London: Robert Hale, 1941; new edition, ed. Paul Edwards. Santa Barbara: Black Sparrow Press, 1985.

"What Books for Total War." *Saturday Night: The Canadian Weekly* 57 (10 October 1942): 16; reprinted in *Critical Views on Canadian Writers: Morley Callaghan,* ed. Brandon Conron. Toronto: McGraw-Hill Ryerson Ltd., 1975, pp. 55-59.

Wyndham Lewis: An Anthology of his Prose. Ed., with an introduction, by E.W.F. Tomlin. London: Methuen, 1969.

Wyndham Lewis on Art: Collected Writings, 1913-1956. Ed. Walter Michel and C.J. Fox. London: Thames and Hudson/ New York: Funk and Wagnalls, 1969. (Includes "Canadian Nature and its Painters", pp. 425-29.)

Wyndham Lewis The Artist: From 'Blast' to Burlington House. London: Laidlaw and Laidlaw, 1939.

PART II: PUBLICATIONS ON LEWIS AND HIS CANADIAN ASSOCIATES

Bridson, D.G. *The Filibuster: A Study of the Political Ideas of Wyndham Lewis.* London: Cassell and Co., 1972.

Carter, Thomas H., ed. "Wyndham Lewis Number." *Shenandoah* 4 (Summer-Autumn 1953).

Chapman, Robert T. *Wyndham Lewis: Fictions and Satires.* London: Vision Press, 1973.

Cookson, William, ed. "Wyndham Lewis Special Issue." *Agenda* 7-8 (Autumn-Winter 1969-70).

Cooney, Seamus, ed. *Blast 3.* Co-edited by Bradford Morrow, Bernard Lafourcade and Hugh Kenner. Santa Barbara: Black Sparrow Press, 1984.

Daniels, Mary F. *Wyndham Lewis: A Descriptive Catalogue of the Manuscript Material in the Department of Rare Books, Cornell University Library,.* Ithaca, New York: Cornell University Library, 1972.

Dasenbrock, Reed Way. *The Literary Vorticism of Ezra Pound and Wyndham Lewis: Towards the Condition of Painting.* Baltimore and London: The Johns Hopkins University Press, 1985.

Edwards, Paul. *Wyndham Lewis: Art and War.* Chronology and catalogue of plates by Catherine Wallace. London: Published by the Wyndham Lewis Trust in association with Lund Humphries/Imperial War Museum, 1992.*

Enemy News: Newsletter of the Wyndham Lewis Society (1978-present). Succeeds *Lewisletter.*

Exhibit of Paintings and Books by Wyndham Lewis. Toronto: Art Gallery of York University, 1964.*

Fairley, Barker. "Canadian War Pictures." *The Canadian Magazine* 54 (November 1919): 2-11.

Farrington, Jane. *Wyndham Lewis.* London: Lund Humphries/ Manchester: Manchester City Art Gallery, 1980.*

Frye, H. Northrop. "Neo-Classical Agony." *The Hudson Review* 10 (Winter 1957): 592-98.

——. "Wyndham Lewis: Anti-Spenglerian." *Canadian Forum* (June 1936): 21-22.

Fulford, Robert. "An Englishman's Life in a Disgusting Spot Called Toronto." *Maclean's Magazine* 76 (24 August 1963): 45.

——. "It's time to remember why Wyndham Lewis blasted Toronto's cold." *Toronto Star,* 16 October 1982.

Gift from the Douglas M. Duncan Collection and the Milne-Duncan Bequest/ Le don provenant de la collection Douglas M. Duncan et le legs Milne-Duncan. Ottawa: National Gallery of Canada, 1971. Organization and catalogue by Pierre Théberge, with essays by Norman J. Endicott and Alan Jarvis.*

Grigson, Geoffrey. *A Master of Our Time: A Study of Wyndham Lewis.* London: Methuen and Co., 1951; reprinted London: Folcroft Library Editions, 1971.

Hammond, Arthur. "The Three Lives of Wyndham Lewis." *The Globe Magazine, The Globe and Mail* (Toronto), 28 September 1963: 15.

Handley-Read, Charles. *The Art of Wyndham Lewis.* London: Faber and Faber, 1951. Includes a critical evaluation by Eric Newton.

Harries, Meiron and Susie. *The War Artists: British Official War Art of the Twentieth Century.* London: Michael Joseph in association with the Imperial War Museum and the Tate Gallery, 1983.

Jackson, A.Y. *A Painter's Country: The Autobiography of A.Y. Jackson.* Toronto: Clarke, Irwin & Co., 1958; memorial edition, 1976.

——. Letter to C.J. Fox, 24 January 1965; and typescript interview with C.J. Fox, c. 1965. C.J. Fox Collection, London. (Jackson's recollections of Wyndham Lewis.)

Jameson, Fredric. *Fables of Aggression: Wyndham Lewis, the Modernist as Fascist.* Berkeley, Los Angeles, London: University of California Press, 1979.

James, Philip. "Vision and Satire in the Art and Fiction of Wyndham Lewis." Unpublished University of Toronto doctoral thesis, 1972.

Jarvis, Alan. *Douglas Duncan: A Memorial Portrait.* Ed. Alan Jarvis. Toronto: University of Toronto Press, 1974.

Kahma, David. "Wyndham Lewis and the Archangel Michael." *Spectrum* 4 (Autumn): 176-191.

Kenner, Hugh. Introduction, *Self Condemned* by Wyndham Lewis. Chicago: Regnery, 1965, pp. 7-15.

——. Introduction, *Wyndham Lewis.* Santa Barbara: Santa Barbara Museum of Art, 1957.*

——. "The Last European." *Canadian Literature,* no. 36 (Summer 1968): 5-13. Reprinted in *Wyndham Lewis in Canada,* ed. George Woodcock.

——. *The Pound Era.* Berkeley: University of California Press, 1971; London: Faber and Faber, 1972, 1975.

——. *Wyndham Lewis.* Norfolk, Connecticut: New Directions Books, 1954. The Makers of Modern Literature series.

Kush, Thomas. *Wyndham Lewis's Pictorial Integer.* Ann Arbor, Mich.: UMI Research Press, c. 1981.

Laurette, Patrick Condon. *Wyndham Lewis: A Centennial Salute.* Halifax: Art Gallery of Nova Scotia, 1982.*

McLuhan, Herbert Marshall, with Harley Parker. *Counterblast.* Toronto: Privately printed, 1954; New York/ Toronto: Harcourt, Brace and World/McClelland and Stewart, 1969.

——. "Explorations." *The Varsity Graduate* (May 1964): 53-57.

——. "The Global Lewis." *Lewisletter,* no. 5 (October 1976): 11.

——. *The Gutenberg Galaxy: The Making of Typographic Man.* Toronto: University of Toronto Press, 1962.

——. *Letters of Marshall McLuhan.* Selected and ed. by Matie Molinaro, Corinne McLuhan, William Toye. Toronto: Oxford University Press, 1987.

——. "Lewis's Prose Style", in *Wyndham Lewis: A Revaluation: New Essays,* ed. Geoffrey Meyers. London: The Athlone Press/ Montreal: McGill-Queen's University Press, 1980, pp. 64-67.

——. *The Mechanical Bride: Folklore of Industrial Man.* New York: Vanguard Press, 1951.

——. Radio reviews of *Self Condemned* and *The Demon of Progress in the Arts.* Canadian Broadcasting Corporation, 21 August 1955. Printed text in Cornell.

——. "Wyndham Lewis." *The Atlantic Monthly* 224 (December 1969): 93-98.

——. "Wyndham Lewis: His Theory of Art and Communication." *Shenandoah* 4 (Summer/Autumn 1953): 76-88.

——. "Wyndham Lewis: Lemuel in Lilliput." *St Louis Studies in Honour of St. Thomas Aquinas,* II. St. Louis, 1944, pp. 58-72.

Marchand, Philip. *Marshall McLuhan: The Medium and the Messenger.* Toronto: Random House, 1989.

Materer, Timothy. *Wyndham Lewis the Novelist.* Detroit: Wayne State University, 1976.

Meyers, Jeffrey. *The Enemy: A Biography of Wyndham Lewis.* London and Henley: Routledge and Kegan Paul, 1980.

——, ed. *Wyndham Lewis: A Revaluation: New Essays.* London: The Athlone Press; Montreal: McGill-Queen's University Press, 1980. (Includes Meyers's introduction and essay, "Self Condemned", pp. 226-37.

Michel, Walter. *Wyndham Lewis: Paintings and Drawings.* With an introductory essay by Hugh Kenner. Berkeley and Los Angeles: University of California Press/ London: Thames and Hudson/ Toronto: McClelland and Stewart, 1971.

"Ninth Year of the Original Christian Culture Series: 1942-1943...." Windsor: Assumption College, 1942. (Prospectus for lecture series.)

Pictures from the Douglas M. Duncan Collection. Selected and introduced by Frances Duncan Barwick. Toronto: University of Toronto Press, 1975.

Powe, B.W. *The Solitary Outlaw.* Toronto: Lester and Orpen, Dennys, 1987, pp. 21-66.

Pritchard, William H. *Wyndham Lewis.* New York: Twayne Publishers, 1968.

——. *Wyndham Lewis.* Profiles in Literature. London: Routledge and Kegan Paul, 1972.

Reid, John. "Journey out of Anguish." *Canadian Literature,* no. 39 (Winter 1969): 93-98. (Reprinted in *Wyndham Lewis in Canada.)*

Rothenstein, John. *Wyndham Lewis and Vorticism.* London: The Tate Gallery, 1956.*

Schenker, Daniel. *Wyndham Lewis: Religion and Modernism.* Huntsville: University of Alabama Press, 1992.

Smith, Rowland. "Wyndham Lewis and the Sanctimonious Ice-Box." *The Dalhousie Review* 52 (Summer 1972): 302-8. (Review of *Wyndham Lewis in Canada.)*

Some Paintings, Drawings and Prints from the Douglas Duncan Collection. Preface by Kenneth Saltmarche, introduction by Alan Jarvis. Windsor, Ontario: Willistead Art Gallery, 1967.*

Symons, Julian. "Friends of the Enemy: Reassessing the uncomfortable art of Wyndham Lewis." *Times Literary Supplement* (10 July 1992): 16-17.

Tippett, Maria. *Art at the Service of War: Canada, Art, and the Great War.* Toronto: University of Toronto Press, 1984.

Tomlin, E.F.W. *Wyndham Lewis.* Writers and their Works no. 64, The British Council. London: Longmans, Green and Co., 1969.

Wagner, Geoffrey A. *Wyndham Lewis: A Portrait of the Artist as the Enemy.* London: Routledge and Kegan Paul, 1957/ New Haven: Yale University Press, 1957.

Wallace, Catherine. "Art for posterity? The commissioned war art of Percy Wyndham Lewis." *Imperial War Museum Review,* no. 6 (Autumn 1991): 51-61.

Watson, Sheila M. "A Collection." *Open Letter,* Third Series (1974). (Reprints "Wyndham Lewis: A Question of Portraiture", "The Great War: Wyndham Lewis and the Underground Press", "Canada and Wyndham Lewis the Artist", "Artist Ape as Crowd-Master", "Myth and Countermyth", and includes "Unaccommodated Man", mostly concerned with Lewis's *The Lion and the Fox.*)

——. "The Artist as Crowd-Master." *The Varsity Graduate* (Toronto) (May 1964).

——. "The Great War: Wyndham Lewis and the Underground Press", *artscanada* 24, no. 11, issue 114 (November 1967): 1-17. (Includes 34 reproductions and a 45 rpm record of Lewis reading from *One-Way Song* at Harvard University in 1940, and Marshall McLuhan recalling Lewis.)

——. "Wyndham Lewis: A Question of Portraiture." *Tamarack Review* 29 (Autumn 1963): 90-98.

——. "Wyndham Lewis and Expressionism." Unpublished University of Toronto doctoral thesis, 1965. 2 vols.

Wees, William C. *Vorticism and the English Avant-Garde.* Toronto: University of Toronto Press, 1972.

Wheeler, Monroe, ed. *Britain at War.* Text by T.S. Eliot, Herbert Read, E.J. Carter and Carlos Dyer. New York: The Museum of Modern Art, 1941.*

Wilson, Andrew, Introduction, *Wyndham Lewis: 1882-1957.* (London: Austin/Desmond Fine Arts, 1990.*

Woodcock, George. "Editorial: Criticism and Other Arts." *Canadian Literature*, no. 49 (Summer 1971): 9. (Reviews of *Wyndham Lewis: Paintings and Drawings* and *Wyndham Lewis on Art.*)

——. "The Enemy of Man." *Canadian Literature,* no. 17 (Summer 1963): 57-60. (Review of *The Letters of Wyndham Lewis.*)

——. "The Intellectual Fury." *The New Yorker* 31 (4 June 1955): 104-5. (Review of *Self Condemned,* etc.)

——. "Making it Up to a Snubbed Artist." *Daily Times* (Victoria, B.C.), 17 July 1971.

——, ed. "Wyndham Lewis in Canada", special issue of *Canadian Literature*, no. 35 (Winter 1968). Reprinted, with additions, in book form, 1971; see below.

——, ed. *Wyndham Lewis in Canada.* With an introduction by Julian Symons. Vancouver: University of British Columbia Publications Centre, 1971. Canadian Literature Series, no. 2.

Wyndham Lewis. Foreword by Michael Ayrton. London: Redfern Gallery, 1949.*

PART III: ARCHIVAL SOURCES

Wyndham Lewis Collection, Department of Rare Books, Olin Library, Cornell University, Ithaca, New York
Wyndham Lewis Papers, Imperial War Museum, London
Marshall McLuhan Papers, National Archives of Canada, Ottawa
Father J. Stanley Murphy Papers, Assumption University Archives, University of Windsor, Windsor, Ontario
Lorne Pierce Papers, Queen's University Archives, Kingston, Ontario
Private individuals

Endnotes

Introduction (13-23)

1. "Representative Opinions", typescript, 3 December 1940, H.O. McCurry Papers, Archives, National Gallery of Canada, Ottawa. The punctuation and spelling are as they appear in the original document.
2. Lewis to Geoffrey Stone, 7 December 1940. *The Letters of Wyndham Lewis*, ed. W.K. Rose [Norfolk, Connecticut: New Directions, 1963], p. 282, no. 263. Hereafter, citations from this volume are indicated as "Rose," followed by the letter-number.
3. "The Importance of the Visual Arts", typescript, n.d. (c. December 1940), H.O. McCurry Papers, Archives, National Gallery of Canada. A note in another hand at the bottom of the title-page reads: "Unearthed & rec'd for filing July 30th 1945."
4. Lewis to Geoffrey Stone, n.d. [c. December 1940], Cornell. The relevant passage reads as follows: "There are no *closed doors* here, and there are a dozen which I have not even approached as yet— They are very cut off from the States and England, and welcome the talented intruder." Lewis was, of course, to revise this early and optimistic impression.
5. Catalogue note in *Vorticist Exhibition* (London: Doré Galleries, 1915); quoted in Dennis Farr, *English Art: 1740-1940* (London: Oxford University Press, 1984), pp. 212-13.
6. "Introduction", *Wyndham Lewis and Vorticism* (London: Tate Gallery, 1956), p. 5.
7. "Blueprint to the Vortex", *Blast 1*, ed. Wyndham Lewis, foreword by Bradford Morrow (Santa Barbara: Black Sparrow Press, 1981; first published 20 June 1914): v.
8. For a complete list of one-man and group exhibitions of Lewis's work in Canada, see the "Canadian Exhibition History" appendix to this catalogue.
9. "What Went Wrong", *Studio International* (July/August 1971): 42.
10. Michael Durman, "Cork's Vorticism: What Went Wrong?", *Enemy News*, No. 9 (December 1978): 4-5, 7.
11. *The Letters of Wyndham Lewis* (1963), p. 264.
12. For a discussion, see Thomas Dilworth's essay in this catalogue, "Out of Canada: Lewis's North American Writings."
13. Lewis to Frank Morley, 7 October 1941, Rose, no. 279, p. 301; *America, I Presume* (New York: Howell and Soskin, 1940), p. 229.
14. This document declares that "My son Percy Wyndham Lewis was born on the 18th day of November 1882 at Amherst, Nova Scotia in the Dominion of Canada and was therefore in the 18th day of November last seventeen years old and no more." Wyndham Lewis Collection, Department of Rare Books, Olin Library, Cornell University, Ithaca, New York. All subsequent endnote references to this collection are indicated as "Cornell."
15. The Do-Nothing Mode: An Autobiographical Fragment", *Agenda (Wyndham Lewis Special Issue)* 7 (Autumn/Winter 1969-70): 216-18. Among Charles E. Lewis's publications were *Reveries of an Old Smoker: Interpreted with Reminiscences of Travel and Adventures* (Toronto: Hunter Rose, 1881), *Briar Wreathes: Prose and Verse* (London and New York: Eyre and Spottiswood, 1899), and a series of seven "Sketches" of his service in the American Civil War, printed in England in the late 1890s.
16. *Ibid.*: 217. C.E. Lewis entered West Point Military Academy in 1861, and in 1862, on the outbreak of the Civil War, he resigned to join the Rebel forces, only to switch allegiance and become an Abolitionist, enlisting with the Northern army under General Sheridan.
17. *Ibid.*: 219.
18. *History of Toronto and County of York, Ontario*, vol. 2 (Toronto: C. Blackett Robinson, 1885), p. 141. In addition, this much-admired citizen was a member of the York Pioneer and Historical Society for thirty-one years.
19. Lewis to Geoffrey Stone, n.d. [December 1940], Rose no. 264, p. 283.
20. The *Dictionary of Canadian Biography* entry on François Romain (1768-1832, a place-holder and militia officer in Quebec, the son of François Audivert, *dit* Romain, indicates that he "belonged to the third generation of a family whose forebear had come from Italy to New France early in the 18th century." He and his father were keepers of the Quebec Library, an institution founded in 1779, and "may thus be considered the first Canadians to have exercised the profession of Librarian in Lower Canada", as well as the co-organizer of the first free public school in Quebec (Yvon Thériault, *Dictionary of Canadian Biography*, vol. 7 [Toronto: University of Toronto Press, 1987], p. 658.) Romain is not a common surname in Quebec: there are only five Romains in the 1992 Quebec City telephone, four of them residents of the suburb of Village-des-Hurons, and nineteen in the Montreal book; whereas twenty-nine Romains and one Romaine are currently listed in the Toronto directory. The Huron Indian Romains may, of course, have adopted the name from the "Italian" Romains of Quebec City, perhaps as a result of intermarriage.
21. *Landmarks of Canada: What Art Has Done for Canadian History* (Toronto: J. Ross Robertson, 1917), p. 127.
22. Lewis to Stone, 15 January 1941, Rose no. 266, p. 285.
23. "Hill 100: Outline for an Unwritten Novel", *Wyndham Lewis in Canada*, ed. George Woodcock (Vancouver: University of British Columbia Publications Centre, 1971), pp. 90-95.
24. "Exile's Letters", *Ibid.*, p. 85.
25. Quoted in Jeffrey Meyers, *The Enemy: A Biography of Wyndham Lewis* (London: Routledge and Kegan Paul, 1980), p. 262.
26. "Nature's Place in Canadian Culture", *Wyndham Lewis in Canada*, p. 56.
27. C.J. Fox to Robert Stacey, July 1992. Peter Caracciolo detects a strong interest on Lewis's part in North American Indian mythology and iconography, particularly rites of sacrifice, as manifested in his close reading of Sir James Frazer's *The Golden Bough* (see P. Caracciolo, "'Carnivals of Mass-Murder': The Frazerian Origins of Wyndham Lewis's *The Childermass*", in *Sir James Frazer and the Literary Imagination: Essays in Affinity and Influence*, ed. Robert Fraser [London: Macmillan, 1990]). Caracciolo points out in a letter to Robert Stacey (1 July 1992) that Lewis's wartime short-story, "The French Poodle", first published in *The Egoist* in 1919, "notes affinities with the Otawa *[sic]* and Huron tribes" in the naming of the dog "Carp," the totem of an Ottawa Indian clan. One of the protagonists of this tale of mascot-sacrifice is called James Fraser, who asks, "'Must we be savage?'"–to which his shellshocked partner replies that the "beginning of a period" of unprecedented savagery is at hand. In the outline of "Hill 100", Lewis quotes the legendary graffito written on the hull of their abandoned ship by the lost party dispatched by La Salle to sail down the Mississippi: "'NOUS SOMMES TOUS SAUVAGES'" (p. 95). Caracciolo also points to Lewis's 1912 drawing, *Indian Dance* (M 69).
28. This biographical outline is derived from such references as Walter Lewis's entry on William Chisholm in the *Dictionary of Canadian Biography*, vol. 7 (Toronto: University of Toronto Press, 1988), pp. 177-79; Hazel C. Mathews's *Oakville and the Sixteen* (Toronto: University of Toronto Press, 1953); and the Oakville chapter of Mary Byers' and Margaret McBurney's *The Governor's Road* (Toronto: University of Toronto Press, 1982).
29. For a description and pictures of this house, see David and Suzanne Peacock, *Old Oakville: A character study of the town's early buildings and the men who built them* (Willowdale: Hounslow Press, 1979), pp. 56-63.
30. Hazel C. Mathews, *Oakville and the Sixteen...*, pp. 318-19.
31. Jeffrey Meyers, *The Enemy: A Biography of Wyndham Lewis* (London: Routledge & Kegan Paul, 1980), p. 251.
32. "The Do-Nothing Mode": 220.
33. Lewis to Stone, 15 January 1941. Further, Lewis's Canadian-period address-book (Cornell) lists such relatives as Frederick Lewis, Charles Austen Lewis, and Harry and Pierrette Romain, all of Toronto; Harry Lewis, of Scarborough, Ontario; Evelyn Ethel Lewis, of Long Island, New York; Alfred Lewis, of White Springs Farm, near Geneva, New York; and, in Montreal, Gordon Lewis, and the firm of Lewis, Apedaile and Hanson Inc., Lewis Building.
34. "Address to French-Canada. C.B.C.", holograph MS, n.d. [c. 1942?], Cornell.
35. Albert Lewis to Charles E. Lewis, 2 May 1899, Cornell. Query: where now is that early sketchbook?
36. See endnote 106 in Part II of Catharine Mastin's essay in this catalogue for a discussion of Vernon Van Sickle's introduction to Lewis's writings and thought in Vancouver, British Colmbia.

THE TALENTED INTRUDER: "A QUESTION OF FORCE MAJEURE" (PAGES 24-29)

1. Lewis to Mary Borden Turner, n.d. (Summer 1915), *The Letters of Wyndham Lewis*, ed. W.K. Rose (Norfolk, Conn.: New Directions, 1963), no. 66, p. 74. Hereinafter, all references to this volume are indicated as "Rose", followed by the assigned letter-number and page-number.
2. Wyndham Lewis, *Rude Assignment: A Narrative of My Career Up-to-date* (London: Hutchinson and Co. Ltd., 1950; new edition Santa Rosa: Black Sparrow Press, 1984), p. 138.
3. Foreword, *Guns* (London: Goupil Gallery, 1919), unpaginated.
4. *A Canadian Gun-Pit* was first exhibited in North America in a show held at the Anderson Galleries, New York, in June-July 1919, which later travelled to the Canadian National Exhibition, Toronto (August-September 1919) and the Art Association of Montreal (October-November 1919). *The Canadian War Memorials* exhibition included fifty-four of Lewis's battlefront pictures, as well as several studio works, such as his other major wartime canvas, *A Battery Shelled* (1919; Imperial War Museum, London, England), which was painted at the behest of the British War Records Office.
5. "Canadian War Pictures", *The Canadian Magazine* (November 1919).
6. As quoted by Jeffrey Meyers, *The Enemy: A Biography of Wyndham Lewis* (London and Henley: Routledge and Kegan Paul, 1980), p. 249.
7. Lewis to Robert Hale, Rose, no. 268, p. 288.
8. "Biographical information" (c. 1940-43), Wyndham Lewis Collection, Department of Rare Books, Olin Library, Cornell University, Ithaca, New York. All subsequent endnote references to this collection are hereafter indicated as "Cornell."
9. Lewis to T. Sturge Moore, 15 July [1941], Rose, no. 273, p. 292.
10. Lewis to Eric Kennington, 26 January 1942, Cornell.
11. As related by B.W. Powe in *The Solitary Outlaw: Trudeau, Lewis, Gould, Canetti, McLuhan* (Toronto: Lester and Orpen, Dennys, 1987), p. 41.
12. Lewis, "Canadian Address Book", n.d. (c. 1940-45), and "American Address Book", n.d. (c. 1939-40), both Cornell. For a fuller examination of Lewis's pursuit of his roots, see the Introduction to this catalogue.
13. Among Lewis's explorations of similar themes are such now-unlocated works as *Christopher Columbus* (1913-14), *Arctic Summer: Coronation Gulf* (late 1930s) and *Captain Cook in Ellesmere Land* (late 1930s). The sequence also included *Landscape with Northmen* (1936-37), *The Harbour* (1936), *Nordic Beach* (c. 1936) and *The Armada* (1937). For illustrations of these latter works, see Walter Michel, *Wyndham Lewis: Paintings and Drawings* (Toronto: McClelland and Stewart, 1971).
14. John Reid, "Journey Out of Anguish", in *Wyndham Lewis in Canada*, ed. George Woodcock (Vancouver: University of British Columbia Publications Centre, 1971), p. 97.
15. MacDermot knew several Canadian artists, including Charles Comfort and Arthur Lismer (with whom he had founded the Toronto branch of the National Film Society in 1936), and put Lewis in contact with John Grierson, director of the National Film Board in Ottawa (see MacDermot to Lewis, 30 April 1940, Cornell). MacDermot also suggested that Lewis make the acquaintance of the modernist Montreal painter and critic John Lyman (1886-1967), who in 1939 co-founded the Contemporary Art Society; in a letter of 22 March 1940 (Cornell), Lyman expressed the hope of being able to arrange a time when Lewis could talk before the Society. And MacDermot offered the walls of his home for a private exhibit of Lewis's pictures (see MacDermot to Lewis, 19 November 1940, Cornell).
16. John Reid to Lewis, n.d. (Spring 1940), Cornell.
17. MacDermot to Lewis, 24 June 1940, Cornell.
18. See Schaefer to Lewis, 12 December 1939, Cornell.
19. *America, I Presume* (London and Brusells: Howell and Soskin, 1940), pp. 237-38.
20. Lewis to MacDermot, 19 November 1940, Rose, no. 259, p. 277.

THE TALENTED INTRUDER: "MY TUDOR PERIOD": WYNDHAM LEWIS IN TORONTO (PAGES 30-72)

1. That same month, Roy Greenaway, a *Toronto Star* reporter and gifted amateur painter who previously had befriended Ernest Hemingway when he joined the *Star* in 1923, invited the Lewises to dine with himself, his wife, and Frederick S. Haines, principal of the Ontario College of Art. The dinner was to be held at the Women's University Club; an alternative arrangement proposed by Greenaway was a Sunday tea at which Mrs. Greenaway's moving pictures of "winter north of Sudbury" and the Gaspé peninsula would be shown (Greenaway to Lewis, 18 November 1940, Cornell).
2. Geoffrey Stone, 25 January 1942, Rose, no. 288, p. 311.
3. Lewis to Stone, 5 December 1940, Rose, no. 262, p. 281.
4. Lewis to Mary Hutchinson (30 June 1942), Cornell.
5. Lewis to Archibald MacLeish, 18 April 1942, Cornell.
6. Anne Lewis, "The Hotel", *Wyndham Lewis in Canada*, p. 26.
7. Lewis to Geoffrey Stone, 7 December 1940, Rose, no. 263, p. 282.
8. Lewis to Stone, 20 November 1940, Rose, no. 260, p. 278.
9. Lewis to Stone, December 1940, Cornell.
10. Lewis to Stone, n.d. (early December 1940), Cornell.
11. Lorne Pierce, "A Recollection of Wyndham Lewis", *Wyndham Lewis in Canada*, p. 62.
12. A.Y. Jackson to C.J. Fox, 2 January 1965, C.J. Fox, London.
13. *Toronto Daily Star*, 18 November 1940.
14. Lewis, "C.B.C. talk" (i.e. for the CBC broadcast, "Can Democracy Be Defined?", delivered on 12 December 1940), pp. 1-10, Cornell.
15. "Address to French Canada", December 1940, pp. 1-2., Cornell.
16. "Address to French-Canada", n.d. (c. 1940), Cornell. On the cover-sheet of the holograph MS of this broadcast at Cornell is written, in Lewis's hand, the date "tentatively" Thursday, 12/ 23". The errors in French grammar and orthography are in the original.
17. Mary Stewart, in an interview with Catharine Mastin, 10 September 1991.
18. *Ibid.*
19. *Ibid.*
20. *Ibid.*
21. As quoted in the transcript of an interview with C.J. Fox, c. 1965, p. 3, C.J. Fox, London.
22. Mary Stewart, in an interview with Catharine Mastin, 10 September 1991.
23. Amy Stewart, 17 February 1991, and Mrs. Mary Stewart, 10 September 1991, in interviews with Catharine Mastin.
24. A.Y. Jackson to C.J. Fox, 2 January 1965, C.J. Fox, London.
25. "Wyndham Lewis' Portrait of J.S. McLean Presented", *Toronto Daily Star*, 18 April 1941.

26. *Ibid.*

27. Lewis had probably seen the painting at J.S. McLean's Toronto residence. McLean's private art collection consisted chiefly of works by members of the Group of Seven (1920-1932) and the Canadian Group of Painters (1933-1954). See *The J.S. McLean Collection of Canadian Painting* (Toronto: Art Gallery of Ontario, 1968). *Mining Town* was in McLean's collection in 1941 and is now in the Art Gallery of Ontario. McLean was a regular patron of Douglas Duncan's Picture Loan Gallery, where many of the Lewis drawings in his collection were acquired. The version of the portrait reproduced in Michel's *catalogue raisonnée* (plate 148) is clearly a preliminary one, lacking either the books or the painting in the background that are present in the final state.

28. "Speech at the unveiling of the J.S. McLean Portrait", 1941, Cornell.

29. All that is known about *The Red Hat* is that it showed a "front view of the head and shoulders of the sitter who is holding a cigarette and wearing a tall hat." See Walter Michel, *Wyndham Lewis...*, p. 344.

30. Catherine Johnson, curator of European art, National Gallery of Canada, to Catharine Mastin, 16 April 1992.

31. R.J. Sainsbury to R.H. Hubbard, 17 April 1964, Registration Papers, National Gallery of Canada, Ottawa.

32. For information regarding J.S. McLean's loans to Lewis, see note 104.

33. For a discussion of Lewis's amours, see chapter seven of Jeffrey Meyers, *The Enemy...*; for references to the repression of Anne Lewis's talents in art, see the comments of Corinne McLuhan, as quoted by Meyers (p. 288).

34. "Lecture on the Visual Arts", 1943-44, p. 5, Cornell.

37. Lewis made a present of the drawing to Pierce, who subsequently sent him a cheque for $30. See Lewis to Pierce, 13 October 1941, Cornell.

38. Pierce, "A Recollection...", p. 63.

39. Lewis to T.S. Eliot, n.d. (c. 1941), Cornell. Le Pan's first collection, *The Wounded Prince and Other Poems*, was published in 1948.

40. Douglas LePan, in an interview with Catharine Mastin, 16 February 1991.

41. Lewis, "Appointment Register for LePan portrait", on the *verso* of a letter to Marcia Christophorides, n.d. (c. September-October 1941), Cornell.

42. *Bright Glass of Memory: a set of four memoirs* (Toronto et *al.*: McGraw-Hill Ryerson Ltd., 1979), p. 114.

43. *Ibid.*, p. 118.

44. *Ibid.*

45. Lewis to Leonard Amster, n.d. (c. August 1940), Rose, no. 256, p. 274.

46. His comments on these artists are contained in the undated "Portrait lecture" (c. 1943-44), unpaginated, Cornell.

47. *Ibid.*

48. *Ibid.*

49. Lewis to Archibald McLeish, 21 October 1951, Rose, no. 302, p. 280.

50. Lewis's *Catnap* (1942; M 1011), which belongs to the knitting series, could not be located for inclusion in this exhibition.

51. Lewis also vainly sought portrait commissions from the president of the Algoma Steel Co., Sir James Dunn, and the Premier of Ontario, Mitchell Hepburn. See Robert Stacey's essay in this catalogue for a detailed discussion of these failed opportunities, in the context of the series of imaginative works that inadvertently resulted.

52. As indicated in a letter from Lewis to J.S. McLean, 7 July 1941, Cornell. Lewis asked McLean to buy *The Red Hat* and fifteen drawings but was unable to sell the painting, and consequently could not raise sufficient money to pay for steerage tickets to England. He tried to return home again in the fall of 1941, again unsuccessfully.

53. Late in 1941 H.O. McCurry of the National Gallery of Canada had placed Varley's name with the Department of War Services in the hope of getting work for him. In February 1942 he was commissioned to draw portraits of soldiers in Kingston for the Ministry of Public Information, a job for which, however, he received no advance, and which he misinterpreted by making oil paintings, which the director of the department rejected. However, the government eventually purchased one of the works, and left the other two with Varley to sell.

54. For a detailed discussion of F.H. Varley's portrait commissions, see Christopher Varley, *Frederick H. Varley: A Retrospective* (Edmonton: Edmonton Art Gallery, 1980).

55. If Lewis did not see Heward's work in Toronto at the 1942 Canadian Group of Painters exhibition, held at the Art Gallery of Toronto, he is certain to have known it by 1945, for he spoke at the opening of the exhibition *Three Montreal Painters: Anne Savage, Ethel Seath and Prudence Heward*, held early that year at the Willistead Art Gallery, Windsor (see typed exhibition list, Exhibition Files, Art Gallery of Windsor).

56. Lewis to Theodore Spencer, 28 January 1942, Cornell.

57. Lewis to Alfred Barr, 24 November 1941, Cornell.

58. Although the title of the latter work is given as *Still Life: Figures in the Belly of a Bird* by Walter Michel, the inscription in Lewis's hand on the *verso* clearly reads *Duck*.

59. The whereabouts of *Crucifixion, IV*, formerly in the collection of the late John Reid, is unknown. See Michel, *Wyndham Lewis...*, M 983, plate 154, for an illustration.

60. "Towards an Earth Culture", *Wyndham Lewis On Art: Collected Writings, 1913-1956*, ed. Walter Michel and C.J. Fox (London and New York: Thames and Hudson/Funk and Wagnalls, 1969), pp. 382-86. Lewis earlier developed these ideas in the lectures presented at Assumption College, Windsor in 1943 and 1944 (discussed in Section III of this essay), and these in turn largely formed the content of his book *America and Cosmic Man* (1948).

61. J.W.G. Macdonald, as cited in Joyce Zemans, *Jock Macdonald: The Inner Landscape* (Toronto: Art Gallery of Ontario, 1981), p. 97. Lewis may well have seen Macdonald's "modalities" in April 1941, when they were included in a four-man exhibition at the Art Gallery of Toronto.

62. For reproductions of the Milne sequences, see Ian M. Thom ed., *David Milne* (Vancouver: Vancouver Art Gallery, 1991).

63. "The Artist and Society", August 1948, p. 14, Cornell.

64. See Marshall McLuhan and Bruce R. Powers, *The Global Village: Transformations in World Life and Media in the 21st Century* (New York and Oxford: Oxford University Press, 1989); and Lewis, "Keep Culture Alive", unpaginated, Cornell. See also the lectures Lewis delivered at Assumption College in 1943 and 1944, Cornell.

65. "The End of Abstract Art", *The New Republic* (1 April 1940): 439.

66. "Abstract Art", August 1943, p. 1, Cornell.

67. "The End of Abstract Art", pp. 438-39.

68. Lewis wrote about regionalism in "Is a Canadian Renaissance Likely?", n.d. (c. 1943), Cornell, and "Canadian Nature and its Painters", n.d. (c. 1943), Cornell (part of which appeared in *The Listener* in August 1946, a longer, revised version being published in *Wyndham Lewis in Canada)*.

69. Jack Shadbolt, in conversation with Catharine Mastin, 4 October 1992. For further information about this historic event, see Michael Bell and Frances K. Smith, *The Kingston Conference Proceedings* (Kingston: Agnes Etherington Art Centre, 1991).

70. For information on these bodies, see Christine Boyanoski, *The 1940s: A Decade of Painting in Ontario* (Toronto: Art Gallery of Ontario, 1984).

71. Lewis to Cass Canfield, 1 November 1941, Cornell.

72. Lewis to Naomi Mitchison, 31 May 1945, Rose, no. 316, p. 354.

73. "Canadian Nature and Its Painters", *Wyndham Lewis in Canada*, p. 27.

74. "Is A Canadian Renaissance Likely?", p. 3.

75. *Ibid.*, pp. 3-4. Thoreau MacDonald wrote to Carl Schaefer on 21 April 1941, "Mr. Lewis says he considers you the best painter he's seen in these woods, better than [Charles] Burchfield." *(Notebooks: Thoreau MacDonald*, ed. John Flood [Moonbeam, Ontario: Penumbra Press, 1980], p. 111.)

76. Lewis to R.D. Jameson, 14 February 1942, Rose, no. 292, p. 317. Ironically, "Is a Canadian Renaissance likely?", which was probably intended for *Saturday Night* magazine, was not accepted for publication.

77. John Reid, "Journey Out Of Anguish", p. 101.

78. *Ibid.*, p. 102.

79. For further information, see Joan Murray, *Canadian Artists of the Second World War* (Oshawa: Robert McLaughlin Gallery, 1980).

80. This large exhibition was organized by the Museum of Modern Art in New York and supplemented by loans from the National Gallery of Canada. It was opened in Toronto by Lewis's friend and patron the Right Hon. Malcolm MacDonald, then High Commissioner for Britain in Canada. See "Britain-at-War Exhibition, Opened by M. Macdonald, Draws Crowd to Art Gallery", *The Globe and Mail*, 15 November 1941.

81. The catalogues of the 1940-41 O.S.A. annual exhibition list the following artists as residing on Grenville: E. Grace Coombs, Adrian Dingle, Helen R. FitzGerald, Stanley C. Knapp, Marion Long, Manly MacDonald, Charles MacGregor, William John Patterson, Tom Roberts and Donald Stewart. Other artists associated with this street were the painters F.H. Varley and Yvonne McKague (Housser) and the photographer John Steele. At no. 23 Grenville was the Loomis and Toles Co. art supplies store and, at no. 66, Malloney's Art Gallery, where several members of the Group of Seven exhibited; also on the street was the Roberts Gallery, whose origins dated back to the late nineteenth century. See Rosemary Donegan, "Whatever Happened to Queen Street West? A History of Art Scenes and Communities", *Fuse* 10 (Fall 1986): 17.

82. As Thoreau MacDonald informed Carl Schaefer on 10 March 1941, "A well-known Englishman, Mr Wyndham Lewis, is in Lawren's studio." *(Notebooks...*, p. 110.) Lewis probably kept this studio until June. No. 86-A Isabella Street, not far from the Tudor Hotel, was Lewis's next studio. See Lewis to J.S. McLean, 5 August 1941, Cornell.

83. "Portraits from Memory", unpublished typescript, Charles F. Comfort Papers, National Archives of Canada, Ottawa, unpaginated.

84. Lewis also befriended a gold-mining prospector by the name of Keith MacIver, who lived behind the Studio Building in the shack formerly inhabited by Tom Thomson, an affiliate of the Group of Seven. For further details on their acquaintance, see A.Y. Jackson, *A Painter's Country: The Autobiography of A.Y. Jackson* (Vancouver and Toronto: Clarke, Irwin and Co., 1958), p. 129., and "A.Y. Jackson recalls", *Maclean's Magazine* (1 September 1956): 46.

85. "On Canada", *Wyndham Lewis in Canada*, p. 23.

86. "Nature's Place in Canadian Culture", p. 52.

87. Lewis to Malcolm MacDonald, 8 August 1943, Rose, no. 320, p. 359. Rose (p. 359) notes that in an earlier draught of this letter, Lewis explained himself as follows: "My subject was only incidentally `Canadian Painting': I wanted to defend Jackson against the sort of criticism that treats the nature-painters as out-of-date `romantics'. It is rather like defending Augustus John against the aspersions of the Bloomsburies (as in fact I did).... With the case of Jackson it is simply a case of a French Impressionist (of a period when Impressionism was moving over into what [Roger] Fry called Postimpressionism) going out into the Canadian Bush and struggling with a much harsher nature than Monet or Sisley ever had to meet. Fundamentally, the problem is *Nature*, rather than *Jackson*."

88. A.Y. Jackson, *A Painter's Country*, p. 128.

89. Jackson to C.J. Fox, 2 January 1965.

90. Carl Schaefer, in an interview with Catharine Mastin, 11 February 1991.

91. See Helen Marzolf, *Scottie Wilson: The Canadian Drawings* (Regina: Dunlop Art Gallery, 1989).

92. See G. Blair Laing, *Memoirs of an Art Dealer* (Toronto: McClelland and Stewart, 1979), p. 29. Roberts Gallery was purchased by the Wildridge family in 1947, after which it relocated on Yonge St. south of Bloor.

93. Lewis to J.S. McLean, 1 December 1942, Cornell.

94. As it happens, several of Lewis's Toronto acquaintances and patrons were then on the Acquisitions Committee of the A.G.T., including J.S. McLean, A.Y. Jackson, Douglas Duncan, Barker Fairley, Isabel McLaughlin (b. 1903), and the chief curator, Martin Baldwin. The Gallery's Executive Board then consisted of Vincent Massey (honorary president), John M. Lyle (president), Col. R.S. McLaughlin (vice-president), J.S. McLean (vice-president), R.Y. Eaton (hon. vice-president), Edgar G. Burton (hon. secretary), Martin Baldwin (curator), and W.G. Hay (treasurer).

95. Douglas Duncan is listed in the catalogues of these exhibitions as having submitted Lewis's work.

96. Another such show was *The Canadian Armed Forces Art Exhibition*, held between 14 and 29 November 1942 at Hart House, University of Toronto. The A.G.T. regularly borrowed several exhibitions from other institutions, such as *Augustus John* (May 1943), *Henri Rousseau* (January 1943), and *Americans 1942*. For a complete listing of exhibitions held at the gallery during the 1940s, see Karen McKenzie and Larry Pfaff, "The Art Gallery of Ontario: Sixty Years of Exhibitions 1906-1966", *RACAR* 7 (1980): 62-91.

97. Jackson, A.J. Casson, Franklin Carmichael, Arthur Lismer, C.W. Jefferys, Charles Comfort, Lorne Pierce, J.S. McLean, Bertram Brooker, B.K. Sandwell (who had commissioned Lewis to write articles for *Saturday Night)*, and H.O. McCurry were all members of the Arts and Letters Club. Source: membership lists, Archives of the Arts and Letters Club, Toronto, Ontario.

98. Early-1940s exhibitions at the Arts and Letters Club included: *Paintings by David Milne and Carl Schaefer from the J. S. McLean Collection* (January 1941); *J. W. Beatty Memorial Exhibition* (October 1941); *Thoreau MacDonald: Paintings and Drawings* (December 1942); and *Paintings by J.S. Hallam and Franklin Carmichael* (February 1943). Source: exhibition files and scrapbooks, Arts and Letters Club, Toronto.

99. As is indicated in the Chronology section of this catalogue, Lewis took three trips to Ottawa between 1940 and 1943. See Introduction of this essay for an account of the December 1940 visit. In the first week of June 1941 Lewis visited Leonard Brockington, H.O. McCurry and Gladstone Murray in Ottawa. See Wyndham Lewis to Anne Lewis, n.d. (c. 6 June 1941), Cornell. Lewis made one other trip to Ottawa in April 1943, in connection with the commissioned *A Canadian War Factory* (no. 58). See Lewis to Malcolm MacDonald, 10 February 1943, and Lewis to H.O. McCurry, 17 April 1943, both Cornell.

100. The Hayden Street or "Studio" group consisted of twenty-four members who shared a studio space on Hayden Street, just south of Bloor off Yonge Street, not far from where Lewis had his studio and his apartment, and only a few steps from the Picture Loan Gallery.

101. As is noted in the introduction to this catalogue, Frye attended a lecture Lewis gave in Toronto, and he may well have encountered him at the Picture Loan Gallery through his wife, Helen Kemp Frye, a member of the Picture Loan Society whose name appears in Lewis's Canadian-period address book (Cornell). However, their relations likely were cool, as Frye was not a friendly critic of Lewis's writings, as can be seen from his attack on Lewis's attempts to debunk Oswald Spengler, which was published in *Canadian Forum* in 1936; he would go on to include a detailed hostile critique of Lewis in his favourable review of Geoffrey Wagner's *Wyndham Lewis: A Portrait of the Artist as the Enemy* (New Haven and London, 1957), entitled "Neo-Classical Agony" (*The Hudson Review* 10 [Winter 1957]: 592-98).

102. See C.J. Fox, *Wyndham Lewis and E.J. Pratt: A Convergence of Strangers* (St. John's, Newfoundland: Memorial University, 1983).

103. See Rose, no. 281, p. 303; no. 286, p. 309; no. no. 287, p. 311; no. 293, p. 318; no. 314, p. 352; and no. 316, p. 354.

104. On the basis of existing correspondence and documents recording Lewis's income during his five years in North America, he earned over $12,000 from art sales, portrait commissions, lecture fees and his teaching salary. In addition, he borrowed approximately $3,000 from various Canadian, American and British friends and acquaintances. Together, these figures are equivalent, in today's dollars, to roughly $140,000, or $28,000 per year. Taking into account the fact that the buying power of the dollar was then twice what it is today, Lewis made the equivalent of approximately $56,000 per annum: roughly three times the average annual income of an ordinary Canadian wage-earner during the war. (For further information on average annual incomes, see Bell and Smith, *The Kingston Conference Proceedings*.) Known income sources: *Portrait of J.S. McLean*, $1,500; *Douglas LePan*,

$100; four *Saturday Night* articles, $120; three C.B.C. talks, $105; Christian Culture Series lecture, $100; Marygrove College lecture, $75; War Artists Advisory Commission for *A Canadian War Factory*, $1,500; Assumption College lecture fees, $2,000; Basilian Fathers portrait commission, $450, *Mrs. Paul Martin*, $700; *Mrs. Ernest William Stix*, $500; *Mrs. George Gellhorn*, $50; *Dr. Erlanger*, $1,500; St. Louis Museum of Art talk, $150; *James Taylor*, $300; Detroit Institute of Arts lecture, $75; Hemingway and Tolstoy lecture, $100. Other income, with approximate/estimated value: *Chancellor Capen*, at least $1,500; *Mary McLean*, c. $500; *Mrs. R.J. Sainsbury*, c. $500; purchases by the Art Gallery of Toronto for two works, c. $100; *Tom Cori*, c. $300; sales of artwork to J.S. McLean, c. $450-$600; Art Club of Chicago lecture, c. $100; advances and royalties for *Anglosaxony*, unknown; sale of *Crucifixion IV* to John Reid, c. $50; two Newberry portrait drawings, c. $50 each; *Head of W.R. Valentiner*, c. $50; *Mrs. Henry Ford II*, unknown (possibly not paid for), Portrait of Miss X. Loans (most probably not repaid): Iris Barry, 1941-42, $205; Geoffrey Stone, 7 December 1940, $150; Lorne Pierce, October 1941, $30; A.Y. Jackson, 9 July 1941, $100; James Johnson Sweeney, $50; John Burgess, 24 November 1942, $400, and 23 June 1943, $200; J.S. McLean, 27 July 1942, *via* McLean's secretary Mr.McKechnie, $200; Felix Giovanelli and Marshall McLuhan, $450-500; E.P. Richardson, unknown (c. $100?); Malcolm MacDonald, 1945, $750. Douglas Duncan had also loaned Lewis money, but he did not keep records of the debt. Malcolm MacDonald paid the back rent on Lewis's London studio of £800. According to his friend Norman Endicott, the independently wealthy Douglas Duncan "took no salary and sometimes paid deficits" of the Picture Loan Gallery. "His own income had increased from the '$2300' of about 1928, but until the early 1960s it apparently never exceeded fifty-five hundred a year, an extraordinary figure in view of the number of pictures he bought." ("Douglas Moerdyke Duncan: A Memoir", *Gift from the Douglas M. Duncan Collection and the Milne-Duncan Bequest* [Ottawa: National Gallery of Canada, 1971], unpaginated.) This is backed up by another close associate of Duncan's, Alan Jarvis, who noted in the same publication that "The myth that DMD was the indulged scion of a wealthy family is quite false. He lived modestly, sometimes austerely, and his lack of interest in clothes and money became part of the Duncan legend in the public mind.... DMD never wanted either wealth or any indulgences for himself, yet his generosity to others was astonishing. I once saw him slip a Craven `A' box across a restaurant table to a young Canadian artist; the packet contained ten one-hundred-dollar bills."

105. Lewis to John Rothenstein, 17 August 1943, Cornell.

106. The extensive correspondence between Lewis and David Kahma is in Cornell. Kahma's "Wyndham Lewis and the Archangel Michael" (*Spectrum* 4 [Autumn 1960]: 176-91) includes first printings of numerous letters sent from Lewis to Kahma, passages from which are reprinted in Rose. Shirley Allen, the widow of the Lewis enthusiast Vernon Van Sickle, records that "In the early '40s David [Kahma] was a newcomer to a small group of writers and artists encouraged by Mrs. Lilette Mahon. I never met her, but knew of her as a widow with a grown son, a house and a comfortable income, who wanted to have a sort of salon - a very unusual ambition among Vancouver matrons, then and now!... Mrs. Mahon met Vernon when he read from his work-in-progress at the West End Writer's Group, and offered him a room in her house in which to write. This arrangement gradually evolved into full-time residence for several years. Vernon had been fascinated by Lewis and his ideas since the mid-30's, starting with *Men Without Art*, and would have introduced those ideas, or at least put them forward, at Mrs. Mahon's soirées, and it's very likely that David encountered them there" (Shirley Allen to Catharine Mastin, 11 February 1992). Among attendees at these evenings were such noted Vancouverites as the painter Jack Shadbolt and the photographer John Varley, son of Frederick Varley.

107. Lewis to H.O. McCurry, 3 December 1940, Director's Files, National Gallery of Canada, Ottawa. See also Joan Murray, *Canadian Artists of the Second World War*, p. 8.

108. Kenneth Clark to Vincent Massey, 27 July 1942, Wyndham Lewis, Second World War Papers (1942-48), Art Department, Imperial War Museum, London, England.

109. Lewis to Kenneth Clark, 17 November 1942, Cornell, and Lewis to Reille Thomson, 27 March 1943, Cornell.

110. Lewis to Malcolm MacDonald, 25 March 1943, Cornell.

111. It is likely that Lewis either started the canvas over again or substantially reworked it. He claimed to have finished the painting in Toronto in the spring of 1943, but began working on it again during the summer of 1943, after his move to Windsor.

112. Lewis to Malcolm MacDonald, 19 January 1944, Wyndham Lewis, Second World War Papers (1942-48), Imperial War Museum, London.

113. For a detailed account of this transaction, see Wyndham Lewis, Second World War Papers (1942-48), Imperial War Museum.

114. Lewis recommended Maritain's *Art and Scholasticism, and Other Essays* (New York, 1930) to the class he went on to instruct at Assumption, the French philosopher being his employers' "supreme contemporary authority" (Lewis to John Burgess, 17 July 1943, Rose, no. 518, p. 357). In a later letter to the same correspondent he confessed that "I must say I like him" (24 November 1943, Rose, no. 329, p. 370). In 1949 Lewis denounced Gilson, however, "as a *clerc*" on the pattern of those impugned by Julian Benda in his defence of intellectual detachment, *La trahaison des clercs* (Lewis to J.E. Palmer, 18 March 1949, Rose, no. 430, p. 486).

115. "Religious Expression in Contemporary Art: Rouault and Original Sin", as cited in *Wyndham Lewis on Art*, p. 372.

116. *Ibid.*, p. 380.

117. *Ibid.*, pp. 374-75.

118. *Ibid.*, p. 376.

119. Lewis, "Modernism in Art", 1943, p. 13, Cornell.

120. *Self Condemned* (Santa Barbara, California: Black Sparrow Press, 1983), p. 290.

121. See "Woman Gets Hair Wave As All Her Belongings Burn in Tudor Hotel", *Toronto Daily Star*, 15 February 1943. This melodramatic scenario may have been designed to garner sympathy, as virtually all of Lewis's known commissioned portraits and MSS materials from this period are presently accounted for, and most are included in this exhibition.

122. "On Canada", *Wyndham Lewis in Canada*, p. 24.

THE TALENTED INTRUDER "A SOMEWHAT DECEPTIVE ADDRESS": WYNDHAM LEWIS IN WINDSOR (PAGES 73-100)

1. Lewis to John Burgess, 17 August 1943, Rose, no. 324, p. 364.

2. The Lewises stayed at the apartment of Mrs. Delores Sills.

3. Lewis to Fr. J. Stanley Murphy, 12 February 1943, Assumption College Archives, Assumption College, Windsor.

4. Lewis to Burgess, 17 July 1943, Rose, no. 318, p. 357.

5. See correspondence (all at Cornell) from Lewis to: Leonard Brockington, 13 August 1941; Florence Lamont, 25 September 1941 and 5 October 1941; Frank Morley, 17 October 1941; James Johnson Sweeney, 13 October 1941; Cass Canfield, 1 November 1941; Archibald MacLeish, 7 November 1941; Alfred Barr, 17 November 1941, 24 November 1941; R.D. Jameson, 4 December 1941 and 15 February 1942; and Charles Dollard, 16 March 1942. In his search for such a position, Lewis had been inspired the examples of Carl Schaefer, who was awarded a Guggenhiem Fellowship to paint in Vermont in 1941, and André Biéler, resident artist and professor of art at Queen's University, Kingston since 1936.

6. Lewis to Burgess, 17 August 1943.

7. Lewis to McLuhan, 5 December 1943, Rose, no. 331, p. 372. The professor to whom Lewis was referring may have been J.D. Grant, chairman of the Department of English, University of Toronto, who invited Lewis to speak to the Graduate English Club (see Grant to Lewis, 8 February 1943, Cornell).

8. In his description of the development of the Windsor cityscape, Larry L. Kulisek records that "The French system of land division had encouraged a stringing out of settlement along the Detroit R. Over time communities were established (Sandwich) or sprang up around some function such as the ferry dock (Windsor), a distillery (Walkerville) or an auto maker's plant (Ford City). The transformation of the industrial base by the auto industry attracted rapid population growth and increased demands of administering the metropolitan area as a single functioning unit." The population of Windsor had grown from 21,000 in 1908

to 105,000 in 1928, an increase "almost entirely due to employment offered in the automobile industry.... During the Depression unemployment reached 30% of the work force, immigration ceased and the area suffered from outmigration. WWII production of war materials and postwar demand for automobiles meant employment and population gains." ("Windsor", *The Canadian Encyclopedia*, vol. IV, 2nd ed. (Edmonton: Hurtig Publishers, 1988), p. 2314.

9. It was incorporated as a city in 1892.
10. "Artist Finds Pupils Responsive," *Windsor Daily Star*, 5 August 1943.
11. Dr. D. Barath, in an interview with Catharine Mastin, 12 June 1992.
12. Marshall McLuhan, "My Friend Wyndham Lewis", *Atlantic Monthly* (December 1969): 93.
13. Lewis to Eliot, 13 March 1945, Rose, no. 341, p. 380.
14. See Jacques Maritain, Christian Culture Series brochure, 1943, Cornell. Lewis and Maritain also shared an interest in Georges Rouault. See Jacques Maritain, introduction to Rouault retrospective exhibition, held at the Cleveland Museum of Art and at New York's Museum of Modern Art, 1953. Lewis probably first met Maritain in the fall of 1942 through Fr. Stan Murphy. Maritain was in Toronto in mid-October through mid-November, teaching at St. Michael's College. See Murphy to Lewis, 12 September 1942, Cornell. Lewis and Maritain met one another in the fall of 1943, when Maritain was visiting Assumption College to receive the Annual Christian Culture Series Award Gold Medal.
15. For illustrations of works discussed in the preceding paragraphs see, Michel, *Wyndham Lewis: Paintings and Drawings*. In 1943 David Milne was also painting still lifes, domestic interiors, and portraits of women knitting and reading.
16. "Lecture i (Windsor)", c. 1943, p. 2A, Cornell.
17. *Ibid.*, pp. 7, 11-12.
18. Lewis to Malcolm MacDonald, 27 July 1943, Rose, no. 319, p. 359.
19. "Abstract Art", 1943, unpaginated, Cornell.
20. As many of these lectures are undated, it is not possible to determine the precise course contents for "The ABC of the Visual Arts." Several, however, can be dated to c. 1943, and it would seem likely that they pertained to this course, as most of Lewis's other Assumption College lecture MSS are dated.
21. "Lecture on the Visual Arts", subtitled "The ABC of the Visual Arts", c. 1943, p. 1, Cornell.
22. "Assumption College Lecture", c. 1943, unpaginated, Cornell.
23. The idea of the cultural melting-pot was an elaboration of notions first set forth, but much more critically than here, in *Paleface: The Philosophy of the 'Melting Pot'* (London: Chatto & Windus, 1929).
24. *America and Cosmic Man*, p. 12.
25. "The Frontiers of Art", c. 1943, pp. 3, 5, points 8, 1, Cornell.
26. In early 1943 a symposium was held to deal with the lasting effects of war and a solution to world peace, the texts for which, published in *Prefaces to Peace: A Symposium* (New York: cooperatively published by Simon and Schuster, Doubleday, Doran and Company, Inc., Reynal and Hitchcock Inc., and Columbia University Press, 1943), consisted of the following: "One World", by Wendell L. Willkie; "The Problems of Lasting Peace", by Herbert Hoover and Hugh Gibson; "The Price of Free World Victory", by Henry A. Wallace; and "Blue-print for Peace", by Sumner Wells. The published findings of this symposium make clear that global peace and harmony were actively being sought by the more enlightened of current American political leaders. Willkie's address, based on his travels to meet with diplomats from various countries outside the immediate war zone, promoted the concept of world political and economic union. Similarly, Wallace saw the United States as taking a leadership role in the promotion of disarmament and the prevention of an escalating arms race. For Lewis's being referred to H.J. Ford's *The Rise and Growth of American Politics* (New York: MacMillan Company, 1898) by Marshall McLuhan, see McLuhan to Lewis, 26 October and 2 December 1943, *Letters of Marshall McLuhan*, ed. Matie Molinaro, Corinne McLuhan and William Toye (Toronto *et al.*: Oxford University Press, 1987), pp. 135, 139.
27. "Naturalism", Heywood Broun Lecture Series, 1943, p. 6., Cornell.
28. *America and Cosmic Man*, pp. 12, 16.
29. *Ibid.*, p. 26.
30. *Ibid.*, p. 179.
31. "Creative Literature", Group I, 2 February 1944, unpaginated, Cornell.
32. "Creative Literature No. 2", 26 February 1944, unpaginated, Cornell.
33. *Ibid.*
34. McLuhan to Lewis, 24 July 1943, *Letters of Marshall McLuhan*, p. 129.
35. McLuhan to Lewis, 17 August 1943, *Ibid.*, p. 130.
36. *Mrs. George Gellhorn* (M 1041), reproduced on plate 145 of Michel's *Wyndham Lewis...*, could not be located for inclusion in this exhibition.
37. McLuhan to Lewis, 1 February 1944, *Letters of Marshall McLuhan*, p. 153.
38. "About Myself", c. 1944, unpaginated, Cornell.
39. "The Role of Art in Ordering Nature", 21 February 1944, Cornell.
40. Lewis to Charles Nagel, 20 August 1943, Cornell.
41. "Chicago Lecture", 29 February 1944, pp. 18, 19, Cornell.
42 Lewis was paid $1,500 for this painting, the commission for which came through Mrs. Gellhorn. See McLuhan, "My Friend Wyndham Lewis": 94. The canvas (M P108, reproduced on plate 148 in Michel's *Wyndham Lewis...*), is in the collection of the Washington University School of Medicine, St. Louis.
43. Lewis to Fr. J. Stanley Murphy, 23 March 1944, Assumption College Archives.
44. Murphy to Lewis, 25 April 1944, Cornell.
45. Murphy to Lewis, 25 March 1944, Cornell.
46. Copies of *The Basilides* are housed in the Assumption College Archives. Another photograph of D.L. Dillon, probably also used as a study for the oil portrait, is in a box of Lewis's photographs at Cornell.
47. Catharine Mastin, in an interview with Dr. D. Barath, 12 June 1992.
48. "Assumption College, Page of Notes for the Basilian Fathers", c. 1944, Cornell.
49. "Chicago Lecture", 29 February 1944, p. 20., Cornell.
50. "Draft Note", 1944, Cornell, indicates that Fathers Muckle, Dillon, Kennedy and Macdonald were living in different places.
51. Murphy to Lewis, 25 March 1944, Cornell.
52. "Final Assumption Lecture: The Nature of Criterion in the Fine Arts", summer 1944, p. 15., Cornell.
53. Murphy to Lewis, 13 August 1945, Cornell. Lewis eventually sold this portrait to a private individual from the 1956 Tate Gallery retrospective exhibition, *Wyndham Lewis and Vorticism. Thirty Personalities* was published in London by Desmond Harmsworth in 1932.
54. Murphy, "Wyndham Lewis at Windsor", *Wyndham Lewis in Canada*, p. 40.
55. Murphy to Lewis, 13 August 1945, Cornell.
56. See Lewis to Felix Giovanelli, 5 September 1943, Cornell.
57. Pauline Bondy, in an interview with Catharine Mastin, 24 November 1990.
58. *Ibid.*
59. *Ibid.*

60. *Ibid.*
61. Philip Marchand, *The Medium and the Messenger: Marshall McLuhan* (Toronto: Random House, 1989), p. 72. The information is derived from Marshall McLuhan's article, "My Friend Wyndham Lewis": 97.
62. Murphy to Lewis, 25 March 1944, Cornell.
63. See H. Marshall McLuhan Papers, National Archives of Canada, Ottawa, Ontario, and *Letters of Marshall McLuhan*, passim.
64. McLuhan to A.J.M. Smith, 12 October 1945, pp. 2, 4, A.J.M. Smith Papers, Thomas Fisher Rare Book Library, University of Toronto. Lewis met Smith during his lecture at the University of Michigan in Ann Arbor in March 1945.
65. *Ibid.*
66. McLuhan to Lewis, 15 April 1953, *Letters of Marshall McLuhan*, p. 236.
67. As cited in Marchand, *The Medium and the Messenger...*, p. 72.
68. For further details regarding McLuhan loans to Lewis, see note 105 of the second section of this catalogue essay.
69. Pauline Bondy, in an interview with Catharine Mastin, 24 November 1990.
70. Lewis to Felix Giovanelli, 9 November 1943, Cornell. Lewis mentions receiving $25 for portraying Mrs. Giovanelli, a remarkably small sum for such a highly realized work.
71. Another St. Louis-period portrait of a young boy is *Tom Cori* (M P107, reproduced on plate 148 of Michel's *Wyndham Lewis...*). The sitter was the son of Dr. Gerty Cori, who became professor of Biological Chemistry at Washington University in 1947, in which year she and her husband were joint winners of the Nobel Prize in Medicine and Physiology.
72. Lewis probably met Marion Trowell through the Windsor Art Association, on whose board she then sat, serving as a publicity person.
73. Martin's autobiography, *A Very Public Life*, was published in two volumes, in 1983 and 1986.
74. Martin and Lewis had corresponded before the latter's arrival in Windsor; in 1942 Lewis sent Martin a copy of *Anglosaxony: A League That Works* (see Lewis to Martin, 11 June 1942, Cornell). Martin, a friend of the novelist Morley Callaghan, had been first president of the Border Cities branch of the League of Nations Society, accompanied Vincent Massey on a speaking tour of Canada on League of Nations work for peace in 1933, and was Canadian government delegate to the Assembly of the League of Nations, Geneva, in 1938.
75. Martin to Lewis, 18 October 1944, Cornell.
76. Lewis to Martin, n.d. (c. February-April 1945), Cornell.
77. Mrs. Eleanor Martin, in an interview with Catharine Mastin, 24 August 1990.
78. *Ibid.*
79. *Ibid.*
80. Lewis received $750 for the portrait; see Paul Martin to Lewis, 22 February 1945, Cornell.
81. Martin to Lewis, "Tuesday", 1945, Cornell.
82. For further information on local artistic activities, see Elizabeth Burrell, *Windsor Celebrates 100 Years of Visual Art* (Windsor: Art Gallery of Windsor, 1992).
83. Valerie Conde, "City Gets Art Gallery", *Windsor Star*, 25 September 1945.
84. Lewis to Duncan, 17 July 1943, private collection.
85. "New Show", *Windsor Star*, 27 January 1945; "Artist Will Be Speaker", *Windsor Star*, 3 February 1945.
86. Lewis to E.P. Richardson, 15 October 1943, Cornell.
87. Newberry to Lewis, 9 April 1945, Cornell.
88. "Hemingway, Tolstoi and War", Cornell.
89. Lewis, "The Problem of Beauty", n.d. (c. March 1944), pp. 3, 4, 5, 5a, 13, Cornell.
90. Richardson to Jeffrey Meyers, 19 January 1978, quoted in *The Enemy...*, p. 285.
91. According to Lewis, "It...is quite impossible to find accommodation except in a hotel. Here in Ottawa one even is legally debarred from renting an apartment (flat) or house: only officials and the military and naval offices are allowed to do that...." (Lewis to Augustus John, 19 June 1945, Rose, no. 344, no. 383.)
92. While in Ottawa, Lewis attempted to sell some drawings to the National Gallery of Canada, leaving with H.O. McCurry for consideration of purchase the following works: *American Midinette, Woman Reading the Newspaper, Woman and Teacup, Teacups, (woman partly appearing), Girl Reading, Girl Seated.* See Malcolm Macdonald to H.O. McCurry, 29 May 1945, Director's Files, Archives, National Gallery of Canada, Ottawa.
93. Lewis to Malcolm Macdonald, n.d. (1945), Cornell. This undated letter, written after Lewis returned to London, contains the remarks which suggest that MacDonald had taken care of this debt.
94. Sir Harold Nicolson, *Diaries and Letters: 1939-1945* (London, 1945), as quoted in John Robert Colombo, *Colombo's Canadian Quotations* (Edmonton: Hurtig Publishers, 1974), p. 382.

CONCLUSION (PAGES 102-105)

1. Lewis to Duncan, note accompanying change-of-address form, n.d. (c. October 1943), private collection.
2. Meyers, *The Enemy...*, p. 262.
3. *The Solitary Outlaw...*, p. 31.
4. Meyers, *The Enemy...*, p. 136.
5. *Ibid.*, p. 138.
6. Lewis to McLuhan, 4 February 1945, H. M. McLuhan Papers, National Archives of Canada.
7. Geoffrey Grigson, "The Ogre in the Black Hat", *Blessings, Kicks and Curses: A Critical Collection* (London and New York: Allison and Busby, 1982), p. 36.
8. "Wyndham Lewis: his Theory of Art and Communication", *Shenandoah* 4 (Summer-Autumn 1953): 80, 83, 85.
9. "Wyndham Lewis Recalled", vinyl recording supplement to *artscanada*, issue no. 114 (November 1967), of a reading of *One-Way Song*, given by Lewis at Harvard University in 1940.
10. Lewis to Lady Waterhouse, 27 January 1942, Rose, no. 291, p. 316.
11. "I Can Take It", holograph MS, n.d. (c. 1941), Cornell.
12. *America and Cosmic Man*, p. 7.
13. McLuhan to Pound, 22 July 1951, *Letters of Marshall McLuhan*, p. 227. In this letter, McLuhan went on (p. 227) to complain that the impact of the book was "nil. We resent or ignore such intellectual bombs. We prefer to compose human beings into bombs and explode political and social entities. Much more fun. Lewis clears the air of fug. We want to get rid of people entirely." B.W. Powe notes in *The Solitary Outlaw* that McLuhan had underlined, in the University of Toronto's copy of *America and Cosmic Man*, Lewis's claim that "the world is becoming one big village", suggesting that this may be one of the origins of his concept of the "global village."
14. "Prospect", *Canadian Art* 81, vol. 19 (October 1962): 363.
15. Two recent installations at the Art Gallery of Windsor, Rita McKeough's *Embrace* (1990) and Rod Strickland's *Beyond the Sweet Sea* (1990), question, as Lewis did in the 1940s, the concept of progress and contemplate the consequences of industrialization.

16. Philip Marchand, McLuhan's biographer, noted in an article entitled "Mexico and Canada: A contrast in cultural identity" *(The Toronto Star,* 25 September 1992), that "Forty years ago, the communications theorist Marshall McLuhan said of the Royal Commission on Canadian Culture that produced the Canada Council, 'The Royal Commission is squarely in line with our bureaucrats and Victorian patriarchs in supporting that culture is basically an unpleasant moral duty. According to this view, everything that people do spontaneously and with gusto, everything connected with industry, commerce, sport, and popular entertainment is merely vulgar.'' Marchand concludes, "Things haven't changed much in 40 years. The attitude is partly a product of our habit, ingrained over centuries, of deferring to officialdom, whether it be the royal bureaucrats of New France or the arts bureaucrats of modern day Ottawa.

"MAGICAL PRESENCES IN A MAGICAL PLACE": FROM *HOMAGE TO ETTY* TO *THE ISLAND* (PAGES 107-155)

1. Wyndham Lewis to J.S. McLean, 1 December 1942, holograph draught, Wyndham Lewis Collection, Department of Rare Books, Cornell University Library, Ithaca, New York. All subsequent endnote references to this collection are indicated as Cornell.
2. "Chronological Outline", *The Art of Wyndham Lewis* (London: Faber and Faber, 1951), p. 47.
3. "Wyndham Lewis: An Assessment", *Wyndham Lewis* (London: Lund Humphries, in association with the City of Manchester Art Galleries, 1980), p. 21.
4. *Rude Assignment: A narrative of my career up-to-date*, ed. Toby Foshay (Santa Barbara: Black Sparrow Press, 1984; first published London: Hutchinson & Co., 1950), p. 140.
5. *Wyndham Lewis: Paintings and Drawings* (Toronto: McClelland and Stewart, 1971), p. 137.
6. *Ibid.*, p. 143.
7. McLean to Lewis, 3 June 1941, TLS, Cornell.
8. Lewis to McLean, 13 June 1941, holograph draught, Cornell.
9. "On Canada", n.d., holograph MS, Cornell; first published in *Canadian Literature*, no. 35 (1968), reprinted in *Wyndham Lewis in Canada*, ed. George Woodcock (Vancouver: University of British Columbia Publications Centre, 1971), p. 29.
10. *Courage: The Story of Sir James Dunn* (Fredericton: Brunswick Press, 1961), pp. 235-39.
11. Walter Sickert, quoted in Charles Handley-Read and Eric Newton, *The Art of Wyndham Lewis*, p. 70.
12. *Courage*, p. 246. A further connection with the British art scene was made through the marriage of Anne Dunn, Sir James's daughter by his second wife, Irene Clarice, the ex-Marchioness of Queensberry, to the painter Rodrigo Moynihan.
13. *Ibid.*, p. 240. Lewis may have had Dunn, or at least culturally aquisitive capitalists like him, in mind when he complained in *America and Cosmic Man* (1948) that "The odd rich man who has a collection of the more enterprising type of pictures, etchings, sculpture, ceramics, is to be found in most places. But these pieces are generally European. So that solves nothing for the American artist."
14. See Kim Sloan, *Victorian Painting in the Beaverbrook Art Gallery* (Fredericton: The Beaverbrook Art Gallery, 1989).
15. Lewis to Sir James Dunn, 13 June 1941, holograph draught, Cornell.
16. Dunn to Lewis, 23 June 1941, TLS, Cornell.
17. Lewis to Dunn, 4 July 1941, TLS, Cornell.
18. Bickell, as it happens, was an art connoisseur, collector and benefactor on a par with Dunn himself, and like him was involved in heavy industry in Ontario's northland. The president of McIntyre Porcupine Mines Ltd., headquartered, like Algoma Steel, at 25 King St. West (where yet another great benefactor of the Art Gallery of Toronto, William P. Wood, head of Burlington Steel Co. Ltd, also had his offices), Bickell held court at his estate, "Arcadia," near the Lake Ontario village of Port Credit, just west of Toronto.
19. Lewis to Dunn, 11 August 1941, TLS, Cornell.
20. Lewis's synopsis and notes for this book, dated June 1942, are at Cornell; they were published under the title "Hill 100: Outline for an Unwritten Novel" in *Wyndham Lewis in Canada* (pp. 90-96).
21. *Courage.*, pp. 214-15. In 1947 Dunn purchased "Dayspring," a substantial mansion and spread at the southern New Brunswick holiday resort village of St. Andrews.
22. Wyndham Lewis, "Nature's Place in Canadian Culture", *Wyndham Lewis in Canada*, p. 57. A shorter version of this article—a review of Donald Buchanan's Phaidon Press publication, *Canadian Painters*—appeared in *The Listener* under the title "Canadian Nature and its Painters" (29 August 1946); this was reprinted in *Wyndham Lewis on Art: Collected Writings, 1913-1956*, ed. Walter Michel and C.J. Fox (London: Thames and Hudson/New York: Funk & Wagnalls, 1969), pp. 425-30.
23. Lewis to Marcia Christophorides, 22 September 1941, holograph draught, Cornell.
24. Lewis to Geoffrey Stone, 26 September 1941; quoted in Jeffrey Meyers, *The Enemy: A Biography of Wyndham Lewis* (Boston and London: Routledge and Kegan Paul, 1982), p. 271. On 23 September Lewis had written to the same correspondent, "I am back as you see in this godforsaken city [i.e. Toronto] and have been rushing up and down this tedious land; on `business' errands. I have just returned from the Maritime Provinces, where I went to paint a magnate." *(The Letters of Wyndham Lewis*, ed. W.K. Rose [Norfolk, Conn.: New Directions, 1963], no. 277, p. 297. Subsequent endnote references to *The Letters* are indicated as Rose, followed by the numbers assigned to them by the editor.) There are two possible candidates for Dunn-caricatures in *Self Condemned*: the alcoholic Mulligan, "the president of a big concern, clothed like a big shot, with the bullying voice and glassy eye of a tycoon" (p. 207), and "Mr. Cox, the vice-president of a very large corporation" who lived at the King George Hotel "with a floozy of old standing. They were there together for so long that this had become his real home" (p. 208). Dunn kept a suite at Toronto's King Edward Hotel.
25. Although Jeffrey Meyers and Angela Wright, in the chronology sections of *The Enemy* and *Wyndham Lewis: Art and War* (London: Published by the Wyndham Lewis Memorial Trust in association with Lund Humphries, 1992), respectively, state that, in September 1941, Lewis made a "trip to Halifax, Nova Scotia", "in apparently futile search for portrait commissions", no such journey seems to have been made, Bathurst, N.B. being several hundred miles from Halifax. Instead, correspondence indicates that, immediately after failing to get a sitting with Sir James Dunn at his "camp," Lewis returned directly to Toronto; nor was he again to travel to the Maritimes. Anne Lewis concluded her reminiscence, "The Hotel", by expressing regret that "at the end of our stay in Canada the main original purpose of our visit remained incompletely fulfilled; this had been to carry out research into the lives of Wyndham Lewis's grandparents in Canada, and to go back to his birthplace in Nova Scotia"–i.e. Amherst. (*Wyndham Lewis in Canada*, p. 23.)
26. In the end, Hepburn was painted from photographic sources by the Royal Canadian Academician Cleeve Horne in 1958, five years after the former premier's death.
27. Lewis to Lord Carlow, January 1943; quoted in Michel, *Wyndham Lewis...*, p. 135.
28. Had he been in the city in 1940, rather than in New York, he would have been able to see two paintings by Etty, *Dancing Girl* and *The Gladiator*, in the *Loan Exhibit from the Hall Estate*, held at the Art Gallery of Toronto from the 5th to the 29th of that month. These works were borrowed by the gallery from Mr. Fred Hamilton, of Hamilton, Ontario, the executor of the Hall Estate, which, the catalogue foreword explains, "had remained in the Hall family in Nottinghamshire, England, until 1914, when it was sold by the consent of the last male survivor, Francis Hall, who had been born in Canada but who was then living on the Estate, and who brought what he required to Canada, of which this exhibit is a part." I am grateful to Hugh Anson-Cartwright for pointing out this catalogue to me. When in Ottawa, in December 1940, Lewis could have seen Etty's *Seated Nude* and *Kneeling Nude*, both acquired by the National Gallery of Canada in 1926; and when in Montreal, in the spring and early summer of 1941, *The Bivouac of Cupid*, in the collection of the Art Association of Montreal (now the Montreal Museum of Fine Arts).
29. This same dealer, the proprietor of the Savile Gallery, London, in 1930 donated Lord Leighton's *Actaea, Nymph of the Sea Shore* to the National Gallery of Canada.

30. *Seated Female Nude* (listed as *Study of a Female Nude*) and *Nude–Half-Length,* along with another Etty oil entitled *Reclining Nude Model,* were included in the *Exhibition of the Beaverbrook Collection of Paintings and Prints and Some Portraits from the Collection of Sir James Dunn, Bart.,* held at the Bonar Law - Bennett Library of the University of New Brunswick in November 1954; Lewis's *The Mud Clinic* was also in this show. I do not know the present whereabouts or time of acquisition of *Reclining Female Model,* but *Nude–Half-Length* was purchased for Lord Beaverbrook from Christie's, London sale of 3 May 1946.
31. "The Coming Academy", *Sunday Express,* no. 121 (24 April 1921): p. 3; reprinted in *Wyndham Lewis on Art...,* p. 191.
32. *The Pre-Raphaelite Dream* (London: The Reprint Society, 1943; first published as *The Pre-Raphaelite Tragedy* by Jonathan Cape, 1942), p. 28. Gaunt was also the author, with F. Gordon Roe, of *Etty and the Nude* (London, 1943).
33. Jean-Jacques Mayoux, tr. James Emmons, *English Painting from Hogarth to the Pre-Raphaelites* (Geneva: Skira, 1975), p. 172.
34. Introduction, *An Exhibition of Paintings by William Etty* (London: The Arts Council of Great Britain, 1955), p. 5.
35. *Ibid.,* p. 5.
36. Rose MacDonald, "Lewis Exhibit Recalls Sojourn In Toronto", *The Toronto Evening Telegram,* 11 February 1950.
37. *William Etty* (London: Routledge & Kegan Paul, 1958), p. 47.
38. William Etty to Walter Etty, 25 December 1823, York City Reference Library; quoted in Farr, *William Etty,* p. 43.
39. Martin Postle, in *Victorian Painting in the Beaverbrook Art Gallery,* p. 112.
40. *Ibid.,* p. 110.
41. *The Nude: A New Perspective* (Cambridge, Mass.: Harper & Row, 1989), p. 98.
42. *Wyndham Lewis...,* p. 410. However, Michel also suggests that *Homage to Etty* "could have been nothing more than a title assigned by Duncan, picking up a joke or witty remark by Lewis. Lewis I should think didn't care much about what title people put on his pictures, especially not the Toronto ones, which he may well have thought would end up mouldering in some attic anyway." (Walter Michel to Robert Stacey, 7 January 1992.)
43. The full inscription reads: "Wyndham Lewis: `Homage to Etty' 1942/ (the result of a visit to a Toronto home/that sported five *[sic?]* Etty nudes/Colln. Douglas Duncan, Toronto 3235." Duncan's accession-card for the work, now in the Archives of the National Gallery of Canada, reveals that he acquired it on 12 March 1942. Perhaps the first artist to use the titular phrase was the Victorian painter and muralist Daniel Maclise, who, during a pilgrimage to Etty's native York in 1851, inscribed after his own name in the visitor's book at the School of Design, "Homage to Etty!" (Alexander Gilchrist, *Life of William Etty,* vol. 2 [London: David Bogue, 1855], p. 307.)
44. Paul Edwards, *Wyndham Lewis: Art and War* (London: Imperial War Museum, 1992), p. 21. Walter Michel states that "An alternative title, *Norwegian Dance,* is used by the Countess of Drogheda in an undated latter to Lewis [November 1913], now in the Department of Rare Books, Cornell University." *(Wyndham Lewis...,* p. 333.)
45. "Wyndham Lewis at the Goupil", *The New Age* (20 February 1919); reprinted in *Selected Prose: 1909-1965,* ed. William Cookson (New York: New Directions, 1973), p. 427.
46. *Wyndham Lewis...,* p. 99.
47. *Wyndham Lewis...,* p. 108.
48. *Ibid.,* p. 110.
49. "Manifesto", *Blast,* No. 1 (1914) (reprinted Santa Barbara: Black Sparrow Press, 1981): 22, 35.
50. Lewis to J. M. Dent & Son, Ltd., 22 November 1941, TLS, Cornell. The first part of the book Lewis was pitching to Dent, *The Ideas with Which we Fight,* was published in 1941 by Ryerson Press under the title *Anglosaxony: A League that Works.*
51. "The Great War, Wyndham Lewis and the Underground Press", *artscanada* 24, no. 11, issue no. 114 (November 1967): 4.
52. Lewis, *Rude Assignment,* p. 130.
53. *The Enemy...,* pp. 23-24.
54. First published in *The Listener* on 10 May 1951, this essay, in which Lewis announced his retirement as that journal's art critic, was issued in pamphlet form by Black Sparrow Press in 1981.
55. Hugh Kenner, "The Last European", *Canadian Literature,* no. 36 (1968), reprinted in *Wyndham Lewis in Canada,* p. 17.
56. It was here that he wrote not only *The Vulgar Streak* but two short stories with Atlantic beach settings, "The Yachting Cap" and "The Weeping Man" (first published in *Unlucky for Pringle,* ed. C.J. Fox and Robert T. Chapman [London: Vision, 1973], pp. 147-58).
57. *Wyndham Lewis...,* p. 140.
58. "Canada and Wyndham Lewis the Artist", *Canadian Literature,* no. 35 (1968), reprinted in *Wyndham Lewis in Canada,* pp. 68-69.
59. Quoted in *Wyndham Lewis and Vorticism* (London: Tate Gallery, 1956), under No. 87.
60. Michel, *Wyndham Lewis...,* p. 107.
61. This title is a conflation of two versions of a famous line from Edward Fitzgerald's "translation" of the *Rubaiyat* of Omar Khayyam, the relevant quatrain in the fourth and last edition of which (1879) is no. XII:

    A Book of Verses underneath the Bough,
    A Jug of Wine, a Loaf of Bread—and Thou
    Beside me singing in the Wilderness—
    Oh, Wilderness were Paradise enow.

    In the first edition (1859), the last line reads: "And Wilderness is Paradise enow." In the "Passchendaele" chapter of *Blasting and Bombardiering,* Lewis writes of the sandbag dugout that was his temporary home, "All was set for a little picnic of the mind in this cell of a booted anchorite. `The wilderness were paradise enow,' though I had no book of verses with me, but *Das Kapital* which was probably more suitable under the circumstances." (London, 1937; revised edition London: John Calder, 1982, p. 150.)
62. Richard Humphreys, "An Inca Key to `Inca and the Birds'", *Enemy News,* no. 9 (December 1978): 3.
63. *Wyndham Lewis...,* p. 122.
64. Introduction, *Catalogue of an Exhibition of Paintings and Drawings by Wyndham Lewis* (London: Leicester Galleries, 1937), p. 7.
65. *Tarr: The 1918 Version,* ed. Paul O'Keeffe (Santa Rosa: Black Sparrow Press, 1990), p. 299.
66. "The Nude is Dying Out", *Lilliput* 4 (May 1939): 441-43. In Lewis's analysis, "The last really great Nudes were those painted or drawn by Ingres..." (p. 442).
67. See Bertram Brooker, "Nudes and Prudes", *Open House,* ed. W.A. Deacon and Wilfred Reeves (Ottawa: Graphic Publishers, 1931); reprinted in *Documents in Canadian Art,* ed. Douglas Fetherling (Peterborough: Broadview Press, 1987), pp. 66-75. In 1933 eight of Russell's then-controversial but in fact innocuous works were rejected by the C.N.E. hanging committee, an act which induced him, the following year, to rent the entire mezzanine floor of the Automotive Building on the C.N.E. grounds for his hugely popular exhibit. In 1935 the highlight of his one-man show on the premises was his large canvas, *Spirit of the Island,* featuring a life-sized nude figure of a young woman poised on the "diving rock" of Toronto Island. For a commentary on the Russell controversy, see Donald Buchanan, "Naked Ladies", *The Canadian Forum* (April 1935): 273-74.
68. Other indicative examples are John Lyman's *Airplane* (c. 1912; private collection) and *Les Baigneurs* (c. 1912; Musée du Québec); Adrien Hébert's *Bacchanale* (c. 1923; unlocated); Kathleen Munn's *Composition* (c. 1926-28; private collection); Bertram Brooker's *Endless Dawn* (1927; Estate of M.A. Brooker), *Green Movement* (c. 1927; Art Gallery of Ontario), and *Three Figures* (1937; London Regional Art Gallery); Prudence Heward's *Femme au bord de la mer* (1930; Art Gallery of Windsor), and *Girl Under a Tree* (1931; Art Gallery of Windsor); Edwin Holgate's *Bather* (c. 1930; private collection), *Nude in a Landscape* (c. 1930; National Gallery of Canada), *Nude* (1930; Art Gallery of Ontario), *The Bathers* (1937; Montreal Museum of Fine Arts), and *Early Autumn* (1938; National Gallery of Canada), as well as such woodcuts as *Nude Figure* (1924), *Two Figures* (1924), *Nude* (c. 1926), *The Bathers* (c. 1930), and *Nude by a Lake* (c. 1933); Dorothy Stevens's *Nude Bathers on a Rock by a Lake* (Sotheby's, Toronto, May 1992, no.

225); Jean-Paul Lemieux's *Jeunes baigneurs sur le quai* (1936; Hotel des encans de Montreal, November 1989, no. 132); Charles Comfort's *Northern Waters*, of 1926 or '27 (a large watercolour of a female nude sitting on a rock in water, which the artist destroyed in 1960), *Promontory* (1937; also destroyed by the artist), and *Primavera* (1941; Women's Art Association, Toronto); H.G. Glyde's *She Sat Upon a Hill Above the City* (c. 1939; Glenbow Museum, Calgary); and Paul-Emile Borduas's *5.45 ou Nu Vert (Green Nude)* (1945; Sotheby's, Toronto, May 1992, no. 81). The same Sotheby's, Toronto auction catalogue for May 1992 also featured an extraordinary example of an early-Canadian *plein-air* treatment of the nude: the German-born William Raphael's *An Afternoon in the Woods*, dated 1870 (no. 165; see also no. 167.)

69. "Engendering Imaginary Modernism: Henri Matisse's *Bonheur de vivre*", *Genders*, No. 9 (Fall 1990): 55.]
70. *Time and Western Man* (Boston: Beacon Press, 1957; first published London: Chatto and Windus, 1927), p. 239.
71. *The Art of Being Ruled*, ed. Reed Way Dasenbrock (Santa Rosa: Black Sparrow Press, 1989), p. 365.
72. "Wyndham Lewis: His Theory of Art and Communication", *Shenandoah* 4 (Summer-Autumn 1953): 87-88.
73. Thomas Dilworth to Robert Stacey, 23 April 1992. For a discussion of Lewis's reading of Frazer, see Peter L. Caracciolo, "Carnivals of Mass-Murder", in *Sir James Frazer and the Literary Imagination: Essays in Affinity and Influence* (London: Macmillan, 1990).
74. Paul Edwards, "Wyndham Lewis: Art and War", *Wyndham Lewis: Art and War*, p. 49.
75. *Fables of Aggression: Wyndham Lewis, the Modernist as Fascist* (Berkeley: University of California Press, 1979), p. 141.
76. *Wyndham Lewis*, p. 53.
77. In conversation with Robert Stacey, August 1992.
78. Quoted in Charles Estienne, "Des tendences de la peinture moderne. Entretien avec M. Matisse" (1909), trans. in Jack D. Flam, *Matisse on Art* (London, 1973), p. 49.
79. *Wyndham Lewis...*, p. 142.
80. "The New Egos", *Blast*, No. 1: 141.
81. "Media Log", *Counterblast* (New York: Harcourt, Brace and World, 1969), pp. 113-14. This publication was an expansion of McLuhan's privately printed pamphlet, *Counterblast*, of 1954, the first half of which was originally written as a review of the Massey Commission *Report* (1951).
82. *Wyndham Lewis* (Norfolk, Conn.: New Directions, 1954), p. 7.
83. *Ibid.*, p. 94.
84. This was not the first time Lewis had used the title: his typewritten "1917 List", in the Department of Rare Books at Cornell University, includes, under the sub-heading of "Drawings at Pound", the now-lost *Island* (M 236).
85. *Wyndham Lewis...*, p. 344. The typed record of Lewis works in Duncan's possession (Archives, National Gallery of Canada, Ottawa) lists the following works: *Creation Myth No. 17, Two Women on a Beach, Homage to Etty, Creation Myth-Maternal Figure, Centaur [or Satyr] Observing a Group of Girls, Marine Fiesta, Picture of a Picture in the Making* (i.e. *The Mind of the Artist, About to Make a Picture*), and *Bathing Women. He sold Nude Panel, A Party of Girls, Pool of Amazons* and *"...And Wilderness Were Paradise Enow"* to J.S. McLean in the 1940s.
86. The four other works were *Three Martyrs, A Man's Form Falling from a Horse, War News*, and *Marine Fiesta*. Subsequently, seven more works (M 965, 988, 997, 1010, 1011, 1013, and 1014) were returned to Mrs. Lewis by the Toronto antiquarian book dealer and Lewis aficionado Hugh Anson-Cartwright, at Frances Barwick's behest.
87. Omar S. Pound to Robert Stacey, 1 March 1992.
88. *Ibid.* The first instalment or "section" of this three-part novel, *The Childermass*, appeared in 1928; its sequels, *Monstre Gai* and *Malign Fiesta*, came out in 1955. A fourth and final volume, tentatively entitled *The Trial of Man*, was never completed. Could the third title be a deliberate play or variant on that of Lewis's crowded 1942 watercolour, *Marine Fiesta*?
89. John Martin to Robert Stacey, 4 February 1992.
90. Paraphrased from a letter from Walter Michel to Robert Stacey, 7 January 1992.
91. "Notes on the Colour Plates", *Blast 3* (Santa Barbara: Black Sparrow Press, 1984), p. 236.
92. Lewis, *Tarr: The 1918 Version*, p. 52. This passage has led the Canadian novelist Sheila Watson, in her 1964 University of Toronto Ph.D. thesis, "Wyndham Lewis and Expressionism", to go so far as to state that "Bertha Lunken...comes out of the canvases of Böcklin" (p. 386). There are, of course, no "grottoes of teutonic nymphs" in any of the versions of *Die Toteninsel*—which suggests that Lewis's memory of the painting, at least when he was writing *Tarr*, was shaky.
93. "The Great War, Wyndham Lewis and the Underground Press": 7.
94 *Ibid.*: 12.
95. "The Artist Older than the Fish", *The Caliph's Design*, first published in *The Egoist* (1919), reprinted in *Wyndham Lewis The Artist: From 'Blast' to Burlington House* (London: Laidlaw & Laidlaw, 1939); in *Wyndham Lewis on Art*, p. 168; and in *The Caliph's Design*, ed. Reed Way Dasenbrock (Santa Barbara: Black Sparrow Press, 1986), pp. 65-71.
96. Elizabeth Tumasonis, "The Piper among the Ruins: The God Pan in the Work of Arnold Böcklin", *RACAR* 17 (1990): 62, n. 1.
97. Clive Sinclair, "The weight of Guilt", *Times Literary Supplement* (12 June 1992): 18. The closing stage direction of *The Ghost Sonata* reads as follows: *"The room disappears. Böcklin's picture* The Island of the Dead *is seen in the distance, and from the island comes music, soft, sweet, and melancholy."* The Canadian architectural magazine *Construction* noted in 1918 that "The works of Corot, Bocklin, Gaston La Touche, Rene Menard, and Frank Brangwyn, would furnish inspiration for a whole generation of scene painters, whether in the field of poetic fantasy, vivid impressionism, atmospheric mystery, weird and somber imagery, gracious pastoral simplicity, or vigorous emphasis of reality." ("Loew's Theatre, Montreal", *Construction* 11 [February 1918]: 50.)
98. *Howards End* (New York: Alfred A. Knopf, Everyman's Library, 1991), p. 78.
99. "'Hitler's a Böcklin fan, I believe. Isn't he?'" asks Victor Stamp, the left-wing protagonist of Lewis's *Revenge for Love* (London: Cassell, 1937; revised. Santa Barbara: Black Sparrow Press, 1991), p. 147.

    "It is interesting to note", writes Rolf Andree, "...that Hitler ordered the acquisition of 13 paintings [by Böcklin], ofwhich the third version of the *Island of the Dead* and the later version of the *Combat of the Centaurs* were for his private collection (these can no longer be traced and were probably destroyed)." (Introduction, *Arnold Böcklin: 1827-1901* [London: Arts Council of Great Britain/Pro Helvetica, 1971], p. 7.) The three extant versions of his *Kentaurenkampf* (said to reflect his feelings about the Franco-Prussian War) are dated 1871, 1872, and 1872-73, respectively. Lewis, as we have seen, was also captivated by the theme of centaurs and centauresses.
100. The first version of *Die Toteninsel* has belonged to the Kunstmuseum, Basel, since 1920; the second, also dating from 1880, was acquired by the Metropolitan Museum of Art, New York, in 1926; the third, dated 1883, was appropriated from the Berlin art dealer Dr. Fritz Nathan by Hitler in 1939 and has been lost since the end of World War II; the fourth (1884), last located in the collection of Schloss Rohoncz, Lugano, has also been unaccounted for since 1945; and the fifth and last has been in the Museum der bildenenden Kunste zu Leipzig since 1886, the year of its completion. Lewis could have viewed several of these versions on a number of occasions: for instance, during his visits to Berlin of September 1921, November 1930 (out of which came his disastrous *Hitler* of 1931), September 1932, January 1934, and October 1937, encompassing a period in which the third and fourth *Toteninsels* were present in the city. While in Munich in September 1928 he would have had the opportunity to see the third version at the Kunsthandlung Galerie Heinemann. And in the course of his first and second trips to New York, in November 1931 and December 1939-March 1940, he could have studied the second version at the Metropolitan Museum.
101. Introduction, *Arnold Böcklin...*, pp. 7-8.
102. *Böcklin*, vol. 7, part 75 of the *Masters of Art: A Series of Illustrated Monographs Issued Monthly* (Boston: Bates & Guild Co., 1906), p. 120.
103. *Ibid.*, p. 122.

104. Catalogue note on *The Island of the Dead* (Metropolitan Museum of Art, New York), in *Arnold Böcklin...*, p. 31. The castle was inherited by Vittoria Colonna, Michaelangelo's muse and friend. Other suggestions for Böcklin's inspiration include Pondikonisi, near Corfu, and the Ponza Islands in the Gulf of Gaeta; on the other hand, one commentator contends that Böcklin based his entire composition on a photograph taken by Franz Schensky of the rocky island of Helgoland in 1893 (see Hans Günther Sperlich, "Lichregie", *A. Böcklin: 1827-1901*, vol. I [Darmstadt: Mathildenhöhe, 1977], p. 138). At any rate, the "source" of *The Island* might just as well have been the island cemetery in Venice, visited by Lewis in October 1922, or the "M"-shaped isle of Capri, a short boat-ride from Ischia.)

105. *The Demon of Progress in the Arts* (London: Methuen & Co., 1954), p. 45.

106. For the commentary on *The Island* of which these remarks are a free translation, see Norbert Schneider, "Böcklins »Toteninsel«", *Arnold Böcklin 1827-1901*, vol. I (Darmstadt: Mathildenhöhe, 1977), pp. 106-25.

107. Tumasonis, "The Piper among the Ruins...": 56, 59.

108. *The Demon of Progress in the Arts*, p. 46.

109. "The Credentials of the Painter", *The English Review*, Part I, no. 34 (January 1922): 33-38; Part II, no 34 (April 1922): 391-96; reprinted in *Creatures of Habit and Creatures of Change*, ed. Paul Edwards (Santa Rosa: Black Sparrow Press, 1989), p. 74.

110. "French Realism", in "The Caliph's Design", Wyndham Lewis the Artist..., pp. 273-74; reprinted in *Wyndham Lewis on Art*, p. 160. The fact that, in revising *The Caliph's Design* for republication, Lewis altered his original 1919 text to include Böcklin's and Burne-Jones's names indicates that something or someone had recently brought these artists favourably to his attention. His estimation of Burne-Jones improved over the years: whereas, in the April 1919 issue of *The English Review*, he had written of "a Burne-Jonesesque wallow of sentiment" ("What Art Now?"), in *The Listener* for 22 April 1948 he referred to him as "so dazzlingly successful a pioneer of surrealism" ("The Brotherhood"). In 1968 Geoffrey Grigson affirmed that Lewis "liked–this rather surprised me–Burne-Jones (but then consider the likeness of the close verticals of Burne-Jones...and Lewis), at least when Burne-Jones remained vertical and linear and managed to keep clear of sentimentality." ("The Ogre in the Black Hat", *Blessings, Kicks and Curses: A Critical Collection* [London/ New York: Allison & Busby, 1982], p. 33.)

111. *Arnold Böcklin...*, p. 31.

112. Norman Douglas, "Sirens", *The English Review* (May 1909): 213; reprinted in *Siren Land* (London, 1911). Also for the May 1909 issue of *The English Review*, the editor, Ford Madox Hueffer, had accepted Lewis's "The Pole"–the first of his writings to be published. "The Island of Typhoëus" was reprinted in Douglas's *Summer Islands, Ischia and Ponza* (London, 1931).

113. "The Visual World of Wyndham Lewis", pp. 20-21.

114. "A Child of the Century", *Bandits in a Landscape: A study of Romantic Painting from Caravaggio to Delacroix* (London: The Studio Ltd., 1937), p. 127. On 10 April 1937 Lewis wrote to Gaunt to thank him for the book, and expressing a desire to "hear more about these romantic ancestors of yours..." (Rose, no. 233, p. 245).

115. The identification of this painting was made by Jeffrey Meyers in *The Enemy...* (p. 259).

116. *Bandits in a Landscape*, p. 73.

117. *Symbolist Art* (New York: Praeger Publishers, 1972), p. 151.

118. "'Art' lecture", delivered at Assumption College, Windsor, 4 February 1944, holograph MS, Cornell.

119. "Art Lecture", delivered at Assumption College, Windsor, 28 January 1944, holograph MS, Cornell.

120. (London: Chatto and Windus, 1931), pp. 66-67. First published in *The Enemy*, No. 3 (1929).

121. Meryl Secrest, *Salvador Dali: A Biography* (New York: E. P. Dutton, 1986), p. 125. Lewis had a high opinion of Fuseli, and although he criticized those who aped his "tragic female contortionists", there is a definite Fuseli-esque "distortionism" in such Lewis figure drawings as *Eighteenth Century Amazons* and *Two Vorticist Figures*, both from 1912. Reviewing the Arts Council's *Henry Fuseli* exhibition for *The Listener* on 16 February 1950, he described the subject as a "super-illustrator, a rip-roaring romantic with a classical training, and he comes to us recommended by Blake as the only real person in England at that time." *(Wyndham Lewis on Art*, p. 404). Besides the work discussed below, Dali's Böcklin-tributes include *L'Ile des Morts* (1934) and *Chevalier de la mort* (1935).

122. "Super-nature versus Super-real", *Wyndham Lewis the Artist*, reprinted in *Wyndham Lewis on Art*, pp. 328-29.

123. Farrington, *Wyndham Lewis*, p. 53.

124. *The Englishness of English Art: An Expanded and Annotated Version of the Reith Lectures Broadcast in October and November 1955* (London: The Architectural Press, 1955), p. 122.

125. *Painting in England: 1525 to 1975* (New York: New York University Press, 1976), p. 230.

126. See G. Sawyer, *Journal of the Courtauld and Warburg Institutes* (London, 1951): 134.

127. *Olympian Dreamers: Victorian Classical Painters, 1860-1914* (London: Constable, 1983), p. 22.

128. *The Demon of Progress in the Arts*, p. 45.

129. *A Fable of Modern Art* (New York and London: Thames and Hudson, 1980), caption to plate 5; see also p. 32.

130. "Art Chronicle", *The Criterion* 2 (October 1924), reprinted in *Creatures of Change and Creatures of Habit...* (p. 106); and "Matisse and Derain", in "The Caliph's Design", p. 105.

131. Paul Edwards argues that the "continuity between the figures and their landscape" found in such early Lewis works as *Sunset among the Michaelangelos, Figure Composition, Second Composition* and *Two Mechanics* invites a comparison with "the lyrical harmony between man and nature suggested by the arabesque in Matisse's *Bonheur de Vivre* of 1905-6." ("Wyndham Lewis: Art and War", p. 21.) For a discussion of this seminal but complex and conflict-raising work, see the aforementioned article by Margaret Werth, "Engendering Imaginary Modernism: Henri Matisse's *Bonheur de vivre.*" Werth contends that "Matisse's image of the *bonheur de vivre* encompasses a catalog of infantile fantasies, a sequential imagining of a mythic infantile sexuality", as well as offering "a repertoire of poses and types of the Nude"; she concludes with a question: "is this innocence, irony, or idiocy?" (pp. 54, 68-69).

132. *Henri Matisse* (New York: Harry N. Abrams, 1973), p. 112.

133. "Picasso", *The Kenyon Review* (Spring 1940), reprinted in *Wyndham Lewis on Art*, pp. 353-54, and *Creatures of Habit and Creatures of Change*, pp. 295-96. On 4 January 1940 J.S. McLean had written to Lewis, then based in New York, to express regret that he had not been able to secure his services as a guide to the MOMA's Picasso exhibition during a last-minute weekend visit to the city. He took the opportunity of this letter to inform Lewis that Douglas Duncan, whom he had previously met in Toronto, and the Russian-born painter Paraskeva Clark, would be calling on him at his hotel on their own imminent pilgrimage to see the show.

134. *Ibid.*, p. 357.

135. *Picasso: Forty Years of his Art* (New York: Museum of Modern Art, 1939), p. 99.

136. *The Literary Vorticism of Ezra Pound & Wyndham Lewis: Towards the Condition of Painting* (Baltimore and London: The Johns Hopkins University Press, 1985), pp. 104-5.

137. "The Objective of Art in Our Time", *Wyndham Lewis The Artist*, p. 357.

138. *The Demon of Progress in the Arts* (London: Methuen & Co. Ltd., 1954), p. 79.

139. "Guess Who's Coming to Lunch?", *Naked Authority: The Body in Western Painting, 1830-1908* (Cambridge: Cambridge University Press, 1990), p. 114.

140. *Ibid.*, p. 124. The references are to G. Mauner, *Manet: Peintre-Philosophe* (Pennsylvania, 1975), and A.C. Hanson, *Manet and the Modern Tradition* (New Haven and London: Yale University Press, 1977).

141. The Raimondi connection was made by Ernest Chesneau in 1864. Lewis referred to the Giorgione painting in *Tarr*, this time while describing the salon of another German female resident in Paris, the pretentious Fräulein Lipmann: "The `Concert' of Giorgione did not hang there for nothing" (p. 130). A now-unlocated drawing entitled *Fête Champêtre* is included in Lewis's "1917 List", which Walter Michel suggests "may contain the titles of some `Obscenities' as Ezra Pound called them in a letter to John Quinn of 11 April 1917." *(Wyndham Lewis...*, p. 448.)

142. *Manet and the Modern Tradition*, p. 92.

143. Jean Clay, "Ointments, Makeup, Pollen", *October* 27 (Winter 1983): 5.

144. *"Introduction au catalogue de l'exposition Manet"* (Paris: Musée de l'Orangerie, 1932), in P. Callier, ed., *Manet raconté par lui-même et par les amis* (Paris, 1953), p. 198.

145. "The Artist Older than the Fish", *The Caliph's Design*, p. 66.

146. Pointon, "Guess Who's Coming to Lunch?", pp. 113-34. In Pointon's view, *Le Déjeuner* "interrogates the symbolic function of women in the organisation of the world through pictorial representation and in so doing renders allegory problematic. In other words, the painting does not construct an allegory but it foregrounds allegory as actually problematic." (*Ibid.*, p. 113.)

147. "Picasso", *The Caliph's Design*, pp. 109, 112.

148. See Douglas Cooper, *Les Déjeuners* (Paris: Cercle d'Art, 1962), and Marie-Laure Bernadac, "De Manet à Picasso: l'eternel retour", in *Bonjour Monsieur Manet* (Paris: Centre Georges Pompidou/Musée d'art modern, 1983), pp. 33-46.

149. *The Renaissance in Italy: Painting, Sculpture, Architecture*, tr. Robert E. Wolf (New York: Harry N. Abrams, 1969), p. 224. Keller elaborates (p. 324): "Certainly no-one could mistake this for a scene from everyday life. The women are not mortal creatures but demigoddesses. Does the one on the left draw water from the fount of eternal life in her priceless crystal vase? Why does the hatless curly-haired youth lie completely in shadow? Can it be that this is a memorial for a dead friend?"—perhaps by Titian, who is believed to have completed the picture, as a commemoration of Giorgione himself? Sir Kenneth Clark takes a much less complicated view, describing the painting as "the first picture in which man was content to do nothing, because he was perfectly in harmony with nature." (*Civilization: A Personal View* [London: British Broadcasting Corp. and John Murray, 1969, 1974], p. 235.)

150. *Wyndham Lewis* (Santa Barbara: Santa Barbara Museum of Art, 1957), unpaginated. Thomas Dilworth proposes that "The right-left distinction may reflect a Christian distinction, here paganised to be Dionysian." (Letter to Robert Stacey, 23 April 1992.)

151. *Fables of Aggression*, pp. 154-57. Marshall McLuhan observed in 1971 that "When Lewis opts for eye values and rationality and civilization, he was at the same time creating, graphically and verbally, art forms that are audio-tactile. Do you think that he really understands that icons and bounding lines are not visual but audile-tactile? Did he understand that `touch' is the acoustic interval? The other point I had in mind is the characters of *The Human Age as angels*. Electrically, it is the sender who is sent, whether on the telephone, or on radio, or TV. We are transported electrically and bodily. Thus the people of the Magnetic City are angels, literally. Good or bad, disembodied intelligences. Lewis seems to have grasped this, perhaps as early as *The Enemy of the Stars* [first published in *Blast*, revised edition 1932]." (McLuhan to Shiela Watson, 17 February 1971, *Letters of Marshall McLuhan*, [Toronto: Oxford University Press, 1987] , p. 424.)

152. *The Childermass: Part I* (New York: Covici, Friede, 1928), p. 145.

153. *America I Presume* (London and Brussels: Howell and Hoskin, 1940), p. 237. The allusion here is probably to the famous Dionne quintuplets, whose "miraculous" birth in Callander, Ontario in May 1934, who created exactly the kind of "youth-cult" that Lewis detested.

154. "The End of Abstract Art", *The New Republic* 102 (1 April 1940): 439.

155. Lewis to Lorne Pierce, 31 May 1941, Rose, no. 270, p. 290.

156. "Public Spirit and Egotistic Mind", typescript, n.d. [1942], Cornell.

157. "Manifesto", *Blast*, No. 1: 22-23.

158. Lewis to James Johnson Sweeney, 30 December 1942, Rose, no. 308, p. 342.

159. Lewis to Naomi Mitchison, 26 January 1943, Rose, no. 310, p. 346.

160. Lewis to Geoffrey Grigson, 13 July 1942, holograph draught, Cornell.

161. Lewis to Mrs. Roy Campbell, 5 January 1944, Rose, no. 333, p. 374.

162. Lewis to E.P. Richardson, 15 October 1943, Rose, no. 327, p. 368. Lewis proposed to Richardson, then assistant director at the Detroit Institute of Arts, "a lecture voicing and elaborating the point of view" expressed in Richardson's book *The Way of Western Art: 1776-1914* (1939), "under such titles as `Isolation in Art,' or `What are Art's Frontiers?'...."

163. Draught notes for lecture on "ordering nature", 1944, holograph MS, Cornell. Lewis's emphases.

164. Untitled lecture draught, n.d. (c. 1943-45), holograph MS, Cornell. Lewis's emphases.

165. *Self Condemned*, ed. Rowland Smith (Santa Barbara: Black Sparrow Press, 1983), p. 324. In a letter to Lewis written from St. Louis on 17 January 1944, McLuhan exclaimed, "But what complete isolation governs the maturing of any thought in this country! You have had a big taste of it." (Cornell; published in *Letters of Marshall McLuhan*, p. 147.)

166. *Wyndham Lewis...*, pp. 135-6.

167. *Ibid*, p. 144.

168. "The Ogre in the Black Hat", p. 33.

169. Charles E. Lewis, "Imagination", *Reveries of an Old Smoker* (Toronto: Hunter, Rose & Co., 1881), p. 171.

170. *Ibid.*, p. 176. In *The Tyro: A Review of the Arts of Painting, Sculpture and Design*, No. 2 (1922), Lewis published an essay by Herbert Read entitled "A Note on Imagination" which begins, "I touch this subject with a barge-pole of deference. It lies, like a rusty kettle, buried beneath the luxurient and tangled undergrowth of transcendental criticism. One would gladly leave it there but for the fact that this protective undergrowth is the most prickly impediment at present blocking progress" (p. 43).

171. *Ibid.*, p. 180.

172. *Ibid.*, p. 193.

173. *Ibid.*, pp. 199-200.

174. "The Visual World of Wyndham Lewis", *Ibid.*, p. 18.

175. *Ibid.*, p. 16.

176. *Ibid.*, p. 16.

177. *Ibid.*, p. 21.

178. *Ibid.*, pp. 23-24.

OUT OF CANADA: WYNDHAM LEWIS'S NORTH AMERICAN WRITINGS (PAGES 157-166)

1. Father Stan Murphy told me this in one of the conversations we had from 1964, when I met him, until his death in 1983.

2. *America I Presume* (New York: Howell, Soskin, 1940), p. 133.

3. *Ibid.*, p. 266.

4. *Ibid.*, pp. 230-31. The warden of Hart House from 1921 to 1947, Bickersteth had joined the Anglican mission in Edmonton in 1911 and served as a lay preacher in the country northwest of the Alberta capital for two years, returning to his native England in 1913. The next year he published his *The Land of Open Doors*, consisting of his letters to Lord Grey, the recently retired governor-general of Canada; this account of his Canadian experiences was republished, with a new introduction by the author, by the University of Toronto Press in 1976.

5. *Ibid.*, p. 232.

6. *Ibid.*, pp. 242-43.

7. *Ibid.*, p. 262.

8. Jeffrey Meyers, *The Enemy: A Biography of Wyndham Lewis* (London: Routledge & Kegan Paul, 1980), p. 262.

9. Torontonians were rightly proud of their university, which was the best in Canada and among the best on the continent until the late 1970s, when it created mega-departments and otherwise undermined the autonomy of the colleges that had made it unique among universities in North America.

Another cause of umbrage may have been the implied mockery of a leader of Toronto's intellectual aristocracy in the person of Vincent Massey (1887-1967). Although Lewis does not acknowledge the fact, Hart House was built and endowed by the Massey Foundation, named after the manufacturer and philanthropist Hart Massey, the father of the future governor-general of Canada, who from 1935 to 1946 was Canada's high commissioner in London.

10. *The Vulgar Streak*, ed. Paul Edwards (Santa Barbara: Black Sparrow Press, 1985), p. 205.

11. *Ibid.*, p. 176.

12. *Ibid.*, p. 221.

13. *Ibid.*, p. 223.

14. *Ibid.*, p. 226.

15. *Anglosaxony: A League that Works* (Toronto: Ryerson Press, 1941), p. 75.

16. *Ibid.*, p. 35.

17. The title was the last thing Lewis and Lorne Pierce decided on. They agreed that the word "Democracy" in a title "makes people shy away." Lewis thought the same of "Freedom" and "Liberty." Initially, he proposed as titles, in order of preference: 1) "Atlantic Man, the Anglosaxon destiny"; 2) "Cosmic Man and Fascist Man, Nazi 'sovereignty' versus 'universalism'"; 3) "The God Pan versus the Nazi Tin-Trumpet, the backgrounds of Anglosaxon collaboration"; and 4) "First Steps in a Cosmic League, Anglo-American confederation." Lewis subsequently vetoed "Cosmic Man and Fascist Man," or any such title as certain to puzzle "the man-in-the-street" because he "would think one meant *comic* and hadn't spelled it properly." Pierce had suggested "Anglosaxon Commonwealth, a League that will work." Lewis considered the subtitle hackneyed and misleading and opposed Pierce's intention to use it as the main title. He proposed the modification of Pierce's suggestion that became the published title. Lewis to Pierce, 30 May, 8 June, 11 June 1941, Queens University Archives, Kingston, Ontario.

18. *Anglosaxony*, p. 38.

19. *Ibid.*, p. 1.

20. Lewis to Pierce, 23 May 1941, Queens University Archives.

21. Lewis to Fr. Stan Murphy, 12 February 1946, Assumption University Archives, Windsor, Ontario.

22. Lewis to Pierce, 17 June and 16 July 1941, Queens University Archives; Pierce to Lewis, 21 August 1941, Cornell.

23. Lewis told reporters at the scene of the Tudor Hotel fire that he had lost to the fire a book-length political study, the library books borrowed to research it, a novel in manuscript, hundreds of drawings and small paintings, and two portraits–one of Mary McLean, the other of Lisa Sainsbury (*Toronto Daily Star* 15 February 1943). About the portraits we know he lied, since they survived and are present in the current exhibition. If they were still in his possession, they were probably in his studio at 22 Grenville Street. Two days before the fire, he had written to Stan Murphy, "For some time I have been assimilating material for a book about American notions of Liberty" (12 February 1943, Assumption University Archives). This suggests that his work had not yet reached the stage of being "a book-length...study." There is no way of knowing whether this material burned. But it, too, may have been safe in his studio.

24. *America and Cosmic Man* (London: Nicholson and Watson, 1948), p. 12.

25. *Ibid.*, p. 16.

26. *Ibid.*, p. 167.

27. *Ibid.*, p. 68.

28. *Ibid.*, p. 134.

29. *Ibid.*, p. 167.

30. *Ibid.*, p. 176.

31. "How Would You Expect the English to Behave?" *Saturday Night* (4 October 1941): 18.

32. "Reasons why an Englishman is an Englishman", *Saturday Night* (15 November 1941): 34.

33. "That 'Now-or-Never' Spirit", *Saturday Night* (13 June 1942): 6.

34. See "Canadian Nature and its Painters", *The Listener* (26 August 1946), reprinted in *Wyndham Lewis on Art: Collected Writings, 1913-1956*, ed. Walter Michel and C.J. Fox (London: Thames and Hudson, 91969), pp. 425-29.

35. *Saturday Night* (10 October 1942): 16.

36. "Journey out of Anguish," *Wyndham Lewis in Canada*, ed. George Woodcock (Vancouver: University of British Columbia, 1971), p. 102. Reid adds that Lewis would never have written this where those in England who knew him could have read it.

37. "On Canada," *Wyndham Lewis in Canada*, pp. 28-29.

38. *Toronto Daily Star*, 15 February 1943.

39. "Chateau Rex", Cornell. Another sketch for an unwritten novel set in Canada is also at Cornell: "Hill 100" (included in *Wyndham Lewis in Canada*, pp. 90-96); for a discussion, see introduction to this catalogue.

40. "Journey out of Anguish," p. 102. These notebooks are further indication that there was no finished manuscript, as Lewis would hardly have saved the notebooks from the fire and allowed a manuscript to perish.

41. For a discussion of the name "Momaco," see the introduction to this catalogue.

42. *Self Condemned*, ed. Rowland Smith (Black Sparrow Press, 1983), p. 179.

43. *Ibid.*, p. 183.

44. *Ibid.*, p. 407.

45. *Ibid.*, p. 384.

46. *Ibid.*, p. 380.

47. *Ibid.*, p. 382. The prototypes of the fictional priests were identified for me by Fr. Stan Murphy.

48. About his teaching duties, he writes to Stan Murphy, "For the *subject:* history would be the simplest, provided it were a period of which I had sufficient knowledge" (12 February 1943, Assumption University Archives).

49. *Self Condemned*, p. 14.

50. *Ibid.*, p. 164.

51. Meyers, *The Enemy...*, pp. 277-78.

52. Anne Wyndham Lewis to Stan Murphy, 14 June 1959, Assumption University Archives.

53. *Self Condemned*, p. 351.

54. While my reading of the novel is original, it is partial. Perhaps the best thorough analysis of *Self Condemned* is by Timothy Materer in *Wyndham Lewis the Novelist* (Detroit: Wayne State University, 1976), pp. 137-51.

55. *The Enemy...*, p. 312.

Contributors

CATHARINE M. MASTIN was educated at York University, Toronto, where she received her Bachelor of Fine Arts in 1986 and her Master of Arts in art history in 1988, her thesis being on the mural-decoration scheme of St. Anne's Church, Toronto, coordinated by J.E.H. MacDonald. Since 1989 she has been curator of Canadian historical art at the Art Gallery of Windsor. Prior to this appointment she taught at York University and was employed by the McMichael Canadian Art Collection, Kleinburg, Ontario, and the Art Gallery of Ontario, Toronto. She has written primarily on Canadian art, including such topics as printmaking, mural decoration, and modernism, and has published catalogues, brochures and essays on such figures as William G.R. Hind, Emily Carr, Franklin Carmichael, and J.E.H. MacDonald.

Since graduating from the University of Toronto in 1972, ROBERT STACEY has worked as a freelance exhibition curator, writer and editor. He is the author of *The Canadian Poster Book: 100 Years of the Poster in Canada* (Toronto: Methuen, 1979), *The Hand Holding the Brush: Self-Portraits by Canadian Artists* (London: London Regional Art Gallery, 1983), *Western Sunlight: C.W. Jefferys on the Canadian Prairies* (Saskatoon: Mendel Art Gallery, 1984), *C.W. Jefferys* (Ottawa: National Gallery of Canada, 1985); is co-author of *Eighty/Twenty: 100 Years of the Nova Scotia College of Art and Design* (Halifax: Art Gallery of Nova Scotia, 1988); contributed an essay to the catalogue of the 1991 Barbican Art Gallery (London) exhibition, *The True North: Canadian Landscape Painting, 1896-1939;* and wrote the introduction to the 1992 reprint of Wyndham Lewis's "lost" 1941 monograph, *The Rôle of Line in Art*. The recipient of several Canada Council and Ontario Arts Council grants, a Social Sciences and Humanities Research Council grant, and a writing award from the Canadian Studies Directorate of the Department of the Secretary of State, in 1991-92 he was the first Research Fellow in Canadian Historical Art at the Canadian Centre for the Visual Arts, National Gallery of Canada, Ottawa.

THOMAS DILWORTH, a native of Toronto, was educated at the University of Toronto, where he received a Bachelor of Arts in English Language and Literature in 1969, a Master of Arts in English Literature in 1970, and Ph.D. degree in English Literature in 1977. The recipient of numerous honours, he is Professor of English at the University of Windsor, in Windsor, Ontario. Among his publications are *The Liturgical Parenthesis of David Jones* (Cambridge: Golgonooza Press, 1979), *Inner Necessities: The Letters of David Jones to Desmond Chute* (Toronto: Hugh Anson-Cartwright Editions, 1984), and *The Shape of Meaning in the Poetry of David Jones* (Toronto: University of Toronto Press, 1988), and essays and articles on Marshall McLuhan, William Blake and James Joyce. He currently is researching and writing the designated biography of David Jones.